SECURITIES LITIGATION AND ENFORCEMENT

IN A NUTSHELL®

MARGARET V. SACHS
Robert Cotten Alston Chair in Corporate Law
University of Georgia School of Law

DONNA M. NAGY
C. Ben Dutton Professor of Law and
Executive Associate Dean
Indiana University Maurer School of Law

GERALD J. RUSSELLO
Partner, Sidley Austin LLP

WEST
ACADEMIC
PUBLISHING

Nutshell Series, In a Nutshell and the Nutshell Logo are trademarks registered in the U.S. Patent and Trademark Office.

© 2016 LEG, Inc. d/b/a West Academic
       444 Cedar Street, Suite 700
       St. Paul, MN 55101
       1-877-888-1330

West, West Academic Publishing, and West Academic are trademarks of West Publishing Corporation, used under license.

Printed in the United States of America

ISBN: 978-0-314-28769-4

ACKNOWLEDGMENTS

References to and quotes from the ABA Model Rules of Professional Conduct are reprinted with permission. © 2016 by the American Bar Association. All rights reserved. This information or any portion thereof may not be copied or disseminated in any form or by any means or stored in an electronic database or retrieval system without the express written consent of the American Bar Association.

OUTLINE

TABLE OF CASES

References are to Pages

SECURITIES LITIGATION AND ENFORCEMENT

IN A NUTSHELL®

CHAPTER 1

AN OVERVIEW OF SECURITIES LITIGATION AND ENFORCEMENT

§ 1.1 INTRODUCTION

Securities litigation and enforcement is a dynamic area of legal practice with important developments occurring on a number of fronts. This Chapter provides an overview of the area, identifying concepts and concerns that later Chapters will explore in greater depth.

The principal federal securities statutes are the Securities Act of 1933 (the Securities Act) and the Securities Exchange Act of 1934 (the Exchange Act). Enacted during the Great Depression and amended numerous times thereafter, these statutes are enforced through civil and administrative actions by the Securities and Exchange Commission (the SEC or Commission); criminal actions by the Department of Justice (the DOJ); and individual, derivative, or class actions by investors.

Contemporaneously with the Securities Act and the Exchange Act, Congress enacted a number of specialized securities statutes targeting specific abuses in the securities markets. These statutes included the Investment Company Act of 1940 (regulation of mutual funds and other companies with assets consisting primarily of securities of other issuers) and the Investment Advisers Act of 1940 (regulation of conflicts of interest and other problems affecting investment advisers).

§ 1.2 THE SECURITIES ACT

The Securities Act is primarily concerned with securities offerings by issuers and those who control them. Applicable to initial public offerings (IPOs) as well as to subsequent offerings by seasoned issuers that have long been publicly held, it emphasizes both the disclosure of information and the prevention of fraud.

§ 1.2.1 THE REGISTRATION REQUIREMENT

Under Securities Act § 5, an issuer making an offering of securities must either file a registration statement with the SEC or find an applicable exemption from registration. The registration statement, which includes certified financial statements, is the Act's centerpiece disclosure document. In reviewing a registration statement, the SEC makes neither an affirmative investigation of the facts set forth therein nor a determination of the merits of the offering.

§ 1.2.2 EXEMPTIONS FROM REGISTRATION

The Securities Act provides numerous exemptions from registration. Litigators need to be familiar with them for three reasons. First, if an issuer fails to satisfy its chosen exemption, the purchasers have the right to rescind under § 12(a)(1). Second, the availability of § 12(a)(2), a private action for material misstatements and omissions, may turn on which exemption the offering of securities was based. Third, the SEC has increased its focus on market manipulation and other types of fraud in the context of unregistered offerings.

The principal exemptions include the following:

Securities Issued by the U.S., State or Local Governments, Banks or Non-Profit Institutions. *See* §§ 3(a)(2) and 3(a)(4).

Intrastate Offerings. Intrastate offerings of securities are sold to residents of a single state by an issuer incorporated and doing most of its business within that state. *See* § 3(a)(11) and Rule 147.

Offerings Under Rule 504 of Regulation D. The SEC adopted Rule 504 pursuant to § 3(b)(1), which authorizes exemptions for offerings not exceeding $5 million where registration is "not necessary in the public interest and for the protection of investors." The Rule 504 offering can be made only by a non-reporting company (*see* § 1.3 *infra*), cannot exceed $1 million, and does not require disclosure of information to investors.

Offerings Under Rule 505 of Regulation D. Rule 505 was adopted pursuant to § 3(b)(1). A Rule 505 offering cannot exceed $5 million. Disclosure of specified information must be made to investors who are not "accredited investors" (a category including certain institutions, certain insiders of the issuer, and individuals with a net worth exceeding $1 million). The offering is limited to 35 purchasers, not including accredited investors.

<u>Offerings Under Regulation A</u>. Regulation A was recently updated and expanded by the SEC pursuant to § 3(b)(2), enacted by Congress as part of the Jobs Act. The Regulation, known colloquially as Regulation A+, is limited to non-reporting companies (*see* § 1.3 *infra*). It authorizes two tiers of offerings, the first capped at $20 million and the second capped at $50 million. The issuer must file an abbreviated registration statement with the SEC.

<u>Private Offerings</u>. This important exemption, set forth in § 4(a)(2), encompasses "transactions by an issuer not involving any public offering." The Supreme Court has limited this exemption to offerings made to persons with "access to the kind of information which registration would disclose" and with the capacity to "fend for themselves." *SEC v. Ralston Purina Co.*, 346 U.S. 119, 125–127 (1953). A quintessential private offering would be an offering to 10 banks, but private offerings can be made to sophisticated individuals (the requisite attributes of whom are somewhat unclear). If offerees are sought by way of general advertising, the offering becomes public and thereby invalid.

<u>Offerings Under Rule 506 of Regulation D</u>. Rule 506 was adopted under § 4(a)(2), giving issuers a "safe harbor" alternative to § 4(a)(2) itself. Rule 506 encompasses offerings of any dollar amount and, in accordance with a directive in the Jumpstart Our Business

Startups Act of 2012 (the JOBS Act), now comes
in two varieties.

Under Rule 506(b), an offering can be made to
an unlimited number of accredited investors and
up to 35 additional investors who must each be
sophisticated—that is, have "such knowledge
and experience in financial and business
matters that he is capable of evaluating the
merits and risks of the * * * investment." Rule
506(b)(2)(ii). Disclosure of specified information
must be made to investors who are not
accredited investors.

Under Rule 506(c), an offering can be made to
an unlimited number of accredited investors but
only to such investors. The issuer must "take[ ]
reasonable steps to verify" that those who buy
meet the "accredited investor" criteria. Unlike
Rule 506(b), Rule 505, and § 4(a)(2), offerees
may be procured through general advertising.
The use of such advertising, however, does not
render the offering "public." *See* Securities Act
§ 4(b), enacted as part of the JOBS Act.

<u>Offerings Under the Crowdfunding
Exemption</u>. This exemption, authorized by
§ 4(a)(6), allows small businesses to raise up to
$1 million through the use of the Internet and
other means of general advertising, subject to
numerous limitations.

<u>Offerings Under Regulation S</u>. Regulation S,
adopted pursuant to Securities Act § 5,

encompasses offerings made outside the United States by domestic or foreign issuers.

§ 1.2.3   LIABILITY PROVISIONS

The Securities Act contains the following liability provisions:

Section 11. Purchasers in registered offerings may sue the issuer and other specified defendants (including underwriters, accountants, directors, and certain officers) for material omissions and misstatements in the registration statement. Defendants need not have acted with "scienter," *i.e.,* intentionally or with an intent to deceive. Non-issuer defendants have "due diligence" defenses.

Section 12(a)(1). Plaintiffs who can establish a violation of § 5 have the right to rescind their purchases.

Section 12(a)(2). Purchasers in registered offerings as well as in some exempt offerings may sue their "sellers" for material omissions and misstatements made "by means of a prospectus" or, in some instances, verbally. Defendants need not have acted with scienter and have a "reasonable care" defense.

Section 17(a). An important enforcement tool of the SEC and the DOJ that is not available to investors, § 17(a) prohibits three sets of fraudulent acts "in the offer or sale of a security," only the first of which requires scienter. *See Aaron v. SEC*, 446 U.S. 680 (1980).

Section 4A(c). Purchasers of securities in an offering made pursuant to SEC rules promulgated under the crowdfunding exemption can sue an "issuer" that made an oral or written material statement or omission in the offering. For these purposes, the term "issuer" includes, among others, a director, partner, or principal executive officer of an issuer. Liability proceeds "as if" it had been created pursuant to § 12(a)(2). As with the latter, the defendants have a "reasonable care" defense.

§ 1.3 THE SECURITIES EXCHANGE ACT OF 1934

The Exchange Act focuses mainly on the secondary trading markets. Its wide-ranging regulation of these markets includes the following aspects of particular significance to securities litigators and enforcement attorneys.

Section 10(b) and Rule 10b-5. From the standpoint of such attorneys, by far the most important provision in the Exchange Act (or anywhere) is § 10(b), which makes it unlawful "[t]o use or employ, in connection with the purchase or sale of any security * * * , any manipulative or deceptive device or contrivance" in contravention of SEC rules. In 1942, the SEC adopted Rule 10b-5, which proscribes fraud in a manner virtually as wide-ranging as § 10(b) itself. The Rule, applicable regardless of the size of the transaction or the securities issuer, serves not only as a general prohibition against fraud "in connection with the purchase or sale of any security" but also as a prohibition against insider trading.

As originally understood, § 10(b) and Rule 10b-5 were enforceable only by the SEC and the DOJ. But beginning in 1946, courts recognized an implied private action that is now established "beyond peradventure." *Herman & MacLean v. Huddleston,* 459 U.S. 375, 380 (1983).

Market Manipulation. The Exchange Act contains numerous provisions that specifically target market manipulation. Besides § 10(b) and Rule 10b-5, these include § 9 (barring various types of manipulative practices involving securities); § 10(a) (authorizing the SEC to adopt rules regulating short sales and stop-loss orders involving securities); § 14(e) (prohibiting "fraudulent, deceptive, or manipulative acts or practices, in connection with any tender offer"); and § 15(c) (prohibiting "any fraudulent, deceptive, or manipulative act or practice" by brokers and dealers). The Exchange Act does not define manipulation, however, and its precise meaning is by no means self-evident.

Disclosure Obligations of Reporting Companies. To reduce the frequency of fraud and manipulation in public markets, the Exchange Act requires that "reporting companies" file reports on a regular basis with the SEC. A number of provisions important to litigators apply only to reporting companies (or to § 12 companies, which comprise the first and second categories listed below).

Reporting companies, which include the vast majority of public companies, fall into any one of the following three categories:

- Companies which, as provided by § 12(b), have a security (equity or debt) listed on a national securities exchange. *See* § 12(a).

- Companies which, as provided by § 12(g), have total assets exceeding $10 million and a class of equity security held by at least 2,000 shareholders of record or 500 such shareholders who are not accredited investors. Not counted are those who acquired their shares through the crowdfunding exemption.

- Companies fitting neither of the above categories that have filed a registration statement under the Securities Act that became effective. *See* § 15(d).

The most significant report that reporting companies must file is the annual report (the 10-K). Also required are quarterly reports (the 10-Q) as well as reports (the 8-K) for special occurrences, such as the dismissal of the company's accounting firm.

<u>Proxy Regulation</u>. Section 14(a) gives the SEC a wide mandate to adopt rules governing solicitation of proxies from shareholders in § 12 companies. From a securities litigator's standpoint, the most important such Rule is Rule 14a-9, which prohibits material omissions or misrepresentations in proxy solicitations. Rule 14a-9 is enforceable by the SEC and the DOJ and also by investors, pursuant to an

implied private action upheld in *J. I. Case Co. v. Borak,* 377 U.S. 426 (1964).

Tender Offer Regulation. The Exchange Act has regulated tender offers since 1968, when Congress enacted amendments known as the Williams Act. The Williams Act does not define "tender offer," which typically refers to a publicized offer, sometimes by a hostile bidder, to buy shares of a public company at an advertised price within a set time period. The regulation established by the Williams Act has three principal aspects: the disclosure of information; the reduction of shareholder coercion; and the prohibition of fraud in connection with any tender offer.

Self-Regulatory Organizations. SROs are industry groups which, although under the SEC's purview, exercise considerable regulatory authority themselves. The most important are the stock exchanges and the Financial Industry Regulatory Authority (FINRA), the product of the 2007 consolidation of the National Association of Securities Dealers with the member regulation, enforcement, and arbitration functions of the New York Stock Exchange. FINRA is also the forum for almost all private securities arbitrations.

§ 1.4 THE PRIVATE SECURITIES LITIGATION REFORM ACT OF 1995

The Private Securities Litigation Reform Act of 1995 (the PSLRA) imposes numerous restrictions on private securities actions, which, as Congress saw it, were filed by lawyers seeking simply to reach a settlement and collect a fee. Some PSLRA restrictions apply to class actions specifically, whereas others apply more broadly.

On the substantive side, the PSLRA gives certain issuers a "safe harbor" which, when satisfied, shields them from claims that they made fraudulent forward-looking statements (*i.e.*, predictions of earnings or of other matters). Other substantive changes include a requirement that plaintiffs prove loss causation; an adjustment to the calculation of damages; and a system of proportionate liability that largely replaces joint and several liability.

Probably the two most important procedural hurdles that the PSLRA imposes on plaintiffs are (i) heightened pleading requirements mandating the setting forth of specific facts and (ii) a stay on discovery pending resolution of a defendant's motion to dismiss.

The PSLRA also contains many provisions specifically directed at class actions, including those requiring the court to appoint a "lead plaintiff," as well as a "lead counsel"; restricting "professional plaintiffs" from serving as lead plaintiffs; and prohibiting class representatives from receiving greater awards than other class members.

§ 1.5 THE SECURITIES LITIGATION UNIFORM STANDARDS ACT OF 1998

As originally enacted, the Securities Act and the Exchange Act preserved state law actions. After the enactment of the PSLRA, its supporters complained that plaintiffs' lawyers were avoiding its restrictions by filing class actions in state court.

In 1998, Congress enacted the Securities Litigation Uniform Standards Act (the SLUSA), which preempted class actions for securities fraud under the common law and statutes of all 50 states. With limited exceptions, investors are now barred from bringing state-law class actions, whether in state or federal court, that allege fraud in connection with the purchase or sale of a "nationally traded security" (encompassing those listed on the New York Stock Exchange, the American Stock Exchange, or the NASDAQ). The SLUSA also authorizes federal courts to stay discovery in state court of any private action (whether or not a class action) while a federal action is pending.

§ 1.6 THE SARBANES-OXLEY ACT OF 2002

In the wake of the massive accounting frauds at Enron, WorldCom, and other large public companies, Congress enacted the Sarbanes-Oxley Act (the SOX). Among other things, the SOX heightened corporate disclosure obligations, enhanced federal regulation of attorneys and accountants, established new securities crimes, and lengthened the limitations period for private securities fraud actions.

§ 1.7 THE DODD-FRANK ACT OF 2010

Enacted in response to the 2008 financial crisis, the Dodd-Frank Act dramatically increased the degree of government oversight of large financial institutions and established new consumer financial protections. Features of special importance for securities litigation and enforcement attorneys include: the facilitation of private actions against credit rating agencies by relaxing the pleading requirements for plaintiffs seeking damages under Rule 10b-5; the establishment of monetary incentives and protections for whistleblowers who provide the SEC with "original information" about possible securities law violations; the grant of authority to the SEC to impose civil monetary penalties in administrative proceedings; and the clarification of the SEC's right to sue against aiders and abettors who recklessly provide substantial assistance to a primary violator of the federal securities laws.

§ 1.8 THE JUMPSTART OUR BUSINESS STARTUPS ACT OF 2012

Enacted in 2012, the JOBS Act seeks to facilitate the raising of capital by small businesses. Its provisions include the exemption from Securities Act registration known as "crowdfunding"; a private cause of action for material misstatements or omissions in offerings made pursuant to the crowdfunding exemption; the authority for the SEC to adopt "Regulation A+"; and an increase in the number of shareholders sufficient to trigger reporting company status.

§ 1.9 THE COURTS

Besides providing a forum for securities actions, the federal courts play a substantial role in shaping the substantive law of securities litigation. There are two main reasons. First, the federal securities laws are written in broad language (such as § 10(b)'s prohibition against "any manipulative or deceptive device or contrivance"), with critical terms often not defined (such as "manipulation"). As Congress undoubtedly expected, courts have had to step in to supply the missing content.

The second reason involves a happenstance of timing. Many basic securities litigation questions reached the courts in the 1960s and 1970s, an era of judicial activism on many fronts. Thus, just when the Supreme Court was ruling expansively on civil liberties and criminal defense, it was also upholding implied private actions under Rule 10b-5 and Rule 14a-9. Likewise during this period, the lower federal courts recognized an implied private action under § 14(e), read Rule 10b-5 to prohibit insider trading, and granted Rule 10b-5 a substantial international reach. While later decisions and legislation curtailed some of the more expansive interpretations, the rights and duties upheld during the 1960s and 1970s have largely remained in place.

The Supreme Court has an impact by virtue of both what it decides and what it fails to decide (and thereby leaves to the lower courts for resolution). For example, the Court has yet to say whether recklessness satisfies Rule 10b-5's scienter requirement, even though forty years have passed since it first posed but declined to answer that question. *See Ernst & Ernst v. Hochfelder*, 425 U.S. 185, 193 n.12 (1976).

§ 1.10 THE SECURITIES AND EXCHANGE COMMISSION

The SEC is an independent agency charged with enforcing the federal securities laws, composed of five members appointed by the President and confirmed by the Senate for five year terms, no more than three of whom can come from the same political party. Since its founding, the SEC has played a formidable and multi-faceted role in the development of the federal securities laws.

The SEC's range of activities includes the adoption of rules to implement the federal securities statutes; the initiation of administrative actions against securities law violators as well as the adjudication of those actions; the filing of enforcement actions in federal court; the filing of amicus briefs on federal securities issues in private actions in which it is not a party; the provision of testimony, or more informal input, to Congress when Congress considers legislation amending the securities statutes.

Of the SEC's five main divisions, the most important from the standpoint of securities litigators and enforcement lawyers is the Enforcement Division. That Division conducts investigations and, where appropriate, files administrative or court actions against securities law violators. Where criminal prosecution appears warranted, the matter is referred to the DOJ.

§ 1.11 THE DEPARTMENT OF JUSTICE

The DOJ has exclusive authority over criminal enforcement of the federal securities laws. Even when the SEC refers a case, it is the DOJ that makes the final decision as to whether to indict. Moreover, the DOJ prosecutes numerous securities cases that do not originate with the SEC.

In general, the Securities Act and the Exchange Act ground criminal and civil actions on the same violations. Criminal actions nonetheless have two distinctions: a special state of mind requirement, pursuant to which the defendant must have acted "willfully," or, in some instances, "knowingly" (which may, or may not, mean the same thing as "willfully"); and a unique burden of proof—namely, "proof beyond a reasonable doubt" rather than the preponderance standard applicable to civil actions.

§ 1.12 SOCIAL AND ECONOMIC FORCES

Social and economic forces have always had a substantial impact on securities litigation and enforcement. As noted previously, the enactment of the Securities Act and the Exchange Act was driven by the 1929 crash and the disastrous bear market of 1929–1932.

Today, the Internet has generated huge consequences by creating new opportunities for obtaining information as well as for deception, since vast audiences can now be reached by tricksters who operate anonymously. Moreover, the Internet's global reach generates substantial jurisdictional questions.

In addition, the Internet aside, the internationalization of the securities markets that began in the 1960s has had, and continues to have, significant ramifications for securities litigation and enforcement. The Supreme Court and Congress have both recently weighed in on the extraterritorial reach of the federal securities antifraud provisions. *See Morrison v. Nat'l Austl. Bank Ltd.,* 561 U.S. 247 (2010) (reading § 10(b) and Rule 10b-5 to reach securities transactions occurring on U.S. exchanges or otherwise in the United States) and Exchange Act § 27(b) (authorizing the SEC and the DOJ, but not private parties, to prosecute extraterritorial securities fraud that involves domestic conduct or domestic effects).

Most devastating for investor confidence and for the economy has been the mortgage meltdown, the collapse of Bear Stearns, the Lehman Brothers bankruptcy, and the federally orchestrated bailouts of AIG, Merrill Lynch, and other large financial firms in 2008. Much like the 1929 crisis, the 2008 crisis resulted in the deepest and longest recession in 70 years.

§ 1.13 THE EFFICIENT CAPITAL MARKETS HYPOTHESIS

The Efficient Capital Market Hypothesis (the ECMH) has been a highly influential economic theory that has had, and continues to have, a substantial impact on securities law in general and securities litigation and enforcement in particular. For example, the ECMH provides the premise for the fraud-on-the-market and puffery doctrines that are developed in later Chapters.

The doctrines and legislation draw on the widely accepted "semi-strong" version of the ECMH. That version posits that once information becomes public, it is quickly impounded into securities prices.

A distinction is sometimes made between informational efficiency (requiring only that prices react quickly to new public information) and fundamental efficiency (requiring in addition that prices reflect the true value of the shares). Thus, a market can be informationally efficient and not fundamentally efficient.

Markets tend to become efficient as the result of heavy trading by sophisticated investors, many of them institutions, based on what they and their advisers cull from available public sources about the securities and the companies that issue them. Not all public markets are efficient markets. Public markets that are thinly traded or have few or no institutional investors are unlikely to be efficient. The IPO market is prototypically inefficient, whereas the market for New York Stock Exchange-traded securities is prototypically efficient.

Debates among both scholars and judges swirl over whether and to what extent markets are inefficient because of trading driven by psychological factors such as faddishness and overestimation or underestimation of risk.

CHAPTER 2

SECTION 10(b) OF THE EXCHANGE ACT AND RULE 10b-5

§ 2.1 INTRODUCTION

Rule 10b-5 is the leading anti-fraud weapon in the federal securities laws. Its reach is vast, embracing fraud in the largest public corporations as well as in the smallest close corporations. Likewise varied are its forms of enforcement: individual and class actions by investors, civil and administrative actions by the Securities and Exchange Commission (SEC or Commission), and criminal actions by the Department of Justice (DOJ).

The SEC adopted Rule 10b-5 in 1942 pursuant to § 10(b) of the Exchange Act. Section 10 reads in pertinent part:

> It shall be unlawful for any person, directly or indirectly, by the use of any means or instrumentality of interstate commerce, or of the mails, or of any facility of any national securities exchange— * * *
>
> (b) To use or employ, in connection with the purchase or sale of any security registered on a national securities exchange or any security not so registered, * * * any manipulative or deceptive device or contrivance in contravention of such rules and regulations as the Commission may prescribe as necessary

or appropriate in the public interest or for the
protection of investors.

Rule 10b-5 encompasses virtually as much as
§ 10(b) itself:

It shall be unlawful for any person, directly or
indirectly, by the use of any means or
instrumentality of interstate commerce, or of the
mails or of any facility of any national securities
exchange,

(a) to employ any device, scheme, or artifice
to defraud,

(b) to make any untrue statement of a
material fact or to omit to state a material fact
necessary in order to make the statements
made, in the light of the circumstances under
which they were made, not misleading, or

(c) to engage in any act, practice, or course of
business which operates or would operate as a
fraud or deceit upon any person, in connection
with the purchase or sale of any security.

As is apparent, Rule 10b-5 and § 10(b) say nothing
about private enforcement. Beginning with *Kardon v.
Nat'l Gypsum Co.*, 69 F. Supp. 512 (E.D. Pa. 1946),
however, lower federal courts recognized an implied
private action for violations of the Rule. The Supreme
Court upheld the implied private action in a footnote
in *Superintendent of Ins. v. Bankers Life & Cas. Co.*,
404 U.S. 6, 13 n.9 (1971), While initially offering no
rationale for the implication, the Court later
observed that "the theory * * * [was] to supplement"

actions by the SEC and the DOJ. *Musick, Peeler & Garrett v. Emp'rs Ins.*, 508 U.S. 286, 291 (1993). *See Tellabs, Inc. v. Makor Issues & Rights, Ltd.*, 551 U.S. 308, 313 (2007) (collecting cases acknowledging this theory). The Court recently described the implied private action as "settled." *See Janus Capital Group, Inc. v. First Derivative Traders*, 564 U.S. 135, 144 (2011).

The courts (rather than the SEC) have been the principal interpreters of Rule 10b-5. Recognizing the implied private action has been only one aspect of this interpretative project (albeit an important one). Another aspect has been identifying the elements of that action as well as those of SEC and the DOJ and giving the elements substantive content. Courts construing Rule 10b-5 have faced (and continue to face) formidable challenges given the confluence of the following:

Broad Language. Section 10(b) and Rule 10b-5 are broadly worded, offering few bright lines as to how far the Rule's prohibition extends. Moreover, the language of the Section and the Rule is especially uninstructive with respect to matters that bear exclusively on the implied private action (such as standing or reliance), since neither provision was written with private actions in mind.

Limited History. In the course of enacting the Exchange Act in 1934, Congress made only scant references to § 10(b) in the floor debates and official reports. Moreover, the administrative history of the Rule is likewise of limited substantive value.

Multiple Enforcement Contexts. As mentioned, Rule 10b-5 is enforceable in criminal actions as well as in various types of civil actions. Interpretations of the Rule in one context may have undesirable ramifications when applied in other contexts.

Shifting Policies. Until the mid-1970s, the Supreme Court gave § 10(b) and Rule 10b-5 a relatively liberal reading in order to protect gullible investors from exploitation. *See, e.g., Affiliated Ute v. United States*, 406 U.S. 128, 151–154 (1972). Thereafter, the Court came to see at least some investors as essentially puppets of lawyers who sue simply to reach a settlement and collect a fee. Curtailing frivolous private securities actions thus became an important judicial policy. *See, e.g., Blue Chip Stamps v. Manor Drug Stores*, 421 U.S. 723, 739–747 (1975). But this policy of retrenchment has not invariably driven the result in specific cases. For example, the Court has recently reaffirmed fraud-on-the-market, without which most Rule 10b-5 class actions could not be brought. *See Halliburton Corp. v. Erica P. John Fund, Inc.*, 134 S. Ct. 2398 (2014).

The vastly diminished status of investor protection as a policy animating the interpretation of Rule 10b-5 emerged from *Morrison v. National Australia Bank, Ltd.*, 561 U.S. 247 (2010), a decision addressing the Rule's extraterritorial reach (*see* § 12.2 *infra*). Taking up that reach for the first time, the Court read Rule 10b-5 narrowly without confronting the impact of its reading on investor protection.

In addition, beginning in the 1970s, the Court adopted approaches to statutory interpretation that have carried significant consequences for the interpretation of § 10(b) and Rule 10b-5. Those approaches consist of strict construction, constriction of implied private actions, and disregard for legislative history.

The Influence of the Efficient Capital Markets Hypothesis. The Efficient Capital Markets Hypothesis (ECMH) posits, in its widely-accepted semi-strong form, that the price of a security traded in an efficient market reflects all publicly available information. *See* § 1.13 *supra*. The ECMH has provided the premise for various doctrinal innovations, including fraud-on-the-market (*see* § 2.8.2 *infra*), the "truth-on-the-market" defense (*see* § 2.8.2 *infra*), and the "puffery" defense (*see* § 2.3.1 *infra*).

The Absence of Dependable Analogies. Because § 10(b) and Rule 10b-5 prohibit fraud, they virtually invite judicial analogies to common law deceit. The Supreme Court has sometimes embraced that analogy. *See, e.g., Dura Pharm., Inc. v. Broudo*, 544 U.S. 336, 341 (2005). But the Court has pulled back from it as well. *See, e.g., Stoneridge Inv. Partners, LLC v. Scientific-Atlanta, Inc.,* 552 U.S. 148, 162 (2008). The deceit analogy is at best far from perfect, since Congress intended the federal securities laws to "rectify perceived deficiencies in the available common-law protections." *Herman & MacLean v. Huddleston,* 459 U.S. 375, 389 (1983).

Another obvious potential analogy is Rule 14a-9, the subject of Chapter 4 *infra.* Adopted by the SEC pursuant to § 14(a) of the Exchange Act, Rule 14a-9 prohibits material misstatements and omissions in proxy solicitations and, like Rule 10b-5, can be enforced in implied private actions as well as in actions by the SEC and the DOJ. Yet the proxy voting context involves distinctive considerations that may render Rule 14a-9 (at least some of the time) a less than reliable benchmark for interpreting Rule 10b-5.

Subsequent Congressional Enactments. Congress has not ceded control of § 10(b) and Rule 10b-5 entirely to the courts. Its most significant contribution in this regard has been the Private Securities Litigation Reform Act of 1995 (the PSLRA), which makes maintenance of private securities actions more difficult by stiffening the pleading requirements (*see* immediately below and § 2.6 *infra*); providing a safe harbor for fraud involving forward-looking statements (*see* § 2.3.8 *infra*), establishing an affirmative requirement of loss causation (*see* § 2.9 *infra*), adjusting the calculation of damages (*see* § 2.10 *infra*), and creating a scheme of proportionate liability (*see* § 2.10.1 *infra*).

Additional aspects of the PSLRA that apply exclusively to class actions are addressed in Chapter 6 *infra*.

Likewise important for Rule 10b-5 purposes is the Sarbanes-Oxley Act of 2002 (the SOX). That Act lengthened the statute of limitations for private actions under the Rule (*see* § 2.13 *infra*). In addition, it empowered the SEC to expand the scope of the "duty to disclose" upon which Rule 10b-5 liability often turns by authorizing the agency to adopt "real time" disclosure rules for reporting companies. *See* § 2.2 *infra*. Other aspects of the SOX are considered in connection with SEC enforcement (*see* Chapter 9 *infra*) and SEC regulation of accountants and attorneys (*see* Chapter 10 *infra*).

Finally, the Dodd-Frank Act of 2010 (the Dodd-Frank Act) has made significant contributions to the Rule 10b-5 landscape. Those addressed in this Chapter include expanded SEC authority to sue aiders and abettors (*see* § 2.12.1 *infra*) and controlling persons (*see* § 2.12.3 *infra*). Other Rule 10b-5-related aspects of the Dodd-Frank Act are covered in Chapter 9 (SEC enforcement), Chapter 12 (international securities fraud), and Chapter 13 (arbitration).

In considering Rule 10b-5, it is important to keep in mind certain critical procedural matters. These involve pleading, dismissal of actions, discovery stays, and the burden of proof, as follows:

<u>Pleading</u>. The Federal Rules of Civil Procedure apply to all civil complaints filed in federal court. Rule 8 provides that plaintiffs need only plead "a short and plain statement of the claim showing that [they are] entitled to relief." The Supreme Court has extracted an additional unstated requirement from Rule 8— that the allegations in the complaint qualify as "plausible." *Ashcroft v. Iqbal*, 556 U.S. 662 (2009).

Rule 9 sets the standard for "Pleading Special Matters," with Rule 9(b) providing that in "all averments of fraud or mistake, the circumstances constituting fraud or mistake shall be stated with particularity." Courts construe Rule 9(b) to require particularity in the pleading of what material misstatements or omissions were made, who made them, and where and when they were made.

The pleading burdens on private plaintiffs grew even greater with the enactment of the PSLRA, which added § 21D(b)(1) to the Exchange Act:

In any private action arising under [the Exchange Act] in which the plaintiff alleges that the defendant—

(A) made an untrue statement of a material fact; or

(B) omitted to state a material fact necessary in order to make the statements made, in the light of the circumstances in which they were made, not misleading;

The complaint shall specify each statement alleged to have been misleading, the reason or reasons why the statement is misleading, and, if an allegation regarding the statement or omission is made on information and belief, the complaint shall state with particularity all facts on which that belief is formed.

While at first blush this provision appears to pertain only to the pleading of material omissions and misstatements, it actually has a broader reach than that. For example, the requirement to plead "the reason or reasons why the statement is misleading" bears on materiality and reliance. The PSLRA also substantially raised a private plaintiff's burden of pleading scienter by adding § 21D(b)(2) to the Exchange Act. That provision is addressed in § 2.6 *infra*.

<u>Dismissal of Actions and Discovery Stays</u>. The above-mentioned heightened pleading requirements for private plaintiffs must be considered in light of two other Exchange Act provisions that were added by the PSLRA. One is § 21D(b)(3)(A), which states that in any private action arising under the Exchange Act, "the court shall, on the motion of any defendant, dismiss the complaint" if the heightened requirements in § 21D(b) are not met. The other is the equally significant § 21D(b)(3)(B), which requires a court to stay discovery during the

pendency of any such motion to dismiss. This mandatory stay of discovery while a dismissal motion is pending allows for only a limited exception when a "court finds upon motion of any party that particularized discovery is necessary to preserve evidence or to prevent undue prejudice to that party."

<u>Mandatory Sanctions</u>. A final noteworthy provision added to the Exchange Act by the PSLRA is § 21D(c). That provision requires the court to review every private action at the time of final adjudication to determine whether a party or attorney has committed a violation of Rule 11(b) of the Federal Rules of Civil Procedure—for example, filing a motion for purposes of delay, making a frivolous legal argument, or offering a factual contention that lacks evidentiary support. In the event a violation is found, § 21D(c) makes sanctions mandatory and establishes as the presumptive sanction an award of the opposing party's attorney's fees and expenses. *See* § 21D(c)(2)–(3).

<u>Burden of Proof</u>. For the small percentage of Rule 10b-5 civil actions that reach the trial stage, the burden of proof is a "preponderance-of-the evidence"—that is, "more likely than not." *Herman & MacLean v. Huddleston*, 459 U.S. 375, 390 (1983).

This Chapter examines the elements of Rule 10b-5, with emphasis upon the Rule's private enforcement. It is divided into the following sections: the requirement of manipulation or deception (§ 2.2 *infra*); materiality (§ 2.3 *infra*); the "in connection with" requirement (§ 2.4 *infra*); scienter (§ 2.5 *infra*); pleading scienter (§ 2.6 *infra*); the purchaser-seller requirement (§ 2.7 *infra*); reliance (§ 2.8 *infra*); loss causation (§ 2.9 *infra*); damages (§ 2.10 *infra*); primary liability (§ 2.11 *infra*); secondary liability (§ 2.12 *infra*); the statute of limitations (§ 2.13 *infra*); and the overlap between Rule 10b-5 and the express private fraud actions under the Securities Act and the Exchange Act (§ 2.14 *infra*).

Later chapters draw upon the elements of Rule 10b-5 in connection with securities class actions (Chapter 6 *infra*); insider trading (Chapter 7 *infra*); market manipulation (Chapter 8 *infra*); SEC enforcement (Chapter 9 *infra*); criminal enforcement (Chapter 11 *infra*); and international securities fraud (Chapter 12 *infra*).

§ 2.2 THE REQUIREMENT OF MANIPULATION OR DECEPTION

Section 10(b) prohibits, in connection with the purchase or sale of a security, "any manipulative or deceptive device or contrivance" in contravention of rules adopted by the SEC for the protection of investors. *See* § 2.1 *supra* (setting forth the text of § 10(b)). Thus, the scope of § 10(b)—and hence also that of Rule 10b-5—turns on the meaning of the phrase "manipulative or deceptive," regardless of whether the action is private or governmental.

The term "manipulative" has a specialized meaning, which is explored in Chapter 8 *infra*. Our focal point here is the meaning of the term "deceptive"—traditionally the more nettlesome problem for the securities litigator.

Certain basic propositions about deception are important to bear in mind:

- Deceptive statements include outright misrepresentations as well as statements that mislead by omission. Both fall within the explicit text of Rule 10b-5(b), which appears in § 2.1 *supra*.

- Statements that mislead by omission include "so-called 'half-truths'—literally true statements that create a materially misleading impression." *SEC v. Gabelli*, 653 F.3d 49, 57 (2d Cir. 2011), *rev'd on other grounds sub nom. Gabelli v. SEC*, 133 S. Ct. 1216 (2013).

- A defendant's secret intention not to honor a promise may render materially misleading his affirmative statement (or statements). *Wharf (Holdings) Ltd. v. United Int'l Holdings, Inc.*, 532 U.S. 588, 596 (2001).

- Deception may occur in the absence of a statement of any kind. This form of deception is captured by subsections (a) and (c) of Rule 10b-5, set forth in § 2.1 *supra*, which prohibit "schemes to defraud" as well as acts which "operate as a fraud." These prohibitions may encompass the following:

so-called "pure silence" cases, *see Chiarella
v. United States*, 445 U.S. 222, 228 (1980)
("[O]ne who fails to disclose material
information prior to the consummation of a
transaction commits fraud only when he is
under a duty to do so."); and

cases involving deceptive conduct, *see
Stoneridge Inv. Partners, LLC v. Scientific-
Atlanta, Inc.*, 552 U.S. 148, 158 (2008)
("Conduct itself can be deceptive;" there
need not be "a specific oral or written
statement before there could be liability
under § 10(b) or Rule 10b-5.").

The scope of deception is wide, but "it irreducibly
entails some act that gives the victim a false
impression." *United States v. Finnerty*, 533 F.3d
143, 148 (2d Cir. 2008).

The sections that follow address aspects of
deception that are far less settled. These include
issues involving both material misstatements and
omissions (§ 2.2.1 *infra*) as well as those involving
material omissions in particular (§ 2.2.4 *infra*).

§ 2.2.1   THE BASIC PARAMETERS
OF DECEPTION

The basic parameters of § 10(b)'s deception
element are set forth in *Santa Fe Indus., Inc. v.
Green*, 430 U.S. 462 (1977). To understand *Santa Fe*'s
holding and implications, some background about the
case is essential.

Background. Santa Fe, owner of more than 90% of the shares of Kirby, merged with Kirby in accordance with Delaware's short-form merger statute. That statute required the approval of the merger by the parent's board, but not by the minority shareholders, who likewise had no right to be told about the merger in advance. The only remedy available to those shareholders under the then-existing Delaware law was that of appraisal—the right to be bought out by the parent at a judicially determined "fair" price (which might in the end be higher, lower, or identical to the merger consideration).

The plaintiffs, minority shareholders of Kirby, did not pursue appraisal. Suing Santa Fe instead under § 10(b) and Rule 10b-5, they set out two claims seeking to have the merger set aside or to obtain damages calculated according to the "fair value" of their shares:

Principal Claim—that the merger itself, as well as the amount of the merger consideration, constituted breaches of fiduciary duty actionable as "fraud" under Rule 10b-5. They did not allege a misrepresentation or omission, however, since the information that they received about the merger, albeit after-the-fact, was accurate.

Additional Claim—that Santa Fe's failure to give them advance notice of the merger was an omission actionable under Rule 10b-5.

The Court's Rejection of the Principal Claim. The Court rejected the principal claim mainly on the basis of the language in § 10(b) prohibiting any "manipulative" or "deceptive" device or contrivance. The defendant's alleged breaches were not "manipulative," the Court ruled, since manipulation is a specialized term of art that does not encompass garden-variety mismanagement. *See id.* at 476–477. Moreover, the breaches were not "deceptive," since deception requires an omission or a misrepresentation and here neither was alleged. *Id.* at 474. Finally, the breaches did not qualify as "fraud" under Rule 10b-5, since the interpretation of Rule 10b-5 is governed by the language of § 10(b). *Id.* at 472.

In Part IV of its decision, the Court deemed the language of § 10(b) to be "dispositive," but added that "even if it were not," other considerations likewise counseled in favor of rejecting the principal claim. *Id.* at 477. First, the Exchange Act is aimed mainly at achieving "full disclosure," whereas insuring the fairness of a merger is at best a "tangential" goal and thus an unsound guide for construing § 10(b). *See id.* at 477–478. Second, minority shareholders dissatisfied with a merger have long had an appraisal remedy, although the Court cautioned that "the existence of a particular state-law remedy is not dispositive of the question whether Congress meant to provide a similar federal remedy." *Id.* at 478. Third, to federalize the minority shareholders' claim would likely also lead to the federalization of a wide variety of other management-type claims governed by state law, a development that should occur only if Congress explicitly so directs. *Id.* at 479.

It bears noting that not long after *Santa Fe*, the Delaware Supreme Court reinterpreted Delaware's appraisal remedy for the benefit of minority shareholders. *See Weinberger v. UOP, Inc.*, 457 A.2d 701 (Del. 1983). It is widely supposed that this reinterpretation may have been driven at least in part by the desire to reduce the likelihood that Congress would intervene to level the playing field on minority shareholders' behalf.

The Court's Analysis of the Additional Claim. Unlike the principal claim, the additional claim involved an omission—the failure to give the minority shareholders advance notice of the merger. But in footnote 14, the Court held that the omission lacked "materiality," an essential element of § 10(b) and Rule 10b-5. *See* 430 U.S. at 474 n.14. *See also* § 2.2.2 *infra*. The reason for the lack of materiality, the Court explained, was that the minority shareholders could not have used the omitted information to enjoin the merger (or, for that matter, to pursue any other state law remedy).

The Court's rationale implied that the additional claim might have been cognizable if the minority shareholders had a state law remedy (and then lost it on account of the fraud). This possibility is discussed in § 2.2.2 *infra*.

§ 2.2.2   THE CLAIM RECOGNIZED BY *GOLDBERG v. MERIDOR*

Footnote 14 of *Santa Fe*, discussed immediately above, served as the predicate for the Second Circuit's landmark decision in *Goldberg v. Meridor*,

567 F.2d 209 (2d Cir. 1977). There the court upheld the viability of a Rule 10b-5 claim premised on a fiduciary duty breach where the breach involved a misrepresentation or omission that led to the loss of a state remedy. To appreciate *Goldberg*'s significance and controversiality, some brief background about the case is necessary.

Background. The directors of a subsidiary approved the issuance of stock to the parent but withheld from its minority shareholders information concerning the substantial insufficiency of the merger consideration as well as the fact that a majority of the subsidiary's directors were beholden to the parent. Challenging their failure to receive this information, the minority shareholders brought a Rule 10b-5 derivative action on behalf of the subsidiary. The minority shareholders could not sue on their own account due to Rule 10b-5's purchaser-seller requirement, which limits standing to sue to those who bought or sold the security in question (*see* § 2.7 *infra*). Here the subsidiary, not its shareholders, sold the stock to the parent.

Holding and Reasoning. The Second Circuit held that the above facts constituted actionable deception under § 10(b) and Rule 10b-5 for the following reasons:

- A corporation can be "deceived" despite the fact that a majority of its directors acted knowingly for their own benefit. As the court observed: It is a "now widely recognized ground that there is deception of the corporation (in effect, of its minority shareholders) when the corporation is influenced by its controlling shareholder to engage in a transaction adverse to the corporation's interests (in effect, the minority shareholders' interests) and there is nondisclosure or misleading disclosures as to the material facts of the transaction." *Goldberg*, 567 F.2d at 217.

- Unlike the minority shareholders in *Santa Fe*, who had no remedy under Delaware law for enjoining the merger, the minority shareholders in *Goldberg* had such a remedy under New York law and could have used the omitted information in that connection. That utility rendered the omitted information material. *Goldberg*, 567 F.2d at 220. *See also* § 2.3 *infra* (discussing materiality under § 10(b) and Rule 10b-5).

- Given the materiality of the omitted information, the shareholders' claim differed from the garden-variety mismanagement claims that Part IV of *Santa Fe* sought to insulate from federalization. *See Goldberg*, 567 F.2d at 220–221. *See also* § 2.2.1 *supra* (discussing *Santa Fe*).

While that difference may be valid as far as it goes, there is nonetheless some tension between Part IV of *Santa Fe* and a *Goldberg* claim, since the latter is invariably intertwined with state law. That intertwining becomes evident upon considering the elements of a *Goldberg* claim, described immediately below.

Elements of a *Goldberg* Claim. Minority shareholders must establish the four elements in order to prevail on a *Goldberg* claim:

(1)   that they received information containing a misrepresentation or omission with respect to the merger or other transaction at issue;

(2)   that if they had known the truth, they could have utilized a state law remedy;

(3)   that if they had pursued that state law remedy, they would have had "a reasonable probability of ultimate success." *Healey v. Catalyst Recovery of Penn., Inc.*, 616 F.2d 641, 647–648 (3d Cir. 1980); and

(4)   that the state law remedy has since become "lost," that is, it is no longer available based on the state's procedural and/or substantive law.

For decisions outside the Second Circuit that have followed *Goldberg*, *see*, *e.g.*, *Healey*, *supra*; *Alabama Farm Bureau Mut. Cas. Co. v. Am. Fidelity Ins. Co.*, 606 F.2d 602, 614 (5th Cir. 1979); *Kidwell ex rel. Penfold v. Meikle,* 597 F.2d 1273, 1292 (9th Cir. 1979).

Considerations Relevant to the Viability of a *Goldberg* Claim. The viability of a *Goldberg* claim is arguably affected by certain developments under § 14(a) of the Exchange Act and Rule 14a-9, to which § 10(b) and Rule 10b-5 are sometimes analogized (*see* § 2.1 *supra*). One such development involves the Seventh Circuit's rejection of the *Goldberg* decision. The others involve *Virginia Bankshares, Inc. v.*

Sandberg, 501 U.S. 1083 (1991), and the lower court decisions issued in its wake.

The Seventh Circuit's Rejection of *Goldberg*. The Seventh Circuit rejected the approach taken by *Goldberg* and its progeny in *LHLC Corp. v. Cluett, Peabody & Co.*, 842 F.2d 928 (7th Cir. 1988). Rather than asking whether the omission or misrepresentation led to the loss of a state remedy, the Seventh Circuit held, the focus should be the fraud had an effect on an investment decision. Only if it did does the plaintiff have a cause of action. A good illustration comes from *LHLC* itself, where the transaction at issue was Cluett's sale of all the stock of its wholly-owned subsidiary (Lytton) to LHLC. More than half the purchase price was attributable to the value of Lytton's inventory, misrepresented by Cluett in a letter to LHLC received after the transaction had closed. Since the misrepresentation did not affect LHLC's "investment decision," it was held not to be actionable, despite its conceivable relevance to a lawsuit by LHLC against Cluett. *See id.* at 931–932.

The Supreme Court's Decision in *Virginia Bankshares*. In *Virginia Bankshares*, the plaintiff used § 14(a) and Rule 14a-9 to challenge a misrepresentation in a proxy statement that urged approval of a merger. That approval was assured based on the shares controlled by management, regardless of how the minority shareholders voted. 501 U.S. at 1099. At issue was whether the plaintiff could show, despite the superfluousness of the minority shareholders' vote, a causal connection between the fraudulent proxy statement and her injury. *See id.* Attempting to establish that connection, the plaintiff argued that knowledge of the truth would have enabled her to initiate a state law remedy to void the merger on conflict-of-interest grounds. *See id.* at 1101. Finding that remedy not to have been lost, the Supreme Court was able to sidestep the soundness of the lost state remedy argument. *Id.* at 1107. By deeming that argument unsettled, the Court may have undercut the *Goldberg* line of cases.

Lower Court Decisions After *Virginia Bankshares*. After *Virginia Bankshares*, lower federal courts have allowed the loss of a state remedy to satisfy causation under § 14(a) and Rule 14a-9 when the shares controlled by management guaranteed the approval of the transaction in question. *See, e.g., Wilson v. Great Am. Indus., Inc.*, 979 F.2d 924 (2d Cir. 1992). *See also Howing Co. v. Nationwide Corp.,* 972 F.2d 700, 709–710 (6th Cir. 1992) (accepting a lost state remedy argument in connection with claim made under § 13(e) of the Exchange Act). By accepting lost state remedy arguments in the Rule 14a-9 context, these courts may have bolstered the *Goldberg* line of cases.

§ 2.2.3   DECEPTIVE OPINIONS

Another aspect of § 10(b)'s deception element involves the question whether an opinion is a "fact" the misrepresentation or omission of which can be actionable. The Supreme Court took up this question in *Virginia Bankshares v. Sandberg*, 501 U.S. 1083

(1991), a decision involving § 14(a) and Rule 14a-9. At issue was the misrepresentation of the directors' opinion regarding the fairness of the price offered to shareholders in a merger in exchange for their stock. The Court concluded that while an opinion constitutes a "fact," it is not actionable simply because it is material and "misstate[s] the speaker's reasons." *Id.* at 1095. It must also be "false or misleading about its subject." *Id.* at 1095–1096. Thus, the directors' assertion that $42 per share was a "fair price" would be actionable under Rule 14a-9 only so long as (i) the directors did not believe that $42 was a fair price and (ii) the price was not fair in fact. *Cf. id.* at 1109 (Scalia, J., concurring in part and concurring in the judgment).

The Supreme Court recently reaffirmed these requirements in *Omnicare, Inc. v. Laborers District Council Construction Industry Pension Fund,* 135 S. Ct. 1318, 1327 (2015), a decision involving § 11 of the Securities Act. Other aspects of *Omnicare* that bear specifically on § 11 are discussed in § 3.4 *infra.*

The *Virginia Bankshares/Ominicare* requirements are routinely imported into Rule 10b-5 decisions involving deceptive opinions. *See, e.g., Mayer v. Mylod,* 988 F.2d 635, 639 (6th Cir. 1993); *Special Situations Fund III QP, L.P. v. Deloitte Touche Tohmatsu CPA, Ltd.,* 96 F. Supp. 3d 325 (S.D.N.Y. 2015); *Battle Constr. Co. v. InVivo Therapeutics Holdings Corp.,* 101 F. Supp. 3d 135 (D. Mass. 2015).

§ 2.2.4   SILENCE AS DECEPTION

The general rule is that silence constitutes deception under Rule 10b-5 only when there is an affirmative duty to disclose. *See, e.g., Basic Inc. v. Levinson*, 485 U.S. 224, 239 n.17 (1988); *Chiarella v. United States*, 445 U.S. 222, 235 (1980); *In re Time Warner Sec. Litig.*, 9 F.3d 259, 267 (2d Cir. 1993).

The Supreme Court's decision in *Chiarella*, an insider trading case examined extensively in § 7.3 *supra*, stands as the Court's principal discussion of silence-as-deception. Chiarella was employed by a financial printer that had been retained by companies planning to make tender offer bids. Gleaning the names of the target companies from confidential documentation supplied to his employer, Chiarella bought stock in the targets prior to the public announcement of the bids. Despite his exploitation of material inside information, the Court concluded that he had not defrauded the shareholders on the other side of his transactions in violation of Rule 10b-5: "[T]he element required to make [his] silence fraudulent—a duty to disclose—is absent in this case." 445 U.S. at 232. In extensive dicta, the Court noted that his silence would have constituted deception had he been an officer or director of a company in which he bought shares, since his position would have bestowed on him fiduciary duties owed to the company and its shareholders. *See id.* at 228–229.

Application of the general rule requires an understanding of when a duty to disclose can arise. Such a duty may be rooted in a line-item requirement; in the duty to update or correct; or in the common law. After considering each of these, brief mention will be made of a matter closely related to the duty to disclose—namely, Regulation FD.

<u>Line-Item Requirements</u>. The Securities Act's registration requirement (*see* § 1.2.1 *supra*) and the Exchange Act's annual and periodic disclosure requirements (*see* § 1.3 *supra*) impose on issuers an affirmative duty to disclose information about a wide range of matters. These matters include the results of business operations, financial position, transactions involving directors and other related persons, and known trends or uncertainties (including pending litigation) that the issuer expects will have a materially favorable or unfavorable impact on net sales or revenues.

Most of these disclosures take the form of "line-items" in Regulations S-X (for accounting-related information) and S-K (for all other information). These line-items must be included in the following:

<u>any registration statement</u> (on a Form S-1, for example) covering an offering of securities not exempt from the Securities Act's registration requirement (*see* § 1.2.1 *supra*);

<u>the annual report</u> (the 10-K) and <u>quarterly reports</u> (10-Qs) filed by a reporting company (defined in § 1.3 *supra*). Particularly sweeping are the disclosure requirements set out in Item 303(a) of Regulation S-K, which is often referred to as MD & A disclosures ("Management's Discussion and Analysis").

Moreover, various Exchange Act provisions impose additional disclosure obligations for specific transactions or events:

- § 14(a) imposes disclosure requirements in connection with proxy solicitations in a § 12 company (*see* § 1.3 *supra*);

- § 13(d) requires disclosure in connection with the acquisition of more than five percent of a class of equity security of a § 12 company (*see* § 1.3 *supra*);

- § 14(d) requires disclosure when a tender offer is the means of accomplishing the acquisition of more than five percent of a class of equity security of a § 12 company (*see* § 1.3 *supra*); and

- § 14(e) prohibits fraud in connection with tender offers in all companies. *See* Chapter 5 *infra*.

The schedules required to be filed with the SEC on the occurrence of these transactions or events (*i.e.*, Schedule 14A, Schedule 13D, or a Schedule TO) contain highly detailed line-item requirements, many of which draw upon the line-items set out in Regulations S-X and S-K.

In addition, reporting companies must also file reports (the 8-K) for special occurrences, including changes in control of the issuer; bankruptcy or receivership; change in accountants; resignation of directors; change in fiscal year; changes in the issuer's Code of Ethics; or waiver of a provision in the

Code of Ethics. For most items, the 8-K must be filed within four business days of the triggering event. Moreover, for a limited number of items, there is a safe harbor for failure to timely file an 8-K that offers protection from liability in Rule 10b-5 actions brought by either the government or private parties.

Even considered as a totality, these requirements fall considerably short of a mandate to provide "continuous disclosure" of all material events. Whether and to what extent a continuous disclosure system eventually emerges turns on how the SEC chooses to utilize its rulemaking power under Exchange Act § 13(*l*), enacted as part of the SOX. That provision authorizes the SEC to adopt rules requiring reporting companies to make public disclosure of information "on a rapid and current basis" as it deems "necessary or useful for the protection of investors and in the public interest."

<u>The Duty to Update</u>. Various federal appeals courts recognize a "duty to update" that operates as an exception to an issuer's general right to remain silent about new material information. *See, e.g., Finnerty v. Stiefel Labs., Inc.,* 756 F.3d 1310 (11th Cir. 2014); *Weiner v. Quaker Oats Co.,* 129 F.3d 310, 318 (3d Cir. 1997); *In re Time Warner Sec. Litig.,* 9 F.3d 259 (2d Cir. 1993).

The duty to update attaches only to future-oriented statements. *See IBEW Local Union No. 58 Pension Trust Fund & Annuity Fund v. Royal Bank of Scot. Grp.,* 783 F.3d 383, 390 (2d Cir. 2015). It imposes an obligation to modify or supplement such statements which, although accurate when made, have since become inaccurate or misleading due to subsequent developments. Updating is necessary, however, only to the extent that the prior statements remain "alive" in the minds of reasonable investors. *See Weiner*, 129 F.3d at 318.

Courts interpret the duty to update restrictively in order to avoid creating a system of "continuous disclosure" by indirection. Thus, the Second Circuit declined to find a duty to disclose a marketing plan so significant that it required board approval. *See San Leandro Emergency Med. Grp. Profit Sharing Plan v. Philip Morris Cos.*, 75 F.3d 801, 809 (2d Cir. 1996). Moreover, the Third Circuit has held the duty "appli[cable] only in 'narrow circumstances' involving more fundamental corporate changes such as mergers, takeovers, or liquidations, as well as when subsequent events produce an 'extreme' or 'radical change' in the continuing validity of the original statement." *City of Edinburgh Council v. Pfizer, Inc.*, 754 F.3d 159, 176 (3d Cir. 2014) (quoting *In re Burlington Coat Factory Sec. Litig.*, 114 F.3d 1410, 1433–1434 (3d Cir. 1997)). *See also Finnerty*, 756 F.3d at 1319–1320 (finding duty to update when insiders traded on the basis of secret information).

The Seventh Circuit, on the other hand, has rejected the imposition of a duty to update altogether. *See Stransky v. Cummins Engine Co.*, 51 F.3d 1329, 1332 (7th Cir. 1995). It has done so on the basis of the language in Rule 10b-5(b) prohibiting "any untrue statement of material fact or [omitting] to state a material fact necessary in order to make the statements made, *in the light of the circumstances under which they were made*, not misleading." *Id.* (emphasis by the court). In the Seventh Circuit's view, this language "implicitly precludes basing liability on circumstances that arise after the speaker makes the statement." *Id.*

The Duty to Correct. The duty to correct attaches to a historical statement later discovered to have been false when made. It does not matter that the speaker uttered the falsehood unintentionally or that she believed it to be true when she said it.

Most courts recognize some form of a duty to correct a false statement made by the issuer or one of its officials. *See, e.g., In re IBM Corporate Sec. Litig.*, 163 F.3d 102, 109 (2d Cir. 1998); *In re Burlington Coat Factory Sec. Litig.*, 114 F.3d 1410, 1430–1431 (3d Cir. 1997); *Stransky v. Cummins Engine Co.*, 51 F.3d 1329, 1331 (7th Cir. 1995). A duty to correct has also been recognized in connection with a false statement made by an accountant in a certified opinion. *See Overton v. Todman & Co.*, 478 F.3d 479, 486–487 (2d Cir. 2007).

An important related question is whether, and to what extent, an issuer has a duty to correct a false statement made by a third party. Virtually all courts agree that there is no such duty unless the statement can be attributed to the issuer or one of its officials. *See Eisenstadt v. Centel Corp.,* 113 F.3d 738, 744 (7th Cir. 1997); *State Teachers Ret. Bd. v. Fluor Corp.*, 654 F.2d 843, 850 (2d Cir. 1981). Moreover, any such attribution would have to render the issuer (or the official) the "maker" of the statement in accordance with *Janus Capital Group, Inc. v. First Derivative*

Traders, 564 U.S. 135 (2010), discussed in § 2.11.1 *infra*. Unlikely to satisfy *Janus*, at least without more, is the issuer's "entanglement" with the preparation of the third-party's report. *Cf. Cooper v. Pickett*, 137 F.3d 616, 623–624 (9th Cir. 1997); *Raab v. General Physics Corp.*, 4 F.3d 286, 289 (4th Cir. 1993); *Elkind v. Liggett & Myers, Inc.*, 635 F.2d 156, 163 (2d Cir. 1980). Likewise problematic from the standpoint of *Janus* would be the issuer's after-the-fact adoption of the third-party's statement. *Cf. In re Cypress Semiconductor Sec. Litig.*, 891 F. Supp. 1369, 1377 (N.D. Cal. 1995), *aff'd mem. sub nom. Eisenstadt v. Allen*, 113 F.3d 1240 (9th Cir. 1997) .

<u>Fiduciary Relationships and Other Duties at Common Law</u>. When deciding whether a disclosure duty exists under Rule 10b-5, courts frequently look to the common-law. Consider *Chiarella v. United States*, 445 U.S. 222 (1980), where the Supreme Court drew on a fiduciary duty set forth in the Restatement (Second) of Torts to ground its observation that Rule 10b-5 liability attaches to officers and directors who trade in their company's securities while failing to disclose material information. *Id.* at 228 (quoting Restatement (Second) of Torts § 551(2)(a) (1976)).

Moreover, courts have relied on fiduciary disclosure duties to impose Rule 10b-5 liability not only on officers and directors but also on issuers who buy or sell their own securities while withholding material information from the public. *See Castellano v. Young & Rubicam, Inc.*, 257 F.3d 171, 179 (2d Cir. 2001); *Shaw v. Digital Equip. Corp.*, 82 F.3d 1194

(1st Cir. 1996); *McCormick v. Fund Am. Cos.*, 26 F.3d 869, 875–876 (9th Cir. 1994); *Jordan v. Duff & Phelps, Inc.*, 815 F.2d 429, 435–439 (7th Cir. 1987).

A Brief Word About Regulation FD. An important issue relating to the duty to disclose involves Regulation FD (for "Fair Disclosure"), applicable only to reporting companies (*see* § 1.3 *supra*). To be sure, Regulation FD does not compel these companies to disclose information. But it does prohibit them from engaging in selective disclosure of information to securities analysts or to other favored constituencies by requiring that any such disclosure be shared with the general public.

Regulation FD is enforceable only in actions brought by the SEC. Moreover, it specifically provides that "[n]o failure to make a public disclosure required solely by [Regulation FD] shall be deemed to be a violation of Rule 10b-5." Regulation FD, Rule 102. For further discussion of Regulation FD, *see* § 7.8 *infra*.

§ 2.3 MATERIALITY

To be actionable under § 10(b) and Rule 10b-5, the omitted or misstated fact must be "material" in nature. The materiality element has its origins in common law deceit and appears explicitly in Rule 10b-5(b), which is set forth in § 2.1 *supra*.

The applicable standard of materiality comes from *TSC Indus., Inc. v. Northway, Inc.*, 426 U.S. 438 (1976), which involved the materiality of an omission under § 14(a) of the Exchange Act and Rule 14a-9 (*see*

Chapter 4 *infra*). After noting the objective nature of the materiality inquiry, the Court set out the following standard:

> An omitted fact is material if there is a substantial likelihood that a reasonable shareholder would consider it important in deciding how to vote. It does not require proof of a substantial likelihood that disclosure of the omitted fact would have caused the reasonable shareholder to change his vote. * * * Put another way, there must be a substantial likelihood that the disclosure of the omitted fact would have been viewed by the reasonable investor as having significantly altered the "total mix" of information made available.

Id. at 445–449. *See Basic, Inc. v. Levinson*, 485 U.S. 224, 232 (1988) (adopting *Northway* standard of materiality for purposes of § 10(b) and Rule 10b-5). *See also Matrixx Initatives, Inc. v. Siracusano*, 563 U.S. 27 (2011) (reaffirming applicability of *Northway* standard of materiality to Rule 10b-5).

Several aspects of the *Northway-Basic* standard are important to keep in mind. It is a contextual standard, as the "total mix" prong makes explicit. Thus, a fact that might otherwise qualify as material might nonetheless be rendered immaterial once a subsequent paragraph in the same document, or a different document, is taken into account. Moreover, materiality assessments are made from the standpoint of the "reasonable investor," who is presumed to know more than the reasonable person does about such matters as how markets work, the difference between equity and debt, and the time value of money.

While the *Northway-Basic* standard is the overarching materiality standard, courts have developed additional considerations that provide guidance in specific types of situations. Those considerations are discussed in the sections that follow.

§ 2.3.1   PUFFERY

A misstatement is immaterial if it constitutes "puffery"—that is, if it is so vague as to be meaningless to the reasonable investor. *See, e.g., City of Pontiac Policemen's & Firemen's Ret. Sys. v. UBS AG*, 752 F.3d 173, 183 (2d Cir. 2014). Puffery is, by its nature, not amenable to objective confirmation. *See, e.g., Oregon Pub. Emps. Ret. Fund v. Apollo Grp. Inc.*, 774 F.3d 598, 606 (9th Cir. 2014).

The puffery doctrine (sometimes called the puffery defense) arose initially in securities cases involving brokers. *See, e.g., Rotstein v. Reynolds, Inc.*, 359 F.Supp. 109, 113 (N.D. Ill. 1973) (characterizing as "puffery" the statement that a stock was "red-hot"). Now expanded in scope, the puffery doctrine is today frequently invoked defensively by corporations and their managers seeking to show the immateriality of statements that they have made about their firms. *See, e.g., Nathenson v. Zonagen, Inc.*, 267 F.3d 400, 419 (5th Cir. 2001) (characterizing as puffery the description of a drug as a " 'fast-acting,' 'improved formulation' ").

Like the materiality inquiry in general, the puffery inquiry in particular often involves an examination of the context in which the statement appears. *See, e.g., Glassman v. Computervision Corp.*, 90 F.3d 617, 635–636 (1st Cir. 1996) (taking into account in puffery inquiry other statements made by the company).

Evidence of puffery can include the defendant's lack of knowledge that the statement was false. *See, e.g., Zaluski v. United Am. Healthcare Corp.*, 527 F.3d 564, 574–575 (6th Cir. 2008). Put differently, there is a relationship between puffery and a lack of scienter. On the other hand, a statement can sometimes qualify as puffery even where the defendant knew it to be false. *See UBS*, 752 F.3d at 183 (noting that the "[p]laintiffs' claim that these statements were knowingly and verifiably false when made does not cure their generality").

§ 2.3.2　THE RELEVANCE OF STATISTICAL SIGNIFICANCE

Can defendants establish the immateriality of an omitted fact simply by showing that the fact lacked statistical significance? The Supreme Court addressed this question in *Matrixx Initiatives, Inc. v. Siracusano*, 563 U.S. 27 (2011). At issue was a pharmaceutical company's failure to disclose the existence of reports indicating that its cold remedy had led some users to lose their sense of smell. The number of reports was statistically insignificant, prompting the company to seek a bright-line rule

that statistical insignificance equals immateriality.
The Court rejected such a rule as follows:

> Given that medical professionals and regulators
> act on the basis of evidence of causation that is
> not statistically significant, it stands to reason
> that in certain cases reasonable investors would
> as well. * * * This is not to say that statistical
> significance (or the lack thereof) is irrelevant—
> only that it is not dispositive of every case.

Id. at 43.

§ 2.3.3   PRICE MOVEMENTS
IN EFFICIENT MARKETS

When a Rule 10b-5 action involves securities
traded in an efficient market, the market itself
typically serves as the stand-in for the reasonable
investor. Thus, suppose that the price of the security
changes significantly following the company's public
correction of a previously misstated fact. That price
change suggests that the fact was important to the
market, and thus material. *See, e.g., In re Merck &
Co., Inc. Sec. Litig.*, 432 F.3d 261, 274 (3d Cir. 2005).
The case for materiality could likely be overcome,
however, if, for example, the price change was
industry-wide, or market-wide.

Suppose in the alternative that no price change
occurred after the company's public correction of the
misstatement. While the lack of change points
toward   immateriality,   reality   may   be   more
complicated. For example, the truth may have leaked
to the market prior to the official date of the

correction, with the result that the correction, when it came, made no difference. Or some other piece of news, whether from the company or elsewhere, may have emerged at the same time as the correction and dissipated the correction's effects. Proof of the impact of the leakage or other news item, while likely difficult to make, would have relevance for the materiality analysis.

§ 2.3.4   THE DISTINCTION BETWEEN HARD AND SOFT INFORMATION

Materiality is typically easier to assess when the information is "hard" rather than "soft." Hard information is rooted in historical or objective fact (*e.g.*, the plant burned to the ground yesterday). Soft information, on the other hand, has a subjective or futurist aspect (*e.g.*, the corporation is considering a merger; a competitor's new product may soon put the corporation out of business). The sections that follow present considerations relevant to assessing the materiality of various types of soft information— merger negotiations and other contingent events (§ 2.3.5 *infra*); and forward-looking statements (§ 2.3.6 *infra*).

§ 2.3.5   THE PROBABILITY/MAGNITUDE TEST

In *Basic Inc. v. Levinson*, 485 U.S. 224 (1988), the Supreme Court upheld the probability/magnitude test as the benchmark for assessing the materiality of merger negotiations. *See id.* at 238–240. The *Basic* decision is likewise significant for two other reasons as well—its adoption of the *Northway* standard as

the materiality standard under Rule 10b-5, *see* § 2.3
supra, as well as for its endorsement of the claim of
fraud-on-the-market, *see* § 2.8.2 *infra*.

The *Basic* defendants had repeatedly issued false
denials concerning their company's participation in
merger negotiations. As the Court noted, merger
negotiations are a species of contingent event, since
whether the merger will eventually occur cannot be
known at the time that it is being negotiated. The
contingency dimension complicates the assessment
of what would be regarded as important by the
reasonable investor, making additional guidance
desirable.

Seeking to provide such guidance, the Court
endorsed the probability/magnitude test, which the
Second Circuit, the "Mother Court" of securities law,
had long used in connection with merger negotiations
in particular as well as with contingent events more
broadly. The probability/magnitude test involves
" 'balancing of both the indicated probability that the
event will occur and the anticipated magnitude of the
event in light of the totality of the company activity.' "
Id. at 237 (quoting *SEC v. Tex. Gulf Sulphur Co.*, 401
F.2d 833, 849 (2d Cir. 1968)). The Court remanded
the case for consideration under this test.

Does the probability/magnitude test apply to
contingent events other than merger negotiations?
The Court affirmatively left that question open. *See
Basic*, 485 U.S. at 260 n.9. Prior to *Basic*, lower courts
applied the test to other types of contingent events.
See, e.g., Harkavy v. Apparel Indus, Inc., 571 F2d
737, 740–742 (2d Cir. 1978) (application to a clothing

manufacturer's plan to introduce a new line of sportswear). After *Basic*, that pattern has continued. *See, e.g., United States v. Smith*, 155 F.3d 1051, 1065 (9th Cir. 1998) (application to forecasts tipped in insider trading).

The probability/magnitude test is often easier to recite than to apply. To be sure, assessments of magnitude can be relatively easy, since corporate events such as mergers are frequently of clear-cut importance. But assessments of probability are often considerably more challenging. Transactions such as mergers, leveraged buyouts, or initial public offerings are often conditioned on numerous factors that cannot be predicted, such as market conditions, availability of financing, resolution of antitrust, and other regulatory issues.

Further confounding assessments of probability is the fact that these assessments are typically made after the merger or other event in question has occurred (or failed to occur). The event's occurrence contributes to the perception that the probability at the relevant earlier point was higher than it may actually have been, just as the event's non-occurrence has the opposite effect. This phenomenon—known as hindsight bias—can impact the fact-finding of a judge or jury (or even the SEC or the DOJ).

§ 2.3.6   FORWARD-LOOKING STATEMENTS

In the 1970s, the SEC began encouraging companies to disclose, in filed documents or otherwise, forward-looking statements such as earnings projections and statements of future plans.

But companies worried that by making such disclosure, they would render themselves vulnerable to fraud actions when their predictions failed to come true.

The SEC responded by adopting Rule 175 (under the Securities Act) and Rule 3b-6 (under the Exchange Act), which, at least to a limited extent, encouraged issuers to disclose forward-looking information. These rules apply only to forward-looking statements that appear in SEC filings. In addition, they provide no insulation from fraud liability when the forward-looking statement "was made or reaffirmed without a reasonable basis or was disclosed other than in good faith." Because the existence of bad faith and a reasonable basis are generally questions of fact for which a hearing is necessary, these rules do not ordinarily enable defendants to obtain a dismissal at an early stage of litigation involving forward-looking statements.

Sturdier insulation comes from the judicially created bespeaks caution doctrine (*see* § 2.3.7 *infra*) and the statutory safe harbor for forward-looking statements (*see* § 2.3.8 *infra*). For either to apply, the statement at issue must qualify as "forward-looking." Since a given statement can refer to the future as well as to the present (or the past), categorization can be difficult. One approach is to focus on whether the aspect of the statement alleged to be false is forward-looking. Consider how the First Circuit applied this approach to the statement that the company " 'has on hand and has access to sufficient sources of funds to meet its anticipated * * * needs' " in *In re Stone &*

Webster, Inc. Sec. Litig., 414 F.3d 187, 211 (1st Cir. 2005). Reasoning that the plaintiffs had alleged that the defendants had misrepresented the company's "present access to funds," the court concluded that the statement was not forward-looking. *Id.* at 212–13.

A different approach was taken by the Fifth Circuit to the statement that " 'the challenges unique to this period are now behind us' " in *Harris v. Ivax Corp.*, 182 F.3d 799, 805 (11th Cir. 1999). Rejecting the significance of the present-tense verb, the court deemed the statement forward-looking because "[w]hether the worst of Ivax's challenges were behind it was a matter verifiable only after the chairman so declared." *Id. See Julianello v. K-V Pharm. Co.*, 791 F.3d 915, 921 (8th Cir. 2015) (following this same approach).

Another classification issue arises when the defendant offers a list of factors, only some of which involve the future. Confronting such a list of factors that were expected to impact the company's business in the third quarter, the *Ivax* court treated the entire list as forward-looking. It offered three justifications for so doing. First, to do otherwise would cause corporate officers to say less rather than more. Second, a mixed list will be treated as forward-looking only if it contains assumptions, the presence of which should serve as a red flag for investors. Finally, the defendant will be protected only where it provides meaningful cautions. *See Ivax*, 182 F.3d at 805–807.

§ 2.3.7   THE BESPEAKS CAUTION DOCTRINE

Under the bespeaks caution doctrine, an omitted or misstated forward-looking statement is immaterial as a matter of law if accompanied by cautions flagging the potentiality of an outcome different from the one predicted. *See, e.g., SEC v. Merchant Capital, LLC*, 483 F.3d 747, 767 (11th Cir. 2007); *Emp'rs Teamsters Local Nos. 175 & 505 Pension Trust Fund v. Clorox Co.*, 353 F.3d 1125, 1131–1132 (9th Cir. 2004); *In re Donald J. Trump Casino Sec. Litig.*, 7 F.3d 357 (3d Cir. 1993). The doctrine is a corollary of the contextual nature of materiality. *See Trump*, 7 F.3d at 364.

For the doctrine to apply, the cautions must be "substantive and tailored to the specific future projections, estimates or opinions" at issue. *Id.* at 371–72. These non-boilerplate cautions prevent the forward-looking statement from having an impact on the "total mix" of information.

An illustration comes from the Third Circuit's decision in *Trump*, above. At issue there was the following assertion in a prospectus offered in connection with an IPO: "The Partnership believes that funds generated from the operation of [the partially-built casino known as] the Taj Mahal will be sufficient to cover its debt service." *Id.* at 369. This assertion appeared after a detailed discussion of various specific risks that could materialize and prevent the bondholders from being repaid, including those emanating from the casino business in general, the casino's lack of operating history and its size and complexity. *Id.* at 370. Moreover, the assertion was followed by the statement that "[n]o assurance can be given, however, that actual operating results will meet the Partnership's expectations." *Id.* at 371. The court dismissed the action by granting the defendants' motion to dismiss under Rule 12(b)(6) of the Federal Rules of Civil Procedure for failure to state a claim. *Id.* at 377.

By authorizing dismissal at a very early stage of the litigation, the bespeaks caution doctrine may increase companies' willingness to make forward-looking statements. It may do something else as well—namely, eliminate weak actions prior to the discovery phase of the litigation and thereby spare the defendants the time and expense that discovery entails.

Does the bespeaks caution doctrine provide the basis for dismissal where the plaintiff can show that the defendant did not believe the prediction when he made it? One court has given a negative answer on the ground that a positive one "would allow, if not encourage, fraud and non-disclosure on the part of corporate actors." *Gurfein v. Sovereign Grp.,* 826 F. Supp. 890, 908 n.20 (E.D. Pa. 1993).

Because the bespeaks caution doctrine applies to both reporting companies and non-reporting companies, as well as to any type of issuer or transaction, it can come into play when the more highly restricted statutory safe harbor for forward-looking statements, described in § 2.3.8 *infra*, is not available.

§ 2.3.8   THE STATUTORY SAFE HARBOR FOR FORWARD-LOOKING STATEMENTS

As part of the PSLRA, Congress provided a safe harbor for forward-looking statements by adding § 21E to the Exchange Act (and § 27A to the Securities Act). This safe harbor is explicitly limited to private actions (and thus does not come into play in actions brought by the SEC or the DOJ). Moreover, it applies only when the issuer of the securities is a reporting company (*see* § 1.3 *supra*). In addition, it excludes from its purview certain types of issuers (*e.g.*, partnerships and limited liability companies) and transactions (*e.g.*, initial public offerings and tender offers).

The statutory safe harbor authorizes three alternative prongs for dismissing a private fraud action involving a forward-looking statement:

The "Bespeaks Caution" Prong. The forward-looking statement must be "identified as a forward-looking statement, and [be] accompanied by meaningful cautionary statements identifying important factors that could cause actual results to differ materially from those in the forward-looking statement." § 21E(c)(1)(A)(i). As its text suggests, this ground was inspired by the judicially-created bespeaks caution doctrine, discussed in § 2.3.7 *supra*.

The Immateriality Prong. The forward-looking statement must be "immaterial." § 21E(c)(1)(A)(ii). For example, the statement might amount to puffery (*see* § 2.3.1 *supra*) or it might fail to satisfy the probability/magnitude test (*see* § 2.3.5 *supra*).

The Actual Knowledge Prong. The plaintiff must be unable to show that the defendant made the forward-looking statement "with actual knowledge" of its falsity. § 21E(c)(1)(B). With this prong, Congress ratcheted up the scienter standard from recklessness to "actual knowledge" for private fraud actions involving forward-looking statements.

During the pendency of a motion to dismiss based on any of these prongs, discovery is stayed. *See* § 21E(f).

The "bespeaks caution" prong has generated a number of questions. One is what makes a cautionary statement "meaningful." *See In re Harman Int'l Indus., Inc. Sec. Litig.*, 791 F.3d 90, 103–108 (D.C. Cir. 2015) (discussing this question). A general caution does not qualify, just as it fails to qualify under the judicially-created bespeaks caution doctrine. *See id.* Also problematic is a caution which remains the same even when changes occur in the relevant risks. *See Asher v. Baxter Int'l, Inc.*, 377 F.3d 727 (7th Cir. 2004). Moreover, while the defendant does not have to include every "important factor," what if he omits the one that is "such a market-driver that it dwarfs" the others in importance? *See Harris v. Ivax Corp.*, 209 F.3d 1275, 1276 (11th Cir. 2000) (raising this question but not answering it).

Another question prompted by the "bespeaks caution" prong is whether it matters that the defendant knew about the risks omitted from the forward-looking statement. To be sure, the legislative history is explicit that the defendant's knowledge (the subject of the actual knowledge prong) is not a proper focus of the inquiry under the bespeaks caution prong (a reading consistent with the fact that the two prongs are connected by the word "or"). While acknowledging this history, the Second Circuit has asked Congress for additional guidance on the following "thorny" issue: "May an issuer be protected by the meaningful cautionary language prong of the safe harbor even where his cautionary statement omitted a major risk that he knew about at the time he made the statement?" *Slayton v. American Express Co.*, 604 F.3d 758, 771–772 (2d Cir. 2010). *Cf. In re Stone & Webster Inc. Sec. Litig.*, 414 F.3d 187, 212 (1st Cir. 2005) (describing the safe harbor as "surprising," "curious," and "a license to defraud").

§ 2.4 THE "IN CONNECTION WITH" REQUIREMENT

The "in connection with" requirement emerges from the language of § 10(b) and Rule 10b-5, each of which prohibits fraud "in connection with" the purchase or sale of any security. The language is silent, however, concerning the nature of the necessary connection, as is the legislative history. Thus, judicial decisions provide the key source of guidance regarding the substance of the requirement. That substance is discussed in § 2.4.1 *infra*.

Rule 10b-5's "in connection with" requirement became the model for the requirement of the same name contained in the Securities Litigation Reform Act (the SLUSA), enacted by Congress in 1998. For discussion of the SLUSA's "in connection with" requirement, *see* § 6.5 *infra*.

§ 2.4.1   *SEC v. ZANDFORD*

The Supreme Court's principal exposition to date of Rule 10b-5's "in connection with" requirement came in *SEC v. Zandford*, 535 U.S. 813 (2002). The defendant was a stockbroker charged with selling securities over a two-year period from the account of his elderly, ailing client and misappropriating the money for his own use without the client's knowledge or permission. At issue was whether the fraud practiced on the client occurred "in connection with" the purchase or sale of a security. The Court held that it did, reversing the circuit court (which had in turn reversed the trial court).

As the Supreme Court saw it, the fraud perpetrated on the client and the sales of the securities from the client's account "coincided," that is, they were not "independent events," since "each sale was made to further respondent's fraudulent scheme." *Id.* at 820. The Court clarified its holding by contrasting several situations in which no such "coincidence" arose:

- the situation "in which, after a lawful transaction had been consummated, a broker decided to steal the proceeds and did so;"

- the situation "in which a thief simply invested the proceeds of a routine conversion in the stock market;"

- the situation in which "a broker . . . takes advantage of the fiduciary relationship to induce his client into a real estate transaction."

Id. at 820, 825 n.4. As these examples illustrate, finding a "coincidence," and meeting the "in connection with" requirement more generally, turns on more than the simultaneity or close temporal succession of the fraud and the securities transaction (if any). Thus, after *Zandford*, the Fourth Circuit has undertaken to identify some additional relevant factors. *See* § 2.4.2 *infra*.

The Supreme Court also focused its "in connection with" inquiry on the presence of a "coincidence" when examining whether § 10(b) and Rule 10b-5 encompass the misappropriation theory of insider trading. *See United States v. O'Hagan*, 521 U.S. 642, 656 (1997), discussed in § 7.4 *infra*.

§ 2.4.2   OTHER CONSIDERATIONS REGARDING THE "IN CONNECTION WITH" REQUIREMENT

The Fourth Circuit made a significant contribution to "in connection with" analysis with its decision in *SEC v. Pirate Investor LLC*, 580 F.3d 233 (4th Cir. 2009). *See, e.g., Serra v. Banco Santander P.R.*, 747 F.3d 1, 6 (1st Cir. 2014) (applying the Fourth Circuit's approach).

At issue in *Pirate* was a fraudulent "Super Insider Tip E-Mail" sent in "waves" by a publisher of investment newsletters to more than 800,000 subscribers. The email touted the profits that would come from buying shares in an unnamed company prior to the company's upcoming announcement of an important and favorable transaction that had been privately acknowledged by one of its senior officers. The email advised that the company's name would be revealed for a payment of $1,000. More than a thousand people made that payment. Some of them purchased the shares, leading to surges in the stock price, which surges were noted in later waves of the email that in turn precipitated additional $1,000 payments. No officer of the company had in fact made the representations described in the e-mail and the transaction in question did not occur.

After a bench trial, the trial court concluded that the SEC had established the "in connection with" requirement, as well as the other elements of a Rule 10b-5 cause of action. On appeal, the Fourth Circuit found that it needed more guidance on the "in connection with" inquiry than *Zandford* provided. To aid that inquiry, it identified the following four non-exclusive factors:

- first, "whether a securities sale was necessary to the completion of the fraudulent scheme." *Pirate*, 580 F.3d at 244 (citing *Zandford*, 535 U.S. at 820–821);

- second, "whether the parties' relationship was such that it would necessarily involve trading in securities." *Id*. This factor finds at least

implicit support in *Zandford,* which involved
a stockbroker-client relationship. *See* § 2.4.1
supra.

- third, "whether the defendant intended [the
  fraud] to induce a securities transaction." *Id.*
  This factor likewise finds implicit support in
  Zandford, which approved SEC decisions that
  premised "in connection with" determinations
  on the defendant's intent. *See Zandford*, 535
  U.S. at 820.

- fourth, "whether material misrepresentations
  were 'disseminated to the public in a medium
  upon which a reasonable investor would
  rely.'" *Pirate,* 580 F.3d at 244 (quoting
  Semerenko v. Cendant Corp., 223 F.3d 165,
  176 (3d Cir. 2000)). As the Fourth Circuit
  noted, this factor originated in the Second
  Circuit's landmark decision in *SEC v. Texas
  Gulf Sulphur Co.*, 401 F.2d 833 (2d Cir. 1968)
  (en banc), which held that "Rule 10b-5 is
  violated whenever assertions are made * * *
  in a manner reasonably calculated to
  influence the investing public." *Id.* at 862.

To satisfy the fourth factor, the misrepresentations
at issue must be material. *See Pirate*, 580 F.3d at 249.
Recall that materiality is also an independent
element of the cause of action. *See* generally § 2.3
supra.

Applying these factors, the Fourth Circuit
concluded that the first, third, and fourth cut in favor
of the SEC. Consider the court's observation

concerning the first factor (the necessity of a securities sale to the scheme)—"[T]he fraud was not complete when investors paid $1,000 to learn the identity of the company." *Pirate*, 580 F.3d at 246. The reason was that "the defendants also needed those investors to purchase the stock thereby increasing the stock price so as to boost the credibility of the solicitation e-mail to obtain more $1,000 payments." *Id.*

Consider next the third factor (the defendants' intent that the fraud "induce a securities transaction"). Of critical importance, the court noted, was that the misrepresentations about the forthcoming transaction that were attributed to the senior officer appeared not only in the initial e-mail but also in the later document naming the company (for which investors paid). The reason to include these misrepresentations in the later document was to prompt its recipients to buy shares in the company. If the fraud was designed only to elicit payments of the $1000 fee, the repetition of the fraud would have served no purpose. *Id.* at 248.

Consider also the fourth factor ("whether material misrepresentations were disseminated to the public in a medium upon which a reasonable investor would rely"). The court acknowledged that relying on Internet investment advice was arguably something that a reasonable investor would not do. *Id.* at 250. But it found this argument inapposite given the fourth factor's underlying purpose—namely, to give speakers notice of their potential liability for misstatements appearing in media that investors trusted, regardless of the seeming remoteness of those media to the securities markets. The court explained that the e-mails at issue in this case did not raise notice issues, since the defendants sent them only to subscribers to Internet investment newsletters, that is, only to those who evidenced a willingness to rely on such media in the first place.

The Fourth Circuit determined that the only factor cutting against the SEC was number two (a relationship that "would necessarily involve trading in securities"). *Id.* at 252. The court noted that the case at bar did not present a relationship analogous to the broker-client relationship presented by *Zandford. Id.* at 247.

The Fourth Circuit held that the SEC met its burden in establishing the "in connection with" requirement, despite its failure to satisfy the second factor. The SEC's success under these circumstances underscores the court's admonition that the factors merely "guide the inquiry" and do not amount to "mandatory requirements." *Id.* at 244.

§ 2.5 SCIENTER

Scienter, a Latin word for "knowingly," is a term used to describe a person's state of mind at the time he or she took action or failed to take action. An action taken with scienter is taken intentionally, or at least recklessly. On the other hand, an action taken negligently, or even grossly negligently, is said to lack scienter.

Understanding Rule 10b-5's scienter requirement involves familiarity in the first instance with its substantive content, which is discussed in § 2.5.1 *infra*. Likewise of critical importance are the relevant pleading rules, the subject of § 2.6 *infra*.

§ 2.5.1   *ERNST & ERNST v. HOCHFELDER*

The Supreme Court addressed whether § 10(b) and Rule 10b-5 require proof of scienter in *Ernst & Ernst v. Hochfelder*, 425 U.S. 185 (1976). To make sense of the decision, familiarity with the underlying facts is essential.

The plaintiffs, clients of a small brokerage firm, were persuaded by its president (Nay) to invest in "escrow accounts" that purportedly offered a high rate of return but were actually fictitious. Nay misappropriated for his own benefit the funds that the plaintiffs surrendered for deposit in those accounts. Nay eventually committed suicide, which led to the revelation of the fraud and the firm's insolvency. The clients thereupon brought a Rule 10b-5 action against Ernst & Ernst, the firm's auditor, on the theory that the accountants had "aided and abetted" the fraud by negligently overlooking practices that enabled it to escape notice, principally the "mail rule," pursuant to which only Nay could open mail addressed to him.

The Court held that proof of scienter was an essential element of § 10(b) and Rule 10b-5. Since the plaintiffs had not alleged scienter on the part of Ernst & Ernst officials, the lawsuit was doomed to failure, allowing the Court to sidestep the question whether

aiders and abettors were appropriate Rule 10b-5
defendants. *See id.* at 191 n.7. The Court did not
reach the viability of aiding and abetting liability for
almost another 20 years, rejecting it in *Central Bank,
N.A. v. Interstate Bank, N.A.*, 511 U.S. 164 (1994),
discussed in § 2.12.1 *infra.*

The Court upheld the scienter requirement
primarily on the basis of § 10(b)'s prohibition against
the use of "any manipulative or deceptive device or
contrivance." *See* § 2.1 *supra* (setting forth the text of
§ 10(b)). Turning to a 1934 Webster's dictionary for
definitions of the words in this phrase, the Court
concluded that § 10(b) "clearly connotes intentional
conduct." *Hochfelder*, 425 U.S. at 201. The Court also
drew support from testimony offered by Thomas G.
Corcoran in the House Hearings on the Exchange
Act. Corcoran, "a spokesman for the drafters" [who
had been recruited to work on New Deal legislation
by then-Professor Felix Frankfurter], testified that
§ 10(b) prohibited "cunning" or "manipulative"
devices. *Id.* at 202. In the Court's view, Corcoran's
formulation signaled that § 10(b) was limited to
intentional conduct. *Id.* at 204.

The Court considered, but rejected, the argument
that negligence should suffice because it satisfies the
Securities Act's express remedies. *See id.* at 200–201.
Those remedies, discussed in Chapter 3 *infra*, involve
procedural restrictions not germane to Rule 10b-5. If
negligence were to satisfy Rule 10b-5, the Court
explained, the Rule would become vastly more
popular than those express remedies, thereby
"nullify[ing] the effectiveness of the * * * procedural

restrictions" attached to the latter, a development which, without more, would contradict the intent of Congress. *Id.* at 210.

The Court acknowledged that Rule 10b-5, if "[v]iewed in isolation," might be read to allow liability on the basis of negligence. *Id.* at 212. The Court concluded, however, that this reading could not carry the day, since § 10(b), the parent statute, so clearly compelled the opposite interpretation. *See id.* at 212–214.

What then is the substance of Rule 10b-5's scienter requirement? The *Hochfelder* Court had two things to say:

- First, "the term 'scienter' refers to a mental state embracing intent to deceive, manipulate, or defraud." *See id.* at 193 n.12.

- Moreover, reckless may, or may not, suffice as scienter for these purposes. *See id.* The Court was able to avoid addressing this issue, since there was no allegation that Ernst & Ernst had been reckless.

The question whether recklessness suffices, discussed in § 2.5.2 *infra*, was not the only scienter-related question that the *Hochfelder* Court left dangling. There was also the question of the decision's applicability to actions filed by the government, discussed in § 2.5.3 *infra*.

§ 2.5.2   RECKLESSNESS AS SCIENTER

As noted in § 2.5.1 *supra*, the *Hochfelder* Court declined to address whether recklessness constitutes scienter under § 10(b) and Rule 10b-5. The Court has thereafter declined to do so four more times—in *Aaron v. SEC*, 446 U.S. 680, 686 n.5 (1980); *Herman & MacLean v. Huddleston*, 459 U.S. 375, 378 n.4 (1983); *Tellabs, Inc. v. Makor Issues & Rights, Ltd.*, 551 U.S. 308, 319 n.3 (2007); and *Matrixx Initiatives, Inc. v. Siracusano*, 563 U.S. 27, 48 (2011).

This silence notwithstanding, every federal circuit court to confront the issue has held recklessness to be sufficient. *Tellabs*, 551 U.S. at 319 n.3. To be sure, these courts do not all define recklessness the same way. *See id.* Yet among the many circuit definitions, the following formulation has carried significant weight:

> [R]eckless conduct may be defined as . . . highly unreasonable [conduct], involving not merely simple, or even inexcusable negligence, but an extreme departure from the standards of ordinary care, and which presents a danger of misleading buyers or sellers that is either known to the defendant or is so obvious that the actor must have been aware of it.

Sundstrand Corp. v. Sun Chem. Corp., 553 F.2d 1033, 1045 (7th Cir. 1977).

The *Sundrand* definition has given rise to a number of permutations. For example, the Fifth Circuit requires " 'severe recklessness,' " which is " 'limited to those highly unreasonable omissions or misrepresentations that involve not merely simple or even inexcusable negligence, but an extreme departure from the standard of ordinary care, and that present a danger of misleading buyers or sellers which is either known to the defendant or is so obvious that the defendant must have been aware of it.'" *Nathenson v. Zonagen Inc.*, 267 F.3d 400, 408 (5th Cir. 2001) (quoting *Broad v. Rockwell Int'l Corp.*, 642 F.2d 929, 961–962 (5th Cir. 1981)). On the other hand, the First Circuit has observed that recklessness " 'does not include ordinary negligence, but is closer to being a lesser form of intent.'" *Fire & Police Pension Ass'n v. Abiomed, Inc.*, 778 F.3d 228, 240 (1st Cir. 2015) (quoting *Greebel v. FTP Software, Inc.*, 194 F.3d 185, 188 (1st Cir. 1999)).

§ 2.5.3   THE NECESSITY FOR SCIENTER IN SEC AND DOJ ACTIONS

The *Hochfelder* Court sent mixed signals regarding the implications of its decision for government actions—that is, to SEC actions (both administrative and judicial) and to DOJ actions (all of which are criminal). On the one hand, the Court identified the question for decision as "whether a *private cause of action for damages* will lie under § 10(b) and Rule 10b-5 in the absence of any allegation of scienter." *Id.* at 193 (emphasis added). On the other hand, the reasons it offered for requiring scienter—namely, statutory language and legislative history, discussed in § 2.5.1 *supra*—are arguably as relevant, if not more relevant, to expressly-created government actions than to private actions created by judicial implication.

Five years later, in *Aaron v. SEC*, 446 U.S. 680 (1980), the Court held that *Hochfelder* applied to government actions as well. The *Aaron* Court explained its holding by pointing to *Hochfelder*'s reliance on statutory language and legislative history: "In our view, the rationale of *Hockfelder* [sic] ineluctably leads to the conclusion that scienter is an element of a violation of § 10(b) and Rule 10b-5, regardless of the identity of the plaintiff or the nature of the relief sought." *Aaron*, 446 U.S. at 691.

One final issue, involving *Hochfelder* and criminal actions, merits attention. When a Rule 10b-5 action is criminal, the DOJ must prove that the defendant acted "willfully," as required by Exchange Act § 32(a). *See* § 11.2.1 *infra*. That requirement in turn prompts the question, to which there is as yet no answer—namely, whether scienter is subsumed by "willfulness" or retains independent significance in the criminal context. *See* § 11.2.1 *infra*.

§ 2.5.4   CIRCUMSTANTIAL EVIDENCE AS PROOF OF SCIENTER

As the Supreme Court has recognized, proof of scienter under Rule 10b-5 "is often a matter of inference from circumstantial evidence." *Herman & MacLean v. Huddleston*, 459 U.S. 375, 390 n.30 (1983). The First Circuit compiled the following list of factors that may provide evidence of scienter in a Rule 10b-5 action alleging material misstatements or omissions:

- insider trading [at suspicious times and in suspicious amounts];

- divergence between internal reports and external statements on the same subject;

- closeness in time of an allegedly fraudulent statement or omission and the later disclosure of inconsistent information;

- evidence of bribery by a top company official;

- existence of an ancillary lawsuit charging fraud by a company and the company's quick settlement of that suit;

- disregard of the most current factual information before making statements;

- disclosure of accrual basis information in a way which could only be understood by a sophisticated person with a high degree of accounting skill; and

- the self-interested motivation of defendants in the form of saving their salaries or jobs.

Greebel v. FTP Software, Inc., 194 F.3d 185, 196 (1st Cir. 1999).

Notice that some of these types of evidence may be more accessible than others. Certain of them may appear in public documents, whereas others may be obtained only through the mechanisms of discovery, such as interrogatories or depositions.

§ 2.5.5 THE PROBLEM OF CORPORATE SCIENTER

The typical way for the plaintiff to establish the scienter of a corporate defendant is by proving the individual scienter of the corporation's director(s) or senior officer(s) who uttered or approved the fraud. *See Teamsters Local 445 Freight Div. Pension Fund v. Dynex Capital, Inc.*, 531 F.3d 190, 195 (2d Cir. 2008). But suppose the speaker lacks the requisite scienter. Should the plaintiff be allowed to show the corporation's scienter based on what was known by another high-ranking individual? A few courts have suggested an affirmative answer. *See, e.g., Teamsters*, 531 F.3d at 195; *In re WorldCom, Inc., Sec. Litig.*, 352 F.Supp.2d 472, 497 (S.D.N.Y. 2005).

Aggregation assumes that high-ranking corporate officials tend to share information, even if that sharing cannot be proven. At least some of the time, however, sharing does not occur, making the imposition of liability arguably unfair.

§ 2.5.6   THE DISTINCTION BETWEEN GOOD AND BAD MOTIVES

The question sometimes arises as to whether a person acts with scienter if he or she intentionally misrepresents (or omits) a material fact with an arguably praiseworthy motive. For example, consider the CEO of a potential takeover target who denies to a reporter the existence of merger negotiations to prevent a run-up in the stock price (which would make the transaction substantially less attractive to a potential bidder).

Securities fraud cases generally draw the same distinction between motive and intent that is common in criminal law—namely, proof of motive often evidences an intent to deceive, but an intent to deceive does not require a nefarious motive. The Supreme Court has underscored that a nefarious motive is not necessary by refusing to insulate "white lies" from Rule 10b-5 liability: "[W]e think that creating an exception to a regulatory scheme founded on a prodisclosure legislative philosophy, because complying with the regulation might be 'bad for business,' is a role for Congress, not this Court." *Basic Inc. v. Levinson*, 485 U.S. 224, 239 n.17 (1988).

§ 2.6 PLEADING SCIENTER

When it comes to pleading scienter, several statutory provisions come into play. The oldest one is Rule 9(b) of the Federal Rules of Civil Procedure, noted previously in § 2.1 *supra*. Rule 9(b) applies to private actions and also to those brought by the SEC. The remaining provisions, which were added to the Exchange Act in 1995 as part of the PSLRA, apply to private actions only.

Rule 9(b) of the FRCP, which governs the pleading of all civil complaints filed in federal court alleging violations of Rule 10b-5. It reads as follows:

> In all averments of fraud or mistake, the circumstances constituting fraud or mistake shall be stated with particularity. Malice, intent, knowledge, and other condition of mind of a person may be averred generally.

By allowing general allegations of a "condition of mind," Rule 9(b) may seem at first blush to set a rather low bar for pleading scienter under Rule 10b-5. But in cases involving claims of securities fraud, many courts—most particularly the Second Circuit—put additional teeth into Rule 9(b), requiring plaintiffs (including the SEC) to allege specific facts giving rise to a strong inference of scienter. The Second Circuit also developed the so-called "motive and opportunity" test, under which plaintiffs could successfully plead a "strong inference" of scienter by alleging facts "establishing a motive to commit fraud and an opportunity to do so." *In re Time Warner, Inc., Sec. Litig.*, 9 F.3d 259, 269 (2d Cir. 1993). Alternatively, plaintiffs could satisfy the "strong inference" standard by alleging "facts constituting circumstantial evidence of either reckless or conscious behavior." *Id.*

§ 21D(b)(2) of the Exchange Act, which governs the pleading of all complaints filed in federal court under the Exchange Act by private plaintiffs seeking money damages. This provision establishes a uniform standard for pleading state of mind that draws on the Second Circuit's "strong inference" phraseology noted in the preceding paragraph:

> In any private action arising under [the Exchange Act] in which the plaintiff may recover money damages only on proof that the defendant acted with a particular state of mind, the complaint shall, with respect to each act or omission alleged to violate [the Exchange Act], state with particularity facts giving rise to a strong inference that the defendant acted with the required state of mind.

The Supreme Court construed § 21D(b)(2)'s "strong inference" standard in *Tellabs, Inc. v. Makor Issues*

& Rights, Ltd., 551 U.S. 308 (2007), discussed in § 2.6.1*infra*. There the Court observed that despite its incorporation of the Second Circuit's language, Congress did not mean also to incorporate the Second Circuit's caselaw construing that language. *See id.* at 322.

§ 21D(b)(3)(A) of the Exchange Act, which requires a court, on the motion of any defendant, to dismiss a complaint for failure to meet § 21D(b)'s pleading requirements.

§ 21D(b)(3)(B) of the Exchange Act, which imposes an automatic stay of discovery during the pendency of a dismissal motion, unless the court finds that "particularized discovery is necessary to preserve evidence or to prevent undue prejudice to that party." In effect, the provision creates a default rule allowing discovery "only after the court has sustained the legal sufficiency of the complaint." *SG Cowen Sec. Corp. v. U.S. Dist. Court for N. Dist. of Cal.*, 189 F.3d 909, 912–13 (9th Cir. 1999) (emphasis omitted). The provision does not apply to "discovery received in response to discovery requests properly issued before any stay arose." *Petrie v. Elec. Game Card, Inc.*, 761 F.3d 959, 967 (9th Cir. 2014).

Courts vary considerably regarding what constitutes "undue prejudice." One court equated "undue prejudice" with "improper or unfair detriment" and noted that it fell short of " 'irreparable harm.' " *Med. Imaging Ctrs. of Am., Inc. v. Lichtenstein*, 917 F. Supp. 717, 720 (S.D. Cal. 1996). Elaborating further, the court went on to say that it would find "undue prejudice" in circumstances where the stay would effectively "shield[ ] [defendants] from eventual liability for any material violations of the securities laws," that is, from liability that might attach in the event that the pending dismissal motion were denied. *Id.* at 721 n.3. In contrast, the Ninth Circuit, perhaps (or perhaps not) intending to refer only to the pending dismissal motion and not to future ones in the event that the present one was denied, held that "as a matter of law, failure to muster facts sufficient to meet the [PSLRA]'s pleading requirements cannot constitute the requisite 'undue prejudice' to the plaintiff justifying a lift of the discovery stay under [§ 21D(b)(3)(B)]". *SG Cowen*, 189 F.3d at 913.

§ 2.6.1   *TELLABS, INC. v. MAKOR ISSUES & RIGHTS, LTD.*

In *Tellabs, Inc. v. Makor Issues & Rights, Ltd.*, 551 U.S. 308 (2007), the Supreme Court addressed what it takes to successfully plead "a strong inference" of scienter in accordance with § 21D(b)(2), set forth in § 2.6.1 *supra*. Moreover, as was noted in the latter section, the fact that Congress borrowed the "strong inference" phraseology from the Second Circuit did not reflect an intention to incorporate that Circuit's caselaw regarding the meaning of those words.

Looking to § 21D(b)(2)'s legislative history, the *Tellabs* Court concluded that Congress meant to ratchet up the pleading standard. 551 U.S. at 321. The Court undertook to give content to that standard by drawing on "the PSLRA's twin goals: to curb frivolous, lawyer-driven litigation, while preserving

investors' ability to recover on meritorious claims."
Tellabs, 551 U.S. at 322. In expounding on that
content, it made the following important points:

- When ruling on a motion to dismiss for failing
  to state a Rule 10b-5 claim, courts must accept
  as true the factual allegations of the
  complaint, just as they would on a motion to
  dismiss involving a claim of a different sort.
  Id. at 322.

- In evaluating the allegations pertaining to
  scienter, courts must examine the allegations
  globally. That is, "[t]he inquiry * * * is
  whether *all* of the facts alleged, taken
  collectively, give rise to a strong inference of
  scienter, not whether any individual
  allegation, scrutinized in isolation, meets that
  standard." *Id.* at 322–323.

- The scienter inquiry is "inherently
  comparative," requiring courts to consider
  "plausible opposing inferences." *Id.* at 323. It
  is with reference to these inferences that the
  ones favoring the plaintiffs must emerge as
  "strong"—that is, "powerful" or "cogent" or
  "compelling." *Id.* at 324. The inferences
  favoring the plaintiffs do not, however, have
  to qualify as "irrefutable." *Id.*

- Pleading a "strong inference" of scienter
  requires that "a reasonable person * * * deem
  the inference of scienter *cogent and at least as
  compelling* as any opposing inference one
  could draw from the facts alleged." *Id.* at 324

(emphasis added). Thus, under the majority's view, in the event of two equally plausible inferences, one favoring the plaintiff and the other the defendant, the plaintiff would carry the day. In contrast, under the view expressed in concurring opinions by Justices Scalia and Alito, a "strong inference" ought to require an inference that is more likely than not. Under their view, in the event of two equally plausible inferences, one favoring each side, the plaintiff would lose.

§ 2.6.2   THE GROUP PLEADING DOCTRINE

Prior to the enactment of the PSLRA, most courts recognized the so-called group pleading doctrine:

> In cases of corporate fraud where the false or misleading information is conveyed in prospectuses, registration statements, annual reports, press releases, or other "group-published information," it is reasonable to presume that these are the collective actions of the officers. Under such circumstances, a plaintiff fulfills the particularity requirement of Rule 9(b) by pleading the misrepresentations with particularity and where possible the roles of the individual defendants in the misrepresentations.

Wool v. Tandem Computers, Inc., 818 F.2d 1433, 1439–1440 (9th Cir. 1987). Whether that doctrine survives the PSLRA, however, is a subject on which courts currently divide. This division was acknowledged, but not addressed, by the Supreme Court in *Tellabs. See* 551 U.S. at 326 n.6.

Courts currently rejecting this doctrine focus on the language in § 21D(b)(2), set forth in § 2.6 *supra*, which requires the allegation of "facts giving rise to a strong inference that *the* defendant acted with the required state of mind." *See id.* at 326. (emphasis added). In their view, the words " 'the defendant' may only reasonably be understood to mean 'each defendant' in multiple defendant cases, as it is inconceivable that Congress intended liability of any defendants to depend on whether they were all sued in a single action or were each sued alone in several separate actions." *Southland Sec. Corp. v. INSpire Ins. Solutions, Inc.*, 365 F.3d 353, 364–365 (5th Cir. 2004). Accord *Winer Family Trust v. Queen,* 503 F.3d 319, 337 (3d Cir. 2007).

This rationale has not always carried the day, particularly in the Southern District of New York. Thus, one judge in that district has observed that "[t]he group pleading doctrine does not depend on whether defendants are sued in separate actions or in a single action" but "simply recognizes, solely for pleading purposes, that some corporate documents, including SEC filings and the like, generally are not created by a single author, but by a group of corporate insiders involved in the daily management of a company." *In re BISYS Sec. Litig.,* 397 F. Supp. 2d 430, 440 (S.D.N.Y. 2005). *See City of Pontiac Gen. Emps.' Ret. Sys. v. Lockheed Martin Corp.*, 875 F. Supp. 2d 359, 374 (S.D.N.Y. 2012) (collecting cases and noting that "most judges in this District have continued to conclude that group pleading is alive and well").

§ 2.6.3   PLEADING ANONYMOUS SOURCES

Another contentious issue concerns the PLSRA's impact on scienter allegations resting on unnamed or anonymous sources. In an influential post-*Tellabs* decision, the Seventh Circuit held that while such allegations should not be completely "ignored," they nonetheless should be "discounted"—and "steep[ly]" so in the typical case. *Higginbotham v. Baxter Int'l, Inc.*, 495 F.3d 753, 757 (7th Cir. 2007). The court explained its holding by noting that "[i]t is hard to see how information from anonymous sources could be deemed 'compelling' or how we could take account of plausible opposing inferences. Perhaps these confidential sources have axes to grind. Perhaps they are lying. Perhaps they don't even exist." *Id.*

But soon thereafter, the Seventh Circuit itself distinguished *Higginbotham* in *Makor Issues and Rights, Ltd. v. Tellabs, Inc.*, 513 F.3d 702 (7th Cir. 2008) (*Tellabs II*). There the court noted that the *Higginbotham* complaint not only featured anonymous sources but in addition depicted those sources "merely as three ex-employees of [the defendant company] and two consultants." *Tellabs II*, 513 F.3d at 712. In contrast, the *Tellabs II* complaint contained "numerous" sources "consist[ing] of persons who from the description of their jobs were in a position to know at first hand the facts to which they are prepared to testify * * * . The information that the confidential informants are reported to have obtained is set forth in convincing detail, with some of the information, moreover, corroborated by multiple sources." *Id.* While acknowledging that a complaint with named sources "would be better," the *Tellabs II* court declared that "the absence of proper names does not invalidate the drawing of a strong inference from informants' assertions." *Id.*

Much like the Seventh Circuit in *Tellabs II*, courts in general may be more receptive to allegations based on anonymous sources "when their positions and/or job positions are described in sufficient detail to indicate that it is likely they actually knew the facts underlying their allegations." *In re Gentiva Sec. Litig.*, 932 F. Supp. 2d 352, 376 (E.D.N.Y. 2013). For the various positions taken by federal district courts within the Second Circuit regarding how to assess scienter pleading resting on anonymous sources, see *id.*

§ 2.6.4 PLEADING INSIDER TRADING AS A "MOTIVE AND OPPORTUNITY" FOR FRAUD

Corporate insiders who themselves trade in an issuer's securities presumably have a motive to conceal bad news from other investors until they have executed their own trades, and their control over an issuer's disclosure policies gives them a clear opportunity to deceive those other investors. Thus, both before and after the PSLRA, many Rule 10b-5 plaintiffs have sought to meet the standard for pleading scienter by providing evidence that corporate officials traded in the issuer's stock at the time of the material misstatement or omission alleged in the complaint.

Courts, however, have been clear in holding that mere allegations of insider trading, without more, are insufficient to meet the "strong inference" pleading standard. To meet that standard, the complaint must include specific facts demonstrating that the insider trading is "unusual" or "suspicious." *See, e.g., Pugh v. Tribune Co.*, 521 F.3d 686, 695 (7th Cir. 2008); *In re Silicon Graphics Sec. Litig.*, 183 F.3d 970, 986 (9th Cir. 1999).

Such unusualness or suspiciousness occurs only when the insider trading is " 'dramatically out of line with prior trading practices at times calculated to maximize the personal benefit from undisclosed inside information.' " *Id.* at 986 (quoting *In re Apple Computer Sec. Litig.*, 886 F.2d 1109, 1117 (9th Cir. 1989)). Among the pertinent considerations are "the amount of profit from the sales, the portion of stockholdings sold, the change in volume of insider sales, and the number of insiders selling." *In re Scholastic Corp. Sec. Litig.*, 252 F.3d 63, 74–75 (2d Cir. 2001). *See City of Taylor Gen. Emps. Ret. Sys. v. Magna Int'l Inc.*, 967 F. Supp. 2d 771, 798–799 (S.D.N.Y. 2013). *See also Fla. State Bd. of Admin. v. Green Tree Fin. Corp.*, 270 F.3d 645, 659 (8th Cir. 2001).

§ 2.7 THE PURCHASER-SELLER REQUIREMENT

Private Rule 10b-5 plaintiffs suing for damages must satisfy the "purchaser-seller requirement"—

that is, they must have bought or sold the securities in question. The requirement is inapposite when the plaintiffs is the SEC or the DOJ. The sections that follow discuss the requirement (§ 2.7.1 *infra*), possible exceptions (§ 2.7.3 *infra*), and an alternative that is sometimes available (§ 2.7.4 *infra*).

§ 2.7.1   *BLUE CHIP STAMPS v.*
MANOR DRUG STORES

The Supreme Court upheld the purchaser-seller requirement in *Blue Chip Stamps v. Manor Drug Stores*, 421 U.S. 723 (1975). That decision is noteworthy not only for its holding but also for its articulation of a policy that has continued to play a critical role in the interpretation of § 10(b) and Rule 10b-5—the need to curb vexatious private litigation.

The facts of *Blue Chip Stamps* are unusual as well as important for purposes of understanding the decision's parameters. The plaintiffs, retailers whose businesses had previously used the trading stamps provided by the defendant, had thereafter become eligible to purchase shares in an offering of the defendant's common stock as the result of an antitrust consent decree. The plaintiffs alleged that the prospectus circulated in connection with the offering had painted the defendant's future with a pessimistic brush, prompting them not to buy. In their view, the pessimistic portrayal had been intended to chill their purchases so as to permit the shares to be offered to the public at a higher price in the future.

The question for the Court was whether the non-purchasing plaintiffs could sue for damages. In holding that they could not, the Court adopted the Second Circuit's view that standing to sue is limited to actual purchasers or actual sellers. *See Birnbaum v. Newport Steel Corp.*, 193 F.2d 461 (2d Cir. 1952). In deference to the Second Circuit's seminal decision, the purchaser-seller requirement is still sometimes called the "*Birnbaum* rule."

To justify the purchaser-seller requirement, the Court focused on its utility in curbing vexatious Rule 10b-5 litigation. Attention was also given to the language of § 10(b), pursuant to which the fraud must occur "in connection with the purchase or sale of a security;" to the legislative defeat in the 1950s of proposed amendments adding the phrase "any attempt to purchase or sell;" and to the fact that only purchasers and sellers can pursue the express non-derivative private actions authorized by the Exchange Act and the Securities Act. In a decision more than thirty years thereafter that involved the SLUSA, the Court disavowed any "in connection with" underpinning to the *Blue Chip Stamps* holding and maintained that the purchaser-seller requirement was driven principally by policy considerations. *See Merrill Lynch, Pierce, Fenner & Smith Inc. v. Dabit*, 547 U.S. 71 (2006), discussed in § 6.5.1 *infra*.

In the view of the *Blue Chip Stamps* Court, Rule 10b-5 litigation "presents a danger of vexatiousness different in degree and in kind from that which accompanies litigation in general." 421 U.S. at 739.

This danger is due partly to the fact that the settlement value to the plaintiffs outstrips their chances of winning at trial, so long as they can avoid pre-trial dismissal. *Id.* at 740. The settlement value is enhanced by the lawsuit's capacity to thwart the defendants' routine business activity, a capacity exacerbated when the plaintiffs misuse the liberal federal discovery rules. *Id.* Moreover, the defendants are poorly positioned to challenge testimony by non-trading plaintiffs regarding what they would have done differently in the absence of the fraud, since such testimony would involve matters "totally unknown and unknowable to the defendant." *Id.* at 746. By excluding all non-traders from the litigation pre-trial, the purchaser-seller requirement confines the plaintiff class to those whose account of the relevant events is more likely to be believable. *Id.* at 747.

The Court acknowledged that the purchaser-seller requirement sometimes leaves investors who were deceived into not buying or not selling without a federal securities remedy. *Id.* at 743. But it maintained that the advantages of the requirement outweighed the disadvantages. *Id.* at 749.

The Court took pains to show that it had not pulled the policy of curbing vexatious litigation out of a hat. Rather, the Court insisted, Congress applied that policy in drafting the Exchange Act's sister statute, the Securities Act, § 11 of which permits the court to require the plaintiffs to post a bond to cover litigation expenses. *See id.* at 740–741. Since the 1930s Congress attached importance to combatting strike suits, the Court reasoned, that policy is an appropriate tool for shaping the contours of the Rule 10b-5 private action. *See id.* at 741.

§ 2.7.2   STANDING TO SUE FOR CONTRACT HOLDERS

Under Exchange Act §§ 3(a)(13) and 3(a)(14), respectively, the term "purchase" is defined to include "a contract to purchase securities" and the term "sale" is defined to include "a contract to sell securities." Based on these definitions, the *Blue Chip Stamps* Court took the position that a "purchaser" for Rule 10b-5 purposes includes someone with a contract to purchase and a "seller" includes someone with a contract to sell. *See id.* at 735, 750–751.

This conclusion may not be as inevitable as the Court suggests, since the Exchange Act defines "purchase" and "sale," not "purchaser" and "seller" as such. Be that as it may, the Court's clear stance on the matter provides a basis for Rule 10b-5 standing that adds an important string to a litigator's bow. *See, e.g., Griggs v. Pace Am. Grp., Inc.,* 170 F.3d 877 (9th Cir. 1999).

In *Wharf (Holdings) Ltd. v. United Int'l Holdings, Inc.,* 532 U.S. 588, 594–595 (2001), the Supreme Court held that a contract to buy or sell securities provides standing to sue even if the contract is oral. In so holding, the Court rejected the idea that some plaintiffs could obtain standing by fabricating an oral contract, thereby producing the very vexatious litigation that the purchaser-seller requirement was intended to curtail. Such a development was unlikely, the Court insisted, because the defendants would be able to offer objective evidence that a contract did not exist, thereby countering the plaintiffs' testimony to the contrary. Thus, the situation was different from the one discussed in *Blue Chip Stamps*—namely, where the testimony of non-trading plaintiffs that they would have traded in the absence of the fraud does not lend itself to refutation by objective evidence. *See id.*

§ 2.7.3 POSSIBLE EXCEPTIONS TO THE PURCHASER-SELLER REQUIREMENT

One of the most important—and elusive—aspects of *Blue Chip Stamps* is whether or to what extent it shuts the door on the creation of exceptions to the purchaser-seller requirement. In Part IV of its opinion, the Court acknowledged that creating an exception for the plaintiff retailers would not have been altogether unreasonable. Not only were they a small, circumscribed sub-set of the total investor universe. 421 U.S. at 754. In addition, given their previous dealings with the defendants, they were more likely to have relied on the allegedly fraudulent prospectus than someone who was "a complete stranger." *Id.* Why then did the Court not create an exception? One possibility is that no exceptions are allowed. Indeed, the Court noted that to allow the plaintiff retailers to sue "would leave the *Birnbaum* rule open to endless case-by-case erosion depending on whether a particular group of plaintiffs was thought by the court in which the issue was being litigated to be sufficiently more discrete than the world of potential purchasers." *Id.* at 755. Another possibility is that a necessary—albeit not sufficient—condition for allowing an exception is that the exception have predated the *Blue Chip Stamps* decision: "[W]e have been unable to locate a single decided case from any court in the 20-odd years of litigation since the *Birnbaum* decision which would support the right of persons who were in the position of respondent here to bring a private suit under Rule 10b-5." *Id.* at 751.

In the wake of *Blue Chip Stamps*, courts have struggled with whether to allow various exceptions to the purchaser-seller requirement, including the following:

The Injunction Exception. Prior to *Blue Chip Stamps*, this exception was available to plaintiffs who sought injunctive relief rather than damages. One argument for continuing to allow such an exception is that plaintiffs who are not seeking damages may represent a lesser threat of vexatious litigation. No clear consensus view has emerged. Compare *Cowin v. Bresler*, 741 F.2d 410 (D.C. Cir. 1984) (Bork, J.) (rejecting the injunction exception) and *Cartica Mgmt., LLC v. Corpbanca, S.A.*, 50 F. Supp. 3d 477, 481, 489–91 (S.D.N.Y. 2014) (same) with *Trump Hotels & Casino Resorts, Inc. v. Mirage Resorts, Inc.,* 140 F.3d 478, 486 (3d Cir. 1998) (open question). *See also Trustcash Holdings, Inc. v. Moss*, 668 F Supp. 2d 650, 658–659 (D.N.J. 2009) (identifying arguments for and against the injunction exception and then concluding that the arguments against are "stronger").

<u>The Forced Seller Exception</u>. Prior to *Blue Chip Stamps,* this exception was available to investors who were obliged to sell their shares— say, pursuant to a short-form merger. One reason to doubt the survival of this exception is that the very notion of a seller (or a buyer, for that matter) may involve someone who made an investment decision. *Cf. Isquith by Isquith v. Caremark Int'l, Inc.,* 136 F.3d 531, 535 (7th Cir. 1998). No such decision, however, was made by a forced seller, precisely because he was forced to sell. Moreover, since he was forced to sell, he cannot be said to have relied on the fraud. On the other hand, to allow an exception for forced sellers does not open the door to the entire world, since it would encompass only those investors who incurred the obligation to sell. To be sure, allowing the *Blue Chip Stamps* plaintiffs to sue would likewise not have opened the door to the entire world. But those plaintiffs had no *Birnbaum* era exception to invoke, whereas there was an exception for forced sellers.

Lower courts are divided about whether the "forced seller" exception survives *Blue Chip Stamps.* Compare *7547 Corp. v. Parker & Parsley Dev. Partners, L.P.,* 38 F.3d 211, 228–29 (5th Cir. 1994) (exception survives) with *Isquith,* 136 F.3d at 535–536 (exception unlikely to have survived).

The forced seller exception is sometimes called the fundamental change exception, on the theory that the investor's connection to the company in question has, by dint of the sale, undergone a "fundamental change." *Cf. Id.* at 536.

<u>De Facto Seller Exception</u>. Prior to *Blue Chip Stamps*, this exemption was available to trust beneficiaries who alleged fraud in connection with trades made by their trustees. As potential exceptions to the purchaser-seller requirement go, this one is probably relatively strong, since it is not apt to foment vexatious litigation and does not open the door to the entire world. Some courts, however, limit its availability to those who participated in the investment decisions made by the trustee. *See, e.g., Wendt v. Handler, Thayer & Duggan, LLC*, 613 F. Supp. 2d 1021, 1028–1029 (N.D. Ill. 2009) (participation essential). But *see Ross v. Abercrombie & Fitch Co.*, 257 F.R.D. 435, 448–450 (S.D. Ohio 2009) (participation not essential).

§ 2.7.4   SECTION 29(b) AS A POSSIBLE ALTERNATIVE

At least some plaintiffs who are unable to satisfy the purchaser-seller requirement may nonetheless be able to bring an action under Exchange Act § 29(b), which provides that "[e]very contract made in violation of any provision of this Act or rule or regulation thereunder, and every contract * * * the performance of which involves the violation of * * * any provision of this Act or rule or regulation thereunder, shall be void * * * ." The Supreme Court has held that this provision "confers a 'right to rescind' a contract void under the criteria of the statute." *Transamerica Mortgage Advisors, Inc. v. Lewis*, 444 U.S. 11, 19 (1979) (quoting *Mills v. Elec. Auto-Lite Co.*, 396 U.S. 375, 388 (1970)).

To obtain rescission under § 29(b), the plaintiff must establish that:

(1) the contract involved a "prohibited transaction," (2) he is in contractual privity with the defendant, and (3) he is "in the class of persons the Act was designed to protect."

Reg'l Props., Inc. v. Fin. & Real Estate Consulting Co., 678 F.2d 552, 559 (5th Cir. 1982). In *Regional*, the court found these elements satisfied by a real estate developer that wished to rescind its contracts with a securities broker for the marketing of limited partnerships. The broker had not complied with the Exchange Act's broker registration requirement, thereby rendering the performance of the contracts a "prohibited transaction." 678 F.2d at 561. Moreover, the developer was found to be within the class of people the Act was designed to protect. The court reasoned that not only does § 29(b) "not in terms limit the class of persons who may invoke its contractual voidness provisions to investors." *Id.* In addition, the action furthers the purposes of the Exchange Act by enforcing the statutory requirements applicable to securities brokers. *Id.* at 561–562.

§ 2.8 RELIANCE

Reliance, also known as transaction causation, is one of two causation requirements applicable to private actions under § 10(b) and Rule 10b-5. The other one is loss causation, discussed in § 2.9 *infra*). Neither reliance nor loss causation comes into play when the plaintiff is either the SEC or the DOJ.

Courts imported Rule 10b-5's reliance element from tort law. *See Meyer v. Greene*, 710 F.3d 1189, 1194 (11th Cir. 2013). As traditionally conceived, this element focuses on whether the plaintiff relied on the defendant's fraud when deciding to buy or sell the securities in question. *See Erica P. John Fund, Inc. v. Halliburton Co.*, 131 S. Ct. 2179, 2185 (2011); *Wilson v. Comtech Telecomms. Corp.*, 648 F.2d 88, 94 (2d Cir. 1981).

To ease the burden on plaintiffs, courts have upheld various presumptions of reliance. The presumptions each facilitate class actions by allowing common reliance issues to predominate over individual ones. *See* § 6.3.1 *infra*. The presumptions are, however, also available to plaintiffs suing individually or derivatively.

The following sections discuss three presumptions of reliance—for omissions (*see* § 2.8.1 *infra*); for fraud-on-the-market (*see* § 2.8.2); and for fraud-created-the-market (*see* § 2.8.3 *infra*). Attention then turns to when the plaintiff must show that her reliance was justifiable (§ 2.8.4 *infra*).

§ 2.8.1   THE PRESUMPTION FOR OMISSIONS

In *Affiliated Ute Citizens v. United States*, 406 U.S.
128 (1972), the Supreme Court upheld a presumption
of reliance for Rule 10b-5 plaintiffs who challenge an
omission. In *Affiliated Ute*, Native Americans of the
Ute tribe brought a Rule 10b-5 action against a bank
and two bank employees. The bank served as the
transfer agent for the stock of the company formed to
allocate tribal assets. The defendants allegedly
purchased the plaintiffs' shares without disclosing
the existence of a secondary market in which the
stock traded at a higher price. The Court held that
the plaintiffs did not have to prove their reliance on
the absence of the information that the defendants
had impermissibly withheld:

> Under the circumstances of this case, involving
> primarily a failure to disclose, positive proof of
> reliance is not a prerequisite to recovery. All that
> is necessary is that the facts withheld be
> material * * * .

Id. at 153–154. Although not using presumption
phraseology, the Court is broadly understood to have
granted the plaintiffs a rebuttable presumption of
reliance. *See, e.g., Stoneridge Inv. Partners, LLC v.
Scientific-Atlanta, Inc.*, 552 U.S. 148, 159 (2008).

What were the "circumstances" that led the
presumption of reliance to attach? According to one
view, the key was that the parties "had dealt directly
with each other and there clearly was a duty of
disclosure owed." *Laventhall v. Gen. Dynamics Corp.*,
704 F.2d 407, 413 n.4 (8th Cir. 1983). According to

the most widely accepted view, however, the key was that the fraud involved an omission. While unstated by *Affiliated Ute,* the rationale for presuming reliance in the case of an omission is the "unique difficulty of proving reliance on a failure to disclose material information of which the plaintiff did not know." *Grubb v. FDIC,* 868 F.2d 1151, 1163 (10th Cir. 1989).

A presumption confined to omissions prompts a host of questions. One is what to do in a case in which both omissions and misrepresentations are alleged. The standard answer is that the presumption does not apply "unless the case can be characterized as one that *primarily* alleges omissions." *Binder v. Gillespie,* 184 F.3d 1059, 1064 (9th Cir. 1999) (emphasis added). But when should omissions be said to predominate? Some courts simply count the number of omissions and misrepresentations alleged in the complaint and determine which is larger. *See, e.g., Cavalier Carpets, Inc. v. Caylor,* 746 F.2d 749, 757 (11th Cir. 1984). Other courts dig deeper, seeking to discover the true nature of the matter to which the plaintiffs object. *See, e.g., Starr v. Georgeson S'holder, Inc.,* 412 F.3d 103, 109 n.5 (2d Cir. 2005); *Joseph v. Wiles,* 223 F.3d 1155, 1162–1163 (10th Cir. 2000).

Sometimes it can be difficult to know whether to characterize something as an omission or a misrepresentation in the first place. Consider a so-called "half-truth"—that is, a statement which, while literally true, omits details that make it materially misleading, thereby lying somewhere between an

affirmative lie and the failure to say anything at all.
Does the *Affiliated Ute* presumption apply to a half-
truth? Courts divide on this question. Compare
Hoxworth v. Blinder, Robinson & Co., 903 F.2d 186,
202 (3d Cir. 1990) (answering affirmatively) with *In
re Enron Corp. Sec., Deriv. & ERISA Litig.*, 610 F.
Supp. 2d 600, 631 n.33 (S.D. Tex. 2009) (answering
negatively). One way of approaching this question is
to ask whether proving reliance on the half-truth at
issue would be as onerous as proving reliance on an
omission.

The defendants are entitled to try to rebut the
presumption (as to some or all of the plaintiffs). A
common way to do so is to show that the plaintiff(s)
did not read the document in question and therefore
are not entitled to a presumption of reliance on the
omission that the document allegedly contains.

§ 2.8.2 THE FRAUD-ON-THE-MARKET PRESUMPTION

In *Basic Inc. v. Levinson*, 485 U.S. 224 (1988), the
Supreme Court upheld a much more comprehensive
solution to the reliance problem than it had offered
in *Affiliated Ute*. The *Basic* solution, recently
reaffirmed in *Halliburton Co. v. Erica P. John Fund,
Inc. (Halliburton II)*, 134 S. Ct. 2398 (2014), took the
form of an alternative Rule 10b-5 claim known as
"fraud-on-the-market." *See Asher v. Baxter Int'l, Inc.*,
377 F.3d 727, 731–732 (7th Cir. 2004) (contrasting
the traditional Rule 10b-5 claim and the fraud-on-
the-market claim). When available, the latter
features a rebuttable presumption of reliance capable

of encompassing misrepresentations, omissions, or a combination thereof.

The fraud-on-the-market claim is anchored in the efficient capital markets hypothesis—the idea that the price of a security traded in an efficient market reflects all relevant public information. *See* § 1.13 *supra*. A plaintiff trading in such a market is presumed to rely directly on the security's market price in making her investment decision and thereby indirectly on any public fraud that distorted the price. The presumption transforms reliance into a common issue (thereby facilitating class certification, a subject discussed more fully in § 6.3 *infra*).

This presumption has a number of dimensions that command our attention. These include the identification of its prerequisites; the indicators of market efficiency; the form that rebuttal can take; and the availability of the presumption when the defendant is a securities analyst instead of the issuer.

The Prerequisites. The fraud-on-the-market presumption is available only if the plaintiffs prove that (i) the stock traded in an efficient market (*see* § 2.8.2 *infra*); (ii) the challenged misrepresentation or omission was material (*see* § 2.3 *supra*); and (iii) the fraud was publicly disseminated. *See Halliburton II*, 134 S. Ct. at 2408.

How do courts distinguish between efficient and inefficient markets? The principal post-*Basic* judicial touchstone for measuring market efficiency consists of the following set of five factors, known as the

"*Cammer* factors," due to their having originated in *Cammer v. Bloom*, 711 F. Supp. 1264 (D.N.J. 1989):

> (1) the average weekly trading volume; (2) the number of securities analysts following the stock; (3) the number of market makers; (4) whether the company was entitled to file an S-3 Registration Statement, if relevant, and (5) evidence of a cause and effect relationship between unexpected news and stock-price changes.

Gariety v. Grant Thornton LLP, 368 F.3d 356 (4th Cir. 2004) (citing the *Cammer* factors and applying them); *McIntire v. China MediaExpress Holdings,* 38 F. Supp. 3d 415, 423 (S.D.N.Y. 2014) (same). *Cf. In re DVI, Inc., Sec. Litig.,* 639 F.3d 623, 634 n.16 (3d Cir. 2011) (observing that the *Cammer* factors have been endorsed by seven of the twelve circuit courts), abrogated on other grounds by *Amgen, Inc. v. Conn. Ret. Plans & Trust Funds*, 133 S. Ct. 1184 (2013).

Another well-regarded set of factors, sometimes used in combination with the *Cammer* factors, originated in *Krogman v. Sterritt*, 202 F.R.D. 467 (N.D. Tex. 2001):

> (1) the company's market capitalization, *i.e.*, the number of shares multiplied by the share price; (2) the bid-ask spread, *i.e.*, the difference between the prices at which investors are willing to buy the stock in question and current shareholders are willing to sell that stock; and (3) the float, *i.e.*, the percentage of shares that is publicly-owned.

See id. at 477–478. *See Unger v. Amedisys Inc.*, 401 F.3d 316, 323 (5th Cir. 2005) (applying both the *Krogman* and *Cammer* factors); *McIntire*, 38 F. Supp. 3d at 431–433 (same).

The Court has drawn a distinction among the prerequisites to the fraud-on-the-market presumption in terms of *when* the plaintiffs must establish them: proof of both efficiency and publicity must be made at the certification stage, whereas proof of materiality is inapposite at certification but essential at trial or summary judgment. *See Amgen Inc.*, 133 S. Ct. at 1191. For the rationale underlying this differentiation, *see* § 6.3 *infra*.

Finally, the Court has disallowed two other prerequisites. One was loss causation, rejected in *Erica P. John Fund, Inc. v. Halliburton Co. (Halliburton I)*, 563 U.S. 804 (2011), and discussed further in § 6.3.1 *infra* in connection with class certification. Loss causation is an independent element of the Rule 10b-5 private action. *See* § 2.9 *infra*. The other disallowed prerequisite was price impact, rejected in *Halliburton II*, 134 S. Ct. at 2415. Price impact is nonetheless relevant to the rebuttal of the presumption, a subject discussed immediately below.

<u>Rebuttal</u>. The defendants have several options for rebutting the fraud-on-the-market presumption, although not all of them can be utilized at the certification stage:

- Lack of Price Impact. This form of rebuttal can be attempted at certification as well as at

summary judgment or trial. *See Halliburton
II,* 134 S. Ct. at 2414–2415. To succeed, the
defendants must show that the alleged fraud
had no impact on the market price. *Id.* at
2414. *See also McIntire,* 38 F. Supp. 3d at 434–
435 (holding rebuttal to have failed on this
basis); *Aranaz v. Catalyst Pharm. Partners,
Inc.,* 302 F.R.D. 657, 671–672 (S.D. Fla. 2014)
(same).

- Lack of Materiality. This form of rebuttal,
often referred to as the truth-on-the-market
defense, can be attempted at summary
judgment or trial but not at certification. *See
Amgen Inc.,* 133 S. Ct. 1184, 1191 (2013). For
the reasons underlying this distinction, *see*
§ 6.3.1.

  To succeed, the defendants must show that
  the market knew the truth and thus was not
  fooled by the fraud. *See Basic,* 485 U.S. at 248.
  For a decision upholding a truth-on-the-
  market defense at summary judgment, *see In
  re Apple Computer Sec. Litig.,* 886 F.2d 1109
  (9th Cir. 1989). For a decision rejecting such a
  defense and denying summary judgment, *see
  Kaplan v. Rose,* 49 F.3d 1363, 1377 (9th Cir.
  1995).

- Price Insensitivity of Specific Plaintiffs. This
form of rebuttal can be attempted at the
certification stage in order to show that the
named plaintiffs are inadequate or atypical.
See, e.g., In re Winstar Commc'ns Sec. Litig.,
290 F.R.D. 437, 444–445 (S.D.N.Y. 2013). *See*

generally § 6.3 (discussing certification requirements). Moreover, in a lawsuit not of the class action variety, this form of rebuttal is appropriate at summary judgment or trial.

To succeed, the defendants must show that the plaintiffs in question did not rely on the market price in making their trades. *Basic*, 485 U.S. at 249. For a successful attempt at the bench trial of a case that the judge characterized as "extraordinary," *see Gamco Investors, Inc. v. Vivendi, S.A.*, 927 F. Supp. 2d 88 (S.D.N.Y. 2013). There the defendant proved that the plaintiffs, sophisticated investors, made the investment decisions at issue on the basis of a model that did not take market price into account. *See id.* at 102.

<u>Applicability to Non-Issuer Defendants</u>. The defendants in *Basic* consisted of the issuer and various individual insiders, as did those in *Amgen* and *Halliburton I* and *II*. Can the presumption of reliance attach if the defendant is a securities analyst or some other non-issuer entity or person? The Second Circuit has held that "[i]t * * * does not matter, for purposes of establishing entitlement to the presumption, whether the misinformation was transmitted by an issuer, an analyst, or anyone else." *In re Salomon Analyst Metromedia Litig.*, 544 F.3d 474, 481 (2d Cir. 2008). The few district courts outside the Second Circuit that have considered the issue so far agree. *See, e.g., In re HealthSouth Corp. Sec. Litig.*, 257 F.R.D. 260, 279 (N.D. Ala. 2009); *In*

re Credit Suisse-AOL Sec. Litig., 253 F.R.D. 17, 28 (D. Mass. 2008).

§ 2.8.3 THE FRAUD-CREATED-THE-MARKET PRESUMPTION

The third presumption of reliance is part of an alternative Rule 10b-5 claim known as fraud-created-the market. Applicable only to primary offerings and unconnected to the efficient capital market hypothesis, this claim asserts that the defendants marketed securities that would have been unmarketable absent the fraud.

The Supreme Court has yet to address fraud-created-the-market and the circuits are divided. For positive decisions, *see Regents of Univ. of Ca. v. Credit Suisse First Boston (USA), Inc.*, 482 F.3d 372 (5th Cir. 2007); *Ross v. Bank South, N.A.*, 885 F.2d 723 (11th Cir. 1989); *T.J. Raney & Sons, Inc. v. Fort Cobb, Okla. Irrigation Fuel Auth.*, 717 F.2d 1330 (10th Cir. 1983). For negative decisions, *see Malack v. BDO Seidman, LLP*, 617 F.3d 743 (3d Cir. 2010); *Eckstein v. Balcor Film Investors*, 8 F.3d 1121 (7th Cir. 1993). *See also Penn. Pub. Sch. Emps. Ret. Sys. v. Morgan Stanley & Co.*, 772 F.3d 111, 120 (2d Cir. 2014) (not addressing the question but collecting decisions in opposition).

What does it mean for securities to be unmarketable? Three definitions have emerged:

Economic Unmarketability. This definition requires that the securities in question "could 'not have been offered on the market at any price' absent the fraudulent scheme." *Ross*, 885 F.2d at 729 (quoting *Shores v. Sklar*, 647 F.2d 462, 474 n.2 (5th Cir. 1981) (en banc)).

"Patently Worthless" Enterprise. This definition requires that the enterprise offering the securities be a "sham" or a "hoax." *Abell v. Potomac Ins. Co.*, 858 F.2d 1104, 1122 (5th Cir. 1988), judgment vacated on other grounds sub nom. *Fryar v. Abell*, 492 U.S. 914 (1989) .

Legal Unmarketability. This definition requires the existence of a legal bar to the marketing of the securities in question. *Raney*, 717 F.2d at 1333.

Opponents of the presumption argue that virtually any security can be marketed at some price, even if that price is very low. They also insist that adoption of the presumption would expand the scope of the implied private action under § 10(b) and Rule 10b-5, something that at least in general, the Supreme Court does not favor. *See, e.g., Stoneridge Inv. Partners, LLC v. Scientific-Atlanta, Inc.*, 552 U.S. 148, 168 (2008).

Defenders of the presumption, on the other hand, stress the desirability of offering a solution to the reliance problem in the inefficient market context. They also say that the various definitions of unmarketability presuppose that the defendants acted intentionally, or at least extremely recklessly, and that such a high level of intentional fraud ought to be actionable.

§ 2.8.4   JUSTIFIABLE RELIANCE

In private Rule 10b-5 actions involving face-to-face transactions, the plaintiff must establish the justifiableness of her reliance. *Harsco Corp. v. Segui*, 91 F.3d 337, 342 (2d Cir. 1996) (collecting cases from various circuits). To do so might be difficult, for example, if, prior to making her investment decision, she had in hand a document that contradicted the fraud on which she purportedly relied, or she had reason to suspect the trustworthiness of the seller. To qualify as unjustifiable, her reliance must be reckless rather than merely negligent. *See, e.g., Brown v. Earthboard Sports USA, Inc.,* 481 F.3d 901, 921 (6th Cir. 2007).

To determine the justifiableness of the plaintiff's reliance, courts delve into the facts of the particular situation and take into account factors such as the following:

> (1) [t]he sophistication and expertise of the plaintiff in financial and securities matters; (2) the existence of longstanding business or personal relationships; (3) access to the relevant information; (4) the existence of a fiduciary relationship; (5) concealment of the fraud; (6) the opportunity to detect the fraud; (7) whether the plaintiff initiated the stock transaction or sought to expedite the transaction; and (8) the generality or specificity of the misrepresentations.

Ashland Inc. v. Morgan Stanley & Co., Inc., 652 F.3d 333, 338 (2d Cir. 2011) (collecting cases and quoting

Brown v. E.F. Hutton Grp., Inc., 991 F.2d 1020, 1032 (2d Cir. 1993)).

A recurring issue is whether a plaintiff can justifiably rely on a statement made outside the four corners of a contract of sale when that contract contains a merger clause (sometimes called an integration clause)—that is, a clause providing that there was no such reliance. Three positions have emerged.

One is that the merger clause by itself "precludes any claim of deceit by prior representations." *Rissman v. Rissman*, 213 F.3d 381, 383–84 (7th Cir. 2000) (collecting cases).

Another is that the merger clause cannot be dispositive due to § 29(a) of the Exchange Act, which provides that "[a]ny condition, stipulation, or provision binding any person to waive compliance with any provision of this chapter or any rule or regulation thereunder, or of any rule of an exchange required thereby, shall be void." Under this view, the merger clause is simply a factor in the justifiable reliance analysis but does not dictate the result. *See, e.g., AES Corp. v. Dow Chemical Co.*, 325 F.3d 174, 180 (3d Cir. 2003).

Yet another is that the merger clause cannot serve even as a factor in the analysis because § 29(a), quoted immediately above, renders it void. *See AES Corp.*, 325 F.3d at 184 (Wallace, J., concurring and dissenting).

Courts have offered each of the following as rationales for the justifiable reliance requirement.

Causation. The justifiable reliance requirement "insures that there is a causal connection between the misrepresentation and the plaintiff's harm." *Zobrist v. Coal-X, Inc.*, 708 F.2d 1511 (10th Cir. 1983).

Protecting Defendants. Without a justifiable reliance requirement, "even the most careful seller is at risk, for it is easy to claim: 'Despite what the written documents say, one of your agents told me something else.' " *Acme Propane, Inc. v. Tenexco, Inc.*, 844 F.2d 1317, 1322 (7th Cir. 1988).

Anti-Fraud. Justifiable reliance "requires plaintiffs to invest carefully" and thereby "promotes the anti-fraud policies of the securities acts by making fraud more readily discoverable." *Banca Cremi, S.A. v. Aex. Brown & Sons, Inc.*, 132 F.3d 1017, 1028 (4th Cir. 1997) (quoting *Dupuy v. Dupuy*, 551 F.2d 1005, 1014 (5th Cir. 1977)).

It would be highly unusual, albeit not unthinkable, for justifiable reliance issues to arise in the context of a fraud-on-the-market action. For example, consider such an action brought by Jane, who, through encounters with a corporate insider to which the rest of the world was not privy, gleaned information that served as a "red flag" to her concerning the reliability of the company's public statements at issue in her litigation. Because of this red flag, she might not be able to justifiably rely on the fraud, even if others could.

§ 2.9 LOSS CAUSATION

Loss causation focuses on whether the defendant's fraud was a significant causative factor in the plaintiff's loss (which might instead have been brought about by market or industry conditions or other factors extraneous to the fraud). Loss causation made its initial entrance into the Rule 10b-5 private action as an import from tort law. But in 1995 as part of the PSLRA, Congress transformed it into a statutory requirement by adding § 21D(b)(4) to the Exchange Act. That provision reads as follows:

> In any private action arising under this Act, the plaintiff shall have the burden of proving that the act or omission of the defendant alleged to violate this Act caused the loss for which the plaintiff seeks to receive damages.

In *Dura Pharmaceuticals, Inc. v. Broudo*, 544 U.S. 336 (2005), the Supreme Court addressed the loss causation requirement in the context of a fraud-on-the-market action. According to the plaintiffs, the defendants made a material misrepresentation when they asserted that the company's asthmatic spray device would soon receive FDA approval. Regarding loss causation, the plaintiffs alleged that the misrepresentation had inflated the security's price on the date of their purchase.

The Court rejected this loss causation allegation as inadequate. The fact that the plaintiffs paid an inflated purchase price, the Court explained, did not mean that they would necessarily lose money when they sold their shares. They might, for example, sell before the fraud became public knowledge (that is, while the price remained inflated). Moreover, even if their sale price fell below their purchase price, the reason might have been unrelated to the fraud. Thus, the Court concluded, the plaintiffs failed to allege "proximate cause" (a turn of phrase, it will be noted, that does not explicitly appear in § 21D(b)(4)).

Why didn't the plaintiffs do a better job of pleading a causative link between the fraud and the loss? It appears that the surrounding facts did not allow them to do so. The company's eventual announcement that FDA approval would not be forthcoming prompted a price drop that was recouped within a week. To be sure, the plaintiffs did lose money, but their losses seem to have been driven by an earlier announcement that "slow drug sales" would likely lead to lower earnings than had previously been expected. The essential frivolousness of the plaintiffs' complaint may have contributed to the Court's expressed concern with strike suits of the sort condemned in *Blue Chip Stamps v. Manor Drug Stores*, a decision discussed in § 2.7.1 *supra*.

Given the failure of the plaintiffs to connect the misrepresentation to their loss, the Court had little to say about the nature of the connection that would have sufficed. In the wake of *Dura*, plaintiffs have successfully pursued two approaches, invoking the first more frequently than the second:

    Corrective Disclosure Theory. This theory involves "(1) identifying a 'corrective disclosure' (a release of information that reveals to the market the pertinent truth that was previously

concealed or obscured by the company's fraud);
(2) showing that the stock price dropped soon
after the corrective disclosure; and
(3) eliminating other possible explanations for
this price drop, so that the factfinder can infer
that it is more probable than not that it was the
corrective disclosure—as opposed to other
possible depressive factors—that caused at least
a 'substantial' amount of the price drop."
FindWhat Investor Grp. v. FindWhat.com, 658
F.3d 1282, 1311–1312 (11th Cir. 2011).

Materialization of the Risk Theory. This
theory, available in the absence of a corrective
disclosure, requires the plaintiffs to show that
the fraud concealed a foreseeable risk of an
event that occurred and caused the loss. *See In
re Omnicom Group, Inc. Sec. Litig.*, 597 F.3d 501
(2d Cir. 2010). For example, an investment
advisor's failure to disclose its non-performance
of due diligence in connection with the activities
of Bernard Madoff, who had control over most of
the advisor's assets, concealed the risk of the
investors' losses due to Madoff's Ponzi scheme.
See In re Beacon Assocs. Litig., 745 F. Supp. 2d
386 (S.D.N.Y. 2010).

There is also the question of the standard
governing the pleading of loss causation. The *Dura*
Court "assume[d], at least for argument's sake," that
neither the pleading requirements of the PLSRA, set
forth in § 2.1 *supra*, nor those of the Federal Rules of
Civil Procedure, impose on the pleading of loss
causation any requirement greater than that of Fed.

R. Civ. P. 8(a)(2), which calls for "a short and plain statement of the claim showing that the pleader is entitled to relief." Lower courts currently divide over whether Fed. R. Civ. P. 9(b)'s plead-fraud-with-particularity standard applies to loss causation. *See Oregon Pub. Emps. Ret. Fund v. Apollo Grp. Inc.*, 774 F.3d 598, 604–605 (9th Cir.2014) (collecting cases in support of each position).

Six years after *Dura*, the Supreme Court returned to loss causation in the context of class certification in *Erica P. John Fund, Inc. v. Halliburton Co.*, 563 U.S. 804 (2011). That decision, known as *Halliburton I* and discussed more fully in § 6.3 *infra*, held that plaintiffs seeking certification need not prove loss causation in order to obtain the fraud-on-the-market presumption of reliance.

§ 2.10 DAMAGES

To recover damages under § 10(b) and Rule 10b-5, a private plaintiff must prove them. Proof of damages is inapposite, however, when it comes to actions by the SEC or the DOJ.

The law of Rule 10b-5 damages is quite undeveloped. The Exchange Act itself has relatively little to say. In addition, there are only a small number of judicial decisions. The smallness of that number results from the fact that even those cases that are tried before a judge or jury tend to settle before reaching the damages phase of the litigation.

Section 10(b) and Rule 10b-5, the texts of which appears in § 2.1 *supra*, say nothing about how to measure damages. This silence is not surprising, since the drafters of those provisions did not anticipate private enforcement. *See id.*

The lower federal courts thus have considerable discretion in addressing this subject. However, they operate under the following constraints:

§ 28(a) of the Exchange Act. This provision, which governs damages under the Exchange Act in general, prohibits the plaintiff from recovering "a total amount in excess of his actual damages on account of the act complained of." This language is widely understood to preclude multiple recoveries for the same wrong as well as punitive damages. *See*, *e.g.*, *Boguslavsky v. Kaplan*, 159 F.3d 715, 721 (2d Cir. 1998); *Pelletier v. Stuart-James Co.*, 863 F.2d 1550, 1557 (11th Cir. 1989).

The Out-of-Pocket Default Measure. In *Affiliated Ute v. United States*, 406 U.S. 128 (1972), discussed earlier in connection with Rule 10b-5's reliance element (*see* § 2.8.1 *supra*), the Supreme Court declared the default measure for Rule 10b-5 damages to be the "out-of-pocket rule" from common law deceit—that is, "the difference between the fair value of all that the [plaintiff] received and the fair value of what he would have received had there been no fraudulent conduct." *Id.* at 155.

The Disgorgement Alternative. The *Affiliated Ute* Court went on to identify an alternative measure of damages for use in "the situation in which the defendant received more than the [plaintiff's] actual loss." *Id.* at 155. For this situation, the Court held, the appropriate measure is disgorgement—that is, "the amount of the defendant's profit." *Id. Cf. Rowe v. Maremont Corp.*, 850 F.2d 1226, 1240–1241 (7th Cir. 1988) (giving reasons for rejecting disgorgement for the case at hand).

The Occasional Relevance of Rescission. In *Randall v. Loftsgaarden,* 478 U.S. 647 (1986), the Court opened up the possibilities still further by assuming (but not actually upholding) the at least occasional appropriateness of rescission—the unwinding of the transaction (or the monetary equivalent). *See id.* at 662. The Court affirmatively did not address, however, the question "whether, assuming that a rescissory recovery may sometimes be proper under § 10(b), plaintiffs in such cases should invariably be free to elect a rescissory measure of damages rather than out-of-pocket damages." *See id.* at 666. *See also Lewin v. Lipper Convertibles, LP,* 756 F. Supp. 2d 432, 440 (S.D.N.Y. 2010) (noting that rescission is rarely granted in Rule 10b-5 cases), vacated in part on other grounds sub nom. *CLIP Assocs., L.P. v. PriceWaterhouse Coopers LLP*, 735 F.3d 114, 122 (2d Cir. 2013).

The 90-Day Bounce-Back Rule. Enacted as part of the PSLRA, § 21D(e)(1) of the Exchange Act is designed to insulate defendants from liability for damages based on the market's temporary overreaction. It does so by capping damages at the difference between the price paid by the plaintiff for the security and "the mean trading price of that security during the 90-day period beginning" on the day the issuer made its corrective disclosure. *Id.* The "mean trading price" is defined as "an average of the daily trading price of that security, determined as of the close of the market each day during the 90-day period." § 21D(e)(3). *See Acticon AG v. China North East Petroleum Holdings Ltd.*, 692 F.3d 34, 41 (2d Cir. 2012) (vacating dismissal based on rebound of trading price due to uncertainty at early stage of litigation regarding why rebound occurred).

The Virtual Necessity of an Event Study. To distinguish the effect of the fraud on the security's price from that of other factors, courts routinely rely on the "event study"—a statistical methodology that assesses the impact of a press release, prospectus, or other disclosure document on the market price of a security. *Cf. In re Vivendi Universal, S.A. Sec. Litig.*, 605 F. Supp. 2d 586, 599 (S.D.N.Y. 2009) (referring to the event study as "almost obligatory" in Rule 10b-5 damages litigation).

§ 2.10.1 PROPORTIONATE LIABILITY

Prior to the PSLRA, Rule 10b-5 defendants became jointly and severally liable for damages in accordance with a system developed by the lower federal courts. *See, e.g., Regents of the Univ. of Cal. v. Credit Suisse*

First Boston, Inc., 482 F.3d 372, 404 (5th Cir. 2007). Under this system, the plaintiff was entitled to recoup the entire amount of the damages from any defendant (who in turn could bring contribution actions against the others). *See id. See also Musick, Peeler & Garrett v. Employers Ins.*, 508 U.S. 286 (1993) (recognizing an implied right to contribution among those who violate Rule 10b-5).

In the wake of lobbying by accounting firms and other so-called deep-pocket defendants, Congress concluded that the joint and several liability system was unfair. Accordingly, as part of the PSLRA, Congress radically upended it by adding § 21D(f) to the Exchange Act. That provision establishes a scheme of proportionate liability under which a defendant (with limited exceptions) is liable exclusively for the fraction of the judgment for which she bears responsibility.

Joint and several liability remains for those defendants who commit their violations "knowingly" (and who may seek contribution from each other pursuant to an express action enacted for this purpose). Whether each defendant acted knowingly as well as how much responsibility he bears for the total wrong are jury questions that must be answered pursuant to special interrogatories. In deciding upon each defendant's respective share, the jury is to take account of "each of the other persons claimed by any of the parties to have caused or contributed to the loss incurred by the plaintiff, including persons who have entered into settlements with the plaintiff." § 21D(f)(3). There is an explicit prohibition against disclosing to the jury how their decisions will affect the award of damages. *See* § 21D(f)(6).

§ 2.10.2 INDEMNIFICATION AND INSURANCE

A recurrent question involves a corporation's right to indemnify its officers and directors for liability for Rule 10b-5 damages. The answer turns largely on whether the litigation ends in a judgment of liability (relatively rare) or in a settlement without a judgment of liability (far more common).

When a court finds a defendant liable for intentionally violating the federal securities laws, courts have long prohibited indemnification on public policy grounds. *See In re Enron Corp. Sec. Deriv. & ERISA Litig.*, 2008 WL 2566867, at *10 (S.D.N.Y. June 24, 2008); *McLean v. Alexander*, 449 F. Supp. 1251, 1266 (D. Del. 1978) (collecting cases). Such a defendant may nonetheless be protected by insurance. *See id.* at 1266 n.51 (noting that exclusionary clauses notwithstanding, "some policies may be more expansive than the courts would permit through indemnification"), *rev'd on other grounds*, 599 F.2d 1190 (3rd Cir. 1979). In the case of a corporate defendant, recovery may come either from insurance or from the corporate treasury (and therefore ultimately from the shareholders themselves).

Where the litigation is settled without a finding of wrongdoing, the situation changes in several respects. Corporations are entitled to indemnify their officers and directors. *See, e.g., Raychem Corp. v. Fed. Ins. Co.*, 853 F. Supp. 1170, 1176–1177 (N.D. Cal.

1994) (collecting cases). In addition, insurance coverage is more likely to be applicable.

For decades, the availability of indemnification and insurance spared individual defendants from having to fund settlements from their own pockets. But some individual defendants have recently been obliged to do precisely that. For example, it made national headlines when the *Worldcom* plaintiffs demanded out-of-pocket payments from outside directors as a condition of settlement.

§ 2.11 PRIMARY LIABILITY

A Rule 10b-5 violation typically involves a number of participants, and the courts have wrestled with determining the relative level of culpability of various actors. Liability can be either "primary" or "secondary" and there are several types of each. The sections immediately following discuss two types of primary liability—liability based on "ultimate authority" (§ 2.11.1 *infra*) and on "scheme liability" (§ 2.11.3 *infra*). Thereafter, various types of secondary liability are considered (§ 2.12 *infra*).

§ 2.11.1 THE ULTIMATE AUTHORITY TEST

Rule 10b-5(b) prohibits any person from "mak[ing] any untrue statement of a material fact" in connection with the purchase or sale of a security. Who qualifies as the "maker" of such a statement? The Supreme Court confronted this question in *Janus Capital Group, Inc. v. First Derivative Traders*, 131 S. Ct. 2296 (2011), a case that involved three independent, albeit related, entities: Janus

Capital Group (JCG), a publicly-held financial services company; Janus Investment Fund (JIF), a family of mutual funds created by JCG; and Janus Capital Management (JCM), a wholly-owned subsidiary of JCG that served as JIF's administrator and investment advisor.

The plaintiffs, JCG shareholders, alleged that the price of JCG stock had been artificially inflated by misrepresentations contained in JIF's prospectuses. Named as defendants were JCM and JCG, the latter as JCM's "controlling person" (*see* § 2.12.3 *infra*). Not named as a defendant was JIF, presumably because it had been at most negligent and thereby insulated from liability under Rule 10b-5 (*see* § 2.5.1 *supra*). Thus, the principal issue was whether JCM should be deemed the "maker" of the misrepresentations in JIF's prospectuses.

Dividing 5–4, the Court set out to read Rule 10b-5 restrictively on the theory that Congress had not created the implied private action. 564 U.S. at 2301. From this perspective emerged the following test:

> For purposes of Rule 10b-5, the maker of a statement is the person or entity with ultimate authority over the statement, including its content and whether and how to communicate it. Without control, a person or entity can merely suggest what to say, not "make" a statement in its own right. One who prepares or publishes a statement on behalf of another is not its maker.

Id. at 2302. By way of illustration, the Supreme Court analogized to "the relationship between a speechwriter and a speaker," stating: "Even when a speechwriter drafts a speech, the content is entirely within the control of the person who delivers it" and "it is the speaker who takes credit—or blame—for what is ultimately said." *Id.* Applying the test, the Court found that it was JIF that "made" all the statements in the prospectuses. JIF had control, even if JCM had done the drafting. *Id.* Moreover, JCG could not be liable as a "controlling person," since such liability attaches only when the controlled person" (in this case, JCM), is also liable. Controlling person liability is a form of secondary liability discussed in § 2.12.3 *infra*.

§ 2.11.2   QUESTIONS PROMPTED BY *JANUS*

The Supreme Court's decision in *Janus Capital Group, Inc. v. First Derivative Traders*, 131 S. Ct. 2296 (2011), discussed immediately above, has given rise to various questions concerning primary liability, including the following:

Attribution plus What? The *Janus* Court observed that "in the ordinary case, attribution within a statement or implicit from the surrounding circumstances is strong evidence that a statement was made by—and only by— the party to whom it is attributed." *Id.* at 2302. In a footnote, however, the Court suggested that attribution by itself might not suffice for liability: "More may be required to find that a person or entity made a statement indirectly, but attribution is necessary." *Id.* at 2305 n.11. What that "more" might be, however, was left unstated. *Cf. SEC v. Daifotis*, 874 F. Supp. 2d 870 (N.D. Cal. 2012) (denying summary judgment and leaving it to the jury to evaluate the CIO's argument that he had not approved the statements attributed to him by the company's web site). Likewise uncertain is what would constitute "implicit" attribution. In any event, JCM could not be liable on an attribution theory, since the prospectuses did not attribute the misrepresentations to it either "explicitly or implicitly." *Janus*, 131 S.Ct. 2034 n.11.

Insiders vs. Entities. An additional important question left open by *Janus* is whether its ultimate authority test applies to corporate insiders (directors, officers, and other corporate officials) or is instead limited to separate corporate entities such as those involved in *Janus* itself. *See Glickenhaus & Co. v. Household Int'l, Inc.*, 787 F.3d 408, 425 (7th Cir. 2015) (applying *Janus* to insiders); *Hawaii Ironworkers Annuity Trust Fund v. Cole*, 2011 WL 3862206, at *2–*4 (N.D. Ohio Sept. 1, 2011) (same). One potent indication that the Court intended across-the-board application was that its announcement of the test, set forth in the block quote above, begins with the words "For purposes of Rule 10b-5." The *Glickenhaus* and *Ironworkers* decisions both make this point.

Certified Financial Statements. Prior to *Janus*, an accounting firm could be primarily liable if it was found to be reckless in certifying a financial statement contained in a Form 10-K or other document filed with the SEC. *Cf. Overton v. Todman & Co.*, 478 F.3d 479, 486–87 (2d Cir. 2007) (involving the accounting firm's failure to correct a certification that was false when made). The same seems to be true after *Janus* as well. *See, e.g., Special Situations Fund III QP, L.P. v. Deloitte Touche Tohmatsu CPA, Ltd.,* 33 F. Supp. 3d 401, 428 n.13 (S.D.N.Y. 2014) (finding the accountant to have had "ultimate authority" over its certification). Moreover, the CEO and the CFO, who must certify the 10-K, including the financials, in accordance with the SOX, are "makers" of any fraudulent statements contained in the documents that they signed. *See In re Smith Barney Transfer Agent Litig.,* 884 F. Supp. 2d 152, 163–164 (S.D.N.Y. 2012) (collecting decisions to this effect).

Multiple Makers? The decisions cited above read *Janus* to allow for the possibility of multiple primary violators. To be sure, the Supreme Court upheld this possibility in seemingly no uncertain terms in *Central Bank v. Interstate Bank, N.A.,* 511 U.S. 164 (1994), the decision famous for abolishing aiding and abetting liability in private Rule 10b-5 actions (discussed in § 2.12.1 *infra*). To temper the significance of that abolition, the Court emphasized that primary liability was a wide umbrella:

Any person or entity, including a lawyer, accountant, or bank, who employs a manipulative device or makes a material misstatement (or omission) on which a purchaser or seller of securities relies may be liable as a primary violator under 10b-5, assuming all of the requirements for primary liability under Rule 10b-5 are met. In any complex securities fraud, moreover, there are likely to be multiple violators; in this case, for example, respondents named four defendants as primary violators.

Id. at 191. But *Janus* sent a different signal with its statement that "attribution . . . is strong evidence that a statement was made by—*and only by*—the party to whom it is attributed." *Janus*, 564 U.S. at 2302 (emphasis added). *See id.* at 2307 (Breyer, J., dissenting) (critiquing *Janus* for being out of cinque with *Central Bank* in this regard). *Cf. Smith Barney Transfer Agent Sec. Litig.*, 884 F. Supp. 2d at 164 (holding primarily liable an officer who signed SEC filings but in dictum deeming the corporation itself to have been merely the "speechwriter").

In suggesting that there might be only one primary violator per situation, *Janus* arguably runs afoul of not only *Central Bank* but also the PSLRA's proportionate liability scheme, under which, with limited exceptions, co-defendants in a private action are liable merely for the fraction of the judgment for which they bear responsibility. *See* § 2.10.1 *supra.* Is it likely that Congress would have implemented proportionate liability in 1995 if it regarded a materially misleading statement as having been made only by "the person with ultimate authority over" it? The arguable conflict with the PSLRA may disincline some courts from reading *Janus* as imposing a one-primary-violator-per-situation rule.

§ 2.11.3 SCHEME LIABILITY

Scheme liability is an alternative theory of primary liability that rests on Rule 10b-5(a) ("to employ any device, scheme, or artifice to defraud") and Rule 10b-5(c) ("to engage in any act, practice, or course of business which operates . . . as a fraud or deceit upon any person"). For the full text of these provisions, *see* § 2.1 *supra*.

The Supreme Court considered the viability of scheme liability in *Stoneridge Inv. Partners v. Scientific-Atlanta, Inc.*, 552 U.S. 148 (2008). At issue in *Stoneridge* was an alleged scheme between Charter Communications, Inc., a cable television services provider, and two of its suppliers. According to the complaint, Charter entered into sham transactions with the suppliers that enabled it to trick its auditor into certifying financial statements containing materially inflated revenues and operating cash flow. The Court held that the suppliers could not be primarily liable because the investors failed to establish their reliance on the suppliers' behind-the-scenes activities. *See* 552 U.S. at 774.

The failure to establish reliance notwithstanding, the Court did not reject the theory of scheme liability as such. Moreover, although dividing 5–3 (with Justice Breyer not participating), the Court was unanimous that § 10(b) encompasses not only misrepresentations and omissions but also all forms of deceptive conduct. *Id.* at 158. Thus, after *Stoneridge*, a scheme liability theory has in principle been available to private plaintiffs able to establish reliance (admittedly a tall order). *See, e.g., Pac. Inv. Mgmt. Co., LLC v. Mayer Brown, LLP,* 603 F.3d 144, 158–159 (2d Cir. 2010). Moreover, "scheme liability" is available to the SEC, which does not have the burden of establishing reliance in the first place. *See, e.g., SEC v. Apuzzo,* 689 F.3d 204, 213 (2d Cir. 2012).

Several circuits have held that to be actionable, the scheme must involve deceptive conduct apart from an omission or misrepresentation, although the latter can certainly be part of the picture. *See, e.g., WPP Lux. Gamma Three Sarl v. Spot Runner, Inc.,* 655 F.3d 1039, 1057 (9th Cir. 2011); *Pub. Pension Fund Grp. v. KV Pharm. Co.,* 679 F.3d 972, 987 (8th Cir. 2012). *See also SEC v. Benger,* 931 F. Supp. 2d 908, 913 (N.D. Ill. 2013) (adopting the view of the 8th and 9th Circuits). If this were not the case, it would seem, plaintiffs seeking to allege garden-variety omissions or misrepresentations that violate Rule 10b-5(b) could avoid the strictures of *Janus* by repackaging their claims as "scheme liability" under Rule 10b-5(a) or Rule 10b-5(c).

There remains the question whether scheme liability survives *Janus*. To be sure, *Janus* did not examine scheme liability directly. But the Court's narrow approach to primary liability does not augur well for scheme liability's ultimate fate.

§ 2.12 SECONDARY LIABILITY

The concept of secondary liability allows plaintiffs to sue more defendants than otherwise would be possible if liability were restricted to primary actors. While secondary liability has increased in importance in the wake of the contraction of primary liability, it is no panacea. The reason is that its availability turns on the ability of the plaintiff to establish that another person or entity committed a primary violation.

A number of possible forms of secondary liability must be considered. The sections that follow discuss aiding and abetting liability (§ 2.12.1 *infra*); conspiracy (§ 2.12.2 *infra*); controlling person liability (§ 2.12.3 *infra*); and respondeat superior liability (§ 2.12.4 *infra*).

§ 2.12.1 AIDING AND ABETTING LIABILITY

In *Central Bank v. Interstate Bank, N.A.*, 511 U.S. 164 (1994), the Supreme Court addressed whether defendants can be liable for aiding and abetting violations of § 10(b) and Rule 10b-5. Such liability would require proof of a Rule 10b-5 primary violation of which the aider and abettor was aware and "substantial assistance" by the aider and abettor in the accomplishment of that violation. *Id.* at 168.

In *Central Bank,* the purported aider and abettor was a bank serving as an indenture trustee. Acting in that capacity, the bank allegedly provided substantial assistance to the bond issuer, which had committed fraud constituting a primary violation of

§ 10(b) and Rule 10b-5. The trustee's substantial assistance took the form of postponing the bond issuer's valuations of real property. Dividing 5–4, the Court held that the trustee could not be liable because § 10(b) and Rule 10b-5 did not encompass aiding and abetting liability, a position contrary to that of every circuit at the time. *Id.* at 169.

The Court offered several justifications for its holding. First and foremost was the fact that the text of § 10(b) did not include aiding and abetting phraseology, despite the fact that the enacting Congress was fully aware of the concept. *Id.* at 175–177. In addition, the Court observed, there is no aiding and abetting liability in any of the express private actions in the Securities Act or the Exchange Act, thereby suggesting that an express private action under § 10(b)—if Congress had chosen to create one—would have eschewed aiding and abetting liability as well. *Id.* at 178–180. An additional relevant consideration, the Court noted, was that aiding and abetting liability does not require proof of the plaintiffs' reliance on the fraud. To accept aiding and abetting liability, therefore, would enable the plaintiffs to sidestep the reliance element and thereby run afoul of the Supreme Court's decisions in the reliance area. *See* 511 U.S. at 180. The Supreme Court's reliance decisions are discussed in § 2.8 *supra*.

To the extent that *Central Bank* rested on the text of § 10(b), it undercut the ability of the SEC to sue aiders and abettors. But less than a year after the decision, Congress safeguarded the SEC's aiding and abetting authority in the PSLRA by adding § 20(e) to the Exchange Act. As originally enacted, § 20(e) allowed the SEC to sue anyone who "knowingly provides substantial assistance to another person" in violating an Exchange Act provision or rule. Interpreting this language, courts divided over whether "knowingly" included "recklessly." Compare *SEC v. Fehn*, 97 F.3d 1276, 1294 (9th Cir. 1996) (requiring actual knowledge) with *SEC v. Pimco Advisors Fund Mgmt, LLC,* 341 F. Supp. 2d 454, 468 (S.D.N.Y. 2004) (not requiring actual knowledge). Congress responded to this division in the Dodd-Frank Act by amending § 20(e) to embrace anyone who provides substantial assistance "knowingly or recklessly." Section 20(e) does not require proof by the SEC that the aider and abettor "proximately caused" the primary violation at issue. *See SEC v. Apuzzo*, 689 F.3d 204, 213 (2d Cir. 2012).

Note that there was no need to safeguard the DOJ's authority to proceed on an aiding and abetting theory, given the separate criminal aiding and abetting provision, 18 U.S.C. § 2(a), which is discussed in § 11.6 *infra*.

§ 2.12.2   CONSPIRACY

Prior to *Central Bank*, plaintiffs could claim that the defendants conspired to violate Rule 10b-5. *See, e.g., Brown v. Hutton Grp.*, 795 F. Supp. 1317 (S.D.N.Y. 1992); *Kronfeld v. First Jersey Nat'l Bank*, 638 F. Supp. 1454, 1468 (D.N.J. 1986). Establishing a conspiracy required proof of "(i) an agreement between the conspirator and the wrongdoer and (ii) a wrongful act committed in furtherance of the conspiracy." *Brown*, 795 F. Supp. at 1324.

Thereafter, however, Rule 10b-5 conspiracy claims have been repeatedly rejected as inconsistent with *Central Bank. See Dinsmore v. Squadron, Ellenoff, Plesent Scheinfeld, & Sorkin*, 135 F.3d 837, 841 (2d Cir. 1998) (collecting cases); *Burnett v. Rowzee*, 561 F. Supp. 2d 1120, 1125 (C.D. Cal. 2008). This seems plausible. Like aiding and abetting, conspiracy does not appear in the text of either § 10(b) or the express liability provisions. Also like aiding and abetting, conspiracy liability does not require proof of reliance. *Cf. Central Bank*, 511 U.S. at 200 n.12 (Stevens, J., dissenting).

What about the right of the SEC to sue for conspiracy? To be sure, Congress restored its right to sue aiders and abettors by enacting § 20(e). *See* § 2.12.1 *supra*. But that provision, which speaks in terms of "substantial assistance" that was "knowingly or recklessly given," does not go so far as to restore the agency's right to sue for conspiracy as well.

The DOJ, on the other hand, can bring conspiracy prosecutions by utilizing the separate criminal conspiracy provision, 18 U.S.C. § 371, discussed in § 11.7 *infra*.

§ 2.12.3 CONTROLLING PERSON LIABILITY

Controlling person liability is the only form of secondary liability explicitly authorized by the Exchange Act (excepting SEC actions under § 20(e) for aiding and abetting, discussed in § 2.12.1 *supra*). The authorization is set forth in § 20(a), which reads as follows:

> Every person who, directly or indirectly, controls any person liable under any provision of this Act or any rule or regulation thereunder shall also be liable jointly and severally with and to the same extent as such controlled person to any person to whom such controlled person is liable (including to the Commission * * *), unless the controlling person acted in good faith and did not directly or indirectly induce the act or acts constituting the violation or cause of action.

The language that specifically allows the SEC to sue results from a recent amendment that was enacted as part of the Dodd-Frank Act. The amendment put to rest a circuit split as to whether § 20(a) was intended for use by private plaintiffs only. Compare *SEC v. J.W. Barclay & Co.*, 442 F.3d 834, 842–843 (3d Cir. 2006) (allowing use by the SEC) with *SEC v. Coffey*, 493 F.3d 1304, 1318 (6th Cir. 1974) (disallowing use by the SEC).

As § 20(a) indicates, controlling person liability requires (i) a primary violation of the Exchange Act and (ii) control by the defendant over the primary violator (who need not be joined as a party to the lawsuit). Even if these elements are established, however, the defendant can avoid liability by showing that he "acted in good faith and did not directly or indirectly induce the act or acts constituting the violation" (the so-called "good faith" defense).

The Meaning of Control. With no test for control set forth in § 20(a) itself, courts have looked to whether the defendant:

(i)   exercised control over the primary violator's general operations; and

(ii)   had the power to control the specific activity at issue in the litigation.

See, e.g., Maher v. Durango Metals, Inc., 144 F.3d 1302, 1305 (10th Cir. 1998) (collecting cases); *Donohoe v. Consol. Operating & Prod. Corp.*, 30 F.3d 907, 911–912 (7th Cir. 1994).

The inquiry is highly fact-intensive, " 'involving scrutiny of the defendant's participation in the day-to-day affairs of the corporation and the defendant's power to control corporate actions.' " *SEC v. Todd*, 642 F.3d 1207, 1223 (9th Cir. 2011) (quoting *Kaplan v. Rose*, 49 F.3d 1363, 1382 (9th Cir. 1994)). Sometimes control is found to reside not in a particular person but rather with a group, such as the corporation's management team. *See, e.g., Arthur Children's Trust v. Keim*, 994 F.2d 1390, 1397 (9th Cir. 1993).

The fact that the defendant serves as an officer or director is not itself dispositive of whether he has control. *See Todd*, 642 F.3d at 1223. It may, however, allow the plaintiff to survive a motion to dismiss. *See, e.g., Adams v. Kinder-Morgan, Inc.*, 340 F.3d 1083, 1108–1109 (10th Cir. 2003) (denying dismissal motions by CEO and CFO); *In re Miller Indus., Inc. Sec. Litig.*, 12 F.Supp. 2d 1323, 1333 (N.D. Ga. 1998) (denying dismissal motion by officers and directors).

A controlling person can be the employer of the controlled person or, alternatively, he can simply be his supervisor. Respondeat superior liability also reaches employers, but not supervisors. *See* § 2.12.4 *infra*.

Culpable Participation. The circuits are divided over whether the plaintiff must show that the controlling person was a "culpable participant" in the primary violator's fraud. Compare *ATSI Commc'ns, Inc. v. Shaar Fund*, Ltd., 493 F.3d 87 (2d Cir. 2007) (endorsing culpable participation); *In re Suprema Specialties Inc. Sec. Litig.*, 438 F.3d 256, 284 n.16 (3d Cir. 2006) (same) with *Lustgraaf v. Behrens.*, 619 F.3d 867, 877 (8th Cir. 2010) (rejecting culpable participation); *Howard v. Everex Sys., Inc.*, 228 F.3d 1057 (9th Cir. 2000) (same) and *In re Stone & Webster, Inc. Sec. Litig.*, 414 F.3d 187, 194 n.4 (1st Cir. 2005) (leaving question open). The conduct constituting culpable participation may take the form of action or inaction, but either instance calls for knowledge of the fraud. *See Belmont v. MB Inv. Partners, Inc.*, 708 F.3d 470, 485 (3d Cir. 2013).

The culpable participation requirement is difficult to square with the language of § 20(a), which puts the burden on the defendant to show his lack of knowledge and involvement. The allure of the requirement, however, is that it may facilitate dismissals in favor of sympathetic defendants at an earlier stage than would otherwise be possible.

In circuits requiring culpable participation, trial courts divide over whether the plaintiff must *plead* culpable participation in order to survive a motion to dismiss. *See id.* at 484 n.20 (acknowledging split within the Third Circuit); *In re MBIA Inc. Sec. Litig.*, 700 F. Supp. 2d 566, 598 (S.D.N.Y. 2010) (acknowledging split within Second Circuit).

The Statutory Defense. To determine whether the defendants have established the statutory defense, courts typically "examine what the defendants could have done under the circumstances to prevent the violation, and then to ask whether the defendants— aware that they could take such measures—decided not to." *Donohoe v. Consol. Operating & Prod. Corp.*, 30 F.3d 907, 912 (7th Cir. 1994). As with the question of control itself, the inquiry is heavily fact-intensive.

Establishing the defense is especially demanding when the defendant is a broker-dealer firm sued in connection with an employee's primary violation. In this instance, the defendant must show that "its supervisory system was adequate and that it reasonably discharged its responsibilities under the system." *Hollinger v. Titan Capital Grp.*, 914 F.2d 1564, 1576 (9th Cir. 1990) (*en banc*).

Why impose a higher standard on broker-dealer firms? The reason is rooted in the protection of the public interest as well as in the fiduciary duty of these firms towards their customers. On the other hand, some defendants outside the broker-dealer context may have to maintain supervisory systems as well in order to establish their defenses. One court has said that the following considerations should determine whether that is the case:

a) whether the controlling person derives direct financial gain from the activity of the controlled person, b) the extent to which the controlled person is tempted to act unlawfully because of the controlling person's policies (*e.g.,* compensation system), c) the extent to which statutory or regulatory law or the defendant's own policies require supervision, d) the relationship between the plaintiff and the controlling person, and e) the demonstration of some public policy need to impose such a requirement.

Kersh v. Gen. Council of Assemblies of God, 804 F.2d 546, 550 (9th Cir. 1986). *See Dellastratious v. Williams,* 242 F.3d 191, 195–196 (4th Cir. 2001) (evaluating whether directors established their defense by looking at their obligations under state law).

The Significance of Joint and Several Liability. Notice that § 20(a), set forth in § 2.12.3 *supra*, speaks of the controlling person's being liable "jointly and severally," the standard to which all private Rule 10b-5 defendants were subject prior to the enactment of the PLSRA. *See* § 2.12.3 *supra*. The PSLRA established a system of proportionate liability, under which a defendant, with limited exceptions, is liable only for the fraction of the judgment for which she bears responsibility. *See id.* The proportionate liability system leaves joint and several liability intact, however, when the defendant acted "knowingly." *See id.* How (if at all) does the PSLRA's proportionate liability interface with the joint and several liability set forth in § 20(a)? The one circuit court decision to consider the question has held that proportionate liability governs liability under § 20(a), with the result that the controlling person can be jointly and severally liable only in the event that he or she is shown to have acted "knowingly." *See Laperriere v. Vesta Ins. Group, Inc.*, 526 F.3d 715, 727–728 (11th Cir. 2008).

§ 2.12.4 RESPONDEAT SUPERIOR

For many years, courts imported into § 10(b) and Rule 10b-5 the tort law doctrine of respondeat superior, which renders an employer vicariously liable for the primary violation of an employee acting within the scope of employment or pursuant to apparent authority. *See, e.g., Hollinger v. Titan Capital Corp.*, 914 F.2d 1564, 1577–1578 (9th Cir. 1990); *In re Citisource, Inc. Sec. Litig.*, 694 F.Supp. 1069, 1078 (S.D.N.Y. 1988). These courts regarded respondeat superior liability, controlling person liability, and primary liability as complementary vehicles for holding participants in securities violations accountable.

But does respondeat superior liability survive *Central Bank, N.A. v. Interstate Bank, N.A.*, 511 U.S. 164 (1994), a decision discussed in § 2.12.1 *supra*? The dissent in *Central Bank* was dubious. *See id.* at 200 n.12 (Stevens, J., dissenting). And that doubt can be readily justified. After all, *Central Bank* rejected aiding and abetting liability largely because of its absence from the text of § 10(b), which does not mention respondeat superior either. Moreover, there is the matter of the overlap between controlling person liability in § 20(a) and respondeat superior, since an employer can be liable for the acts of his employee under either one. Did Congress intend employers to be held liable without recourse to § 20(a)'s good faith defense?

Yet respondeat superior seems to be holding its own thus far. *See, e.g., Southland Sec. Corp. v. INSpire Ins. Solutions, Inc.*, 365 F.3d 353, 384 (5th Cir. 2004) (finding respondeat superior claim to withstand motion to dismiss); *In re Parmalat Sec. Litig.*, 474 F. Supp. 2d 547, 551 (S.D.N.Y. 2007) (upholding respondeat superior claim and stating that *Central Bank* "left respondeat superior untouched"); *Seolas v. Bilzerian*, 951 F. Supp. 978, 983–984 (D. Utah 1997) (finding respondeat superior claim to be harmonizable with the text of § 10(b) and with *Central Bank*). But *see In re Fidelity/Micron Sec. Litig.*, 964 F.Supp. 539, 544 (D. Mass. 1997) (concluding that respondeat superior does not survive).

What accounts for respondeat superior's resilience? One reason may be that § 10(b) and Rule 10b-5 apply to "any person," a term defined by Exchange Act § 3(a)(9) to include "a corporation." To hold a corporation liable requires recourse to "agency principles, since a corporation can act only through its agents." *SEC v. Mgmt. Dynamics, Inc.*, 515 F.2d 801, 812 (2d Cir. 1975). Thus, perhaps there is a basis in the statutory text for respondeat superior liability after all.

§ 2.13 STATUTE OF LIMITATIONS

This section addresses the limitation period governing private actions under Rule 10b-5 only. The periods governing SEC and DOJ actions are considered in § 9.10.5 *infra* and § 11.9 *infra*, respectively.

As originally enacted, the Exchange Act did not contain a limitations period applicable to private actions under § 10(b). The omission is not surprising, since Congress did not have private actions in mind when it enacted that provision.

To supply the limitations period, lower courts for years borrowed the most analogous one from the common law or blue sky law of the relevant state. *See Ernst & Ernst v. Hochfelder*, 425 U.S. 185, 210 n.29 (1976) (acknowledging practice of state law borrowing and observing that "it is not always certain which state statute of limitations should be followed").

The practice of state-law borrowing came to a halt with the Supreme Court's decision in *Lampf, Pleva, Lipkind, Prupris, & Petigrow v. Gilbertson*, 501 U.S. 350 (1991). There the Court held that a private action under Rule 10b-5 "must be commenced within one year after the discovery of the facts constituting the violation and within three years after such violation." *Id.* at 364. In so holding, the Court explicitly patterned itself on the limitations period set forth in § 9(e), an express action for specified forms of market manipulation (*see* § 8.3.1).

The ground shifted again in 2002 with the enactment of the SOX. Section 804 of that Act, enacted as 28 U.S.C. § 1658(b), replaced *Lampf*'s one year/three year structure with a two year/five year structure:

> * * * [A] private right of action that involves a claim of fraud, deceit, manipulation, or contrivance in contravention of a regulatory requirement concerning the securities laws, as defined in section 3(a)(47) of the Securities Exchange Act of 1934, may be brought not later than the earlier of—
>
> (1) 2 years after the discovery of the facts constituting the violation; or (2) 5 years after such violation.

The term "securities laws" is defined in Exchange Act § 3(a)(47) to include, among other statutes, the Securities Act, the Exchange Act, and the SOX.

In *Merck & Co., Inc. v. Reynolds*, 559 U.S. 633 (2010), the Supreme Court put meat on the bones of § 1658(b)(1) by announcing holdings as to three separate but related matters:

The Meaning of "Discovery". The word "discovery" encompasses not only what the plaintiff actually discovered but also what "a reasonably diligent plaintiff would have discovered * * * —whichever comes first." *Id.* at 637.

The Facts That Must Be Discovered. The facts that must be discovered include those pertaining to scienter. *See id.* at 648. Scienter-related facts, the Court explained, ordinarily cannot be gleaned from those that show a statement's falsity. *See id.* at 650. The Court allowed, however, that there is a sub-set of statements as to which falsity does presuppose scienter, such as the statement "I am not married." *Id.*

<u>When the Limitation Period Starts</u>. The clock begins to tick "once the plaintiff did discover or a reasonably diligent plaintiff would have 'discover[ed] the facts constituting the violation'—whichever happens first." *Id.* at 637.

What determines when the plaintiff has discovered enough, whether as to scienter or some other element? The plaintiff has discovered enough, the Court implied, when she, or her reasonably diligent hypothetical counterpart, has sufficient information to plead a claim that can withstand a motion to dismiss. *See id.* at 648–649. *See also City of Pontiac Gen'l Emps. Ret. Sys. v. MBIA, Inc.*, 637 F.3d 169, 174–175 (2d Cir. 2011) (discussing this implication). The actual plaintiff's failure to conduct a reasonable investigation, or any investigation at all, does not affect when this point is reached.

Applying these three holdings to the facts before it, the Court concluded that the plaintiffs' action, which charged Merck with misrepresentations in connection with a pain-killing drug called Vioxx, was "timely." *Id.* at 637, 638, 654. The reason was that prior to two years before the filing of their complaint (on November 6, 2003), the plaintiffs had not discovered, and Merck did not prove that a reasonably diligent plaintiff would have discovered, the necessary facts, particularly with respect to scienter. *Id.* at 654.

The scenario prior to November 6, 2001, had included the following. The FDA approved Vioxx in 1999, at which point it went on the market. Thereafter, a study (called the "VIGOR" study) comparing Vioxx to another pain-killer (Naproxen) showed that patients taking Vioxx suffered more heart-attacks than those taking Naproxen. Merck's explanation was that the risk of heart attacks was lowered by Naproxen, rather than raised by Vioxx. Subsequently, the FDA sent Merck a publicly-disseminated letter instructing the company to inform health care providers that the study results could instead have been due to the detrimental impact of Vioxx. The agency described Merck's statements on the matter as "false, lacking in fair balance, or otherwise misleading," while at the same time acknowledging that the company's interpretation of the study data might be the correct one. During this time, there were also various products liability lawsuits brought by Vioxx users against Merck. These lawsuits contained general allegations that Merck had engaged in intentional concealment.

As the Court noted, the FDA's warning letter failed to evidence scienter on Merck's part. *Id.* at 653–654. Indeed, while faulting Merck's presentation of the possible ways to understand the study, the agency also conceded that Merck's preferred explanation might be valid. *Id.* at 654. Moreover, as to the products liability lawsuits, they contained no specific scienter-related information. *Id.*

§ 2.14   RULE 10b-5 VERSUS THE EXPRESS PRIVATE FRAUD ACTIONS

The Exchange Act and the Securities Act contain the following provisions authorizing express private actions for material misstatements and omissions:

Securities Act § 11. This provision, discussed further in § 3.2 *infra*, allows purchasers in a registered offering to sue the issuer and other specified defendants in connection with a material misstatement or omission in the registration statement. Proof of scienter is not required.

Securities Act § 12(a)(2). This provision, discussed further in § 3.3 *infra*, allows purchasers in a public offering (a category broader than a registered offering) to sue their sellers in connection with a material misstatement or omission in a prospectus or oral communication. Proof of scienter is not required.

Exchange Act § 9(e). This provision, discussed further in § 8.3.1 *infra*, allows an action by purchasers and sellers injured by specified forms of market manipulation. The plaintiff must meet a demanding two-pronged causation requirement: the manipulation must not only cause the plaintiff's damages but also affect the price at which he bought or sold. Moreover, unlike any other private federal securities

remedy, the plaintiff must show that the
defendant acted "willfully."

Exchange Act § 18(a). This provision allows
an action by anyone who buys or sells a security
in reliance on a material misstatement in an
SEC filing "at a price affected by such
misstatement." While the plaintiff need not
establish scienter, she must nonetheless satisfy
several other demanding requirements: actual
reliance on the document in question, a causal
relationship between reliance and damages, and
a causal relationship between the misstatement
and the price paid.

Sometimes conduct may fall within the ambit of
one of these express actions as well as within that of
the implied action under § 10(b) and Rule 10b-5. In
the event of such an overlap, is the express action
exclusive? The Supreme Court considered this
question in *Herman & Maclean v. Huddleston*, 459
U.S. 375 (1983). At issue in *Huddleston* was conduct
actionable under Rule 10b-5 that may also have been
actionable under § 11. The Court allowed the
plaintiffs to proceed with their Rule 10b-5 action on
the ground that the remedies were "cumulative." *Id.*
at 386. It gave several reasons for so doing. First, "the
two provisions involve distinct causes of action and
were intended to address different types of
wrongdoing." *Id.* at 381. That is, § 11 is limited to
omissions and misstatements in a registration
statement and can be brought only against a
specified group of defendants, as to whom scienter is
not required. *See id.* at 381–382. *See* generally § 3.2

infra. Rule 10b-5, on the other hand, requires scienter but has no comparable limitations with respect to where the fraud appears or the identity of the defendants. *See* 459 U.S. at 382.

Moreover, the Court noted its previous endorsement of a cumulative approach in *Ernst & Ernst v. Hochfelder*, 425 U.S. 185 (1976), where it upheld a scienter requirement for Rule 10b-5 partly on the ground that to do otherwise would undermine § 11's procedural restrictions, such as the bond for costs. *See Huddleston*, 459 U.S. at 383–384. Also mentioned by the Court was Congress's failure to override the cumulative approach in 1975—by then a fixture in the caselaw—in connection with its massive overhaul of the federal securities laws that year. *See id.* at 385–386.

In accordance with *Huddleston*, the lower courts have continued to take a cumulative approach to Rule 10b-5 and § 11. *See, e.g., In re Lehman Bros. Mortgage-Backed Sec. Litig.*, 650 F.3d 167, 185 (2d Cir. 2011). The available precedent, albeit sparse, also supports cumulativity for Rule 10b-5 and the other express actions. *See, e.g., Chemetron Corp. v. Bus. Funds, Inc.*, 718 F.2d 725 (5th Cir. 1983) (taking cumulative approach to Rule 10b-5 and § 9(e) in light of *Huddleston*), *reh'g en banc ordered,* 718 F.2d 730 (5th Cir. 1983) (settlement displaced *en banc* hearing); *Berger v. Bishop Inv. Corp.*, 695 F.2d 302, 308 (8th Cir. 1982) (taking cumulative approach to Rule 10b-5 and § 12(a)(2) because only Rule 10b-5 requires scienter); *Wachovia Bank & Trust Co. v. Nat'l Student Mktg. Corp.*, 650 F.2d 342, 356–358

(D.C. Cir. 1980) (taking cumulative approach to Rule 10b-5 and § 18(a) because only Rule 10b-5 requires scienter).

Yet the cumulative approach to remedies may have suffered a blow in the wake of the Supreme Court's recent decision in *Janus Capital Group, Inc. v. First Derivative Traders,* 131 S. Ct. 2296 (2011), discussed in § 2.11.1 *supra.* There the Court rejected the plaintiff's argument in favor of holding the defendant primarily liable partly on the ground that to do so "would read into Rule 10b-5 a theory of liability similar to—but broader in application than"—the control person liability provision (§ 20(a)). The dissent countered this assertion by noting that it contravened *Huddleston. See* 131 S. Ct. at 2310 (Breyer, J., dissenting).

One final point about cumulative remedies is important to bear in mind. If a plaintiff establishes the requisite elements of multiple securities remedies (be the remedies exclusively federal or a combination of state and federal), he cannot recover more than his "actual damages." *See* Exchange Act § 28(a), discussed in § 2.10 *supra.* There may, however, be strategic reasons for alleging multiple causes of action.

CHAPTER 3

LIABILITY UNDER THE SECURITIES ACT FOR MATERIAL MISSTATEMENTS, OMISSIONS, AND FRAUDULENT CONDUCT

§ 3.1 INTRODUCTION

This Chapter examines provisions of the Securities Act that authorize liability for material misstatements, omissions, and fraudulent conduct. Two of these provisions—§§ 11 and 12(a)(2)—create express private actions and encompass registered offerings (although, as we will see, § 12(a)(2) reaches more broadly). The third—§ 17(a)—is enforceable by the Securities and Exchange Commission (the SEC) and the Department of Justice (the DOJ) only.

To be sure, the Securities Act also contains a provision—§ 12(a)(1)—that creates an express private action for violations of § 5 of the Securities Act, which requires the registration of every non-exempt securities offering (*see* § 1.2.1 *supra*). But because registration is not a principal focus of this Chapter, § 12(a)(1) is considered only insofar as it sheds light on its statutory sibling, § 12(a)(2).

This Chapter proceeds as follows: first, § 11 (*see* § 3.2 *infra*); next, § 12(a)(2) (*see* § 3.3 *infra*); then, the features that §§ 11 and 12(a)(2) share (*see* § 3.4 *infra*); thereafter, a version of § 12(a)(2) liability applicable solely in the crowdfunding context (*see* § 3.5 *infra*); and finally, § 17(a) (*see* § 3.6 *infra*).

§ 3.2 SECTION 11

Section 11(a) authorizes a straightforward cause of
action: a purchaser of a security sold pursuant to a
registration statement filed with the SEC may sue
any enumerated defendant if the registration
statement contained a material misstatement or
omission on the date it became effective. Before
considering the enumerated defendants, it is useful
to have in mind the entire cast of persons responsible
for the accuracy of the registration statement:

<u>The Issuer</u>. This is the company whose
securities are sold to the public pursuant to the
registration statement. The issuer's officers and
directors are responsible for the content of the
registration statement and for cooperating with
the auditor and underwriters in their efforts to
confirm the truthfulness of the registration
statement.

<u>The Auditor</u>. This is the accounting firm that
must conduct a detailed audit of the issuer and
certify that the issuer's financial statements
have been prepared in accordance with
Generally Accepted Accounting Principles
(GAAP).

<u>The Underwriters</u>. Occasionally, a small
offering (known as a direct public offering) will
be sold directly to investors without an
underwriter. More commonly, however, the
issuer retains one or more investment banks as
underwriters. The investment bank leading the
effort to sell the securities is known as the

managing underwriter (or lead underwriter), and the other underwriters are "major bracket" or "minor bracket" underwriters, depending on the amount of securities for which they agree to be responsible.

Underwriters are typically compensated with a "spread"—the percentage difference between the consideration paid by investors for the securities and the proceeds from the offering received by the issuer. Underwriters are thus normally paid only if the offering is "closed," thereby possibly tempting some underwriters to close an offering even if they know that the registration statement is misleading. As we shall see, one way in which the Securities Act counters this temptation is to subject underwriters to substantial liability under § 11 if securities are sold pursuant to a misleading registration statement.

The brokers who distribute the securities to investors comprise the "selling group." In contrast to the underwriters, the brokers are not in privity of contract with the issuer.

The Lawyers. The issuer as well as the managing underwriter typically retain lawyers to assist with the preparation of the registration statement and related duties. The issuer's lawyer usually takes the principal role in drafting the registration statement, although the underwriters' lawyer usually also has significant involvement.

§ 3.2.1   SECTION 11's
ENUMERATED DEFENDANTS

The plaintiffs in a § 11 action may state a claim against one or more of the following categories of defendants:

- Signers of the registration statement. Section 6(a) of the Securities Act lists those who must sign the registration statement, and the issuer is among the required signers;

- Every person who was a director of the issuer at the time of registration;

- Every future director who, with his or her consent, was named in the registration statement;

- Any accountant who certified any financial statement contained in the registration statement, where at least one of the material misstatements or omissions at issue appears in the statement that he certified;

- Any other person who certified a part of the registration statement, where at least one of the material misstatements or omissions at issue appears in the statement that he certified; and

- Every underwriter involved in the offering.

Observe that § 11 does not authorize liability for lawyers based on either their drafting of the registration statement or their investigation of its accuracy.

§ 3.2.2   THE PRIMA FACIE § 11 CASE

To establish a prima facie case, the § 11 plaintiff must show:

(i) that the registration statement contains at least one material misstatement or omission; and

(ii) that she purchased shares that can be traced to the registration statement. *See* § 3.2.3 *infra.*

Notice that her prima facie case does not include the traditional common law requirements of scienter or causation. Nor does it include her reliance on the material misstatement or omission, except for one rare circumstance—namely, where she bought the securities after the issuer distributed audited financial statements covering the 12-month period after the effective date of the registration statement. *See* § 11(a). To be sure, the Eleventh Circuit adopted an expansive view of reliance in *APA Excelsior III LP v. Premiere Techs., Inc.*, 476 F.3d 1261, 1273 (11th Cir. 2007), which held that § 11 creates a "presumption of reliance" that fails to attach when the plaintiffs made a "binding pre-registration commitment" to purchase the shares. But *see FHFA v. Bank of Am. Corp.*, 2014 WL 7232339, at *2–3 (S.D.N.Y. Dec. 18, 2014) (rejecting the 11th Circuit's analysis).

Section 11 defendants can assert the following defenses, the first of which is not available to the issuer (whose liability is often described as "strict"):

- the due diligence defenses (*see* § 3.2.4 *infra*);

- the negative causation defense (*see* § 3.2.6 *infra*);

- the plaintiff's knowledge of the misstatement or omission at the time of purchasing the security (*see* § 11(a));

- the statute of limitations defense (*see* § 3.4 *infra*).

§ 3.2.3   SECTION 11's TRACING REQUIREMENT

A § 11 plaintiff can be an original purchaser in the registered offering or else a subsequent purchaser of shares that originated from that offering. *See, e.g., DeMaria v. Andersen*, 318 F.3d 170, 176 (2d Cir. 2003). In either instance, she must be able to "trace" her shares back to the challenged registration statement. *See id.*

The tracing requirement can itself be traced to the Second Circuit's landmark decision in *Barnes v. Osofsky*, 373 F.2d 269 (2d Cir. 1967), which focused on § 11(a)'s reference to a lawsuit by "any person acquiring such security." At least in theory, the court observed, that language can be read in two ways: (1) as confining the plaintiff class to those "acquiring a security issued pursuant to the registration statement," thereby making tracing essential or (2) as including those "acquiring a security of the same nature as that issued pursuant to the registration statement," making tracing inapposite. *See id.* at 271. The court gave several reasons for rejecting the latter reading. One was the implausibility that § 11, "developed to insure proper disclosure in the registration statement," could have been "meant to provide a remedy for other than the particular shares registered." *Id.* at 272. Another was the text of § 11(g), which provides that "[i]n no case shall the amount recoverable * * * exceed the price at which the security was offered to the public." In this connection, the court noted that if the number of shares issued in the registered offering was dwarfed by the number of shares otherwise outstanding, the recovery available to purchasers in the registered offering would be severely compromised. *Id.*

The tracing requirement can be easy to satisfy—or virtually impossible—depending on the circumstances. For example, no difficulty arises when the issuer's only outstanding shares emanated from the registration statement in question. *See, e.g., In re Century Aluminum Co. Sec. Litig.*, 729 F.3d 1104, 1107 (9th Cir. 2013). On the other hand, matters tend to become murky when the outstanding shares emerged from a variety of registration statements (and/or exempt offerings). *See id.* The reason is that investors typically own their shares in "street" name, that is, in the name of their brokerage firm, but brokers ordinarily do not segregate newly-issued shares from previously-issued shares of the same issuer or assign particular shares to particular investors.

Plaintiffs have sometimes offered evidence of the statistical likelihood that their shares derived from the challenged registration statement. But courts have been unreceptive to such statistical arguments. *See, e.g., Krim v. pcOrder.com, Inc.*, 402 F.3d 489, 502 (5th Cir. 2005).

§ 3.2.4   SECTION 11's DUE DILIGENCE DEFENSES

Section 11 prevents the issuer from interposing due diligence defenses. *See* § 11(b). But often, prior to the time the § 11 action is filed, the issuer has become bankrupt, and therefore judgment-proof. Under these circumstances, the plaintiff's ability to recover is apt to depend on whether the non-issuer defendants can successfully mount due diligence defenses.

The nature of the requisite due diligence turns on whether the alleged omission or misstatement appeared in the expertised or non-expertised portion of the registration statement. A portion is deemed "expertised" provided the following three conditions are satisfied: (1) the portion "purport[s] to be made on the authority of an expert;" (2) the expert is an "accountant, engineer, or appraiser, or any person whose profession gives authority to a statement made by him;" and (3) the expert's written consent is attached to the registration statement. *See* § 11(a)(4); *FHFA v. Nomura Holding Am., Inc.*, 68 F.Supp. 3d 439, 467 n.40 (S.D.N.Y. 2014). The bulk of the registration statement is *not* expertised.

Consider a director who wishes to establish his due diligence in connection with a misstatement or omission in the non-expertised portion of the registration statement. The director must show that:

he had, after reasonable investigation, reasonable ground to believe and did believe, at the time such part of the registration statement became effective, that the statements therein were true and that there was no omission to state a material fact required to be stated therein or necessary to make the statements therein not misleading.

§ 11(b)(3)(A). With respect to the expertised portion(s), however, that director has a lesser showing, namely that:

he had no reasonable ground to believe and did not believe, at the time such part of the registration statement became effective, that the statements therein were untrue or that there was an omission to state a material fact required to be stated therein or necessary to make the statements therein not misleading, or that such part of the registration statement did not fairly represent the statement of the expert or was not a fair copy of or extract from the report or valuation of the expert.

§ 11(b)(3)(C).

An expert can be liable only in connection with the portion of the registration statement that he certified. Thus, consider an accountant seeking to establish his due diligence in connection with the audited financial statements. He must show that:

(i) he had, after reasonable investigation, reasonable ground to believe and did believe, at the time such part of the registration statement became effective, that the statements therein were true and that there was no omission to state a material fact required to be stated therein or necessary to make the statements therein not misleading, or (ii) such part of the registration statement did not fairly represent his statement as an expert or was not a fair copy of or extract from his report or valuation as an expert.

§ 11(b)(3)(B).

Notice the similarities between the non-expert's defense for the non-expertised portion and the expert's defense for his expertised portion. Both require a "reasonable investigation" and a "reasonable ground to believe" as well as a belief in the truth of the statement in question.

Contrast the leniency reflected in the non-expert's defense for the expertised portion. No investigation is required. Nor is there a necessity for a reasonable ground to believe, or for an affirmative belief, in the truth of the statements. All that is necessary is that the defendant lack a reasonable ground to believe, and not actually believe, that the statements were untrue.

Suppose a plaintiff challenges statements in both the non-expertised and expertised portions. A defendant's failure to establish his defense regarding the statement in one portion makes him liable, but it is still necessary to ascertain whether he can establish the defense regarding the statement in the other portion. The reason is that § 11 defendants can sue each other for contribution. *See* § 11(f). *See also* § 3.2.7 *infra.* A defendant liable for more misstatements must contribute a greater amount than a defendant who is liable for fewer.

§ 3.2.5   DUE DILIGENCE CRITERIA

The due diligence defenses are centered on the indeterminate concepts of "reasonable investigation" and "reasonable ground for belief." *See* § 3.2.4 *supra.* It is worth noting that § 11(c) provides that "the standard of reasonableness shall be that required of a prudent man in the management of his own property," yet this statement tends to be too general to offer much guidance in specific cases.

A significant gloss on these concepts comes from the seminal § 11 decision in *Escott v. Barchris Constr. Corp.*, 283 F.Supp. 643 (S.D.N.Y. 1968). There the court made an in-depth inquiry as to whether each defendant established his defense regarding the alleged misstatements in the non-expertised portion and likewise those in the expertised portion (namely, the audited financials). In so doing, the court considered each defendants specific position in the company and the exposure to the relevant information that his position afforded him; his role in the preparation of the registration statement; and his education and professional training.

None of the *Barchris* defendants was able to establish a defense with respect to the non-expertised portion. Moreover, the accountants could not establish a defense with respect to the expertised portion. The same was true for the CEO and the CFO.

To be sure, the latter were not "experts." But knowledge of the inner workings of the company was attributed to them, thereby leaving them unable to meet even the low bar for a defense under § 11(b)(3)(c).

In the early 1980s, the SEC made two changes that increased the challenges faced by § 11 defendants in performing their due diligence obligations. Both changes enhanced the speed with which a registered offering can be prepared. One change, called "incorporation by reference," permits certain issuers to incorporate their Exchange Act filings into their registration statements and thus ready them sooner. The other change consisted of the expansion of "shelf registration," which enables certain issuers to make multiple offerings on the basis of a single registration statement.

In response to the resultant uncertainty, the SEC adopted Rule 176, which offers a list of "relevant circumstances" bearing on whether the defendant made a "reasonable investigation" or had a "reasonable ground for belief." Circumstances deemed relevant include the type of issuer, security, and person, as well as reasonable reliance on corporate officials.

The inquiry into due diligence defenses frequently focuses on whether the defendant encountered a "red flag," that is, information that would reasonably lead him to doubt the truthfulness of the misstatement in question. *See, e.g., In re Software Toolworks, Inc.*, 50 F.3d 615, 623–624 (9th Cir. 1994). Faced with a red flag, a defendant is obliged to probe further. *See*

FHFA v. Nomura Holding Am., Inc., 68 F.Supp. 3d 439, 473 (S.D.N.Y. 2014).

Red flags and Rule 176 were among the subjects addressed by *In re WorldCom, Inc., Sec. Litig.*, 346 F.Supp. 2d 628 (S.D.N.Y. 2004), a landmark § 11 decision that denied summary judgment to underwriter defendants. Finding Rule 176 to have been intended merely as a guidepost rather than as a means of reducing a defendant's due diligence obligations, the court held that those obligations remained the same, the availability of incorporation by reference and shelf registration notwithstanding.

Consider also the significance of "red flags" in the *WorldCom* court's analysis. A trial was found necessary to ascertain whether certain such flags should have prompted the underwriters to delve more deeply. The red flag pertinent to the expertised portion was that the issuer's E/R ratio stood below those of its competitors, while the red flag pertinent to the non-expertised portion was that the issuer occupied "a deteriorating financial position in a troubled industry." *Id.* at 683. Since neither item necessarily screamed fraud, concern has arisen that those performing due diligence may overlook what are only later found to constitute red flags.

WorldCom's red flag analysis has prompted another concern as well. Notice that the presence of a red flag created a problem for the defendants in connection with both the expertised and non-expertised portions of the registration statement. That in turn suggests something of a convergence between the defenses relevant to the two portions, however distinct they may appear on the face of the statute.

§ 3.2.6   SECTION 11 DAMAGES AND NEGATIVE CAUSATION

Section 11(e) provides a formula for calculating damages pursuant to which the plaintiff can recover the difference between the amount paid for the security (not exceeding the price at which the security was offered to the public) and

(1) the value thereof as of the time such suit was brought, or

(2) the price at which such security shall have been disposed of in the market before suit, or

(3) the price at which such security shall have been disposed of after suit but before judgment if such damages shall be less than [the damages specified in (1) above].

Two aspects of this formula are important to bear in mind. Notice first in (1) above, the use of the word *value* of the security, as distinct from "amount paid" and "price." The word "value" is designed to take account of the somewhat atypical situation in which the actual value of a security cannot be ascertained simply on the basis of its market value. *See McMahan & Co. v. Wherehouse Entertainment, Inc.,* 65 F.3d 1044, 1048–1049 (2d Cir. 1995). For an example, *see NECA-IBEW Health & Welfare Fund v. Goldman Sachs & Co.,* 693 F.3d 145, 165–167 (2d Cir. 2012).

Second, the formula must be read together with § 11(g): "In no case shall the amount recoverable under this section exceed the price at which the security was offered to the public." Thus, those who sold securities above the offering price lack the right to sue under § 11. *See Initial Public Offering Sec. Litig.*, 241 F.Supp. 2d 281, 347 (S.D.N.Y. 2003).

Section 11(e) also contains a so-called "negative causation" defense pursuant to which a defendant can reduce—or even eliminate entirely—the amount of damages he might otherwise owe:

> [I]f the defendant proves that any portion or all of such damages represents other than the depreciation in value of such security resulting from such part of the registration statement, with respect to which his liability is asserted, not being true or omitting to state a material fact required to be stated therein or necessary to make the statements therein not misleading, such portion of or all such damages shall not be recoverable.

§ 3.2.7 SECTION 11 CONTRIBUTION

Most § 11 defendants are jointly and severally liable for the damages that may be awarded. *See* § 11(f)(1). Under this arrangement, any defendant may be liable for all the damages, but may thereafter obtain contribution from anyone who, "if sued separately, would have been liable to make the same payment, unless the person who has become liable was, and the other was not, guilty of fraudulent misrepresentation." *Id.* Two categories of defendants, however, are treated differently: underwriters and outside directors.

The exception for underwriters is set forth in § 11(e). That provision states that unless an underwriter received a benefit from the issuer not received by the other underwriters, his liability under § 11 is capped at "the total price at which the securities underwritten by him and distributed to the public were offered to the public." Thus, in a $300 million offering, an underwriter who sold $50 million in securities would be liable only for $50 million.

The exception for outside directors—set forth in § 11(f)(2)(A)—was added by the Private Securities Litigation Reform Act of 1995 (the PSLRA). Pursuant to this provision, a § 11 defendant who is an outside director is subject to proportionate (rather than joint and several) liability so long as he did not act "knowingly."

§ 3.3 SECTION 12(a)(2)

Section 12(a)(2) creates an express private action pursuant to which securities purchasers can sue their sellers for material misstatements and omissions made "by means of a prospectus" or, in some instances, orally. This provision reads as follows:

Any person who— * * *

(2) offers or sells a security (whether or not exempted by the provisions of section 3, other than paragraphs (2) and (14) of subsection (a) thereof), by the use of any means or instruments

of transportation or communication in interstate commerce or of the mails, by means of a prospectus or oral communication, which includes an untrue statement of a material fact or omits to state a material fact necessary in order to make the statements, in the light of the circumstances under which they were made, not misleading (the purchaser not knowing of such untruth or omission), and who shall not sustain the burden of proof that he did not know, and in the exercise of reasonable care could not have known, of such untruth or omission, shall be liable . . . to the person purchasing such security from him, who may sue either at law or in equity in any court of competent jurisdiction, to recover the consideration paid for such security with interest thereon, less the amount of any income received thereon, upon the tender of such security, or for damages if he no longer owns the security.

Prior to 1995, § 12(a)(2) was codified as § 12(2) and some courts continue to refer to it in that fashion.

Section 12(a)(2) encompasses initial securities offerings only. To state a claim, the plaintiff must allege:

- that she purchased securities in the offering in question. The necessity of her being a purchaser, rather than merely an offeree, emerges from the statutory language deeming the defendant "liable * * * to the person purchasing such security from him."

- that the sale to her occurred "by means of a prospectus or oral communication." *See* § 3.3.1 *infra*.

- that the prospectus or oral communication contained a materially misleading misstatement or omission. For discussion of materiality, *see* § 3.4 *infra*.

- that the defendant(s) each qualify as a "seller" as that term is defined by case law and SEC rule-making. *See* § 3.3.5 *infra*.

Notice that this list does not include the traditional common law fraud elements of scienter, reliance, or causation.

The defendant(s), including the issuer, can assert any of the following defenses:

- the reasonable care defense (*see* § 3.3.6 *infra*);

- the negative causation defense (*see* § 3.3.7 *infra*);

- the statute of limitations defense (*see* § 3.4 *infra*).

§ 3.3.1   BY MEANS OF A PROSPECTUS

Prior to the Supreme Court's 5–4 decision in *Gustafson v. Alloyd Corp.*, 513 U.S. 561 (1995), § 12(a)(2) was widely understood to be applicable to registered offerings, exempt offerings, offerings that should have been registered (and were thus conducted illegally), and secondary market trading. In the wake of *Gustafson*, § 12(a)(2) still applies to

registered and illegal offerings, but only to some
exempt offerings, and not at all to secondary market
trading.

To understand *Gustafson*'s bright lines, as well as
the various uncertainties that it has spawned, it is
necessary to begin with some background about the
case. The plaintiffs contracted to purchase shares
issued decades earlier by a close corporation. Later
dissatisfied with their purchase, they filed a lawsuit
under § 12(a)(2), alleging that the contract qualified
as a "prospectus" and contained material
misrepresentations.

To show that the contract was a "prospectus," they
invoked the Securities Act's definition of that term,
which appears in § 2(a)(10). The definition states
that a prospectus is "any prospectus, notice, circular,
advertisement, letter, or *communication*, written or
by radio or television, which offers any security for
sale or confirms the sale of any security." *Id.*
(emphasis added). As they saw it, the contract was a
"communication * * * which offers any security for
sale."

The Supreme Court rejected this argument and
offered the following reasons for so doing:

- The meaning of "prospectus" as it appears in
  § 12(a)(2) is *not* driven primarily by § 2(a)(10)
  but rather by an altogether different provision
  of the Securities Act, namely, § 10. *See id.* at
  568–573. The latter provision identifies the
  information required in the "prospectus," the
  principal portion of the registration

statement, which is the document that must be filed with the SEC by an issuer making a non-exempt offering of securities on behalf of itself or its controlling shareholder(s). *See* § 1.2 *supra*. The reach of § 10 is "unqualified," except for "the explicit and well-defined exemptions for securities listed under § 3." *Id.* at 569.

- Section 10 prompts the conclusion that "a prospectus * * * is confined to documents relating to *public offerings* by an issuer or its controlling shareholders." *Id.* (emphasis added).

- In the interests of statutory consistency, the meaning of "prospectus" in § 10 should carry over to § 12(a)(2). *See id.* at 570.

- The plaintiffs were therefore not entitled to use § 12(a)(2) because they did not purchase their shares in a "public offering."

The contours of a "public offering" is the transcendent uncertainty created by *Gustafson*'s conclusion, set forth above, that "a prospectus is confined to documents relating to public offerings." No doubt the term "public offering" includes a registered offering, an offering made in violation of § 5's registration requirement, and at least some exempt offerings. *Cf. id.* at 596 n.1 (Ginsburg, J., dissenting) (observing that "the Court's definition of a public offering * * * encompass[es] both transactions that must be registered under § 5, and transactions that would have been registered had the

securities involved not qualified for exemption under
§ 3").

§ 3.3.2   BY MEANS OF AN "ORAL COMMUNICATION"

The *Gustafson* Court noted, and also seemingly
endorsed, the lower court consensus on the reach of
"oral communication"—namely, that it must "relate
to a prospectus." *Gustafson*, 513 U.S. at 567–568. *See,
e.g.*, *Thompson v. RelationServe Media, Inc.*, 610 F.3d
628, 676 n.69 (11th Cir. 2010) (observing that "the
Supreme Court has made clear that the only oral
communications that count are those that 'relate to a
prospectus' "); *Yung v. Lee*, 432 F.3d 142, 147 n.5 (2d
Cir. 2005) (same).

§ 3.3.3   WHICH EXEMPT OFFERINGS DOES § 12(a)(2) EMBRACE?

To determine which exempt offerings are
reachable under § 12(a)(2), two points are relevant at
the outset. First, an offering is not "public" if it
qualifies as a so-called "private offering" under
§ 4(a)(2) of the Securities Act, an exemption for
"transactions by an issuer not involving any public
offering." *See Yung*, 432 F.3d at 148 (collecting cases
to this effect). The Supreme Court established the
scope of § 4(a)(2) in *SEC v. Ralston Purina Co.*, 346
U.S. 119 (1953), which held a private offering to be
one in which the offerees have "access to the kind of
information which registration would disclose" as
well as the capacity "to fend for themselves." *See id.*
at 125–127. *See also Yung*, 432 F.3d at 149 (holding

that an otherwise private offering does not become "public" by virtue of having been marketed on the basis of a prospectus used in a recent registered offering).

Second, the *Gustafson* Court twice implied that § 12(a)(2) reached at least some exempt offerings. One was its statement that "the term [prospectus]" is confined to a document that, *absent an overriding exemption*, must include the "information contained in the registration statement." *Gustafson, 513 U.S. at* 569 (emphasis added). The other, mentioned earlier in § 3.3.1 *supra*, was its description of the reach of § 10 as "unqualified" except for "the explicit and well-defined *exemptions for securities listed under § 3.*" *Id.* (emphasis added). *See also id.* at 596 n.1 (Ginsburg, J., dissenting) (noting that "I understand the Court's definition of a public offering to encompass both transactions that must be registered under § 5, and *transactions that would have been registered had the securities involved not qualified for exemption under § 3*") (internal citations omitted and emphasis added)).

These preliminary points give rise to two alternative approaches—a "bright-line" approach and a "functional" approach:

> <u>Bright-Line Approach</u>. Under this approach, § 12(a)(2) embraces offerings exempt under § 3 (except for subsections (2) and (14) thereof, excluded on the face of § 12(a)(2)) but not those exempt under § 4. Offerings exempt under § 3 would include § 3's progeny, such as Rule 147, Regulation A, and Rules 504 and 505 of

Regulation D. Similarly, offerings exempt under
§ 4 would include § 4's progeny, such as Rule 506
of Regulation D.

Relevant in this regard are two recent
developments emanating from the JOBS Act.
One of them involves Rule 506. The JOBS Act
directed the SEC to amend Regulation D to
remove the ban on general solicitation and
advertising for Rule 506 offerings where all
purchasers are accredited investors. The SEC
responded to this directive in July 2013 by
adopting new Rule 506(c), which permits
general solicitation and advertising as long as
the issuer "take[s] reasonable steps to verify
that purchasers * * * are accredited investors"
and "[a]ll purchasers of securities sold in any
offering * * * are accredited investors." The
JOBS Act also added to the Securities Act a new
§ 4(b), which provides that securities offered and
sold pursuant to Rule 506 "shall not be deemed
public offerings under the federal securities laws
as a result of general advertising or general
solicitation."

The other recent development involves
Regulation A, updated and expanded by the SEC
in accordance with § 3(b)(2), which was added to
the Securities Act as part of the JOBS Act.
Subsection D of § 3(b)(2) specifies that "[t]he
civil liability provision in § 12(a)(2) shall apply
to any person offering or selling such securities."

Functional Approach. Under this approach,
the statutory source of the exemption does not

necessarily carry the day. The key is instead whether the offering satisfies the § 4(a)(2) exemption, even if it also satisfies a § 3 exemption. Thus, § 12(a)(2) would not apply to an offering exempted by § 3 if the offering simultaneously satisfies § 4a(2). On the other hand, this approach may conceivably enable § 12(a)(2) to reach a Rule 506 offering if the offering does not satisfy § 4(a)(2) absent the Rule 506 safe harbor. Such a situation might arise, for example, when a purchaser was an accredited investor based on net worth but failed to meet the *Ralston Purina* criteria.

§ 3.3.4   FREE WRITING PROSPECTUSES

Prior to reforms made by the SEC in 2005, participants in the registration process faced sharp restrictions regarding their use of materials that supplemented the registration statement. Reforms made in 2005 loosened those restrictions by creating the concept of the "free writing prospectus"—written (or electronic) material allowed to supplement the registration statement so long as certain conditions are satisfied. *See* Securities Act Rules 164 and 433. The free writing prospectus is "public, without regard to its method of distribution" because it is "related to the public offering of securities that are the subject of a filed registration statement." Rule 433(a).

In its release accompanying the 2005 reforms, the SEC placed free writing prospectuses squarely under the § 12(a)(2) umbrella. That release stated that "any seller offering or selling securities by means of the free writing prospectus will be subject to disclosure liability under Securities Act Section 12(a)(2)." Securities Offering Reform, Securities Act Release No. 33-8591, 2005 WL 1692642 at *62 (Aug. 3, 2005).

§ 3.3.5 WHO IS A "SELLER"?

Section 12(a)(2) imposes liability on the person(s) who sold the securities to the purchaser(s), but does not tell us who qualifies as a "seller." *See* § 3.3 *supra* (setting out the statutory text). Nor does the Securities Act elsewhere define that term.

The Supreme Court addressed the definition of "seller" in *Pinter v. Dahl*, 486 U.S. 622 (1988), albeit in connection with § 12(a)(2)'s sister provision— § 12(a)(1), which imposes liability on those who sell securities in violation of § 5—that is, who do so without registering the offering or complying with an exemption. *See* § 1.2 *supra.* The two subparts of § 12 impose liability on sellers based on the same language, with the result that no distinction is typically made as to whom can be sued under each. *See Pinter,* 486 U.S. at 642 n. 20; *Miyahira v. Vitacost.com, Inc.*, 715 F.3d 1257, 1265 (11th Cir. 2013) (applying *Pinter's* definition of "seller" to § 12(a)(2)); *In re Morgan Stanley Info. Fund Sec. Litig.*, 592 F.3d 347, 359 (2d Cir. 2010) (same).

The litigation in *Pinter* began as a lawsuit by a group of individuals, including Dahl, against Pinter, from whom the members of the group acquired title to fractional undivided interests in oil and gas leases that had been sold to them in an allegedly illegal offering. Pinter thereafter counterclaimed against

Dahl for contribution, alleging that Dahl was himself a "seller" by virtue of his role in leading the others to participate in the offering. That role included describing the opportunity to the others (none of whom, with one exception, inspected the properties or conversed with Dahl) and helping them to complete their subscription agreements. The counterclaim took center-stage in the Supreme Court.

The Court began its analysis by holding that the "seller" category encompasses more than those who merely pass title. *Pinter*, 486 U.S. at 644. Critical to this conclusion were the Securities Act's definitions of "sale" and "offer," especially the language "solicitation of an offer to buy" that appears in connection with the latter. *See id.* at 645. Moreover, as the Court saw it, a focus on solicitation "furthers the purposes of the Securities Act," since "[t]he solicitation of a buyer is perhaps the most critical stage of the selling transaction." *Id.* at 646.

With these considerations in mind, the Court held that someone who is not a title passer can nonetheless qualify as a seller if he or she:

- successfully solicits the purchase, and

- is motivated at least in part by a desire to serve his own financial interests or those of the securities owner.

Id. at 647. Finding not "clearly erroneous" the trial court's conclusion that Dahl met the first criterion, the Court remanded for consideration, not undertaken by the trial court, of whether he had also met the second one. *See id.* at 654–655. The Court acknowledged that Dahl had not received a commission, but noted that this was "not conclusive." *Id.* at 654.

Can one § 12(a)(2) "seller" sue another such seller for contribution? Unlike § 11, § 12 does not mention contribution. The *Dahl* Court reserved the question of its availability in the context of § 12(a)(1). *See id.* at 630 n.9. *But cf. Baker, Watts & Co. v. Miles & Stockbridge*, 876 F.2d 1101, 1102 (4th Cir.1989) (*en banc*) (holding that there is no right of contribution under § 12(a)(2)).

Analysis of who is a "seller" must take account of the distinction between "firm commitment" underwriting and best efforts underwriting. In firm commitment underwriting, the underwriters buy the securities from the issuer and resell them, whereas in "best efforts" underwriting, the underwriters do not buy the securities but instead use their best efforts to effectuate the distribution.

Consider first a "best efforts" underwriting. Title to the securities remains with the issuer, who is thus the passer of title and hence a "seller" for purposes of § 12(a)(2). The underwriter may also be a seller, so long as it engages in "solicitation," since its activities on behalf of the issuer's sale are motivated by the underwriting commission it will receive if the offering is successful.

Next, consider "firm commitment" underwriting. Various pre-2005 decisions held that the issuer in this situation—not being the title passer—qualified as a § 12(a)(2) seller only if it solicited in the *Pinter* sense (*see* § 3.3.5 *supra*). These holdings did not sit well with the SEC, which stated as follows in its release on the 2005 reforms:

> We believe that an issuer offering or selling its securities in a registered offering pursuant to a registration statement containing a prospectus that it has prepared and filed * * * can be viewed as soliciting purchases of the issuer's registered securities.

Securities Offering Reform, Securities Act Release 33-8591, 2005 WL 1692642 at *78 (Aug. 3, 2005). Accordingly, the SEC adopted Rule 159A(a), which deems an issuer to be a "seller" under § 12(a)(2) "regardless of the underwriting method used to sell the issuer's securities."

§ 3.3.6   SECTION 12(a)(2)'s REASONABLE CARE DEFENSE

Section 12(a)(2) allows the defendant to avoid liability by establishing a reasonable care defense— namely, that "he did not know, and in the exercise of reasonable care could not have known," about the materially misleading misstatement or omission. The success of such a defense turns heavily on the specifics of the situation. *See, e.g., FHFA v. Nomura Holding Am. Inc.*, 68 F.Supp. 3d 439, 466 (S.D.N.Y. 2014).

Courts have long struggled with whether, and to what extent, this defense replicates the due diligence defense under § 11. *See, e.g., In re Software*

Toolworks, Inc. Sec. Litig., 50 F.3d 615, 621 (9th Cir. 1994). In an important 2005 release, the SEC characterized "reasonable care" under § 12(a)(2) as "less demanding" than "due diligence" under § 11. *See* Securities Offering Reform, Securities Act Release 33-8591, 2005 WL 1692642 at *79 (Aug. 3, 2005). Courts have tended to follow the SEC's lead in this regard. *See Mass. Mut. Life Ins. Co. v. DB Structured Products, Inc.*, 110 F.Supp. 3d 288, 298 (D. Mass. 2015) (collecting cases). *But cf. Sanders v. John Nuveen & Co.*, 619 F.2d 1222, 1228 (7th Cir. 1980) (questioning whether "Congress intended to impose a higher standard of care under § 11 than under § 12(2)").

Several differences between "reasonable care" and its § 11 counterpart merit mention.

First, the "reasonable care" defense can be invoked by an issuer, which is strictly liable under § 11. *See* § 3.2.4 *supra*.

Second, the "reasonable care" defense does not distinguish between the expertised and non-expertised portions of the registration statement (although the location of the fraud might prove relevant to what constitutes "reasonable care" in a given situation).

Third, the "reasonable care" defense does not call for an investigation as such, making it plausible to assume that one might not always be required. For example, it is conceivable, albeit not certain, that a non-investigating defendant could establish his defense by showing that if he had conducted an investigation, it would not have elicited the necessary information. *See In re WorldCom, Inc., Sec. Litig.*, 346 F.Supp. 2d 628, 662 n.40 (S.D.N.Y. 2004).

§ 3.3.7   SECTION 12(a)(2) DAMAGES AND NEGATIVE CAUSATION

Damages under § 12(a)(2) are rescissory in nature, regardless of whether the plaintiff sold the securities in question. Thus, if the plaintiff has not sold the securities, he is entitled to "the consideration paid for such security with interest thereon, less the amount of any income received." But if the plaintiff has sold the securities, he has the right to rescissory damages—"a return of the consideration paid, reduced by the amount realized when he sold the security and any 'income received' on the security." *Randall v. Loftsgaarden*, 478 U.S. 647, 656 (1986).

A defendant in a § 12(a)(2) action can reduce—or even eliminate entirely—the amount of money that the plaintiff would otherwise recover. Authorization comes from § 12(b):

[I]f the person who offered or sold such security proves that any portion or all of the amount recoverable under subsection (a)(2) represents other than the depreciation in value of the subject security resulting from such part of the prospectus or oral communication, with respect to which the liability of that person is asserted, not being true or omitting to state a material fact required to be stated therein or necessary to make the statement not misleading, then such portion or amount, as the case may be, shall not be recoverable.

The "negative causation" defense—enacted in 1995 as part of the PSLRA—is analogous to § 11's negative causation defense. *See* § 3.2.6 *supra.* For an extensive analysis of an unsuccessful attempt to establish the defense, *see FHFA v. Nomura Holding Am., Inc.*, 104 F.Supp. 3d 441, 586–588 (S.D.N.Y. 2015).

§ 3.4 ADDITIONAL SHARED FEATURES OF §§ 11 AND 12(a)(2)

Sections 11 and 12(a)(2) have the following features in common: (i) a materiality requirement; (ii) the capacity to reach misleading statements of opinion; (iii) an applicable provision imposing liability on controlling persons; (iv) a discovery stay provision; (v) pleading standards; (vi) a statute of limitations; and (vii) concurrent state and federal jurisdiction.

Materiality. To be actionable under §§ 11 and 12(a)(2), the misrepresentation or omission must be material in nature. As is true under Rule 10b-5, the standard of materiality comes from *TSC Indus., Inc. v. Northway, Inc.*, 426 U.S. 438 (1976):

"a substantial likelihood that a reasonable shareholder would consider [the information] * * * important" or "a substantial likelihood that the disclosure of the omitted fact would have been viewed by the reasonable investor as having significantly altered the 'total mix' of information made available."

Id. at 449. *See, e.g., Litwin v. Blackstone Group, LP*, 634 F.3d 706, 716–717 (2d Cir. 2011) (applying *Northway* standard to §§ 11 and 12(a)(2)).

The Supreme Court recently reaffirmed the *Northway* standard for purposes of Rule 10b-5 in *Matrixx Initiatives, Inc. v. Siracusano*, 563 U.S. 27 (2011). Emphasizing the context-specific nature of the materiality inquiry, the Court refused to allow the materiality of an issuer's statements about drug side effects to turn on whether those side effects met the threshold of "statistical significance." *Id.* at 43. *See* generally § 2.3.2 (discussing *Matrixx* in connection with Rule 10b-5). In addition, the bespeaks caution doctrine (*see* § 2.3.7 *supra*) and the puffery doctrine (*see* § 2.3.1 *supra*) are typically available under §§ 11 and 12(a)(2) under circumstances in which they would also be available under Rule 10b-5. *See, e.g., City of Pontiac Policemen's & Firemen's Ret. Sys. v. UBS AG*, 752 F.3d 173, 183 (2d Cir. 2014) (dismissing claim as puffery under § 11); *P. Stolz Family P'ship L.P. v. Daum*, 355 F.3d 92, 96–98 (2d Cir. 2004) (applying the bespeaks caution doctrine to allegations under § 12(a)(2) and dismissing all but one of them).

Sections 11 and 12(a)(2) also share a statutory safe harbor for forward-looking statements, which is set forth in § 27A of the Securities Act. This safe harbor closely resembles its Exchange Act counterpart— § 21E (discussed in § 2.3.8 *supra*). As with § 21E, § 27A applies only when the issuer is a reporting company under the Exchange Act. *See* § 27A(a)(1). *See also* § 1.3 *supra* (discussing definition of reporting company). Likewise as with § 21E, § 27A does not apply to IPOs and to certain other transactions. *See* § 27A(b).

<u>Challenges to Certain Opinions</u>. Sections 11 and 12(a)(2) allow challenges to materially misleading statements of opinion, as well as to statements of a more objective variety. The Supreme Court addressed the ways in which opinions can become actionable under § 11, and by extension, under § 12(a)(2), in *Omnicare, Inc. v. Laborers Dist. Council Constr. Indus. Pension Fund*, 135 S.Ct. 1318 (2015).

The *Omnicare* Court held that a misleading opinion disbelieved by the speaker can lead to liability, so long as the opinion is material. *Id.* at 1326. More significantly, the Court identified two circumstances under which even a sincerely-held opinion can be actionable, assuming materiality:

- A sincerely held opinion that includes a misleading "embedded statement[ ] of fact." As an example, the Court cited a CEO's statement that "I believe our TVs have the highest resolution available because we use a patented technology to which our competitors do not have access," where the company does not in fact use a patented technology.

- A sincerely held opinion that misleads by virtue of what it omits about "the inquiry the issuer did or did not conduct or the knowledge it did or did not have."

See id. at 1327, 1332.

Controlling Person Liability. Persons who control those who violate §§ 11 and 12(a)(2) are liable under § 15 of the Securities Act, which reads as follows:

> Every person who, by or through stock ownership, agency, or otherwise, or who, pursuant to or in connection with an agreement or understanding with one or more other persons by or through stock ownership, agency, or otherwise, controls any person liable under Sections 11 or 12, shall also be liable jointly and severally with and to the same extent as such controlled person to any person to whom such controlled person is liable, unless the controlling person had no knowledge of or reasonable ground to believe in the existence of the facts by reason of which the liability of the controlled person is alleged to exist.

This provision is the counterpart of Exchange Act § 20(a), which is discussed in § 2.12.3 *supra* in connection with Rule 10b-5.

Discovery Stays and Pleading Standards. Claims under §§ 11 and 12(a)(2) are subject to § 27(b) of the Securities Act, which empowers a court to stay discovery in all private actions under that Act during the pendency of a motion to dismiss. This provision is the counterpart of Exchange Act § 21D(b)(3)(B), which is discussed in § 2.1 *supra* in connection with Rule 10b-5.

Sections 11 and 12(a)(2) are identically situated with respect to the applicable pleading standards. These standards include Fed. R. Civ. P. 8, which governs all civil complaints filed in federal court and provides that plaintiffs need plead only "a short and plain statement of the claim showing that [they are] entitled to relief."

Sections 11 and 12(a)(2) are not, however, subject to the heightened pleading requirements enacted as part of the PSLRA. Indeed, the PSLRA added those requirements to the Exchange Act (*see* Exchange Act § 21D(b), discussed in § 2.1 *supra*) but not to the Securities Act. Therefore the conclusion seems unavoidable that those requirements—applicable to private claims under Rule 10b-5—do not apply to claims under §§ 11 and 12(a)(2).

But do claims under §§ 11 and 12(a)(2) nonetheless need to satisfy Fed. R. Civ. P. 9(b), which requires particularity in the pleading of fraud or mistake? Most circuits say yes if the complaint "sounds in fraud"—that is, if it "employs the exact same factual allegations" for violations asserted under § 11 [or § 12(a)(2)] and Rule 10b-5, or, if not, if it " 'allege[s] a unified course of fraudulent conduct' and 'rel[ies] entirely on that course of conduct as the basis of [the § 11 or § 12(a)(2)] claim.' " *Rubke v. Capitol Bancorp, Ltd.*, 551 F.3d 1156, 1161 (9th Cir. 2009) (quoting *Vess v. Ciba-Geigy Corp. USA*, 317 F.3d 1097, 1103–1104 (9th Cir. 2003)). *See Wagner v. First Horizon Pharm. Corp.*, 464 F.3d 1273, 1277 (11th Cir. 2006) (collecting cases).

The opposite position has been adopted by the Eighth Circuit, which has held Rule 9(b) irrelevant to §§ 11 and 12(a)(2) in all circumstances. *See In re NationsMart Corp. Sec. Litig.*, 130 F.3d 309, 314–315

(8th Cir. 1997); *Wagner*, 464 F.3d at 1277. But recently the Eighth Circuit has at least implied that may not adhere to that position forever. *See Steambend Props II, LLC v. Ivy Tower Minneapolis, LLC*, 781 F.3d 1003, 1012 (8th Cir. 2015).

There remains the question of how to treat Securities Act claims that are clearly negligence-based. The few decisions to address this question have held that Rule 9(b) does not apply under these circumstances. *See, e.g.*, *In re Suprema Specialties, Inc., Sec. Litig.*, 438 F.3d 256, 272–273 (3d Cir. 2006); *In re Refco, Inc. Sec. Litig.*, 503 F.Supp. 2d 611, 633 (S.D.N.Y. 2007) (finding *Suprema* to be persuasive).

<u>Statute of Limitations</u>. The one year/three year statute of limitations for both §§ 11 and 12(a)(2) is set forth in § 13 of the Securities Act:

> No action shall be maintained to enforce any liability created under Section 11 or Section 12(a)(2) unless brought within one year after the discovery of the untrue statement or the omission, or after such discovery should have been made by the exercise of reasonable diligence * * * . In no event shall any such action be brought to enforce a liability created under Section 11 * * * more than three years after the security was bona fide offered to the public, or under Section 12(a)(2) more than three years after the sale.

A split of authority has developed regarding the operation of the three-year period of repose in the class-action context. The Second Circuit has held that the filing of a class action does not toll the running of the three-year period for those who become members of a subsequently certified class. *See Police & Fire Ret. Sys. of the City of Detroit v. Indymac, MBS, Inc.,*721 F.3d 95, 109 (2d Cir. 2013), *cert. granted sub nom. Pub. Emps.' Ret. Sys. of Miss. v. Indymac MBS, Inc.,* 134 S.Ct. 1515 (2014), *cert. dismissed as improvidently granted*, 135 S.Ct. 42 (2014). Thus, if certification is denied after the three-year period expires, the members of the might-have-been class cannot sue individually unless, prior to that expiration, they protected themselves by filing individual actions or by intervening in the class action. In contrast, the Tenth Circuit has held that the filing of a class action does toll the period of repose. *See Joseph v. Wiles,* 223 F.3d 1155, 1166–1168 (10th Cir. 2000).

Another set of questions has arisen in the wake of the enactment of the Sarbanes-Oxley Act of 2002 (the SOX) § 804 (now 28 U.S.C. § 1658(b)), which replaced the one year/three year structure governing the limitation period applicable to Rule 10b-5 with a two year/five year structure. *See § 2.13 supra.* Instead of referring to Rule 10b-5 (or to § 10(b)) specifically, however, § 804 refers to private securities law "claim[s] of fraud, deceit, manipulation, or contrivance." The question has thereby arisen whether this phraseology embraces some or all claims under §§ 11 or 12(a)(2). In general, courts have given a negative answer, offering as their rationale that § 804 encompasses only those claims requiring proof of scienter, whereas §§ 11 and 12(a)(2) do not require such proof. *See In re Alstom*

SA Sec. Litig., 406 F.Supp. 2d 402, 413 & n.5 (S.D.N.Y. 2005) (collecting cases).

But that rationale raises yet another question: whether § 804 applies at least to those §§ 11 and 12(a)(2) claims that "sound in fraud" (and are thereby subject to Rule 9(b)). In *Alstom*, the court rejected such application on the ground that it would "create[ ] uncertainty * * * for defendants as to when their exposure to liability ends" as well as empower the plaintiffs "to prescribe what statute of limitations would apply to their claims by how skillfully they draft the complaint." *Id.* at 417–418. *Cf. In re Exxon Mobil Corp. Sec. Litig.*, 500 F.3d 189, 197–198 (3d Cir. 2007) (rejecting the application of § 804 to Rule 14a-9 claims that "sound in fraud").

<u>Concurrent State and Federal Jurisdiction</u>. Claims under §§ 11 and 12(a)(2) may be brought in state or federal court in accordance with § 22(a) of the Securities Act. The concurrent jurisdiction afforded by § 22(a) stands in sharp contrast to the exclusive jurisdiction mandated by § 27 of the Exchange Act.

But the Securities Act's grant of concurrent jurisdiction only goes so far. That is, if the complaint is a class action and alleges a material misstatement or omission in connection with the sale of a "nationally traded security" (encompassing those listed on the New York Stock Exchange, the American Stock Exchange, or the NASDAQ), it may be filed in federal court only. *See* § 16 of the Securities Act.

§ 3.5 THE CROWDFUNDING EXEMPTION AND § 12(a)(2)-TYPE LIABILITY

The JOBS Act amended the Securities Act to include a new crowdfunding exemption in § 4(a)(6). That exemption authorized the SEC to promulgate rules (now termed "Regulation Crowdfunding") that allow small businesses to raise up to $1 million through the use of the Internet and other means of general advertising (subject to a host of restrictions and limitations). Such offerings must be conducted through registered broker-dealers or through funding portals, which both the SEC and FINRA will regulate.

Congress likewise added to the Securities Act a new § 4A(c), which authorizes an express private action by someone who, having purchased securities from an "issuer" using the crowdfunding exemption, wishes to challenge a material misstatement or omission in a "written or oral communication" provided in the course of the offering. The term "issuer" is defined broadly to "include[ ] any person who is a director or partner of the issuer, and the principal executive officer or officers, principal financial officer, and controller or principal accounting officer of the issuer (and any person occupying a similar status or performing a similar function) that offers or sells a security in a transaction exempted by the provisions of § 4(6), and any person who offers or sells the securities in such offering." Curiously, Congress categorized this express action as one brought "as if the liability were created under § 12(a)(2)." § 4A(c)(B).

The issuer can defend on the basis that it "did not know, and in the exercise of reasonable care could not have known, of such untruth or omission." § 4A(c)(2)(A). The issuer can invoke § 12(b) (the causation defense) and § 13 (the statute of limitations), "as if the liability were created under § 12(a)(2)." § 4A(c)(1)(B).

§ 3.6 FRAUD UNDER § 17(a)

Section 17(a) prohibits fraud in the offer or sale of securities, whether in an initial offering of securities or in secondary market trading. A potent enforcement tool in the arsenal of the SEC as well as the DOJ, § 17(a) reads as follows:

It shall be unlawful for any person in the offer or sale of any securities by * * * the use of any means or instruments of transportation or communication in interstate commerce or by the use of the mails, directly or indirectly—

(1) to employ any device, scheme, or artifice to defraud, or

(2) to obtain money or property by means of any untrue statement of a material fact or any omission to state a material fact necessary in order to make the statements made, in the light of the circumstances under which they were made, not misleading, or

(3) to engage in any transaction, practice, or course of business which operates or would operate as a fraud or deceit upon the purchaser.

As is apparent, § 17(a) closely parallels Rule 10b-5 (set out in § 2.1 *supra*). This parallelism is not an accident. When drafting Rule 10b-5 in 1942, the SEC used § 17(a) as a model.

Given this textual parallelism, it is not surprising that the actions under § 17(a) and Rule 10b-5 have several overlapping elements. Thus, like Rule 10b-5, § 17(a) requires an omission or misrepresentation that is "material" in nature. *See SEC v. Monarch Funding Corp.*, 192 F.3d 295, 308 (2d Cir. 1999). Also like Rule 10b-5, the material omission or misrepresentation need *not* appear in (or be linked to) an official document such as a registration statement or a prospectus.

But the overlap between the two actions is far from complete. For example, unlike Rule 10b-5, which prohibits fraud involving "the purchase or sale," § 17(a) prohibits fraud involving *"the offer* or sale." *See id.* at 308 (emphasis added).

Moreover, unlike Rule 10b-5, which requires scienter in all instances (*see* § 2.5 *supra*), § 17(a) does so only when § 17(a)(1)—but not §§ 17(a)(2) or 17(a)(3)—is at issue. *See Aaron v. SEC*, 446 U.S. 680, 695–702 (1980). The *Aaron* Court reached this conclusion largely on the basis of examining the statutory text. *See id.* at 695–697.

The DOJ and the SEC are differently situated when it comes to the scienter element. In contrast to the SEC, the DOJ cannot sidestep proof of scienter when proceeding under § 17(a)(2) or § 17(a)(3). The reason emerges from Securities Act § 24, which conditions criminal liability on proof that the defendant acted "willfully." For a discussion of the willfulness requirement, *see* § 11.2.1 *infra.*

Can investors sue under § 17(a)? The statutory text says nothing about a private action, leaving it to the courts to decide whether to recognize such an action by implication. The Supreme Court has repeatedly reserved the question. *See, e.g., Bateman Eichler, Hill Richards, Inc. v. Berner*, 472 U.S. 299, 304 n.9 (1985); *Herman & MacLean v. Huddleston*, 459 U.S. 375, 378 n.2 (1983). The consensus among the lower federal courts, however, is that § 17(a) should be available only to the government. *See Maldonado v. Dominguez*, 137 F.3d 1, 7–8 (1st Cir. 1998) (collecting cases). But *see AFA Private Equity Fund 1 v. Miresco Inv. Servs.*, 2005 WL 2417116, at *5–7 (E.D. Mich. Sept. 30, 2005) (holding private actions under § 17(a) to be viable in the Sixth Circuit and denying the defendant summary judgment on the plaintiff's § 17(a) claim).

CHAPTER 4

PROXY FRAUD—SECTION 14(a) OF THE EXCHANGE ACT AND RULE 14a-9

§ 4.1 INTRODUCTION

Shareholders in public corporations typically vote by proxy when electing directors or approving mergers or other corporate transactions. To safeguard the integrity of their decision-making, Congress enacted § 14(a) of the Exchange Act, a provision that gives the Securities and Exchange Commission (the SEC or the Commission) broad authority to adopt rules governing proxy solicitations in § 12 companies (*see* § 1.3 *supra*). Section 14(a) reads as follows:

> It shall be unlawful for any person, by the use of the mails or by any means or instrumentality of interstate commerce or of any facility of a national securities exchange or otherwise, in contravention of such rules and regulations as the Commission may prescribe as necessary or appropriate in the public interest or for the protection of investors, to solicit or to permit the use of his name to solicit any proxy or consent or authorization in respect of any security (other than an exempted security) registered pursuant to section 12 of this title.

Among the rules adopted by the SEC pursuant to § 14(a) is Rule 14a-9, subsection (a) of which prohibits material omissions or misrepresentations in proxy solicitations:

No solicitation subject to this regulation shall be made by means of any proxy statement, form of proxy, notice of meeting or other communication, written or oral, containing any statement which, at the time and in the light of the circumstances under which it is made, is false or misleading with respect to any material fact, or which omits to state any material fact necessary in order to make the statements therein not false or misleading or necessary to correct any statement in any earlier communication with respect to the solicitation of a proxy for the same meeting or subject matter which has become false or misleading.

Id. Certain opinions may be "facts" capable of misstatement or omission for these purposes. *See Virginia Bankshares, Inc. v. Sandberg*, 501 U.S. 1083, 1095–1096 (1991), discussed in § 2.2.3 *supra.*

As is apparent, neither Rule 14a-9 nor § 14(a) mentions private enforcement. The Supreme Court nonetheless recognized an implied private action under the statute and Rule in *J. I. Case Co. v. Borak*, 377 U.S. 426 (1964), on the basis of two rationales that it later disavowed when rejecting an implied private action under § 17(a) of the Exchange Act. *See Touche Ross & Co. v. Redington*, 442 U.S. 560, 577–578 (1979). In making those disavowals, however, the Court explicitly refrained from questioning the existence of an implied private action under § 14(a). *See id.* at 577. Nor did the Court later question that action when directly addressing § 14(a) and Rule 14a-9 in *Virginia Bankshares* (*see* § 4.4 *infra*).

Private Rule 14a-9 actions have been enveloped by the Private Securities Litigation Reform Act (the PSLRA), the principal target of which was Rule 10b-5. *See* § 2.1 *supra*. The PSLRA provisions applicable to private Rule 14a-9 actions include the following:

- those pertaining to class actions specifically (*see* Chapter 6 *infra*);

- the safe harbor for forward-looking statements (§ 21E), which is discussed in connection with Rule 10b-5 in § 2.3.8 *supra*;

- the loss causation requirement (§ 21D(b)(4)), discussed in § 2.9 *supra*;

- those that heighten requirements for pleading material omissions and misstatements (§ 21D(b)(1)), discussed in connection with Rule 10b-5 in § 2.1 *supra*, and for pleading state of mind, at least to the extent discussed in § 4.3 *infra*;

- the automatic stay of discovery during the pendency of motions to dismiss for failure to satisfy the pleading requirements (§ 21D(b)(3)(A)), discussed in connection with Rule 10b-5 in § 2.1 *supra*; and

- proportionate liability (§ 21D(f)), discussed in connection with Rule 10b-5 in § 2.10.1 *supra*.

Liability under § 14(a) and Rule 14a-9 extends to those who "solicited or permitted the use of [their] names to solicit," in accordance with the text of § 14(a) set forth above. That phraseology includes not only the soliciting company and its insiders but also outsiders such as an investment bank that allows its fairness opinion to be attached to the proxy statement. *See, e.g., Herskowitz v. Nutri/System, Inc.*, 857 F.2d 179 (3d Cir. 1988); *City P'ship Co. v. Lehman Bros., Inc.*, 344 F.Supp. 2d 1241, 1246 (D. Colo. 2004); or an accountant who prepared the financial statement attached to the proxy statement. *See, e.g., Adams v. Standard Knitting Mills, Inc.*, 623 F.2d 422 (6th Cir. 1980).

Likewise subject to liability under Rule 14a-9 are "controlling persons," a category addressed by § 20(a) of the Exchange Act. *See, e.g., Smith v. Robbins & Myers, Inc.*, 969 F.Supp. 2d 850, 875 (S.D. Ohio 2013). *See also* § 2.12.3 *supra* (discussing controlling person liability in the context of Rule 10b-5).

Like Rule 10b-5, Rule 14a-9 can be enforced not only by private plaintiffs but also by the SEC (*see* Chapter 9 *infra*) and the Department of Justice (the DOJ) (*see* Chapter 11 *infra*). Unlike Rule 10b-5, however, Rule 14a-9 is rarely utilized by the government, with the result that its enforcement falls largely to investors.

To have standing to sue under Rule 14a-9, the plaintiffs must have the right to vote on the merger or other transaction. *See, e.g., Bricklayers & Masons Local Union No. 5 Ohio Pension Fund v. Transocean Ltd.*, 866 F.Supp.2d 223, 236–237 (S.D.N.Y. 2012). In addition, they must plead and prove the following elements:

- that the alleged misstatement or omission qualifies as material (*see* § 4.2 *infra*);

- that the defendants acted negligently, unless the circumstances are among the small number that call for scienter (*see* § 4.3 *infra*);

- transaction causation (*see* § 4.4 *infra*); and

- loss causation (*see* § 4.5 *infra*).

After examining these elements, this Chapter concludes with a discussion of the statute of limitations (*see* § 4.6 *infra*).

§ 4.2 THE MATERIALITY OF THE ALLEGED MISSTATEMENT OR OMISSION

Rule 14a-9 plaintiffs must establish the materiality of the alleged misstatement or omission. The need for materiality emerges from the Rule itself (*see* § 4.1 *supra*), but the Rule does not provide a standard for making materiality assessments. The Supreme Court filled this void in *TSC Indus., Inc. v. Northway, Inc.,* 426 U.S. 438 (1976), which, after noting that the materiality inquiry was an objective one, announced the following standard:

An omitted fact is material if there is a substantial likelihood that a reasonable shareholder would consider it important in deciding how to vote. * * * It does not require proof of a substantial likelihood that disclosure of the omitted fact would have caused the reasonable investor to change his vote. What the standard does contemplate is a showing of a substantial likelihood that, under all the circumstances, the omitted fact would have assumed actual significance in the deliberations of the reasonable investor as having significantly altered the "total mix" of information available. * * *

Id. at 448–449. By focusing on the impact of the fact in question on the "total mix" of information, the Court calls for a contextual analysis of materiality. For example, a misstatement that might qualify as material if judged in a vacuum might nonetheless be rendered immaterial by information appearing elsewhere in the proxy statement, *see Seinfeld v. Gray*, 404 F.3d 645, 650–651 (2d Cir. 2005), or in widely-disseminated news articles, *see Burkle v. OTK Assocs., LLC*, 2 F.Supp.3d 519, 524 (S.D.N.Y. 2012).

Moreover, the following doctrines can come into play when making materiality determinations under Rule 14a-9:

The Puffery Doctrine. This doctrine deems immaterial statements so vague as to be meaningless. *See, e.g., Bricklayers & Masons Local Union No. 5 Ohio Pension Fund v. Transocean Ltd.*, 866 F.Supp.2d 223, 244 (S.D.N.Y. 2012). *See also* § 2.3.1 *supra* (discussing puffery in connection with Rule 10b-5).

The Probability/Magnitude Test. This test, applicable to merger negotiations or other contingent events, measures materiality by looking at the probability the event will occur combined with the magnitude of the event if it does occur. *See, e.g., meVC Draper Fisher Jurvetson Fund I, Inc. v. Millennium Partners, L.P.,* 260 F.Supp.2d 616, 636 n. 31 (S.D.N.Y. 2003). *See also* § 2.3.5 *supra* (discussing the probability/magnitude test in connection with Rule 10b-5).

The Bespeaks Caution Doctrine. This doctrine deems forward-looking information to be immaterial where the information is surrounded by cautions of the non-boilerplate variety. *See, e.g., Tracinda Corp. v. DaimlerChrysler AG,* 197 F.Supp.2d 42, 76 (D.Del. 2002). *See also* § 2.3.7 *supra* (discussing the bespeaks caution doctrine in connection with Rule 10b-5).

§ 4.3 THE STATE OF MIND REQUIREMENT

Must Rule 14a-9 plaintiffs prove scienter? The Supreme Court has twice deferred the question. *See Virginia Bankshares v. Sandberg,* 501 U.S. 1083, 1090 n.5 (1991); *TSC Indus., Inc. v. Northway, Inc.,* 426 U.S. 438, 444 n.7 (1976).

The lower courts, on the other hand, have for the most part refrained from imposing a scienter requirement, largely because § 14(a) and Rule 14a-9 contain no "words connoting fraud or deception." *Gerstle v. Gamble-Skogmo, Inc.,* 478 F.2d 1281, 1299 (2d Cir. 1973). *See SEC v. Das,* 723 F.3d 943, 953–554 (8th Cir. 2013); *Wilson v. Great Am. Indus., Inc.,* 855 F.2d 987, 995 (2d Cir. 1988). Thus, as these courts see it, Rule 14a-9 requires proof of no more

than negligence. *See, e.g.*, *Beck v. Dombrowski*, 559
F.3d 680, 682 (7th Cir. 2009); *Bond Opportunity
Fund v. Unilab Corp.*, 2003 WL 21058251, at *4
(S.D.N.Y. May 9, 2003) (collecting cases), aff'd, 87
Fed. App'x 772 (2d Cir. 2004).

To be sure, some courts ratchet up to scienter when
the defendant is an outsider. *See, e.g.*, *SEC v.
Shanahan*, 646 F.3d 536, 546–547 (8th Cir. 2011)
(requiring scienter for an outside accountant and
outside directors); *Adams v. Standard Knitting Mills,
Inc.*, 623 F.2d 422, 428 (6th Cir. 1980) (requiring
scienter for an outside accountant). *But see
Herskowitz v. Nutri/System, Inc.*, 857 F.2d 179, 190
(3d Cir.1988) (rejecting scienter requirement in
action against investment banker).

Moreover, when the alleged misstatement or
omission involves a forward-looking statement, the
plaintiffs must show that the defendant acted
"knowingly," in accordance with the safe harbor for
forward-looking statements set forth in § 21E of the
Exchange Act. For a discussion of the safe harbor in
the context of Rule 10b-5, *see* § 2.3.8 *supra*.

There is also authority for ratcheting down from
negligence when the plaintiff seeks injunctive relief
only. *See Ash v. LFE Corp.*, 525 F.2d 215, 220 (3d Cir.
1975) (holding that under these circumstances, "the
test for the purposes of Rule 14a-9 is the objective
sufficiency of the disclosure").

When pleading negligence, must the plaintiffs
"state with particularity facts giving rise to a strong
inference that the defendant acted with the required

state of mind," as required by § 21D(b)(2)? The courts
are divided about whether negligence qualifies as a
state of mind such as to bring that provision into
play. *See Bricklayers & Masons Local Union No. 5
Ohio Pension Fund v. Transocean Ltd.*, 866
F.Supp.2d 223, 240 (S.D.N.Y. 2012) (citing decisions
going both ways and agreeing with the position
espoused in *Beck*). *Compare Beck v. Dobrowski*, 559
F.3d 680, 682 (7th Cir. 2009) (holding § 21D(b)(2)
inapposite because "negligence is not a state of
mind") *with Little Gem Life Scis., LLC v. Orphan
Med., Inc.*, 537 F.3d 913, 917 (8th Cir. 2008) (holding
the opposite).

§ 4.4 TRANSACTION CAUSATION

Private Rule 14a-9 plaintiffs must establish
transaction causation, that is, a causal relationship
between the proxy solicitation and the transaction for
which the shareholders' support was sought. The
Supreme Court has addressed this element twice,
first in *Mills v. Electric Auto-Lite Co.*, 396 U.S. 375
(1970) and again later in *Virginia Bankshares, Inc. v.
Sandberg*, 501 U.S. 1083 (1991).

In *Mills*, the plaintiffs challenged a
misrepresentation in a proxy statement sent to
shareholders in connection with a proposed merger.
The management did not control enough shares to
guarantee the merger's approval, with the result that
the public shareholders controlled the merger's fate.
Those shareholders gave the merger the necessary
support, which in theory they might have done even
if there had been no misrepresentation. Against this

backdrop, the Court addressed the showing that the plaintiffs had to make in order to link the proxy solicitation and the merger.

The Court began by considering the solution upheld by the Seventh Circuit, which was to ascertain whether the terms of the merger were fair, on the theory that fair terms would tend to precipitate approval. *Id.* at 381. The Court rejected this solution on the ground that it would insulate from redress "[e]ven outrageous misrepresentations * * * if they did not relate to the terms." *Id.* at 382. To allow this to happen, the Court explained, "would subvert the congressional purpose of ensuring full and fair disclosure to the shareholders." *Id.*

The Court's own solution was to adopt a presumption that hinged on the materiality of the alleged fraud that became available in situations where, as in *Mills* itself, the approval of the transaction in question required the public shareholders' support:

> Where there has been a finding of materiality, a shareholder has made a sufficient showing of causal relationship between the violation and the injury for which he seeks redress if * * * he proves that the proxy solicitation itself, rather than the particular defect in the solicitation materials, was an essential link in the accomplishment of the transaction. * * *

Id. at 384. The Court explicitly left open the question of what to do when the management controlled enough votes to render those of the public shareholders superfluous. *See id.* at 384 n.7.

More than twenty years intervened between the Supreme Court's *Mills* decision and its next encounter with Rule 14a-9 in *Virginia Bankshares, Inc. v. Sandberg*, 501 U.S. 1083 (1991). During those intervening years, the Court had become quite hostile to implied private actions in general as well as to the one under Rule 10b-5 in particular. *See* § 2.1 *supra.* That hostility, made explicit by the *Virginia Bankshares* Court *see*, *e.g.*, 501 U.S. at 1105, formed the backdrop for its analysis of the question left open by *Mills*—how, if at all, transaction causation can be established when the management controls sufficient votes to approve the transaction without the support of the public shareholders. The plaintiffs attempted to satisfy the *Mills* "essential link" language, set forth in the block quote above, by offering two theories as to why proxy solicitation had been essential: one was to deflect shareholder antagonism and the other was to prevent the shareholders from mounting a state-law challenge to the merger on conflict-of-interest grounds. *See id.* at 1100–1101.

The Court prefaced its consideration of the two theories with the observation that acceptance of either one would expand the scope of the "essential link" that had been contemplated by *Mills*. *Id.* at 1102–03. The Court regarded such an expansion as problematic, given that the legislative history of § 14(a) does not mention private lawsuits at all, let alone lawsuits by those in the plaintiffs' situation. While deeming this silence to be "a serious obstacle,"

the Court did not close the door on expanding the
scope of the "essential link" where to do so "would be
demonstrably inequitable to a class of would-be
plaintiffs with claims comparable to those previously
recognized." *Id.* at 1104. The unclosed door
notwithstanding, the Court's identification of "the
serious obstacle" creates something of an uphill-
battle for any plaintiffs seeking to satisfy transaction
causation where the votes of the public shareholders
are not needed.

Consider the Court's reasons for rejecting the
plaintiffs' first theory—that the solicitation of proxies
was necessary to deflect shareholder antagonism. As
the Court saw it, this theory was too "speculative"
and would, if accepted, allow "[c]ausation [to] turn on
inferences about what the corporate directors would
have thought and done without the minority
shareholder approval unneeded to authorize action."
Id. at 1105. Thus, the Court in effect invites attacks
on any transaction causation argument that can be
deemed unduly speculative.

Now consider the Court's response to the plaintiffs'
second theory—that proxy solicitation was necessary
in order to eliminate a shareholder challenge to the
merger on conflict-of-interest grounds, a challenge
which, according to the defendants, would become
unavailable in the event of a shareholder vote. As the
Court saw it, that vote did not foreclose the state-law
challenge, since the proxy statement had allegedly
not provided the shareholders with full disclosure.
See id. at 1107–1108. Since no state-law remedy had
been lost, the Court took the position that it did not

have to decide whether the loss of such a remedy would provide the predicate for transaction causation. *See id.* at 1107. Thus, while the door to lost state remedy arguments is not wide open, especially given the "serious obstacle" noted above, it is not entirely shut either.

With the door at least somewhat ajar, it is worth noting the various types of lost state remedies that the Court identified as conceivable. One was that the materially misleading proxy statement led the shareholders to forfeit their appraisal rights that state law made available to them in connection with the merger or other transaction. *See id.* Another was that the materially misleading proxy statement prompted the shareholders to forego a state-law challenge to the merger (or other transaction) until after the limitations period had run. *See id.* at 1108.

In the wake of *Virginia Bankshares*, the most frequent type of lost state remedies argument to surface in the case law has involved appraisal rights. *See Cellular Tech. Servs. Co. v. TruePosition, Inc.*, 609 F.Supp. 2d 223, 237 (D. Conn. 2009) (collecting cases). Such an argument met with success in *Wilson v. Great Am. Indus., Inc.*, 979 F.2d 924 (2d Cir. 1992), where the Second Circuit remanded the case in order to ascertain whether the right to appraisal granted by New York law had actually been lost. *See id.* at 932.

Thereafter, *Wilson* has been distinguished on a ground not mentioned by *Wilson* itself—namely, that appraisal was the only remedy available to the shareholders under New York law. *See In re Digital*

Island Sec. Litig., 223 F.Supp.2d 546, 559 (D. Del. 2002). In *Digital*, on the other hand, where Delaware law applied, the shareholders could pursue not only appraisal but also the right to have the merger enjoined. *See id.* at 560. Thus, the court reasoned, it was speculative to assume that, without the fraud, the shareholders would have pursued appraisal, since they might have decided to seek an injunction instead. *See id.* Further exacerbating the speculativeness, the court noted, was the relative unpopularity of the appraisal remedy itself. *See id.* Given that *Virginia Bankshares* had condemned speculativeness, the court rejected the plaintiffs' lost state remedy argument. *See id*; *see also* § 2.2.2 (discussing lost state remedies in the context of Rule 10b-5).

One final observation is in order. Rule 14a-9's transaction causation element is an altogether different animal than the Rule 10b-5 element of the same name. The latter looks to whether the plaintiffs relied on the alleged fraud (*see* § 2.8 *supra*), whereas under Rule 14a-9, reliance on the fraud is inapposite. *See, e.g., Cowin v. Bresler*, 741 F.2d 410, 427 (D.C. Cir. 1984); *Kaplan v. First Hartford Corp.*, 447 F.Supp. 2d 3, 9 (D. Mass. 2006).

§ 4.5 LOSS CAUSATION

Rule 14a-9 plaintiffs must establish loss causation, that is, a causal relationship between the proxy solicitation and the alleged economic harm for which they seek redress. This requirement is set forth in

Exchange Act § 21D(b)(4), which was enacted as part of the PSLRA. That provision reads as follows:

> In any private action arising under this title, the plaintiff shall have the burden of proving that the act or omission of the defendant alleged to violate this title caused the loss for which the plaintiff seeks to recover damages.

This language requires that the plaintiffs plead loss causation as well. *See Dura Pharm., Inc. v. Broudo*, 544 U.S. 336, 346 (2005) (Rule 10b-5 case).

Loss causation requires a direct linkage between the proxy solicitation and the alleged economic harm. Consider as an example *Edward J. Goodman Life Income Trust v. Jabil Circuit, Inc.*, 594 F.3d 783, 797 (11th Cir. 2010), where the proxy statement successfully urged the election of directors as well as the adoption of certain policies which, according to the plaintiffs, had been described in a materially misleading manner. The board thereafter disregarded the policies, and in so doing precipitated the economic harm for which the plaintiffs sought redress. The court explained why, under these circumstances, the plaintiffs could not show loss causation:

> [T]he damages suffered by the shareholders were caused not by the policies that they approved via proxy, but by management's failure to follow those policies. Additionally, the election of directors who violated those policies only indirectly caused the shareholders' loss. * * * [T]he insiders' decision to violate company

policies was not accomplished or endorsed by any proxy solicitation materials.

Id. at 797.

§ 4.6 STATUTE OF LIMITATIONS

This section addresses the limitations period for Rule 14a-9 private actions only. For the period applicable to the SEC, *see* § 9.10.5 *infra*. For the periods applicable to the DOJ, *see* § 11.9 *infra*.

As originally enacted, there was no limitations period in the Exchange Act applicable to private actions under § 14(a). This was to be expected, since Congress did not explicitly authorize private enforcement of § 14(a) in the first place. *See* § 4.1 *supra*. Lower courts used to fill the gap by borrowing the most analogous limitations period from the common law or blue sky law of the relevant state. *See, e.g., Roberts v. Magnetic Metals, Inc.*, 611 F.2d 450, 452 (3d Cir. 1979); *cf. Ernst & Ernst v. Hochfelder*, 425 U.S. 185, 211 n.29 (1976) (discussing the practice of state-law borrowing in connection with Rule 10b-5).

The ground shifted following the Supreme Court's decision in *Lampf, Pleva, Lipkind, Prupris, & Petigrow v. Gilbertson*, 501 U.S. 350 (1991), which rejected the practice of state-law borrowing in the Rule 10b-5 context. In place of that practice, the Court substituted a uniform federal limitations period drawn from Exchange Act § 9(e), which authorizes an express action for specified forms of market manipulation (*see* § 8.3.1). The limitations

period for § 9(e) involves a one year-three year
structure:

> No action shall be maintained to enforce any
> liability created under this section, unless
> brought within one year after the discovery of
> the facts constituting the violation and within
> three years after such violation.

In the wake of *Lampf*, lower courts adopted § 9(e) as
the limitations period for private actions under Rule
14a-9 as well. *See, e.g.*, *Westinghouse Elec. Corp. v.
Franklin*, 993 F.2d 349, 353 (3d Cir. 1993); *Bensinger
v. Denbury Resources, Inc.*, 31 F.Supp. 3d 503, 508
(E.D.N.Y. 2014) (collecting cases).

The ground has *not*, however, shifted again
following the enactment of the Sarbanes-Oxley Act of
2002, § 804 of which replaced *Lampf*'s one year-three
year structure with a two year-five year structure for
private federal securities actions "involv[ing] a claim
of fraud, deceit, manipulation, or contrivance." 28
U.S.C. § 1658(b). This language has been read to
apply only to those actions that require proof of
scienter, which, as noted in § 4.3 *supra*, Rule 14a-9
ordinarily does not. *See, e.g.*, *In re Exxon Mobil Corp.
Sec. Litig.*, 500 F.3d 189, 197 (3d Cir. 2007); *Dekalb
County Pension Fund v. Transocean Ltd.*, 36 F.Supp.
3d 279, 283 (S.D.N.Y. 2014).

But would the two year-five year structure apply
to those Rule 14a-9 actions that allege fraud? Most
courts have not gone down this road. *See DeKalb*, 36
F.Supp. 3d at 283 (collecting cases). To do so, the
Third Circuit has maintained, would undermine "the

principal reason for having time-bars: certainty for defendants." *Exxon,* 500 F.3d at 198.

CHAPTER 5

TENDER OFFER FRAUD—
SECTION 14(e) OF THE
EXCHANGE ACT

§ 5.1 INTRODUCTION

Section 14(e) of the Exchange Act prohibits fraud in connection with a tender offer. It reads as follows:

> It shall be unlawful for any person to make any untrue statement of a material fact or omit to state any material fact necessary in order to make the statements made, in the light of the circumstances under which they are made, not misleading, or to engage in any fraudulent, deceptive, or manipulative acts or practices, in connection with any tender offer or request or invitation for tenders, or any solicitation of security holders in opposition to or in favor of any such offer, request, or invitation. The Commission shall, for the purposes of this subsection, by rules and regulations define, and prescribe means reasonably designed to prevent, such acts and practices as are fraudulent, deceptive, or manipulative.

Section 14(e) was added to the Exchange Act as part of the Williams Act of 1968 (the Williams Act), a set of provisions aimed at regulating tender offers and other acquisitions. Congress enacted the Williams Act in response to an upsurge in tender offers during the 1960s.

A tender offer is a method of accomplishing an acquisition that is opposed by the target's management. In the prototypical tender offer, one company (the bidder) seeks to acquire control of another company (the target) by offering to purchase all or some of the target's shares directly from the target's shareholders, typically at a premium over the market price. The bidder and the target are usually different companies, but occasionally a company makes a tender offer for its own shares in a transaction known as a "self-tender offer." Although tender offers often facilitate hostile acquisitions (*i.e.*, a takeover opposed by the target's management), tender offers may sometimes take place under "friendly" circumstances. *See* § 5.3 *infra.*

This Chapter does not address aspects of § 14(e) that involve insider trading, which are taken up in § 7.5 *infra.* When insider trading is not at issue, the Securities and Exchange Commission (the SEC or the Commission) and the Department of Justice (the DOJ) only rarely undertake to enforce § 14(e). Such enforcement is left largely to investors, who have at their disposal § 14(e)'s implied private action. The implied private action is this Chapter's main subject.

The Chapter proceeds as follows. After a brief overview of the Williams Act (§ 5.2 *infra*), attention turns to the scope of § 14(e) (§ 5.3 *infra*). A discussion of the implied private action follows (§ 5.4 *infra*).

§ 5.2 AN OVERVIEW OF THE WILLIAMS ACT

The principal purpose of the Williams Act is to protect shareholders deciding whether to tender their shares and to do so without siding with either the target or the bidder. *See Rondeau v. Mosinee Paper Corp.*, 422 U.S. 49, 58–59 (1975). The Act consists of the following provisions of the Exchange Act—§§ 13(d), 13(e), 14(d), 14(e), and 14(f). Some of these provisions apply to an acquisition accomplished by any means, whereas others apply only to a tender offer, a term which the statute leaves undefined. The courts have filled the gap with various definitions, which are discussed below.

Section 13(d). This provision provides the marketplace with an early indication that control of a company may be "in play." It applies to any acquirer (whether by tender offer or otherwise) of more than 5% of the shares of a class of equity security of a § 12 company (defined in § 1.3 *supra*). Such an acquirer must, within 10 days of making the acquisition, or "within such shorter time as the Commission may establish by rule," provide the SEC with a report (the Schedule 13D) that discloses his identity, background, source of financing, and any plans to make a later tender offer for the target.

Section 14(d). Unlike § 13(d), § 14(d) applies to tender offers specifically. Each sub-provision of § 14(d) performs a distinct function. Under § 14(d)(1), anyone who makes a tender offer for more than 5% of a class of equity security of a § 12 company (defined in § 1.3 *supra*) must file a Schedule TO with the SEC.

Schedule TO requires disclosure of many items called for by Schedule 13D, along with the terms of the offer and the bidder's financial statements if "material" to the offer. Rules 14d-4 and 14d-6 govern the disclosures that must be made to the target's shareholders about the tender offer.

Under § 14(d)(4), anyone (including the target) who makes a solicitation or recommendation to the target's shareholders concerning a tender offer must file with the SEC a Schedule 14D-9, which mandates many of the same disclosures called for by Schedule TO. In addition, it requires the target to indicate whether it is negotiating with another bidder (a "white knight").

Other subsections of § 14(d) are designed to reduce shareholder coercion as follows:

- The bidder must accept the tendered shares on a pro rata rather than a first-come-first-served basis (§ 14(d)(6) and Rule 14d-8);

- The shareholders may withdraw their tendered shares during the period that the tender offer remains open (§ 14(d)(5) and Rule 14d-7); and

- All tendering shareholders must be paid the same price for their shares (§ 14(d)(7) and Rule 14d-10).

The SEC has also adopted various rules pursuant to § 14(e) that are likewise aimed at reducing coercion. Those rules are noted below in the discussion of § 14(e).

Section 14(f). This provision applies to acquisitions governed by both §§ 13(d) and 14(d). It requires disclosure of arrangements involving a change in the membership of a majority of the target's board of directors that occurs other than by shareholder vote. The disclosure must be made to the SEC as well as to the shareholders denied their franchise not less than 10 days before the new directors assume office.

Section 13(e). Sections 13(d) and 14(d) are each inapplicable when a company purchases its own stock. Such purchases fall instead under § 13(e), which prohibits a § 12 company (defined in § 1.3 *supra*) from "purchas[ing] any equity security issued by it" if doing so would violate SEC rules. Thus, § 13(e) and the rules adopted pursuant to it regulate issuer "buy-backs," so-called "going private transactions" (often structured as leveraged buyouts (LBOs)), and issuer self-tender offers.

Section 14(e). This provision, the text of which is set forth in § 5.1 *supra*, has several characteristics that set it apart from the other Williams Act provisions described above. As is made clear by its text, § 14(e):

- applies irrespective of whether the target is a § 12 company (defined in § 1.3 *supra*), thereby departing from §§ 13(d), 13(e), and 14(d); and

- applies regardless of whether the offer exceeds 5% of the shares, thereby departing from §§ 13(d) and 14(d).

Notice that the last sentence of § 14(e) gives the SEC rule-making authority. Pursuant to that authority, the SEC has adopted Rule 14e-1, which requires that the offer remain open for 20 business days, presumably to give shareholders sufficient time to ponder the disclosures required under § 14(d). The SEC has also adopted Rule 14e-8, which deems it a "fraudulent, deceptive, or manipulative" practice for someone "to publicly announce * * * plans to make a tender offer" if she, among other things, lacks "the intention to commence the offer within a reasonable time and complete the offer."

<u>The Definition of a Tender Offer</u>. As has been noted above, certain Williams Act provisions apply to tender offers specifically. Questions sometimes arise concerning the application of these provisions to transactions which, while admittedly not conventional tender offers, nonetheless arguably call for the sort of regulation that the Williams Act provides. These questions cannot be answered by reference to a statutory definition of "tender offer" because the Williams Act does not provide one. Instead, the Act delegates the definition question to the courts, which in turn have generated two principal approaches.

One approach, known as the *Wellman v. Dickinson* eight-factor approach, determines the existence of a tender offer by reference to the following, not all of which have to be present for a tender offer to be found:

(1) active and widespread solicitation of public shareholders for the shares of an issuer; (2) solicitation made for a substantial percentage of the issuer's stock; (3) offer to purchase made at

a premium over the prevailing market price;
(4) terms of the offer are firm rather than
negotiable; (5) offer contingent on the tender of a
fixed number of shares, often subject to a fixed
maximum number to be purchased; (6) offer open
only for a limited period of time; (7) offeree
subjected to pressure to sell his stock; and
(8) public announcements of a purchasing
program concerning the target company precede
or accompany rapid accumulation of a large
amount of target company's securities.

Wellman v. Dickinson, 475 F.Supp. 783, 823–825
(S.D.N.Y. 1979) (applying the factors to solicitations
made privately to institutions and to individuals),
aff'd on other grounds, 682 F.2d 355 (2d Cir. 1982).
See SEC v. Carter Hawley Hale Stores, 760 F.2d 945,
950–953 (9th Cir. 1985) (applying the factors to a
target's purchases of its own stock on the open
market in response to a hostile tender offer); *Brown
v. Kinross Gold, USA*, 378 F.Supp. 2d 1280, 1285–
1286 (D. Nev. 2005) (applying the factors to a bidder's
transaction occurring prior to public tender offer).

The other approach to the definition of a tender
offer, set forth in *Hanson Trust PLC v. SMC Corp.*,
774 F.2d 47 (2d Cir. 1985), looks to whether the
offerees require Williams Act protection:

[T]he question of whether a solicitation
constitutes a "tender offer" * * * turns on
whether, viewing the transaction in the light of
the totality of the circumstances, there appears
to be a likelihood that unless the pre-acquisition
filing strictures of that statute are followed

there will be a substantial risk that solicitees will lack information needed to make a carefully considered appraisal of the principal put before them.

Id. at 57 (applying this approach to five privately negotiated purchases and one open market purchase). *See E.ON, AG v. Acciona*, SA, 468 F.Supp. 2d 559, 581 (S.D.N.Y. 2007) (applying *Hanson* approach).

§ 5.3 SECTION 14(e)'s SCOPE

The Supreme Court exerted a substantial effect on § 14(e)'s reach with its decision in *Schreiber v. Burlington Northern, Inc.*, 472 U.S. 1 (1985). At issue were two tender offers by Burlington Northern (Burlington) for the shares of El Paso Natural Gas (El Paso)—first, a hostile offer for 25.1 million shares that was later withdrawn and replaced by a friendly offer for 21 million shares at the same price. The first offer was fully-subscribed and the second one oversubscribed, developments which led to significant proration—and thus smaller pay-outs—to those who had subscribed to the first offer.

Suing on behalf of herself and other El Paso shareholders, the plaintiff argued that Burlington's withdrawal of the first offer and substitution of the second one constituted a "manipulative" act that violated § 14(e). As the plaintiff saw it, what Burlington did was substantively unfair, its full disclosure notwithstanding.

Rejecting the plaintiff's argument, the Supreme Court held that all conduct prohibited by § 14(e), including but not limited to manipulation, requires a misrepresentation or omission. To reach this conclusion, the Court pointed to the following:

- A manipulative act entails a misrepresentation or omission for purposes of § 10(b) (*see* § 8.1 *infra*); the common law; and the definition of "manipulative" that appears in the dictionary. *See id*. at 7–8.

- Section 14(e), the text of which is set forth in § 5.1 *supra*, groups manipulative acts with those that are "fraudulent" or "deceptive," words which themselves presuppose a misrepresentation or omission. Words should be judged by the company they keep. *See id*. at 7.

- The main goal of the Williams Act is full disclosure, a purpose served by construing its prohibited acts to require an omission or misrepresentation. *See id*. at 8–9.

In its discussion, the Court ignored a critical difference between the text of § 14(e) (*see* § 5.1 *supra*) and that of § 10(b) (*see* § 2.1 *supra*). While § 10(b) prohibits a "manipulative or deceptive device or contrivance," § 14(e) contains a two-pronged prohibition—one as to "any fraudulent, deceptive or manipulative acts or practices" and the other as to "any untrue statement of a material fact or omit[ting] to state any material fact necessary in order to make the statements made, in the light of the circumstances under which they are made, not misleading." Why have two prongs if they simply duplicate each other? Rather than intending duplication, Congress may have had different goals for each prong—that is, to foster full disclosure through the omission-and-misrepresentation prong and to advance substantive fairness through the "fraudulent, deceptive, or manipulative acts or practices" prong.

By failing even to acknowledge the existence of the two prongs—much less that they might serve different functions—the Court has allowed the federal judiciary to avoid lawsuits by bidders and shareholders challenging a target's defensive tactics. To be sure, this avoidance accords with the policy articulated by *Santa Fe Indus., Inc. v. Green*, 430 U.S. 462 (1977)—namely, to leave traditional state law matters to the state courts unless Congress indicates otherwise. *See id.* at 477–480 (Rule 10b-5 case), discussed in § 2.2.1 *supra*. But conceivably Congress did indicate otherwise in § 14(e), a possibility unmentioned by the Court.

The Court's holding has had two significant consequences. First, § 14(e) claims require the omission or misrepresentation of a material fact, regardless of whether the plaintiff is the SEC, the DOJ, or an investor. The irrelevance of the plaintiff's identity results from the fact that *Schreiber*'s holding is predicated on the statutory text, which applies regardless of the identity of the plaintiff.

Second, tender offer litigation must proceed along two simultaneous tracks: a federal-court track for

§ 14(e) claims (which are subject to exclusive federal jurisdiction under § 27 of the Exchange Act); and a state-court track for state law challenges mounted by bidders and shareholders to defensive tactics by the target's management which are allegedly unfair or constitute a breach of fiduciary duty. The existence of these two tracks may benefit lawyers, but it is not self-evident who the other beneficiaries might be.

§ 5.3.1   THE OMISSION OR MISREPRESENTATION OF A MATERIAL FACT

An omission or misrepresentation can be actionable under § 14(e) only if it is "material," as determined by the same objective and contextual materiality standard that applies to Rules 14a-9 and 10b-5:

> An omitted [or misrepresented] fact is material if there is a "substantial likelihood that a reasonable shareholder would consider it important" or if there is a substantial likelihood that * * * the omitted [or misrepresented] fact would have * * * significantly altered the 'total mix' of information made available.

TSC Indus., Inc. v. Northway, Inc., 426 U.S. 438, 449 (1976) (Rule 14a-9 case). *See Nobles v. First Carolina Commc'ns, Inc.,* 929 F.2d 141, 145 (4th Cir. 1991) (applying *Northway to* § 14(e)); *In re N.Y. Comty. Bancorp, Inc., Sec. Litig.,* 448 F.Supp. 2d 466, 478 (E.D.N.Y. 2006) (equating § 14(e)'s materiality standard with those under Rules 14a-9 and 10b-5).

Moreover, the following doctrines may have a role to play in connection with materiality determinations under § 14(e):

The Puffery Doctrine. This doctrine deems immaterial those statements that are so vague as to be meaningless. *See, e.g., N. Y. Comty. Bancorp*, 448 F.Supp. 2d at 478–479. *See also* § 2.3.1 *supra* (discussing puffery in connection with Rule 10b-5).

The Probability/Magnitude Test. This test, applicable to merger negotiations or other contingent events, measures materiality by looking at the probability the event will occur combined with the magnitude of the event if it does occur. *See, e.g., SEC v. Mayhew,* 121 F.3d 44, 52 (2d Cir. 1997). *See also* § 2.3.5 *supra* (discussing the probability/magnitude test in connection with Rule 10b-5).

The Bespeaks Caution Doctrine. This doctrine deems forward-looking information to be immaterial where the information is surrounded by cautions of the non-boilerplate variety. *See, e.g., Peregrine Options, Inc. v. Farley, Inc.*, No. 90 C 285, 1993 WL 489739, at *12 (N.D. Ill. Nov. 19, 1993). *See also* § 2.3.7 *supra* (discussing the bespeaks caution doctrine in connection with Rule 10b-5).

Not applicable to materiality determinations under § 14(e), however, is the safe harbor for forward-looking statements, set forth in § 21E of the

Exchange Act. That provision explicitly excludes tender offers from its reach. *See* § 21E(b)(2)(c).

One final point merits attention. The material fact alleged to be misrepresented or omitted can take the form of an opinion. An opinion is a "fact" capable of misstatement or omission. *See Omnicare, Inc. v. Laborers Dist. Council Const. Indus. Pension Fund*, 135 S. Ct. 1318, 1326 (2015) (§ 11 case), discussed in § 2.2.3 *supra*.

§ 5.3.2   STATE OF MIND

Prior to the Supreme Court's decision in *Schreiber v. Burlington Northern, Inc.*, 472 U.S. 1 (1985), the need to prove scienter arguably turned on which prong of § 14(e) was at issue. Indeed, based solely on its statutory text (set forth in § 5.1 *supra*), § 14(e) has two prongs—one involving "fraudulent, deceptive, or manipulative acts" (implying the need for scienter) and another involving an omission or misrepresentation (implying no need for scienter). Yet as noted in § 5.3 *supra*, the *Schreiber* Court avoided acknowledging the presence of the second prong, thereby making such an argument more difficult to sustain.

Accordingly, the consensus seems to be that § 14(e) contains a scienter requirement, applicable across the board and defined, as it is under § 10(b) and Rule 10b-5, as a state of mind involving an intent to deceive, intentionality, or recklessness. *See, e.g., In re Digital Island Sec. Litig.*, 357 F.3d 322, 328 (3d Cir. 2004); *Conn. Nat'l Bank v. Fluor Corp.*, 808 F.2d 957, 961 (2d Cir. 1987). Moreover, as with Rule 10b-5, scienter must be pled in accordance with Rule 9(b) of the Federal Rules of Civil Procedure and the enhanced pleading requirements of the Private Securities Litigation Reform Act (the PSLRA). *See, e.g., Digital,* 357 F.3d at 334; *Sodhi v. Gentium, S.p.A.,* 2015 WL 273724, at *3 (S.D.N.Y. Jan. 22, 2015). *See also* §§ 2.1, 2.6 *supra* (discussing these pleading requirements in the context of Rule 10b-5).

§ 5.4 SECTION 14(e)'s IMPLIED PRIVATE ACTION

The implied private action under § 14(e) has several points of commonality with its Rule 10b-5 counterpart. Thus, the action can come into play regardless of the size of the company issuing the securities. There is likewise the need to satisfy various Exchange Act provisions enacted in 1995 as part of the PSLRA, including the following:

- A loss causation requirement for plaintiffs seeking damages (§ 21D(b)(4));

- A scheme of proportionate liability (§ 21D(f));

- Heightened pleading requirements (§ 21D(b)); and

- A set of requirements pertinent to class actions (discussed in Chapter 6 *infra*).

Yet the two implied private actions part company in various respects as well. Consider the Exchange Act's safe harbor for forward-looking statements, which applies to Rule 10b-5 but not to § 14(e). Consider also SEC and DOJ enforcement—which is fairly routine with respect to Rule 10b-5 but relatively infrequent in the case of § 14(e), at least where insider trading is not at issue. Thus, unlike Rule 10b-5, § 14(e) is enforced largely by investors, making it resemble, in this respect at least, § 14(a) and Rule 14a-9 (*see* § 4.1 *supra*).

Liability under the implied private action extends to the "maker" of the omission or misrepresentation as delineated by *Janus Capital Group, Inc. v. First Derivative Traders*, 564 U.S. 135 (2011) (Rule 10b-5 case), discussed in § 2.11.1 *supra. See, e.g., Sodhi*, 2015 WL 273724 at *3 (applying *Janus* to § 14(e)). Likewise subject to liability is anyone who controls the primary violator in accordance with § 20(a) of the Exchange Act. *See, e.g., Flaherty & Crumrine Preferred Income Fund, Inc. v. TXU Corp.*, 565 F.3d 200, 212 n.8 (5th Cir. 2009). *See also* § 2.12.3 *supra* (discussing controlling person liability under § 20(a) in the context of Rule 10b-5).

§ 5.4.1   STANDING TO SUE

In *Piper v. Chris-Craft Indus., Inc.*, 430 U.S. 1 (1977), the Supreme Court held that § 14(e) does not give rise to an implied private damages action that can be used by a defeated bidder against the successful bidder and the target. In so doing, the Court shed some light on the more general question of standing to sue under § 14(e).

The Bidder. The Court held that the bidder lacked standing to sue for damages. *See id.* at 42. To grant such standing, the Court explained, would do nothing to further the main purpose of the Williams Act, namely, to protect the target's shareholders. *See id.* at 41–42.

Does the bidder have standing to sue for an injunction? The Court affirmatively did not address this question. *See id.* at 46 n.33. Several lower courts thereafter have given an affirmative answer. *See, e.g., Torchmark Corp. v. Bixby*, 708 F.Supp. 1070, 1079 (W.D. Mo. 1988); *Humana, Inc. v. American Medicorp*, Inc., 445 F.Supp. 613, 615 (S.D.N.Y. 1977). In so doing, one court relied partly on the following language from *Piper*: "[T]o the extent that the violations are obvious and serious, injunctive relief at an earlier stage of the contest is apt to be the most efficacious form of remedy." *Humana*, 445 F.Supp. at 615 (quoting *Piper*, 430 U.S. at 40 n.26).

<u>The Target</u>. The *Piper* Court affirmatively did not address the target's standing to sue. *See Piper,* 430 U.S. at 42 n28. Lower courts thereafter have allowed the target to sue for injunctive relief on the theory that the target is "frequently in the best position to seek corrective disclosures within a time frame that will optimize the benefit to shareholders of such disclosures." *Florida Commercial Banks v. Culverhouse,* 772 F.2d 1513, 1519 (11th Cir. 1985). *See also Polaroid Corp. v. Disney,* 862 F.2d 987, 1003 (3d Cir. 1988) (collecting cases).

<u>The Target's Shareholders</u>. The *Piper* Court affirmatively did not address whether the target's shareholders have standing to sue. *See Piper*, 430 U.S. at 42 n.28. But it nonetheless suggested that these shareholders might have standing by designating them as § 14(e)'s intended beneficiaries

and by observing that "perhaps" they have standing to sue for damages, including those of them who do not tender their shares. *See id.* at 38–39. Moreover, the Court later appeared to treat their standing to sue for damages as a given in *Schreiber v. Burlington Northern, Inc.*, 472 U.S. 1 (1985), which upheld the dismissal of their action on the ground of their failure to allege an omission or misrepresentation. *See* § 5.3 *supra* (discussing *Schreiber*).

§ 5.4.2   RELIANCE

Does the implied private action under § 14(e) contain a reliance requirement? There appears to be a division of authority on this question.

Courts upholding a reliance requirement have drawn an analogy to Rule 10b-5, where the existence of such a requirement is well-established. *See* § 2.8 *supra. See, e.g., Atchley v. Quonaar Corp.*, 704 F.2d 355, 359–360 (7th Cir. 1983); *Wardrop v. Amway Asia Pacific Ltd.*, 2001 WL 274067 at *3 (S.D.N.Y. Mar. 20, 2001), *aff'd*, 26 Fed. App'x 89 (2d Cir. 2002); *In re ValueVision Int'l, Inc., Sec. Litig.*, 896 F.Supp. 434, 448 (E.D. Pa. 1995). In addition, such courts have presumed reliance when that would be "logical." *Lewis v. McGraw*, 619 F.2d 192, 195 (2d Cir. 1980). Moreover, when the alleged fraud involves an omission, they have applied the presumption for omissions upheld by the Supreme Court in *Affiliated Ute v. United States*, 406 U.S. 128 (1972) (Rule 10b-5 case), discussed in § 2.8.1 *supra. See, e.g., In re Piedmont Office Trust, Inc., Sec. Litig.*, 264 F.R.D.

693, 701 (N.D. Ga. 2010) (applying *Affiliated Ute* to § 14(e)).

The rejection of a reliance requirement under § 14(e) has thus far occurred largely in the Ninth Circuit. *See, e.g., Biotech. Value Fund, LP v. Celera Corp.*, No. C 13–03248 (WHA), 2014 WL 988913, at *9 (N.D. Cal. Mar. 10, 2014) (refusing to dismiss § 14(e) complaint that did not allege reliance); *Rubke v. Capitol Bancorp Ltd.*, 460 F.Supp. 2d 1124, 1131 (N.D. Cal. 2006) (noting the absence of a reliance requirement under § 14(e) in the Ninth Circuit), *aff'd on other grounds*, 551 F.3d 1156 (9th Cir. 2009). This rejection seems to flow, at least in part, from analogizing § 14(e) to § 14(a) and Rule 14a-9, where the implied private action does not require reliance. *See Plane v. McCabe*, 797 F.2d 713, 721 (9th Cir. 1986) (analogizing § 14(e) to § 14(a)). *See also* § 4.4 *supra* (discussing the absence of a reliance requirement in the Rule 14a-9 implied private action).

§ 5.4.3   LOSS CAUSATION

Plaintiffs seeking damages under § 14(e) must establish loss causation, that is, a causal relationship between the fraudulent tender offer and the alleged economic harm for which they seek redress. The loss causation requirement, set forth in Exchange Act § 21D(b)(4) and enacted as part of the PSLRA, reads as follows:

> In any private action arising under this title, the plaintiff shall have the burden of proving that the act or omission of the defendant alleged to

violate this title caused the loss for which the plaintiff seeks to recover damages.

This language requires that the plaintiffs to plead loss causation as well. *See Dura Pharm., Inc. v. Broudo*, 544 U.S. 336, 346 (2005) (Rule 10b-5 case).

To establish loss causation, there must be a direct connection between the fraud and the loss. Such a connection was not established by plaintiffs who alleged that the defendants obtained control of the company by means of a fraudulent tender offer and then used that control to loot the company. *See Gorman v. Coogan*, 2004 WL 60271, at * 20 (D. Me. Jan. 13, 2004).

§ 5.4.4   DAMAGES

Section 14(e) does not identify the measure of damages that governs a private action. This silence is not surprising, given that the private action is implied.

Courts typically require a § 14(e) plaintiff to establish specific damages that flowed from the defendant's violation. The burden of so doing can be daunting:

> While Congress has determined that accurate disclosure is important to shareholders, it would often be impossible for shareholders to prove that on the facts of their particular tender offer accurate disclosure would have affected their decision making in a particular way with concomitant quantifiable monetary loss.

Polaroid Corp. v. Disney, 862 F.2d 987, 1006–1007
(3d Cir. 1988) (directing the lower court to order a
preliminary injunction on behalf of the target, partly
because of the difficulty in establishing damages).
Moreover, in ascertaining whether damages should
be awarded, a court may take into account whether
the price they received for their shares was fair:
"While the issue of fairness is relevant to the issue of
damages, it does not necessarily defeat a plaintiff's
claim of injury." *Plaine v. McCabe*, 797 F.2d 713, 721
(9th Cir. 1986).

§ 5.4.5   STATUTE OF LIMITATIONS

Like its Rule 10b-5 counterpart, the implied
private action under § 14(e) is subject to the
limitations period consisting of the two-year/five-
year structure set forth in 28 U.S.C. § 1658(b) that
was enacted in 2002 as part of the SOX. That
provision reads as follows:

> * * * [A] private right of action that involves a
> claim of fraud, deceit, manipulation, or
> contrivance in contravention of a regulatory
> requirement concerning the securities laws, as
> defined in section 3(a)(47) of the Securities
> Exchange Act of 1934, may be brought not later
> than the earlier of—
>
> (1) 2 years after the discovery of the facts
> constituting the violation; or
>
> (2) 5 years after such violation.

For a decision applying § 1658(b) to § 14(e), *see*
Biotech. Value Fund, LP v. Celera Corp., 12 F.Supp.

3d 1194, 1200 (N.D. Cal. 2014). For a discussion of § 1658(b)'s application to Rule 10b-5, *see* § 2.13 *supra*.

CHAPTER 6
CLASS ACTIONS

§ 6.1 INTRODUCTION

Private securities litigation usually takes the form of a class action. Alternative forms of private securities litigation include derivative actions (that is, actions filed by shareholders on behalf of the corporation) and actions brought solely on behalf of a single individual or entity or a small number of such plaintiffs.

Federal securities class actions are subject to two types of restrictions: those relevant to all forms of private securities litigation and those applicable to class actions only. The first type includes judicially-created restrictions, including Rule 10b-5's purchaser-seller requirement (*see* § 2.7 *supra*) and Rule 14a-9's transaction causation requirement (*see* § 4.4 *supra*) as well as restrictions spawned by the Private Securities Litigation Reform Act (the PSLRA), such as the safe harbor for forward-looking statements (*see, e.g.,* § 2.3.8 *supra*), the loss causation requirement (*see, e.g.,* § 2.9 *supra*), and the heightened pleading requirements (*see, e.g.,* §§ 2.1, 2.6 *supra*).

The focus of this Chapter is on the second type of restrictions—those applicable to class actions only. Some restrictions of this type emanate from Rule 23 of the Federal Rules of Civil Procedure and govern all class actions filed in federal court, irrespective of their subject matter. Others originate in the PSLRA or in the Securities Litigation Uniform Standards Act of 1998 (the SLUSA) and target securities class actions specifically.

This Chapter begins with the selection of the lead plaintiff and the lead counsel (§ 6.2 *infra*) and next moves to certification of securities class actions in general (§ 6.3 *infra*) and Rule 10b-5 actions in particular (§§ 6.3.1–6.3.2 *infra*). Attention then turns to securities class action settlements (§ 6.4 *infra*), the SLUSA (§ 6.5 *infra*), and the interplay between securities class actions and derivative litigation (§ 6.6 *infra*).

§ 6.2 SELECTION OF THE LEAD PLAINTIFF AND THE LEAD COUNSEL

The PSLRA requires a court-appointed "lead plaintiff." *See* Securities Act § 27(a)(3)(B); Exchange Act § 21D(a)(3)(B). As the name implies, the lead plaintiff assumes a leadership role in the litigation. The PSLRA's legislative history suggests that the ideal lead plaintiff is an institution. *See Ravens v. Iftikar*, 174 F.R.D. 651, 661–662 (N.D. Cal. 1997). The text of the PSLRA itself, however, leaves this preference unstated.

When the PSLRA was first enacted, institutional lead plaintiffs were relatively few and far between. In contrast, since 2006, institutions have accounted for in excess of half of the lead plaintiff total. *See* Cornerstone Research, *Securities Class Action Settlements: 2014 Review and Analysis* 16 (2015).

Prior to the PSLRA, securities class action litigation was typically directed by the lawyer whose client managed to be the first to file the class action complaint. To wrest control from that lawyer, the PSLRA establishes the following:

The Notice Requirement. Under the PSLRA, the first filer must notify the other members of the purported class within 20 days after the complaint is filed that the action is pending and that they each have the right to seek appointment as the lead plaintiff. Securities Act § 27(a)(3)(A); Exchange Act § 21D(a)(3)(A). The goal is to reach the most plausible lead plaintiff candidates, not necessarily every class member. *See Greebel v. FTP Software, Inc.*, 939 F.Supp. 57, 63 (D. Mass. 1996).

The Presumption in Favor of the Most Adequate Plaintiff. Under the PSLRA, the court must presume that the most adequate plaintiff is the person or group that: (1) filed the complaint or made a response to the notice requirement; (2) has the largest financial interest in the relief sought; and (3) satisfies the requirements of Rule 23 of the Federal Rules of Civil Procedure. Securities Act § 27(a)(3)(B)(iii); Exchange Act § 21D(a)(3)(B)(iii).

Determining who has the greatest financial interest is typically made by applying the four factors articulated in *Lax v. First Merchants Acceptance Corp.*, 1997 WL 461036 (N.D. Ill. 1997). *See, e.g., In re Millennial Media, Inc., Sec. Litig.*, 87 F.Supp. 3d 563, 569 (S.D.N.Y. 2015).

These factors—known as the *Lax* factors—consist of the following: "(1) the number of shares purchased; (2) the number of net shares purchased; (3) the total net funds expended by the plaintiffs during the class period; and (4) the approximate losses suffered by the plaintiffs." *Lax*, 1997 WL 461036 at *5. The fourth factor is widely understood to be the most important, but divisions abound about how to measure it. *See, e.g., Foley v. Transocean, Ltd.*, 272 F.R.D. 126, 129–130, 130 n.7 (S.D.N.Y. 2011).

The Rule 23 requirements at issue are those of typicality and adequacy. Typicality focuses on whether the candidate with the largest financial interest has "claims or defenses * * * [that] are typical of the claims and defenses of the class." Fed. R. Civ. P. 23(a)(3). Adequacy focuses on whether the candidate "will fairly and adequately protect the interests of the class." Fed. R. Civ. P. 23(a)(4).

The court must decide that the candidate "has made a prima facie showing of typicality and adequacy" before the presumption of most adequate plaintiff can attach. *In re Cendant Corp. Litig.*, 264 F.3d 201, 263 (3d Cir. 2001). Then, if she receives the presumption, other members of the class can try to rebut it by disproving her typicality or adequacy (or both). *See id.* at 263–268. The inquiries into typicality and adequacy tend to be less exhaustive than those made at the certification stage. *See, e.g., In*

re eSpeed Inc. Sec. Litig., 232 F.R.D. 95, 102
(S.D.N.Y. 2005).

The PSLRA presumes in favor of the
candidate that meets the specified criteria,
regardless of whether that candidate is a
"person or group of persons." Courts have
divided over the interpretation of the phrase
"group of persons." Some insist that a group can
serve as lead plaintiff only if its members had a
pre-existing relationship. *Ruland v. InfoSonics
Corp.*, 2006 WL 3746716 at *4 (S.D. Cal. 2006).
The majority of courts permit service by a group
without such a relationship so long as its
members offer evidence that they can "function
cohesively and * * * effectively manage the
litigation apart from their lawyers." *Varghese v.
China Shenghuo Pharm. Holdings, Inc.*, 589
F.Supp. 2d 388, 392 (S.D.N.Y. 2008).

There is also the conceptually distinct,
although not unrelated, matter of whether to
appoint "co-lead plaintiffs." Courts have offered
the following justifications for making such an
appointment—because the novel substantive
questions at issue would benefit from a range of
perspectives, *see Pirelli Armstrong Tire Corp.
Retiree Medical Benefits Trust v. Labranche &
Co.*, 229 F.R.D. 395, 420 (S.D.N.Y. 2004);
because it would permit "diverse representation,
including * * * a state pension fund, significant
individual investors, and a large institutional
investor," *In re Oxford Health Plans, Inc., Sec.
Litig.*,182 F.R.D. 42, 49 (S.D.N.Y.1998); because

distinguishing between two (or more) lead plaintiff candidates is difficult, if not impossible, *see Gluck v. CellStar Corp.*, 976 F.Supp. 542, 549–550 (N.D. Tex. 1997). On the other hand, the Ninth Circuit has, albeit in dictum, suggested that appointing co-lead plaintiffs conflicts with the statutory language: "While the PSLRA allows a group to serve as lead plaintiff, it also consistently refers to the lead plaintiff and most adequate plaintiff in the singular, suggesting that the district court should appoint only one lead plaintiff, whether an individual or a group." *Cohen v. U.S. Dist. Ct. for N. Dist. of Cal.*, 586 F.3d 703, 711 n.4 (9th Cir. 2009).

Availability of Discovery. The presumption in favor of the most adequate plaintiff anticipates a competition among lead plaintiff candidates. Accordingly, "discovery relating to whether a member or members of the purported plaintiff class is the most adequate plaintiff" is available to a plaintiff who "demonstrates a reasonable basis for a finding that the presumptively most adequate plaintiff is incapable of adequately representing the class." Securities Act § 27(a)(3)(B)(iv); Exchange Act § 21D(a)(3)(B)(iv).

Restriction on Professional Plaintiffs. The PSLRA restricts the participation of "professional plaintiffs"—those who frequently file lawsuits against the numerous companies in which they own shares. The restriction is prompted by concern that professional plaintiffs will function merely as lawyers' pawns. In general, a person may serve as lead plaintiff in no more than 5 securities class actions during any 3-year period; however, a court may permit otherwise. Securities Act § 27(a)(3)(B)(vi); Exchange Act § 21D(a)(3)(B)(vi). There is no outright bar likely because it would lead to the frequent disqualification of institutions, Congress's preferred lead plaintiffs.

<u>Selection of the Lead Counsel</u>. The PSLRA provides that, conditioned on the court's approval, the most adequate plaintiff shall select and retain counsel to represent the class. Securities Act § 27(a)(3)(B)(v); Exchange Act § 21D(a)(3)(B)(v).

Most courts regard the lead plaintiff as entitled to receive the lead counsel of her choice, unless that choice is so outrageous that making it demonstrates inadequacy to serve as the lead plaintiff in the first place. *See, e.g., In re Cavanaugh*, 306 F.3d 726, 732–733 (9th Cir. 2002). *See also Cohen*, 586 F.3d at 703 (mandamusing the federal district court that had itself chosen the lead counsel).

§ 6.3 CLASS CERTIFICATION

To proceed as a class action, the court must certify the class in accordance with Rule 23 of the Federal Rules of Civil Procedure. Rule 23 applies to all federal-court class actions, including those filed under §§ 11 and 12(a)(2) of the Securities Act (Chapter 3 *supra*), § 10(b) of the Exchange Act and

Rule 10b-5 (Chapter 2 *supra*), § 14(a) of the Exchange
Act and Rule 14a-9 (Chapter 4 *supra*) and § 14(e)
(Chapter 5 *supra*).

The court's certification ruling carries huge
significance for all concerned. If certification is
denied, most (and possibly all) members of the might-
have-been class will lose the opportunity to recover
because they typically lack the resources to sue
individually. On the other hand, a grant of
certification "may so increase the defendant's
potential damages liability and litigation costs that
he may find it economically prudent to settle and to
abandon a meritorious defense." *Coopers & Lybrand
v. Livesay*, 437 U.S. 463, 476 (1978).

The plaintiff's certification motion often precedes
her motion for the appointment of the lead plaintiff
and the lead counsel. *See, e.g., Desai v. Deutsche
Bank Secs., Ltd.*, 573 F.3d 931, 935–936 (9th Cir.
2009); *Teamsters Local 445 Freight Div. Pension
Fund v. Bombardier, Inc.*, 546 F.3d 196, 198 (2d Cir.
2008). Occasionally, however, these matters are
resolved simultaneously. *See, e.g., In re Turkcell
Iletisim Hizmetler, A.S. Sec. Litig.*, 209 F.R.D. 353,
354-355 (S.D.N.Y. 2002).

In order for the court to grant certification, the
plaintiff must satisfy Rule 23(a) as well as one of the
three subsections of Rule 23(b), typically Rule
23(b)(3). Rule 23(a) imposes four requirements:

- Numerosity. The class is so numerous that
  joinder of all members is impracticable.

- Commonality. There are questions of law or fact common to the class.

- Typicality. The claims or defenses of the representative parties are typical of the claims or defenses of the class.

- Adequacy. The representative parties will fairly and adequately protect the interests of the class.

Rule 23(b)(3) sets forth the following two additional requirements:

- Predominance. The questions of law or fact common to the members of the class predominate over any questions affecting only individual members, and

- Superiority. A class action is superior to other available methods for the fair and efficient adjudication of the controversy.

To find the predominance and superiority requirements satisfied, pertinent matters include:

- the interest of members of the class in individually controlling the prosecution or defense of separate actions;

- the extent and nature of any litigation concerning the controversy already commenced by or against members of the class;

- the desirability or undesirability of concentrating the litigation of the claims in the particular forum; and

- the difficulties likely to be encountered in the management of a class action.

The certification inquiry does not purport to address the substantive strength of the plaintiff's claim(s). But it sometimes reaches the merits, to the extent that to do so becomes necessary to determine the plaintiff's compliance with one (or more) of the certification requirements. *See, e.g., Halliburton Co. v. Erica P. John Fund, Inc.,* 134 S.Ct. 2398, 2416–2417 (2014) (allowing the defendants to prove lack of price impact because of its bearing on whether the predominance requirement had been met).

§ 6.3.1   THE CERTIFICATION CHALLENGE POSED BY THE RELIANCE ELEMENT OF RULE 10b-5

Most securities class actions rest on § 10(b) of the Exchange Act and Rule 10b-5 (the subject of Chapter 2 *supra*). For Rule 10b-5 plaintiffs seeking certification, the single greatest obstacle arises from the reliance element of the cause of action (discussed in § 2.8 *supra*). The reason is straightforward. In the traditional Rule 10b-5 action, each plaintiff must demonstrate her own reliance on the fraud. *See* § 2.8 *supra.* The individual proofs thwart the predominance of common questions required by Rule 23(b)(3) of the Federal Rules of Civil Procedure. *See* § 6.3 *supra.*

The Supreme Court ameliorated the situation somewhat in *Affiliated Ute v. United States,* 406 U.S. 128 (1972). That decision, discussed in § 2.8.1 *supra*, upheld a presumption of reliance for Rule 10b-5 omissions cases on the theory that the absence of something can be difficult to show. Armed with this presumption, Rule 10b-5 plaintiffs can show predominance as long as their allegations consist of omissions only. *See, e.g., Binder v. Gillespie*, 184 F.3d 1059, 1063 (9th Cir. 1999). But when they involve misrepresentations, either entirely or in significant measure, the *Affiliated Ute* presumption becomes inapposite. *See id.* at 1064. As a result, most would-be Rule 10b-5 class actions are left to wither on the vine.

Thereafter, in *Basic, Inc. v. Levinson*, 485 U.S. 224 (1988), the Court provided a more comprehensive solution, which it reaffirmed in *Halliburton Co. v. Erica P. John Fund, Inc. (Halliburton II)*, 134 S.Ct. 2398 (2014). The solution, known as fraud-on-the-market, draws on the efficient capital markets hypothesis—the idea that the price of a security trading in an efficient market reflects all public information, including misinformation. *See* § 1.13 *supra*. Fraud-on-the-market plaintiffs allege that they relied on the fraud indirectly: that is, they relied on the security's price, which the fraud distorted. *See* § 2.8.2 *supra*. Because a presumption attaches to their reliance on the price, common reliance issues predominate over individual ones. *See* § 2.8.2 *supra*.

§ 6.3.2   CERTIFICATION-STAGE PREREQUISITES FOR INVOKING THE FRAUD-ON-THE-MARKET PRESUMPTION

To invoke the fraud-on-the-market presumption at the certification stage, the plaintiffs must show that the stock was traded in an efficient market (*see* § 2.8.2 *supra*); and the fraud was publicly disseminated. *Halliburton II*, 134 S.Ct. at 2408. To be sure, the presumption has a third prerequisite—materiality—which comes into play at trial and summary judgment but has no role at certification. *See Amgen, Inc. v. Conn. Ret. Plans & Trust Funds*, 133 S.Ct. 1184, 1191 (2013). The reason is as follows. To deny certification for lack of materiality would terminate not only the class action itself but also a traditional Rule 10b-5 lawsuit (for which materiality is essential). In contrast, to deny certification for lack of market efficiency or public dissemination would not terminate a traditional Rule 10b-5 lawsuit, as to which such elements are irrelevant. *See id.*

The Court has affirmatively rejected two other prerequisites that had been sought by defendants. One is loss causation, an independent element of the Rule 10b-5 private action, discussed in § 2.9 *supra*. *See Erica P. John Fund Inc. v. Halliburton Co. (Halliburton I)*, 563 U.S. 804 (2011). The other is price impact. *See Halliburton II*, 134 S.Ct. at 2415. To be sure, proof of the lack of price impact can be established by the defendant for purposes of rebutting the presumption, a subject discussed immediately below.

§ 6.3.3   CERTIFICATION-STAGE REBUTTAL OF THE FRAUD-ON-THE-MARKET PRESUMPTION

Defendants are entitled to rebut the fraud-on-the-market presumption at the certification stage on the following grounds:

Lack of Price Impact. The Supreme Court approved such rebuttal in *Halliburton II,* 134 S.Ct. at 2414–2415. To succeed, the defendants must show that the alleged fraud had no impact on the market price. *Id.* at 2414. *See McIntire v. China MediaExpress Holdings,* 38 F.Supp. 3d 415, 434–435 (S.D.N.Y. 2014) (holding rebuttal to have failed on this basis); *Aranaz v. Catalyst Pharm. Partners, Inc.*, 302 F.R.D. 657, 671–672 (S.D.Fla. 2014) (same).

Price Insensitivity of Specific Plaintiffs. This form of rebuttal can be attempted at the certification stage in order to show the lack of adequacy or typicality of the named plaintiffs, and thereby the failure to satisfy Rule 23. *See, e.g., In re Winstar Commc'ns Sec. Litig.*, 290 F.R.D. 437, 444–445 (S.D.N.Y. 2013).

§ 6.4 CLASS ACTION SETTLEMENTS

Because most securities class actions are settled rather than tried, the settlement stage is highly significant. The parameters of settlement are set by Rule 23(e) of the Federal Rules of Civil Procedure as well as by certain PSLRA provisions.

Rule 23(e) establishes requirements for the settlement of any and all class actions filed in federal court. Among the requirements are that the court "direct notice in a reasonable manner to all class members who would be bound by [a proposed settlement]" and that it approve a settlement that "would bind class members * * * only after a hearing and on finding that [the settlement] is fair,

242 CLASS ACTIONS CH. 6

reasonable, and adequate." Fed. R. Civ. P.
23(e)(1),(2). *See, e.g., Wong v. Accretive Health, Inc.,*
773 F.3d 859 (7th Cir. 2014). The court is also
entitled to award "reasonable attorney's fees." Fed. R.
Civ. P. 23(h). *See In re IndyMac Mortg.-Backed Sec.
Litig.,* 94 F.Supp. 3d 517 (S.D.N.Y. 2015).

For class actions brought under the federal
securities laws, the following additional PSLRA
requirements come into play:

- the need to include specified information in
  the notice to class members (*see* Securities Act
  § 27(a)(7), Exchange Act § 21D(a)(7));

- a prohibition against awarding class
  representatives more than other class
  members (*see* Securities Act § 27(a)(4);
  Exchange Act § 21D(a)(4)); and

- a prohibition against awarding attorneys' fees
  that "exceed a reasonable percentage of the
  amount of any damages and pre-judgment
  interest actually paid to the class" (Securities
  Act § 27(a)(6); Exchange Act § 21D(a)(6)).

The PSLRA is silent, however, concerning the role
to be played by the lead plaintiff in the settlement
process. This silence tends to give the trial court
arguably necessary leeway when the lead plaintiff
consists of a group whose members do not see eye to
eye. *Cf. In re BankAmerica Corp. Sec. Litig.,* 350 F.3d
747 (8th Cir. 2003) (upholding the trial court's
approval of the settlement in accordance with its role
as a fiduciary for the absent class members

notwithstanding objections from some members of the lead plaintiff group).

§ 6.5 THE SLUSA

Following the enactment of the PSLRA, some plaintiffs sought to avoid the PSLRA's restrictions by filing securities class actions in state court under state law. To eliminate this tactic, Congress enacted the SLUSA.

The SLUSA bans most state-law class actions that seek damages and that allege, "in connection with the purchase or sale of a covered security," either "an untrue statement of omission of a material fact" or the use or employment by the defendant "of any deceptive device or contrivance." Securities Act § 16(b); Exchange Act § 28(f)(1). A "covered security" includes any that is exchange-traded.

The ban applies regardless of whether the plaintiffs file the class action in state or federal court. If filed in state court, the class action can be removed by the defendants to federal court, from which it may be dismissed or remanded to the state court (in the event that removal is found to have been improper). Remand orders under SLUSA, like remand orders more generally, are not appealable. *Kircher v. Putnam Funds Trust*, 547 U.S. 633 (2006).

The SLUSA contains certain significant explicit exclusions, including the following:

- Actions that are exclusively derivative in nature;

- Actions that involve the fiduciary duties of directors to current shareholders (often referred to as the "Delaware" carve-out); and

- Actions brought by states, their political subdivisions and pension plans.

Another important feature of the SLUSA is its attempt to prevent federal securities plaintiffs from utilizing state court litigation *not* precluded by the SLUSA in order to circumvent the discovery stay provision of the PSLRA. Thus, the SLUSA provides that a federal court hearing a lawsuit subject to the PSLRA, or that has issued a judgment previously in such a lawsuit, may stay discovery in any pending state-court private action. Securities Act § 27(b)(4); Exchange Act § 21D(b)(3)(D). *See, e.g., In re Cardinal Health, Inc., Sec. Litig.*, 365 F.Supp. 2d 866 (S.D. Ohio 2005).

Two additional aspects of the SLUSA merit attention. One is its "in connection with" requirement. The other involves an arguable loophole.

§ 6.5.1   THE SLUSA's "IN CONNECTION WITH" REQUIREMENT

To be precluded by the SLUSA, the fraud must be "in connection with" a covered security. *See* § 6.5 *supra*. The Supreme Court has twice addressed SLUSA's "in connection with" requirement.

First came *Merrill Lynch, Pierce, Fenner & Smith, Inc. v. Dabit*, 547 U.S. 71 (2006), which held that the "in connection with" requirement was intended to track its counterpart under Rule 10b-5 (*see* § 2.4 *supra*), and, like the latter, should be read broadly. 547 U.S. at 85–86. Applying a broad reading, the Court concluded that the SLUSA version encompassed, and thus precluded, a class action by those who "held" their covered securities in response to the fraud rather than sold them. *Id.* at 87.

To be sure, holders likewise cannot sue under Rule 10b-5 due to the purchaser-seller requirement upheld by *Blue Chip Stamps v. Manor Drug Stores*, 421 U.S. 723 (1975). *See* § 2.7 *supra*. Acknowledging this point, the *Dabit* Court noted that holders' claims are especially apt to be vexatious. *See* 547 U.S. at 86. In addition, the Court maintained, it would be "wasteful" and "duplicative" to allow holders' class actions to proceed in state court while the parallel sellers' class actions proceed in federal court under Rule 10b-5. *See id.*

Second came *Chadbourne & Parke LLP v. Troice*, 134 S.Ct. 1058 (2014), which held that fraud "in connection with" a covered security did *not* embrace a class action by purchasers of *uncovered* securities who were fraudulently informed that the latter were backed by *covered* securities. *See* 134 S.Ct. at 1066. This was so, the Court explained, because to be "in connection with" the purchase or sale of a "covered security," the fraud must be "material to a decision by one or more individuals (other than the fraudster) to buy or sell a 'covered security.'" *Id.*

To rationalize this conclusion, the *Troice* Court referenced, among other things, its prior decisions regarding Rule 10b-5's "in connection with" requirement. *See id.* at 1066–1067. The court noted that whenever those decisions found the requirement met, the case "involved victims [other than the fraudster] who took, who tried to take, who divested themselves of, who tried to divest themselves of, or who maintained *an ownership interest* in financial instruments that fall within the relevant statutory definition." *Id.* at 1066 (emphasis in original).

§ 6.5.2   THE SLUSA's ARGUABLE LOOPHOLE

As has been noted, the SLUSA seeks to prevent plaintiffs from circumventing the PSLRA by filing *state law* class actions. *See* § 6.5 *supra.* Some plaintiffs, however, seek to circumvent the PSLRA by filing a state-court class action premised on § 11 or § 12(a)(2) of the Securities Act. *See* Chapter 3 *supra.* When they do, can the defendants make use of the SLUSA's removal provision?

Two hurdles stand in their way. First, the class action is not based on state law. Second, the Securities Act specifically prohibits removal of actions filed in state court under the Act. *See* Securities Act § 22(a).

Courts are deeply divided about how to accommodate the statutory text with the goal of preventing circumvention of the PSLRA. *See Niitsoo v. Alpha Natural Res., Inc.*, 902 F.Supp. 2d 797, 800-801 (S.D.W.Va. 2012) (collecting cases).

§ 6.6 THE INTERPLAY BETWEEN SECURITIES CLASS ACTIONS AND SHAREHOLDER DERIVATIVE LITIGATION

The material misstatements and omissions that typically fuel securities class action litigation often also spawn shareholder derivative litigation. These so-called "tagalong" derivative lawsuits appear to be on the rise.

Derivative litigation is brought on the corporation's behalf by one or more shareholders against those who allegedly wronged the corporation, often on the basis of a breach of fiduciary duty. Under the "internal affairs doctrine," the substantive allegations are governed by the law of the state of incorporation regardless of whether the complaint is filed either outside that state and/or in federal court under diversity jurisdiction.

Although a derivative lawsuit is filed on the corporation's behalf, the reality of the situation is a bit more complex. The corporation can act only through its officers and directors—and those are often the very same people who allegedly committed the breach of fiduciary duty on which the derivative lawsuit is based.

Because directors, rather than shareholders, ordinarily make the corporation's litigation decisions, the law of the state of incorporation ordinarily requires the complaining shareholders to justify the maintenance of the derivative lawsuit where, as is typically the case, the directors have not approved it. Some states—so-called universal demand jurisdictions—require the shareholders to make a demand upon the board to file the lawsuit against the alleged wrongdoers. If, as virtually always happens, the board rejects the demand, the shareholders may proceed with the derivative lawsuit only if they can establish that the demand was wrongly rejected, say, because the directors had a conflict of interest or failed to act with a proper business purpose or on an informed basis.

Other states—so-called demand-excused jurisdictions (with Delaware as the most prominent example)—allow shareholders to forego the formality of the demand if they can show, on the basis of the allegations in the derivative complaint, that demand would be futile. *See Aronson v. Lewis,* 473 A.2d 805, 814 (Del. 1984) (upholding a bifurcated standard for demand futility, consisting of "whether, under the particularized facts alleged, a reasonable doubt is created [either] that: (1) the directors are disinterested and independent, [or] (2) the challenged transaction was otherwise the product of a valid exercise of business judgment").

The requirements for derivative litigation vary with the substantive law of the state of incorporation as well as with the applicable procedural rules (whether in federal or state court), but the threshold inquiry is largely the same—namely, should the decision on whether to proceed with the lawsuit rest with the directors or the shareholders? Only where this inquiry is resolved in a manner that allows the lawsuit to go forward can the court reach the lawsuit's underlying substantive allegations.

Harm to the corporation—not harm to the investors—is the focus of the derivative lawsuit, with the corporation ordinarily receiving any recovery that is obtained. Attorney fees for the successful shareholder are either awarded as part of the judgment or are agreed upon as part of the settlement and then approved by the court pursuant to Rule 23.1(c) of the Federal Rules of Civil Procedure.

CHAPTER 7
INSIDER TRADING

§ 7.1 INTRODUCTION

No federal statute explicitly prohibits the offense of "insider trading." Instead, since the 1960s, when the Securities and Exchange Commission (the SEC) first began to initiate enforcement actions for securities trading on the basis of material nonpublic information, insider trading has typically been prosecuted as a violation of Exchange Act § 10(b) and Rule 10b-5 thereunder. These provisions broadly prohibit fraud "in connection with the purchase or sale of any security." The Department of Justice (DOJ) also prosecutes insider trading as a criminal violation of either Rule 10b-5 or the federal statutes prohibiting mail fraud and wire fraud, 18 U.S.C. §§ 1341 and 1343. Accordingly, federal courts, through their interpretation of what it means to "defraud," have largely shaped the contours of the prohibition of insider trading as currently understood.

A very rich universe of scholarly literature offers a host of arguments as to *why* insider trading should—or should not—be subject to a federal prohibition. Scholars who favor deregulation emphasize that insider trading can benefit securities markets through the swift incorporation of new information into the price of particular securities. Those who support the prohibition argue that other important concerns (including fairness, investor confidence, management integrity and the protection of property rights) far outweigh the temporary efficiency gains that might arise as a side effect of insider trading.

This Chapter traces the development of the law of insider trading. It begins by discussing early attempts by state courts, Congress, and lower federal courts to deal with the problem of insider trading under the common law and the federal securities laws (§ 7.2 *infra*). It then turns to Rule 10b-5 and the Supreme Court decisions establishing or endorsing the classical theory of insider trading (§ 7.3 *infra*) and the misappropriation theory (§ 7.4 *infra*) as well as some lower court decisions and SEC rulemaking that build on those decisions. Section 7.4.4 raises the possibility of a new "deceptive acquisition" theory of insider trading liability and § 7.5 focuses on Rule 14e-3's prohibition of insider trading in connection with tender offers and explores whether the rule constitutes a valid exercise of SEC authority. Section 7.6 examines legislative efforts by Congress, including the Insider Trading Sanctions Act of 1984 (ITSA) and the Insider Trading and Securities Fraud Enforcement Act of 1988 (ITSFEA). Section 7.7 examines the difficulties faced in cases where proof of insider trading must be established by circumstantial evidence. The Chapter concludes with Regulation FD, an SEC initiative designed to prevent the practice of trading securities based on selectively disclosed information (§ 7.8 *infra*).

§ 7.2 INITIAL EFFORTS TO COMBAT AND CURTAIL INSIDER TRADING

§ 7.2.1 THE COMMON LAW

The earliest litigation over insider trading consisted of lawsuits filed in state court by shareholders against corporate officers and directors under a theory of fraudulent nondisclosure. Although an affirmative misstatement is generally required for a plaintiff to plead and prove common law fraud, courts have long recognized a number of circumstances under which a defendant's "pure silence" about material facts in a business transaction may constitute fraudulent conduct. One such circumstance involves transactions in which the parties stand in a fiduciary relationship.

Common law courts varied widely on the issue of whether a fiduciary relationship exists between corporate insiders and shareholders. Under the so-called "majority rule," a director or officer was said to owe fiduciary duties only to the corporation but not to the individual shareholders of the corporation. Thus, in most jurisdictions, corporate insiders were free to exploit whatever informational advantage they possessed. By contrast, the "minority rule" treated officers and directors as fiduciaries to the shareholders as well as to the corporation. Therefore, as a fiduciary, a traditional insider was obligated to share all material facts in his possession before executing a transaction with an existing shareholder.

Some courts sidestepped the fiduciary duty issue and adopted the "special facts" doctrine, which imposed disclosure duties when one party to a transaction had access to highly significant facts unknown to the other party. For example, in *Strong v. Repide*, 213 U.S. 419 (1909), the Supreme Court granted rescission in a case in which the plaintiff-shareholder had sold her stock to an agent of the defendant-director. The company soon after concluded negotiations to sell valuable real estate to the Philippines government, thereby substantially increasing the worth of the company's shares. The Court held that the company's anticipated real estate transaction and the identity of the true purchaser were material facts that the plaintiff was entitled to know prior to the sale of her securities.

Plaintiffs alleging insider trading under the common law of fraud had other hurdles to scale, even in those jurisdictions that generally adhered to the minority rule or special facts doctrine. Two principles, in particular, limited a court's ability to impose liability for an insider's fraudulent nondisclosure. First, officers and directors were said to owe shareholders a disclosure duty only in face-to-face securities transactions. *See Goodwin v. Agassiz*, 186 N.E. 659, 660 (Mass. 1933) (refusing to recognize the breach of a disclosure duty when the traditional insider's securities transactions were carried out over the Boston Stock Exchange). The other limiting principle was that traditional insiders were regarded as fiduciaries only with respect to those investors with pre-existing relationships with the corporation. Thus, there was nothing to prevent corporate insiders from selling their overvalued stock to investors who did not already own shares in the corporation.

To mitigate these common law limitations, a number of jurisdictions allowed shareholders to institute derivative actions against officers and directors who had used the corporation's confidential information to reap "secret profits" in securities transactions. *See, e.g., Brophy v. Cities Service Co.*, 70 A.2d 5 (Del. Ch. 1949); *Diamond v. Oreamuno*, 248 N.E.2d 910 (N.Y. 1969). Notwithstanding the federal prohibition arising under the anti-fraud provisions in § 10(b) and Rule 10b-5, state courts continue to award recovery in derivative actions for insider trading. *See Kahn v. Kolberg Kravis Roberts & Co., L.P.*, 23 A.3d 831, 840 (Del. 2011) ("we find no reasonable public policy ground to restrict the scope of disgorgement remedy in *Brophy* cases— irrespective of arguably parallel remedies grounded in federal securities law").

§ 7.2.2   EXCHANGE ACT § 16(b)
AND SHORT-SWING PROFITS

Section 16 of the Exchange Act was Congress's initial solution to the problem of insider trading. Section 16(a) imposes a reporting obligation upon every officer or director of a company with an equity security registered under § 12 of the Exchange Act, as well as every person "who is directly or indirectly the beneficial owner of more than 10 percent of any class of any equity security" so registered. Pursuant to this obligation, such high level insiders must file with the SEC an initial report on Form 3 within 10 days of becoming an officer, director, or 10 percent beneficial shareholder of the corporation. When such persons change their beneficial ownership (whether through purchases or sales of the company's equity securities), they must file supplementary reports on a Form 4 within 2 business days.

Short-Swing Profits. The mere obligation to report all purchases and sales in a corporation's equity securities is bound to deter some insiders from trading on the basis of confidential corporate information. But Congress intended the principal deterrent for insider trading to stem from Section 16(b), which makes officers, directors, and 10 percent shareholders liable to the corporation, or to shareholders suing on its behalf, for any profits they obtain from "short-swing" trading of the corporation's stock. Such insiders must disgorge to the corporation, or shareholders suing on its behalf, profits from "short swing" trading of the corporation's stock. A trade is considered a "short swing" trade if it is a purchase and sale, or sale and purchase, of the same security within a six-month period. Section 16(b) does not apply, however, if the stock "was acquired in good faith in connection with a debt previously contracted."

As it relates to insider trading, § 16(b) is both too wide and too narrow: it catches legitimate trades by corporate insiders who lack any knowledge of material nonpublic information, and it ignores those trades that *are* based on inside information when the insider has sold stock that was held for at least six months, or when the insider is patient enough to wait for six months to reap the profit off a new purchase. As the Second Circuit noted, § 16(b) "operates mechanically, and makes no moral distinctions, penalizing technical violators of pure heart, and bypassing corrupt insiders who skirt the letter of the prohibition." *Magma Power Co. v. Dow Chem. Co.*, 136 F.3d 316, 320–321 (2d Cir. 1998).

§ 7.2.3   RULE 10b-5 AND THE PARITY OF INFORMATION THEORY

Like common law fraud and deceit actions brought by shareholders against traditional insiders, the first Rule 10b-5 cases that permitted shareholders to sue a traditional insider for insider trading involved face-to-face security transactions. *See, e.g., Kardon v. Nat'l Gypsum Co.*, 73 F.Supp. 798 (E.D. Pa. 1947) (recognizing a private right of action under § 10(b) and Rule 10b-5 against directors and officers who purchase stock of the corporation from others without disclosing material, non-public information).

The scope of Rule 10b-5 expanded considerably in 1961 when the SEC decided *In re Cady, Roberts & Co.*, 40 SEC 907 (1961). The SEC held that Rule 10b-5 prohibited a broker from selling a company's securities on the NYSE on the basis of confidential bad news about the issuer that the broker had received from one of the issuer's directors. It thereby extended the term "insider" to include persons in positions of access to confidential corporate information and "fraud" to include stock market trading. *See also In re Investors Mgmt. Co.*, 44 SEC 633 (1971) (citing *Cady* and imposing Rule 10b-5 liability against non-insider securities professionals who knew or had reason to know that the information they possessed was confidential).

The view that insider trading over anonymous securities markets constitutes a violation of Rule 10b-5 also won acceptance from the federal courts, particularly the Second Circuit. *See, e.g., SEC v. Texas Gulf Sulphur Co.*, 401 F.2d 833 (2d Cir. 1968) (en banc) (finding Rule 10b-5 violations when directors, officers, and employees of a mining company purchased the company's stock over stock exchanges shortly before news of an ore discovery was disclosed to the public). The *Texas Gulf Sulphur* court made clear that "*anyone* in possession of material inside information must either disclose it to the investing public, or, if he is disabled from disclosing it in order to protect a corporate confidence, or he chooses not to do so, must abstain from trading in or recommending the securities concerned while such inside information remains undisclosed." 401 F.2d at 848 (emphasis added). The court explained that the rule was "based in policy on the justifiable expectation of the securities marketplace that all investors trading on impersonal exchanges have relatively equal access to material information." *Id.* That expansive approach to insider trading liability is often depicted as "the parity of information" theory.

In the wake of *Texas Gulf Sulphur*, federal courts began to recognize an implied private right of action for insider trading in circumstances where the plaintiffs were owed disclosure duties by corporate

insiders. There were, however, differences among
circuits in standing, causation, and damages
requirements. *Compare Moss v. Morgan Stanley,
Inc.*, 719 F.2d 5 (2d Cir. 1983) (denying standing of
plaintiffs who sold stock contemporaneously with
defendants who had purchased company stock based
on information that was stolen from the corporation,
because defendants were not fiduciaries of the
plaintiffs, and therefore did not owe a duty of
disclosure); *Wilson v. Comtech Telecomm. Corp.*, 648
F.2d 88, 93 (2d Cir. 1981) (limiting *Shapiro* and
restricting the plaintiff class to those investors who
traded contemporaneously with the defendants);
*Shapiro v. Merrill Lynch, Pierce, Fenner & Smith,
Inc.*, 495 F.2d 228, 241 (2d Cir. 1974) (recognizing
standing for all persons purchasing shares in
company stock from the date of the insiders' sales
until disclosure was made by the company) *with
Fridrich v. Bradford*, 542 F.2d 307, 318 (6th Cir.
1976) (holding that in the absence of proof of a direct
causal relationship, shareholders who sold stock over
an exchange could not recover from directors who
purchased stock based on inside knowledge).
Congress sidestepped those controversies in 1988
when it added a new § 20A to the Exchange Act,
granting "contemporaneous traders" an express right
of action against persons who have violated the
federal securities laws through illegal insider trading
or tipping. *See* § 7.6.2 *infra*.

§ 7.3 THE CLASSICAL THEORY
OF INSIDER TRADING

In *Chiarella v. United States*, 445 U.S. 222 (1980), the Supreme Court curtailed the SEC's and the Second Circuit's expansive approach to insider trading by emphasizing the need for a fiduciary relationship between the parties to a securities transaction. It held that an employee of a printer handling a company's corporate takeover announcements did not violate § 10(b) and Rule 10b-5 by trading the targets' securities based on information he deduced from the announcement documents. The Court held that although the defendant possessed material, nonpublic information, he had no affirmative duty to disclose prior to trading because he was not "a person in whom the sellers had placed their trust and confidence." *Id.* at 232. Thus, "the element required to make [his] silence fraudulent—a duty to disclose—[was] absent in this case." *Id. Chiarella* thus refused to recognize "a general duty between all participants in market transactions to forgo actions based on material, nonpublic information." *Id.* at 233. But in so doing, the Court acknowledged that a failure to abstain from trading would have been actionable under Rule 10b-5 had the securities purchaser been an officer or director who obtained the material nonpublic information through his service to the corporation.

§ 7.3.1   WHO IS AN INSIDER?

By the very terms of the *Chiarella* majority opinion, the classical theory of insider trading liability applies to officers, directors, and controlling shareholders of the corporation because "the relationship between a corporate insider and the stockholders of his corporation gives rise to a disclosure obligation." 445 U.S. at 227. Courts have also extended the classical theory to non-officer employees of the corporation and to the issuer itself. *See, e.g., McCormick v. Fund Am. Cos.*, 26 F.3d 869, 876 (9th Cir. 1994) (emphasizing that "the corporate issuer in possession of material nonpublic information, must, like other insiders in the same situation, disclose that information to its shareholders or refrain from trading with them").

As we shall see, the classical theory likewise governs analysis of securities trading by tippees of classical insiders (§ 7.3.5 *infra*) as well as trading by temporary agents of the corporations (§ 7.3.6 *infra*).

§ 7.3.2   WHAT IS MATERIAL NONPUBLIC INFORMATION?

An insider's obligation under Rule 10b-5 to "disclose or abstain" attaches only when the information can be said to be both "material" and "nonpublic." As we saw in Chapter 2, information is considered "material" if there is a substantial likelihood that a reasonable investor would consider it important in making an investment decision. *See* § 2.3 *supra* (discussing *Basic Inc. v. Levinson,* 485 U.S. 224 (1988)).

Two approaches are used to determine whether information is "nonpublic." Under the first, set forth in *Texas Gulf Sulphur*, for information to be deemed public it "must have been effectively disclosed in a manner sufficient to insure its availability to the investing public." 401 F.2d at 854. The alternative approach is predicated on the efficient capital markets hypothesis (*see* § 1.13 *supra*) and postulates that information is "public" when it is known by a sufficient number of securities analysts or other professionals in the financial community. *United States v. Libera*, 989 F.2d 596, 601 (2d Cir. 1993) ("The issue is not the number of people who possess it but whether their trading has caused the information to be fully impounded into the price of the particular stock. Once the information is fully impounded in price, such information can no longer be misused by trading because no further profit can be made.").

§ 7.3.3 THE "POSSESSION VS. USE" DEBATE

Courts have disagreed about whether an insider is required to abstain from trading securities while that insider is "in possession of" material nonpublic information, or whether the insider is required to abstain only from trading securities "on the basis of" material nonpublic information. This question is often phrased in terms of whether liability for insider trading under Rule 10b-5 should be determined pursuant to a "knowing possession" test or a "use" test. In *SEC v. Adler,* 137 F.3d 1325 (11th Cir. 1998), and *United States v. Smith*, 155 F.3d 1051 (9th Cir. 1998), two federal courts of appeals confronted this question in the context of insider trading claims against a corporate director (in *Adler*) and a corporate officer (in *Smith*). Both circuits rejected the Commission's "knowing possession" position, holding that Rule 10b-5's disclose or abstain obligation prohibits securities trading only *on the basis of* material nonpublic information. The Second Circuit, however, reached precisely the opposite conclusion in *United States v. Teicher*, 987 F.2d 112 (2d Cir. 1993), but the court's views on the issue of "possession vs. use" constituted dictum rather than holding.

§ 7.3.4   RULE 10b5-1

Rather than reconciling the circuits' conflicting positions through case-by-case adjudication, the SEC in August 2000 opted to use its authority under § 10(b) to promulgate Rule 10b5-1, the SEC's first rule designed to regulate insider trading outside the specific context of tender offers. This rule comes close to endorsing a "knowing possession" standard because it focuses liability on whether a person traded securities while "aware" of material nonpublic information.

Subject to several narrowly drawn affirmative defenses, trading "on the basis of" is defined in Rule 10b5-1(b) as trading by someone who "was aware of the material, nonpublic information." According to the SEC's Adopting Release, Rule 10b5-1(c)'s affirmative defenses are designed to provide "appropriate flexibility to persons who wish to structure securities trading plans and strategies when they are not aware of material nonpublic information, and do not exercise any influence over the transaction once they do become aware of such information." Selective Disclosure and Insider Trading, Exchange Act Release No. 43154 (Aug. 23, 2000).

Rule 10b5-1(c)(1)(ii) makes clear that the availability of affirmative defenses is strictly limited to circumstances in which a contract, plan or instruction to trade is "entered into in good faith and not as part of a plan or scheme to evade the prohibitions of the rule."

<u>Financial Institutions and Firewalls</u>. Financial institutions are generally organized into many separate departments, some of which routinely come into contact with material nonpublic information about securities issuers. To prevent confidential information in one sector of the firm (such as an investment banking department) from being imputed to persons working in another sector (such as a trading department), firms typically erect so-called firewalls. Rule 10b5-1(c)(2) codifies the practice of creating firewalls as a separate affirmative defense available to "non-natural" persons. To invoke the affirmative defense, a firm must demonstrates that: (1) the individual making the investment decision on behalf of the firm to purchase or sell the securities was not aware of the information; and (2) the firm had implemented reasonable policies and procedures, taking into consideration the nature of its business, to ensure that individuals making investment decisions would not violate the laws prohibiting trading on the basis of material

nonpublic information. These policies and procedures may include those that restrict any purchase, sale, and causing any purchase or sale of any security as to which the firm has material nonpublic information, or those that prevent such individuals from becoming aware of such information.

§ 7.3.5 TIPPER-TIPPEE LIABILITY

The Supreme Court elaborated on the scope of tipper-tippee liability in *Dirks v. SEC*, 463 U.S. 646 (1983). The petitioner was a securities analyst employed by a broker-dealer firm. He received information from a former officer of Equity Funding of America, a corporation primarily engaged in selling life insurance. The former insider revealed to the analyst that the company's assets were vastly overstated due to fraudulent corporate practices. The analyst investigated the allegations and several current employees corroborated the former director's account. Although neither the analyst nor his firm had traded in the company's stock, the analyst discussed the information he had obtained with a number of investor-clients. Many of these investor-clients sold their shares and avoided huge losses when Equity Funding's fraud subsequently came to light. The SEC investigated the analyst's "tips" to his clients and initiated disciplinary proceedings against him. The analyst received the sanction of a censure after the SEC determined that he had aided and abetted his client's illegal insider trading under § 10(b) and Rule 10b-5. The SEC (and later the D.C. Circuit) took the position that tippees who receive material nonpublic information from a corporate insider become subject to that insider's disclose or abstain obligation to shareholders.

The Supreme Court reversed and found that the analyst had no duty to abstain from using or conveying to his clients the inside information that he obtained from Equity Funding's former and current employees. The Court reiterated the principle in *Chiarella* that only some persons, in some circumstances, would be barred from trading while in possession of material nonpublic information. Although the typical tippee is a complete stranger to a corporation's shareholders, there are some circumstances under which a tippee owes shareholders a disclosure duty that derives from that of the corporate insider. But in the Court's view, a tippee assumes a fiduciary duty to the shareholders only when the insider has breached a duty of loyalty by disclosing the material nonpublic information and the tippee knows or should know that there has been a breach. The test for that breach of the duty of loyalty is whether the insider personally will benefit, directly or indirectly, from the disclosure. "This requires courts to focus on objective criteria, *i.e.*, whether the insider receives a direct or indirect personal benefit from the disclosure, such as a pecuniary gain or a reputational benefit that will translate into future earnings." *Dirks*, 463 U.S. at 663. The Court further observed that "[t]he elements of fiduciary duty and exploitation of nonpublic information also exist when an insider makes a gift of confidential information to a trading relative or friend." *Id.* at 664.

Under this standard, none of the insiders who provided information to the analyst in *Dirks* violated their duty of loyalty to the company's shareholders. The tippers were motivated by a desire to expose the fraud rather than a desire to receive a monetary or other personal benefit—or to make a gift of valuable information. Thus, there was no derivative fiduciary duty that obliged the analyst and his clients to disclose to Equity Funding shareholders the material nonpublic information they received.

§ 7.3.6   TEMPORARY INSIDERS

In a very important footnote, the *Dirks* Court pointed out that the "disclose or abstain" rule applies as well to temporary insiders of a corporation, such as attorneys, accountants, and investment bankers, who are provided with confidential corporate information. *Dirks*, 463 U.S. at 655 n.14. In the Court's view, these "outsiders may become fiduciaries of the shareholders." *Id.* Yet other than noting that "the relationship [itself] must at least imply such a duty [to keep the disclosed information confidential]," *Dirks* did little to shed light on how else one attains this special status. *Id.* Lower courts must therefore articulate their own standards. *See, e.g., SEC v. Ingram*, 694 F.Supp. 1437 (C.D. Cal. 1988) (temporary insider status accorded to stockbroker who had assisted the company with finding a merger partner, and who had been invited to attended pre-merger negotiations where there was an absolute expectation of confidentiality); *SEC v. Mayhew*, 916 F.Supp. 123, 129 (D. Conn. 1995) (concluding that SEC had failed to establish that a business consultant was the "functional equivalent of a fiduciary"), *aff'd without discussion of this issue*, 121 F.3d 44 (2d Cir. 1997).

§ 7.3.7 SECURITIES ANALYSTS AND THE PROBLEM OF SELECTIVE DISCLOSURE

Issuers and their corporate officials regularly interact with securities analysts, often providing them with publicly available information through telephone conversations, letters, in-person meetings, and other types of communications. And to maintain an active level of interest in their company's securities, corporate officials are often tempted to share with analysts information that has yet to be released to the public. The SEC has taken the position that the practice of selective disclosure "leads to a loss of investor confidence in the integrity of our capital markets." *See* Selective Disclosure and Insider Trading, Exchange Act Release No. 43154 (Aug. 15, 2000), 2000 WL 1201556 at *2. But § 10(b) and Rule 10b-5 generally do not prohibit the practice because *Dirks's* "personal benefit" requirement effectively insulated most communications between corporate executives and securities analysts.

The SEC has filled the regulatory gap left open by the insider trading regime under § 10(b) and Rule 10b-5 by promulgating Regulation FD. As explained more fully in § 7.8 *infra*, Regulation FD prohibits reporting companies from making selective disclosures to analysts and other securities professionals. For the definition of a reporting company, *see* § 1.3 *supra*.

§ 7.3.8   WHAT CONSTITUTES A PERSONAL BENEFIT TO THE TIPPER?

Recall the Supreme Court's observation in *Dirks* that an insider's disclosure of material nonpublic information is fraudulent only when the purported tipper breaches a fiduciary duty of trust and confidence by benefitting personally (directly or indirectly) from the disclosure. Lower courts have recently divided over what the government must prove to establish that a tipper received such a personal benefit. This uncertainty will likely be resolved when the Supreme Court issues its decision in *Salman v. United States*, 136 S.Ct. 899, 2016 WL 207256 (cert. granted, Jan. 19, 2016).

The recent controversy over what constitutes a "personal benefit" began with the Second Circuit's decision in *United States v. Newman*, 773 F.3d 438 (2d Cir. 2014). The case was heard on an appeal brought by two portfolio managers at hedge funds who had been convicted of securities fraud and sentenced to prison. At their trial, the government established that analysts at their hedge funds had obtained advanced earnings-related information from employees at Dell and NVIDIA and then subsequently passed that material nonpublic information on, through a chain of tippees, to the defendants. With respect to the personal benefits obtained by the insiders from their disclosures to the analysts (the first of the links in each tipping chain), the evidence established that the NVIDIA insider had disclosed confidential earnings information to a " 'family friend[ ]' that [he] had met through church."

773 F.3d at 452. The insider at Dell likewise disclosed the confidential information to an analyst he had known "for years, having both attended business school and worked at Dell together." *Id.* The evidence further established that Dell insider "sought career advice and assistance" from his former classmate and that "some of this assistance began before [the insider] began to provide tips about Dell's earnings." *Id.*

The Second Circuit, however, reversed the convictions because it disagreed with the jury's finding that "these facts were sufficient to prove that the tippers derived some benefit from the tip." *Id.* As the court saw it, "[i]f this was a 'benefit,' practically anything would qualify." *Id.* Although it acknowledged *Dirks*'s suggestion that "a personal benefit may be inferred from a personal relationship between the tipper and tippee," the court held that "such an inference is impermissible in the absence of proof of a meaningfully close personal relationship that generates an exchange that is objective, consequential, and represents at least a potential gain of a pecuniary or similarly valuable nature." *Id.* The court also emphasized what it drew as a "fundamental insight" from *Dirks*: "that, in order to form the basis for a fraudulent breach, the personal benefit received in exchange for confidential information must be of some consequence." *Id.* Thus, in the court's view, for an insider's disclosure to constitute a fraudulent tip, the tipper must receive something more than the "ephemeral benefit of the value of [the tippee's] friendship." *Id.* (internal quotation marks omitted).

The Ninth Circuit read *Dirks* quite differently in *United States v. Salman*, 792 F.3d 1087 (9th Cir. 2015), in the context of trading tips passed from an investment banker to his older brother, who traded himself while also sharing the information with the defendant. In the Ninth Circuit's view, insistence of proof of a tangible benefit would require courts "to depart from the clear holding of *Dirks* that the element of breach of fiduciary duty is met where an 'insider makes a gift of confidential information to a trading relative or friend.'" *Salman*, 792 F.3d at 1093 (quoting *Dirks*, 463 U.S. at 663). And where there is evidence of a gift, reading *Dirks* to also require a "tangible benefit" would create a nonsensical loophole: "a corporate insider or other person in possession of confidential and proprietary information would be free to disclose that information to her relatives" or friends, and "they would be free to trade on it, provided only that she asked for no tangible compensation in return." *Id.* at 1093-94. The Ninth Circuit therefore concluded that "[p]roof that the insider disclosed material nonpublic information with the intent to benefit a trading relative or friend is sufficient to establish the breach of fiduciary duty element of insider trading." *Id.* at 1094.

§ 7.4   THE MISAPPROPRIATION THEORY

In *United States v. O'Hagan,* 521 U.S. 642 (1997), the Supreme Court addressed whether a securities purchaser, who owed no disclosure duties to the sellers of those securities, nonetheless violates § 10(b) and Rule 10b-5 by trading on the basis of material nonpublic information that he misappropriated from his employer and its client. The defendant, O'Hagan, was a partner at a law firm that represented a bidder regarding a potential tender offer for a target's stock. During his firm's representation of the bidder and before the public announcement of the tender offer, the defendant secretly purchased call options and common shares of the target. He later realized a profit of more than $4 million when he exercised those options and sold his shares upon the bidder's tender offer announcement.

The Supreme Court held that insider trading liability may be predicated on a "misappropriation" theory, which stands as a "complementary" alternative to the classical theory. Under the misappropriation theory, a person commits fraud and thereby violates § 10(b) and Rule 10b-5 when he misappropriates confidential information for securities trading purposes, in breach of a fiduciary duty owed to the source of the information. In contrast to the classical theory of insider trading, which predicates liability on a fiduciary relationship between the trader (or tipper) and the shareholders of the issuing company, the misappropriation theory premises liability on a fiduciary's deception of those who entrusted him with access to confidential information. In this case, O'Hagan owed a duty of trust and confidence to his law firm and its client, and he breached that duty when he secretly traded on the basis of their material nonpublic information. The Court made clear, however, that secrecy was key to liability: "Because the deception essential to the misappropriation theory involves feigning fidelity to the source of information, if the fiduciary discloses to the source that he plans to trade on the nonpublic information, there is no 'deceptive device' and thus no § 10(b) violation—although the fiduciary-turned-trader may remain liable under state law for breach of a duty of loyalty." *O'Hagan,* 521 U.S. at 655.

§ 7.4.1   IDENTIFYING FIDUCIARY-LIKE RELATIONSHIPS

Courts have applied the misappropriation theory in cases involving a broad spectrum of fiduciary or fiduciary-like relationships. *See, e.g., United States v. Willis,* 778 F.Supp. 205, 209 (S.D.N.Y. 1991) (upholding the misappropriation theory against a psychiatrist who traded stock on the basis of material nonpublic information told to him by a patient); *SEC v. Falbo,* 14 F.Supp.2d 508, 523 (S.D.N.Y. 1998) (stating that while a contractor handling electrical work for corporations is not a traditional fiduciary, he was nonetheless placed "in a position of trust and confidence" which he violated when he "used for personal benefit information obtained during the course of his association"). Cases on this issue are often difficult to reconcile. *Compare United States v. Kim,* 184 F.Supp.2d 1006 (N.D. Cal. 2002) (member of the "Young Presidents Association," a national organization of company presidents under the age of 50, did not owe a duty of trust and confidence to fellow club member, despite the club's written requirement that all members must comply with a "confidentiality commitment") *with SEC v. Kirch,* 263 F.Supp.2d 1144, 1147-1150 (N.D. Ill. 2003) (member of a business roundtable owed a "duty of loyalty and confidentiality" to a fellow member where there was an "express policy and understanding that such [nonpublic business] matters were indeed to be kept confidential").

Particularly thorny issues have arisen in the context of misappropriations by family members. *See, e.g., United States v. Reed*, 601 F.Supp. 685 (S.D.N.Y. 1985) (applying misappropriation theory against son who traded on the basis of nonpublic information obtained from father, a corporate director), *rev'd in part on other grounds*, 773 F.2d 477 (2d Cir. 1985); *United States v. Chestman*, 947 F.2d 551, 568 (2d Cir. 1991) (en banc) (reversing conviction of securities broker on the ground that his alleged tipper did not owe a duty of trust and confidence to his wife who had shared with him confidential information about an upcoming transaction involving the sale of her family's company); *SEC v. Yun*, 327 F.3d 1263, 1272 (11th Cir. 2003) (disagreeing with *Chestman* and reasoning that a court's insistence "on either an express agreement of confidentiality or a strictly defined fiduciary-like relationship" would ignore "the many instances in which a spouse has a reasonable expectation of confidentiality").

§ 7.4.2 RULE 10b5-2

Recognizing the uncertainty surrounding whether a particular relationship qualifies as "fiduciary-like," the SEC in 2000 promulgated Rule 10b5-2. Subsection (b) of the rule provides that a person trading or tipping on the basis of material nonpublic information breaches a duty of "trust or confidence" in any one of three circumstances:

(1) when the person receiving the information has agreed to maintain that information in confidence;

(2) when the persons involved in the communication "have a history, pattern, or practice of sharing confidences" that results in a reasonable expectation of confidentiality; and

(3) when the person receives such information from a spouse, parent, child or sibling, unless the person can show affirmatively, based on the particular facts and circumstances of that family relationship, that "he or she neither knew nor reasonably should have known that the person who was the source of the information expected that the person would keep the information confidential."

So far, challenges to Rule 10b5-2's validity have met with mixed success. Compare *United States v. Corbin*, 729 F.Supp.2d 607, 616 (S.D.N.Y. 2010) (holding that Rule 10b5-2(b)(3)'s rebuttable presumption of a fiduciary-like relationship between spouses is a reasonable exercise of the SEC's rulemaking authority under § 10(b) and does not violate defendant's constitutional right to due process) with *SEC v. Cuban,* 634 F.Supp.2d 713, 730–731 (N.D. Tex. 2009) (dismissing complaint and holding that Rule 10b5-2(b)(1) is invalid and unenforceable insofar as it predicates liability on a defendant's mere agreement to maintain information in confidence), *vacated and remanded*, 620 F.3d 551 (5th Cir. 2010). Yet the lower court in *Cuban* also held that a fiduciary-like relationship between a defendant and the source of the information was not essential to liability under the misappropriation theory because the necessary element of deception could be established by a breach of a promise "not to trade on or otherwise use the information for personal benefit." 634 F.Supp.2d at 730. On appeal, the Fifth Circuit vacated the judgment of dismissal and remanded the case for discovery because, in its view, there was "more than a plausible basis to find that the understanding between the [defendant and the source] was that he was not to trade, that it was more than a simple confidentiality agreement." *Cuban*, 620 F.3d at 557. But, at least at this juncture, the Fifth Circuit did nothing to disturb the district court's holdings with respect to Rule 10b5-2(b)(1)'s validity.

§ 7.4.3 TIPPER-TIPPEE LIABILITY UNDER THE MISAPPROPRIATION THEORY

The defendant-attorney in *O'Hagan* had misappropriated confidential client information to personally profit from his own securities trading. Accordingly, the Court had no occasion to address directly the application of the misappropriation theory to cases involving tippee trading. Prior to *O'Hagan*, tippees who traded on the basis of misappropriated information were viewed as co-participants in the misappropriator's breach of fiduciary duty. Thus, tippees incurred Rule 10b-5 liability for their own trading when they knew or should have known that their tippers had breached a fiduciary duty owed to the initial source of the information.

One decision that focuses on this question post-*O'Hagan* is *United States v. Falcone*, 257 F.3d 226 (2d Cir. 2001). The Second Circuit acknowledged that was not present where a tipper conveyed confidential information to a third party but did not himself trade. *Id.* at 233. The court, however, maintained that "*O'Hagan* did not purport to set forth the sole combination of factors necessary to establish the requisite connection in all contexts." *Id.* In the court's view, "*O'Hagan*'s requirement that the misappropriated information 'ordinarily' be valuable due to 'its utility in securities trading' appears to be a more generally applicable factor in determining whether section 10(b)'s 'in connection with' requirement is satisfied." *Id.*

§ 7.4.4   DECEPTIVE ACQUISITION OF MATERIAL NONPUBLIC INFORMATION

In *SEC v. Dorozhko*, 574 F.3d 42 (2d Cir. 2009), the Second Circuit held that when a securities trader makes an affirmative misrepresentation as a means of acquiring material, nonpublic information, no breach of fiduciary duty is necessary to find a violation under § 10(b) and Rule 10b-5. The defendant in *Dorozhko* was a computer hacker who obtained material, nonpublic information and then traded on the basis of that information. Although the hacker clearly misappropriated the information, he did not stand in any type of fiduciary-like relationship with its source.

The Second Circuit rejected the district court's view that *Chiarella* and *O'Hagan* require deception by a fiduciary for insider trading to constitute a violation of § 10(b) and Rule 10b-5. The Second Circuit contrasted fraud by silence, which requires the parties to stand in a fiduciary-like relationship, from fraud through an affirmative misstatement. In the court's view, "[e]ven if a person does not have a fiduciary duty to 'disclose or abstain from trading,' there is nonetheless an affirmative obligation in commercial dealings not to mislead." 574 F.3d at 49. The Second Circuit remanded the case to the district court to consider whether the computer hacking in *Dorozhko* was, in fact, "deceptive." *Id.* at 51. Upon remand, the court granted the SEC summary judgment after the motion went unopposed. *See* SEC Litigation Release No. 21465 (Mar. 29, 2010).

§ 7.5 RULE 14e-3—INSIDER TRADING IN A TENDER OFFER

Corporate transactions involving tender offers frequently present tempting opportunities to profit unlawfully from the use of material nonpublic information. Although "tender offer" is not defined in § 14(e) of the Exchange Act or in Rule 14e-3, the term typically refers to a publicized offer, sometimes by a hostile bidder, to buy shares of a publicly owned company at an advertised price within a confined time period.

Unlike the classical and misappropriation theories of insider trading liability under § 10(b) and Rule 10b-5, no showing of a breach of fiduciary duty is required for an insider trading violation under § 14(e) of the Exchange Act and Rule 14e-3 thereunder. In *United States v. O'Hagan*, 521 U.S. 642 (1997), in addition to violations of § 10(b) and Rule 10b-5, the government charged the defendant with, and the jury convicted him for, illegal trading under § 14(e) and Rule 14e-3(a). The Supreme Court held that, "to the extent relevant to this case," the SEC "did not exceed" its rulemaking authority under § 14(e). 521 U.S. at 667. That provision grants the SEC the authority to promulgate prophylactic measures prohibiting acts that are not themselves fraudulent under the common law or § 10(b), as long as the measures are reasonably designed to prevent fraudulent acts in connection with tender offers. And in the Court's view, Rule 14e-3(a) serves "to prevent the type of misappropriation charged against O'Hagan." *Id*. at 676.

§ 7.5.1   THE SUBSTANTIAL STEP REQUIREMENT

Rule 14e-3(a)'s prohibitions apply only when "the offering person" has "taken a substantial step or steps to commence, or has commenced a tender offer." The SEC has defined "substantial steps" as "activities which substantially facilitate the offer" engaged in after "the formulation of a plan or proposal to make a tender offer by the offeror or person(s) acting on behalf of the offeror." Tender Offers, Exchange Act Release No. 17120, 20 SEC

Docket 1241, 1248 n.23 (Sept. 4, 1980). Courts typically adhere to this broad construction. *See SEC v. Ginsburg,* 362 F.3d 1292, 1304 (11th Cir. 2004) (requirement was met where "there was a meeting between executives, which was followed by due diligence procedures, a confidentiality agreement, and by a meeting between" the defendant and an executive of the target); *SEC v. Mayhew,* 121 F.3d 44, 53 (2d Cir. 1997) (noting that retaining a consulting firm, signing a confidentiality agreement, and holding meetings between company officials constitute "substantial steps"); *SEC v. Maio,* 51 F.3d 623, 636 (7th Cir. 1995) (officials in a meeting "much more serious than any previous discussion between the parties" satisfies substantial step requirement); *SEC v. Musella,* 578 F.Supp. 425, 443–444 (S.D.N.Y. 1984) (retaining a law firm constitutes a "substantial step").

§ 7.5.2   KNOWLEDGE ON THE PART OF THE DEFENDANT

Several courts have held that a defendant does not need to know that the material nonpublic information in his possession pertains to a tender offer for liability to attach under Rule 14e-3(a). *See, e.g., United States v. O'Hagan,* 139 F.3d 641, 650 (8th Cir. 1998) (on remand) (stating that Rule 14e-3(a) "does not require the defendant to have knowledge of [the substantial steps]. Instead, the defendant need only 'know[ ] or have reason to know' that the material information is 'nonpublic and has been acquired directly or indirectly from' the tender offeror in some way."); *SEC v. Ginsburg,* 362 F.3d 1292, 1304

(11th Cir. 2004) (stating that "Rule 14e-3, by its terms, does not require that the offender know or have reason to know that the information relates to a tender offer, so long as the information in fact does relate to a tender offer and the offender knows or has reason to know the information is nonpublic and was acquired by a person with the required status"). This issue, however, may be resolved differently in the context of a criminal proceeding. *See United States v. Cassese*, 290 F.Supp. 2d 443, 450 (S.D.N.Y. 2003) (emphasizing the requirement of willfulness in Exchange Act § 32(a) and concluding that "since there is 'no general duty to refrain from trading on material nonpublic information,' the defendant must have believed that the information related to, or most likely related to, a tender offer in order to impose criminal liability"), *aff'd on other grounds*, 428 F.3d 92 (2d Cir. 2005).

§ 7.6   LEGISLATIVE EFFORTS BY CONGRESS

Before 1984, the SEC had relatively limited ways to enforce federal prohibitions against insider trading. Enforcement actions brought against persons for insider trading—whether litigated or settled—typically resulted in an injunction against future violations and an order that the defendant disgorge the ill-gotten profit gained or loss avoided from the illegal transactions. Alternatively, if the case involved insider trading by a securities professional, such as a broker-dealer or investment adviser, the SEC could pursue an administrative action and impose sanctions including a censure, a temporary suspension, or a permanent bar from the industry. The DOJ could also prosecute the defendant in federal court and typically seek a prison sentence. The SEC, however, could only refer matters to the DOJ for criminal prosecution, as the SEC does not have the power to seek criminal sanctions.

Recognizing that these remedies resulted in an unacceptably low level of deterrence, Congress sought to expand the arsenal of remedies available in insider trading cases with the enactment of the Insider Trading Sanctions Act of 1984 (ITSA) and the Insider Trading and Securities Fraud Enforcement Act of 1988 (ITSFEA).

More recent legislative efforts involving insider trading took form in the Sarbanes-Oxley Act (in the context of pension blackout periods) and with the Stop Trading on Congressional Knowledge (STOCK) Act of 2012.

§ 7.6.1   THE INSIDER TRADING SANCTIONS ACT OF 1984

<u>Treble Penalty Provision</u>. ITSA's most important provision allowed the SEC to seek in federal district court a civil penalty of up to three times the profit gained or loss avoided through a defendant's illegal insider trading or tipping. This penalty is clearly in addition to any disgorgement or criminal fine that may also be ordered. ITSA's civil penalty provision is now set out in § 21A of the Exchange Act.

<u>Options Trading</u>. ITSA also clarified the law of insider trading on options by adding a new § 20(d) to

the Exchange Act. § 20(d) specifies that where trading or tipping on an issuer's securities would violate the Exchange Act, so too would a trade or tip that resulted in the purchase or sale of an option or similar right with respect to that security. Thus, option traders were put on equal footing with shareholders, in terms of their ability to be protected from those with access to material nonpublic information.

§ 7.6.2   THE INSIDER TRADING AND SECURITIES FRAUD ENFORCEMENT ACT OF 1988

With ITSA in place, the SEC quickly escalated its enforcement efforts with respect to insider trading. Yet a number of high-profile scandals in the mid-1980s prompted Congress to respond to the SEC's claim that further measures of deterrence and enforcement were needed. This legislative response took the form of ITSFEA—the Insider Trading and Securities Fraud Enforcement Act of 1988.

Liability for "Controlling Persons". One of ITSFEA's most important provisions extended the treble penalty provision in what is now § 21A to those persons or entities who "control" a person found liable for illegal trading or tipping. Under § 21A(a)(1)(B), the SEC may seek a penalty in federal district court against a controlling person if such controlling person knew or recklessly disregarded the fact that the controlled person was likely to engage in the prohibited acts and failed to take appropriate steps to prevent such acts before they occurred, or if he knowingly or recklessly failed to establish, maintain, or enforce any policy or procedure required under § 15(f) of the Exchange Act or § 204A of the Inv. Advisers Act and the failure substantially contributed to the occurrence of the prohibited acts. Section 21A(3) provides that a court shall determine the penalty imposed on a controlling person "in light of the facts and circumstances," but that it "shall not exceed the greater of $1,000,000 [now 1.2 million (adjusted for inflation)], or three times the amount of the profit gained or loss avoided as a result of such controlled person's violation." Section 21A(b)(2) also explicitly provides that no person shall be subject to a penalty solely by reason of employing someone who violated insider trading laws.

Private Right of Action for Contemporaneous Traders. ITSFEA also added § 20A to the Exchange Act, a provision that establishes an express private right of action for violations of the federal securities laws involving illegal insider trading or tipping. Section 20A eliminates the need for private plaintiffs to show that the insider trader owed them a disclosure duty. Instead, plaintiffs have to establish that they purchased or sold the securities at issue contemporaneously and the defendant violated insider trading laws. Congress chose not to define the term "contemporaneously," preferring instead to rely on the definition that had developed through the case law.

Today, most courts agree that a plaintiff trades "contemporaneously" by trading on the same day or no more than a few days after an illegal trade. Just how many days after is an issue of some dispute. *Compare In re Oxford Health Plans, Inc., Sec. Litig.*, 187 F.R.D. 133, 144 (S.D.N.Y. 1999) (concluding that "[f]ive trading days is a reasonable period between the insider's sales and the plaintiff's purchase to be considered contemporaneous") *with Backman v. Polaroid Corp.*, 540 F.Supp. 667, 671 (D. Mass. 1982) (concluding that purchases two business days after defendant's sales were not contemporaneous). Section 20A also places several limitations on the amount of a defendant's liability. First, § 20A(b)(1) caps the total amount of available damages to "the profit gained or loss avoided in the transaction or transactions that are the subject of the violation." Second, Section 20A(b)(2) provides that any funds that were paid to the SEC as disgorgement may be offset by the "total amount of damages imposed against any person" for the same transaction or transactions. Finally, § 20A(b)(3) clarifies that "[n]o person shall be liable under this section solely by reason of employing another person who is liable under this section, but the liability of a controlling person under this section shall be subject to [Section 20(a)]."

Enhanced Criminal Penalties. ITSFEA amended the Exchange Act in other significant ways. It increased the individual criminal fine available under § 32(a) to a maximum of $1,000,000 and raised the maximum available prison term from 5 to 10 years. For non-natural persons, it increased the maximum criminal fine to 2.5 million. The Sarbanes-Oxley Act subsequently amended § 32(a) to increase the maximum prison sentence to 20 years, and to increase the maximum fine to $5,000,000 for individuals and $25,000,000 for non-natural persons.

Since the enactment of ITSA and ITSFEA, Congress has expanded substantially the SEC's arsenal of remedies in enforcement actions for violations of the federal securities laws including, but certainly not limited to, insider trading. Those legislative efforts unfolded in the Securities Enforcement Remedies and Penny Stock Reform Act of 1990, the Sarbanes Oxley Act of 2002, and the Dodd-Frank Act of 2010, which are discussed extensively in § 9.5.2 *infra*.

§ 7.6.3 INSIDER TRADING DURING PENSION BLACKOUT PERIODS

There is one provision in the SOX that specifically references "insider trading." SOX § 306, which is now codified at 15 U.S.C. § 7244, grew out of the Enron/WorldCom scandals. The provision prohibits any director or executive officer of an issuer of any equity security, directly or indirectly, from purchasing, selling, or otherwise acquiring any security during any blackout period with respect to such security if such person acquires such security in connection with his or her service or employment as a director or executive officer. A "blackout period" is a period of at least 3 consecutive business days during which the majority of company employees are not allowed to make alterations to their retirement/investment plans. As a remedy for breaches of its trading prohibition, § 306(a)(2) provides that an action to recover the profits of the director or executive officer may be instituted at law or in equity in any court of competent jurisdiction by the issuer or on behalf of the issuer if the issuer fails to bring such a suit within 60 days.

§ 7.6.4   THE STOP TRADING ON CONGRESSIONAL KNOWLEDGE (STOCK) ACT

In the Stop Trading on Congressional Knowledge (STOCK) Act of 2012, Pub. L. No. 112–105, Congress sought to clarify the law of insider trading as it pertained to securities transactions by its own members and their staffs. The Act explicitly states that members of Congress and congressional employees, as well as all officers and employees in the executive and judicial branches of the federal government, "are not exempt from the insider trading prohibitions arising under the securities laws, including Section 10(b) of the Securities Exchange Act of 1934 and Rule 10b-5 thereunder." §§ 4(a), 9(b). The Act also added a new § 21A(g) and (h) to the Exchange Act. These provisions make clear that all federal officials, including members of Congress, owe "a duty arising from a relationship of trust and confidence" to the United States Government and its citizens with respect to material nonpublic information obtained in connection with their government service. Section 21A(g) further specifies that members of Congress and congressional employees owe that duty to Congress itself.

§ 7.7 LITIGATING INSIDER TRADING CASES

In criminal litigation, the DOJ must establish the defendant's guilt beyond a reasonable doubt. The SEC's burden in a civil enforcement action is a lower one: liability is established upon a showing of a preponderance of evidence. In either context, insider trading cases often raise difficult questions of proof because evidence that a trader was aware of material nonpublic information at the time of a transaction is often in the sole control of the trader or any alleged tipper. The SEC and the DOJ often have no choice but make their case circumstantially. *See SEC v. Moran*, 922 F.Supp. 867, 890 (S.D.N.Y. 1996) (observing that "[t]he presentation of circumstantial evidence is a well-accepted method" for proving an insider trading case, but finding that the SEC failed to prove that an employee of an investment bank tipped his father to material nonpublic information regarding a potential merger). Although the SEC may work with criminal prosecutors to seek court-orders for wiretaps based on a showing of probable cause, (as it did in connection with the investigation and prosecution of hedge fund trader Raj Rajaratnam and a host of defendants in related actions), wiretap evidence of illegal tipping and trading activity is likely to remain the exception rather than the rule.

§ 7.7.1 SUSPICIOUS TRADING AS PROOF OF POSSESSION

It is well established that suspicious trading activity (in terms of timing and/or amount) can provide circumstantial evidence of possession. But at least one court has concluded that suspicious trading by itself does not give rise to an inference of possession. *See SEC v. Truong*, 98 F.Supp. 2d 1086, 1097 (N.D. Cal. 2000) ("Allowing the SEC to tell a jury that 'because the [defendant's] trading was suspicious, the [defendant] must have possessed some material nonpublic information,' would relieve the SEC of its burden to identify the information, prove its materiality, and prove possession and use by the [defendant].").

§ 7.7.2   USING CIRCUMSTANTIAL EVIDENCE TO ESTABLISH SCIENTER

Even in cases in which it is easy to establish that the defendant was aware of material, nonpublic information at the time of his trade, liability under Rule 10b-5 will attach only if it can also be shown that the defendant acted with "scienter," a "mental state embracing intent to deceive, manipulate, or defraud." *Ernst & Ernst v. Hochfelder*, 425 U.S. 185, 193 n.12 (1976). This showing is generally made in insider trading cases through proof that the defendant knew, or was reckless in not knowing, that the information in his possession was both material and nonpublic. And in tipping cases, the defendant-tippee must also have known or should have known that the tipped information stemmed from a breach of duty on the part of the tipper. Not surprisingly, the government often uses evidence of uncharacteristically large, speculative, or otherwise suspicious trading in proving the defendant's scienter. *See, e.g., SEC v. Warde*, 151 F.3d 42, 48 (2d

Cir. 1998) (noting that co-defendants tipper and tippee "engaged in uncharacteristic, substantial and exceedingly risky investments in [ ] warrants shortly after speaking with one another, suggesting that they discussed not only the inside information, but also the best way to profit from it"); *SEC v. Willis*, 777 F.Supp. 1165, 1173 (S.D.N.Y. 1991) (stating that scienter was plead sufficiently with allegation in complaint concerning "the volume and timing of the trading"); *SEC v. Musella*, 748 F.Supp. 1028, 1039 (S.D.N.Y. 1989) (inferring scienter in part from "the amounts involved and the financing of the trades").

§ 7.8 REGULATION FD

The SEC adopted Regulation Fair Disclosure (FD) in August 2000. Codified at 17 C.F.R. § 243.100 et. seq., the rules are predicated on the view that all investors should have access to an issuer's material disclosures at the same time. *See* Selective Disclosure and Insider Trading, Exchange Act Release No. 43154 (Aug. 15, 2000). But Regulation FD does not categorize the practice of selective disclosure as a fraudulent act or device under § 10(b) and Rule 10b-5. Instead, Regulation FD was promulgated pursuant to Exchange Act § 13(a), which empowers the SEC to regulate the disclosure practices of reporting companies (a term defined in § 1.3 *supra*).

Rule 100 of Regulation FD sets forth a "general rule regarding selective disclosure." As summarized in the SEC's adopting release, the rule requires that whenever:

(1)   an issuer, or person acting on its behalf,

(2)   discloses material nonpublic information,

(3)   to certain enumerated persons (in general, securities market professionals or holders of the issuer's securities who may well trade on the basis of the information),

(4)   the issuer must make public disclosure of that same information

    (a)   simultaneously (for intentional disclosures), or

    (b)   promptly (for nonintentional disclosures).

Accordingly, while Regulation FD does not automatically require covered issuers to promptly disclose all material events as they occur, it does require, as its adopting release makes clear, that when an issuer chooses to disclose material nonpublic information to a person covered by the regulation, the issuer must do so in a manner that provides widespread public disclosure, rather than through selective disclosure to a favored few. Selective disclosures, however, are permissible if the recipients of the information agree to retain the confidentiality of any information imparted.

An issuer may satisfy Regulation FD's requirements for a "public disclosure" by filing a Form 8-K with the SEC or by disseminating "the information through another method (or combination of methods) of disclosure that is reasonably designed to provide broad, non-exclusionary distribution of the information to the public." Rule 101(e).

Failure to comply with Regulation FD subjects the issuer to a host of sanctions, including cease-and-desist orders, civil injunctions, and monetary penalties. The SEC may also initiate enforcement actions against the company officials responsible for causing (or aiding and abetting) the violation. Note, however, that Rule 102 of Regulation FD states specifically that failure to make a public disclosure required solely by Rule 100 would not be deemed to be a violation of Rule 10b-5.

The SEC has initiated a dozen or so enforcement actions charging securities issuers and/or their corporate executives with violations of Regulation FD. In *SEC v. Siebel Systems, Inc.*, 384 F.Supp. 2d 694 (S.D.N.Y. 2005), the only Regulation FD proceeding that was litigated rather than settled, the court held that the allegations in the SEC's complaint did not support its claim that the defendants had privately disclosed material nonpublic information. In doing so, it ruled that neither reasonable inferences nor generalized descriptions based on previous public statements would constitute new material information. A more demanding standard "could compel companies to discontinue any spontaneous communications so that the content of any intended communication may be examined by a lexicologist to ensure that the proposed statement discloses the exact information in the same form as was publicly disclosed." 384 F.Supp. 2d at 705. The court also held that while stock movement is a relevant factor in determining whether the information disclosed is material, it is not dispositive. Thus, the "mere fact that analysts might have considered [the] private statements significant is not, standing alone, a basis to infer that Regulation FD was violated." *Id.* at 707. The court acknowledged, however, that material nonpublic information need not be conveyed as verbal or written statements: "[t]acit communications, such as a wink, nod, or a thumbs up or down gesture, may give rise to a Regulation FD violation." *Id.* at 708 n.14.

CHAPTER 8
MARKET MANIPULATION

§ 8.1 INTRODUCTION

The term "market manipulation," according to the Supreme Court, "connotes intentional or willful conduct designed to deceive or defraud investors by controlling or artificially affecting the price of securities," *Ernst & Ernst v. Hochfelder*, 425 U.S. 185, 199 (1976). That definition, however, raises many more questions than it settles. For example, what, precisely, does it mean to "control" the price of a security? And how is it possible to ascertain whether a security is trading at an "artificial" price? Even more basically, what is the difference between an artificially and a non-artificially priced security?

Courts must establish the contours of the terms "manipulation" and "manipulative" because they appear in, but are not defined by, the federal securities laws. The terms are set out in the titles of § 9 ("Manipulation of Security Prices") and § 10 ("Regulation of the Use of Manipulative and Deceptive Devices") of the Exchange Act and are referenced in Exchange Act §§ 10(b), 14(e), and 15(c).

On three separate occasions, the Supreme Court has emphasized that manipulation is "virtually a term of art when used in connection with securities markets." *See Schreiber v. Burlington Northern, Inc.*, 472 U.S. 1, 6 (1985); *Santa Fe Indus., Inc. v. Green*, 430 U.S. 462, 476 (1977); *Hochfelder*, 425 U.S. at 199. The Court has also stated that the "term refers generally to practices, such as wash sales, matched orders, or rigged prices, that are intended to mislead investors by artificially affecting market activity." *Schreiber*, 472 U.S. at 6 (quoting *Sante Fe*, 430 U.S. at 476).

This Chapter starts by providing several examples of manipulative acts and practice (§ 8.2 *infra*). It then focuses on three distinct types of manipulative activity: securities transactions that create a false impression of active trading (§ 8.3 *infra*); actual securities trading that is conducted for a manipulative purpose (§ 8.4 *infra*); and misleading recommendations and false statements made about particular securities (§ 8.5 *infra*)—conduct that forms the basis of schemes known as "scalping" (§ 8.5.1 *infra*) and "pump and dumps" or "distort and shorts" (§ 8.5.2 *infra*).

§ 8.2 MANIPULATIVE ACTS AND PRACTICES—EXAMPLES

The types of manipulative conduct and schemes that have captured the attention of securities regulators have varied markedly over time. When the federal securities laws were first enacted in 1933 and 1934, Congress's desire to eradicate manipulative activity from the securities markets was propelled, in large part, by testimony and reports of stock pools and other conspiratorial trading schemes thought to have contributed to the stock market crash a few years earlier. Typically, the pools operated to effectuate a series of transactions in a particular security that created the illusion of rapidly rising prices, and the operators would then systematically unload the security to the unsuspecting public before the price dropped and their scam was exposed.

Boiler room operations became a principal concern in the 1950s, and securities regulators sought to slow down, or put out of business altogether, those unscrupulous broker-dealers who used high pressure (and generally misleading) sales tactics over the telephone to generate market activity in stocks of fledgling companies.

In the 1980s, with the scandals that made Michael Milken, Ivan Boesky, and Dennis Levine virtually household names, attention was focused on Wall Street and the staggering profits that could be generated in the securities markets through manipulative activity.

In contrast to these well-known defendants, many of today's market manipulation cases involve far more ordinary types of characters—auto mechanics, tree trimmers, and even law school students—who have managed to use the Internet to perpetrate widespread schemes in a manner that would have been unimaginable to the drafters of the Exchange Act.

Yet practices on Wall Street also continue to occupy the enforcement agenda of the Securities and Exchange Commission (the SEC) and the Department of Justice (the DOJ) as well as the Financial Industry Regulatory Authority (FINRA). In 2003, these federal regulators, together with the Attorneys General from all fifty states, entered into a historic "global settlement" with twelve of the nation's largest investment banks, resolving charges that the firms engaged in fraud and market manipulation through questionable IPO allocation practices and conflicts of interest affecting securities analysts' research reports.

In the aftermath of the 2008 financial crisis, the SEC and other securities regulators turned their attention toward allegations that massive short selling was largely responsible for the sharp declines in the stock prices of the nation's largest financial firms. Some commentators even went so far as to blame manipulative short sellers for the ultimate demise of Bear Stearns (subsequently acquired by J.P. Morgan Chase) and Lehman Brothers (which, prior to its bankruptcy in 2008, was the fourth largest investment bank in the US).

The most recent wave of anti-manipulative enforcement activity has been directed at market abuses pertaining to algorithmic trading. As detailed in Michael Lewis's bestselling book *Flash Boys* (2014), high-frequency securities trading carries with it a dark side, and high profile investigations by the DOJ and the SEC, together with the Commodity Futures Trading Commission (the CFTC) and the New York attorney general, have resulted in a series of charges against several high-frequency trading firms and their traders. Most of these cases involve rapid-fire trades that manipulated the closing share prices of thousands of publicly traded companies during the final seconds of a trading day.

§ 8.3 TRANSACTIONS THAT CREATE THE APPEARANCE OF ACTIVE TRADING

When a person's securities trading creates a false impression that multiple buyers and sellers are actively engaging in securities transactions, the separate concept of market manipulation can simply be viewed as a subcategory of fraud and deception. That is, § 10(b)'s prohibition of deception "in connection with the purchase or sale of any security" (*see* § 2.1 *supra*), encompasses affirmative acts as well as fraudulent statements or material omissions. *See Stoneridge Inv. Partners, LLC v. Scientific-Atlanta, Inc.*, 552 U.S. 148, 158 (2008). (holding that "[c]onduct itself can be deceptive;" there need not be "a specific oral or written statement before there could be liability under § 10(b) or Rule 10b-5").

Examples of deceptive acts that do not involve false or misleading statements are quite common outside of the context of securities transactions: the wolf in "Little Red Riding Hood" engaged in deception when he dressed up as the girl's grandmother; a car salesman engages in deception when he turns back the odometer of the used car he is trying to sell; and the teenager engages in deception when she hands a bartender the driver's license of her 21-year-old sister in exchange for a Budweiser.

Fictitious securities transactions—such as wash sales and matched orders—are likewise a variation of fraud by conduct rather than by false or misleading words.

§ 8.3.1　SECTION 9(a) OF THE EXCHANGE ACT

Section 9(a)(1) of the Exchange Act expressly proscribes "wash sales" and "matched orders" as well as a number of other practices designed to create the appearance of active securities trading. As the Court explained in *Hochfelder*, wash sales are "transactions involving no change in beneficial ownership" and matched orders are "orders for the purchase [or] sale of a security that are entered with the knowledge that orders of substantially the same size, at substantially the same time and price, have been or will be entered by the same or different persons for the sale/purchase of such security." 425 U.S. at 205 n.25. Section 9(a)(1) includes an element of specific intent, namely, that the wash sales or matched orders be engaged in "*[f]or the purpose of* creating a false or misleading appearance of active trading * * * or a false or misleading appearance with respect to the market for any such security" (emphasis added).

A catch-all provision in § 9(a)(2) makes it unlawful to "effect, alone or with [one] or more other persons, a series of transactions in any security other than a government security * * * creating actual or apparent active trading in such security, or raising or depressing the price of such security, *for the purpose of* inducing the purchase or sale of such security by others" (emphasis added). Note again § 9(a)(2)'s element of specific intent.

As initially drafted, § 9(a)'s prohibitions were limited to acts and practices involving securities listed on national securities exchanges. In the Dodd-Frank Act of 2010, however, Congress substantially broadened § 9(a)'s reach by extending the provision to trading in all securities except government securities.

In addition to civil enforcement actions by the SEC and criminal prosecutions by the DOJ, persons who violate § 9(a) can be subject to private litigation under § 9(f). That provision states that any person who "willfully participates in any act or transaction" in violation of § 9 shall be liable "to any person who shall purchase or sell any security at a price which was affected by such act or transaction" for "the damages sustained as a result of any such act or transaction." The provision also authorizes courts, in their discretion, "to assess reasonable costs, including reasonable attorneys' fees, against either party litigant." Although § 9(f) constitutes one of only a few express private remedies in the Exchange Act, at least prior to the Dodd-Frank Act, it was generally viewed as "a dead letter so far as producing recoveries is concerned." 9 Louis Loss & Joel Seligman, *Securities Regulation* 347 (4th ed. 2013).

§ 8.3.2 FICTITIOUS TRADES IN VIOLATION OF RULE 10b-5

Rule 10b-5(a) makes it unlawful "to employ any device, scheme, or artifice to defraud" and Rule 10b-5(c) makes it unlawful "to engage in any act, practice, or course of business which operates * * * as a fraud or deceit upon any person." Those broad prohibitions effectively subsume all acts and practices that would constitute a violation of § 9(a)(1) or (2). In Rule 10b-5 cases alleging market manipulation, however, there is no need to establish that the defendant purchased or sold securities "for the purpose" of inducing securities trading by others.

SEC v. U.S. Environmental, Inc., 155 F.3d 107 (2d Cir. 1998), provides a good illustration as to why most cases involving fictitious securities trading are pursued under § 10(b) and Rule 10b-5's broad anti-fraud prohibitions rather than the explicit anti-manipulation prohibitions in § 9(a). The case involved a scheme on the part of stock promoters and others to manipulate upward the stock price of U.S. Environmental, Inc. (USE) by trading the stock among themselves. Other securities traders, however, were completely unaware of these wash sales and matched orders, and assumed that the rising stock price resulted from the market forces of supply and demand. In a two month period, USE's stock price rose from $.05 to approximately $5.00 a share. The securities broker who executed the trades on the stock promoter's orders persuaded the district court to dismiss the SEC's Rule 10b-5 charges against him on the grounds that he did not share the promoter's ultimate manipulative purpose to raise the stock price. But the Second Circuit reversed that decision on appeal. It held that even if the broker had been "motivated by a desire to obtain compensation rather than by a desire to change USE's market price," he would be liable under § 10(b) "if, with scienter, he effected the manipulative trades." 155 F.3d at 112. The court ultimately concluded that the SEC sufficiently pled scienter given its allegations that the broker either knew or was reckless in not knowing that the buy and sell orders he executed tricked investors into believing that USE's escalating stock price resulted from an active trading market involving legitimate buyers and sellers.

§ 8.3.3   IMPLIED RIGHTS OF ACTION UNDER RULE 10b-5

Private plaintiffs may also state claims under § 10(b) and Rule 10b-5 for illegal market manipulation. To do so successfully, plaintiffs must allege that "(1) they were injured; (2) in connection with the purchase or sale of securities; (3) by relying on a market for securities; (4) controlled or artificially affected by defendant's deceptive or manipulative conduct; and (5) the defendants engaged in the manipulative conduct with scienter." *In re Blech Sec. Litig.*, 961 F.Supp. 569, 582 (S.D.N.Y. 1997) (citing *Ernst & Ernst v. Hochfelder*, 425 U.S. 185, 199 (1976)). Because it is a claim for fraud, market manipulation must be pled with particularity under Fed. R. Civ. P. 9(b). *ATSI Commc'ns, Inc. v. Shaar Fund, Ltd.*, 493 F.3d 87, 101 (2d Cir. 2007). However, because a manipulation claim may involve facts known only by the defendant, the *ATSI* court explained, a plaintiff need not plead manipulation with the same specificity as other misrepresentation claims. *Id.* at 101–102. It need plead with particularity only "the nature, purpose, and effect of the fraudulent conduct and the roles of the defendants." *Id.* at 102. To satisfy this test, the complaint should set forth "what manipulative acts were performed, which defendants performed them, when the manipulative acts were performed, and what effect the scheme had on the market for the securities at issue." *Id.* A private plaintiff's claim for market manipulation must also satisfy the PSLRA's heightened requirement for pleading scienter, which requires particularized "facts giving rise to a strong inference that the defendant intended to deceive investors by artificially affecting the market price of securities." *Id.*

§ 8.3.4 MANIPULATIVE IPO "LADDERING" ACTIVITY

During the so-called high-tech stock market bubble in the late 1990s, several major investment banks may have engaged in practices designed to create the appearance of escalating prices in the secondary market of shares that were recently subject to a particular issuer's hot initial public offering (IPO). More specifically, the SEC alleged that registered representatives at these firms routinely conditioned the allocation of shares at the IPO prices on a client's agreement to purchase additional shares in the aftermarket. For example, in an IPO in which the offering price was $75 a share, a favored client might be allocated 1,000 shares so long as she agreed to purchase 500 additional shares in the aftermarket at successively higher prices. The practice of pre-selling an offering in this manner came to be known as "laddering."

Several investment banks that had been accused of laddering ultimately entered into settlements with the SEC. *See SEC v. Morgan Stanley & Co.*, SEC Litigation Release No. 19050 (Jan. 25, 2005) (consenting to a $40 million penalty); *SEC v.*

Goldman Sachs & Co., SEC Litigation Release No. 19051 (Jan. 25, 2005) (consenting to a $40 million penalty); *SEC v. J.P. Morgan Secs., Inc.*, SEC Litigation Release No. 18385 (Oct. 1, 2003) (consenting to a $25 million penalty). Without admitting or denying liability, these firms agreed to settle charges that they had violated Rule 101 of Regulation M, promulgated under § 10(b) of the Exchange Act. Rule 101 prohibits distribution participants and their affiliated purchasers from bidding for, purchasing, or attempting to induce any person to bid for or purchase, a covered security during a restricted period (that depends on the trading volume associated with the security). In the SEC's view, tie-in agreements for aftermarket purchases are "a particularly egregious form of solicited transactions prohibited by Regulation M * * * because they undermine the integrity of the market as an independent pricing mechanism for the offered security." *See* SEC Division of Market Regulation, Staff Legal Bulletin No. 10 (Aug. 25, 2000). In other words, laddering activity creates an illusion in much the same way that wash sales and matched orders create the illusion of active trading.

Illegal IPO allocation practices were likewise alleged in more than 1,000 private lawsuits under § 10(b) and Rule 10b-5, with alleged damages totaling more than $55 billion. After almost ten years of litigation involving at least 55 investment banks, 300 securities issuers, and more than seven million potential class members, those lawsuits were ultimately consolidated into a class action that settled with the payment of approximately $586 million. *See In re IPO Sec. Litig,* 671 F.Supp.2d 467, 482–91 (S.D.N.Y. 2009) (finding that the settlement was "fair, reasonable and adequate" in accordance with Fed. R. Civ. P. 23(e), and observing that a jury might well have accepted defendants contention that the tie-in agreements were really "underwriters gauging 'indications of interest' as part of the IPO price discovery process").

§ 8.4 ACTUAL TRADING CONDUCTED FOR A MANIPULATIVE PURPOSE

Recall that in *US Environmental,* discussed in § 8.3.2 *supra,* the Second Circuit held that a broker's personal motivation for executing wash sales and matched orders was irrelevant because the trades themselves were manipulative acts proscribed by § 10(b) and Rule 10b-5. Motive, by contrast, plays a very important role in market manipulation cases involving bona fide, arms-length, securities transactions.

In *United States v. Mulheren,* 938 F.2d 364 (2d Cir. 1991), the government alleged that John Mulheren, the chief trader at and general partner of a registered broker-dealer, had conspired to manipulate and engaged in manipulating the stock price of Gulf & Western Industries, Inc. (G & W) in violation of § 10(b) and Rule 10b-5. According to the government, although Mulheren made bona fide purchases totaling 75,000 shares of G & W stock for his firm's accounts, Mulheren's subjective motivation converted what would otherwise have been lawful purchases into illegal ones. That is, the government argued that Mulheren had purchased the G & W shares solely as a favor to Ivan Boesky, who had been planning to sell his substantial block of G & W stock back to the company at the end of the trading day. Mulheren's purchase orders had "dominated" G & W's trading market for the day in question, thereby resulting in a price increase from $44¾ to $45. In appealing his conviction for market manipulation to the Second Circuit, Mulheren argued that the government had failed to prove by a reasonable doubt that he had purchased shares of G & W "for the sole purpose of raising the price at which it traded on the NYSE, rather than for his own investment purposes." 938 F.2d at 366. The court "harbor[ed] doubt" that an investor could lawfully be convicted under Rule 10b-5 for illegal manipulation based solely on the motivation that prompted the trading. *Id.* But it assumed, without deciding, the correctness of the government's view of the law. Instead, the court concluded that Mulheren's conviction could not be sustained because the government had failed to prove that Mulheren even knew of Boesky's substantial holdings in G & W let alone that he agreed to purchase G & W shares to raise the stock price for the benefit of Boesky.

Although the motivations surrounding Mulheren's stock purchases may have been in doubt, the economic effect of those purchases was not: the ¼ point rise in the price of G & W due to Mulheren's trading resulted in Boesky's receiving about $850,000 more for his 3.4 million shares than he would have received had Mulheren not effected the trades. *See* Steve Thel, *$850,000 in Six Minutes—The*

Mechanics of Securities Manipulation, 79 Cornell L. Rev. 219, 255 (1994).

The government's theory of prosecution in *Mulheren* recognized that an increase or decrease in a securities price may often be a foreseeable consequence of transactions effected for legitimate "investment" purposes. Thus, in order to find an unlawful intent to manipulate the price of a particular stock, a jury must find specifically that the defendant intended to move the price of the stock to, or maintain the price of the stock at, an "artificial level," that is, "to a level above [or below] the investment value of the stock as determined by available information and market forces." *United States v. Russo*, 74 F.3d 1383, 1394 (2d Cir. 1996). If Mulheren had traded solely as a favor to ensure that Boesky could sell his stock back to G & W at $45 a share, then Mulheren's trading would have been designed to push the stock price of G & W to an "artificial level."

§ 8.4.1   THE FAILURE TO DISCLOSE ONE'S MANIPULATIVE INTENT

The Second Circuit in *Mulheren* acknowledged, but expressed no view on, an alternative theory that would have rendered Mulheren's trading a violation of Rule 10b-5. Under that theory, Rule 10b-5 is violated when a defendant fails to disclose the subjective "manipulative" intent behind his or her trading decisions. That theory of nondisclosure, however, found acceptance with another Second Circuit panel in *United States v. Regan*, 937 F.2d 823

(2d Cir. 1991), a case decided less than two weeks before *Mulheren*. At trial, the government alleged, and ultimately convinced a jury, that Lee Newberg, a bond trader at Drexel, Burnham, Lambert (Drexel) had sought to depress the price of C.O.M.B. common stock by arranging with Charles Zarzecki, a trader at the arbitrage firm of Princeton/Newport (PN), to sell short a substantial amount of C.O.M.B. stock. Drexel had agreed to underwrite a $25 million dollar offering of convertible bonds for C.O.M.B., and a lower C.O.M.B. stock price would have enabled Drexel to command a higher interest rate for the convertible bonds and therefore make the issue easier to sell. In effecting the short sales, Zarzecki did not disclose that PN was the short seller or that "Drexel was the moving party behind the entire deal." 937 F.2d at 829.

The bond traders in *Regan* argued on appeal that because they did not have a fiduciary relationship with the parties on the other side of their short sales, they were free to remain silent about their motivations for trading, even if they engaged in short sales in the hope of affecting the market price of C.O.M.B. stock. The court rejected this argument, and affirmed the jury's finding that § 10(b) and Rule 10b-5 had been violated. In so doing, the court emphasized that "[f]ailure to disclose that market prices are being artificially depressed operates as a deceit on the market place and is an omission of a material fact." *Id.* (quoting *United States v. Charnay*, 537 F.2d 341, 351 (9th Cir. 1976)). A recorded telephone conversation between the Drexel and PN bond traders, introduced as evidence at trial, unquestionably did much to bolster the government's case that the bond traders' sole purpose in shorting the C.O.M.B stock was to depress the price in the upcoming bond offering for Drexel's benefit.

§ 8.4.2 MARKING THE CLOSE

In *Koch v. SEC*, 793 F.3d 147 (D.C. Cir. 2015), an investment advisor and his company appealed the SEC's decision to impose sanctions based on evidence that the advisor purchased thinly-traded stock from three small banks and made those purchases for the purpose of increasing the price of the shares immediately prior to the close of the market on the last day of the month (a manipulative practice termed "marking the close"). The SEC found that the advisor placed the trades so that higher valuations would appear on his clients' account statements, which were accessible on-line. In reviewing the sufficiency of the evidence (including a "smoking gun" email to the executing broker cautioning him against "appearing manipulative"), the D.C. Circuit concluded that the "burst of trading cannot be explained by anything other than intent to mark the close." 793 F.3d at 153. And the fact that the advisor was not always successful in elevating the price did not negate the SEC's findings. Thus, in the view of the D.C. Circuit, "intent—not success—is all that must accompany manipulative conduct to prove a violation of the Exchange Act and its implementing regulations." *Id.* at 153–154.

§ 8.4.3   MANIPULATIVE SHORT SELLING

Short selling involves the execution of a sell order placed by a person who does not actually own the security that is being sold. Instead, the order is filled with borrowed stock, and the short seller expects that he will be able to cover what is essentially an IOU held by his broker through the purchase of stock at a later time for a lower price. The short seller is therefore hoping to sell high and buy low, in contrast to the more conventional strategic hope of buying low and selling high.

Short sellers perform an important market role by increasing liquidity, promoting efficient price discovery, and facilitating hedging and other risk management activities. However, short selling may also be used to unlawfully manipulate stock prices by creating an artificial appearance of a decline in the price of a stock.

One notorious example of manipulative short selling occurs in a "bear raid," a term used to describe the practice of creating an imbalance of sell-side interest in an effort to drive down the price of an equity security. As the SEC has observed, this "unrestricted short selling could exacerbate a declining market in a security by increasing pressure from the sell-side, eliminating bids, and causing a further reduction in the price of a security by creating an appearance that the security's price is falling for fundamental reasons, when the decline, or the speed of the decline, is being driven by other factors." SEC Final Rule—Amendments to Regulation SHO, Exchange Act Release No. 61595 (Feb. 26, 2010).

Here, however, it is important to recall the Second Circuit's caution in *ATSI Commc'ns, Inc. v. Shaar Fund, Ltd.*, 493 F.3d 87 (2d Cir. 2007) that "short selling—even in high volumes—is not, by itself, manipulative. * * * To be actionable as a manipulative act, short selling must be willfully combined with something more to create a false impression of how market participants value a security." 493 F.3d at 101.

Collusive activity among two or more traders may well be the type of "something more" that creates that negative false impression. Indeed, as financial markets were imploding in 2008, debates about short selling took center stage, with some observers going so far as to blame manipulative short sellers for the collapses of Bear Stearns and Lehman Brothers. Although the SEC emphasized that "we are not aware of specific empirical evidence that the elimination of short sale price tests has contributed to the increased volatility in U.S. markets," SEC officials were concerned nonetheless that short selling in the securities of a wide range of financial institutions "may be causing sudden and excessive fluctuations of the prices of such securities in such a manner so as to threaten fair and orderly markets." Emergency Order Taking Temporary Action to Respond to Market Developments, Exchange Act Release No. 58592, 73 Fed. Reg. 55169 (Sept. 18, 2008). To "prevent short selling from being used to drive down the share prices of issuers even where there is no fundamental basis for a price decline other than general market conditions," the SEC instituted a temporary ban on the short selling of securities in almost 800 financial companies.

The SEC's unprecedented ban on short selling was lifted a month later after the federal government rescued the financial industry with an unprecedented bailout package. After the dust settled, the SEC adopted a number of new measures to more effectively regulate short selling activity.

§ 8.5 RECOMMENDATIONS AND MATERIAL MISSTATEMENTS DESIGNED TO AFFECT MARKET PRICES

Even if § 10(b) and Rule 10b-5 do indeed prohibit securities trading when the sole purpose behind that trading is to raise (or lower) that security's price, it is very difficult unilaterally to affect the market price of a security—and even more difficult to do so to an extent that would cover the transaction costs. Although securities law scholars disagree as to the extent that manipulative *trading* is self-deterring, market manipulators frequently seek to draw in other securities traders by other types of conduct that place upward (or downward) pressure on the market price of a stock. Sometimes the creation of trading momentum can be accomplished with mere recommendations (a practice known as "scalping.") On other occasions, however, manipulators resort to spreading false information to convince others that a stock is undervalued (or overvalued). These latter schemes are known as "pump and dumps" or "distort and short."

§ 8.5.1   SCALPING

Although sometimes viewed and prosecuted as a type of insider trading, scalping can be more generally described as the practice of recommending the purchase of a security to a group of investors while one is simultaneously selling or intending to sell that same security. To be sure, the scalper is trading securities on the basis of the nonpublic information that he is about to publicize in the form of a buy recommendation. But unlike the typical insider trading case, the scalper controls—indeed creates—the very information which, when released, is bound to affect the security's market price. Thus, scalping amounts to making a recommendation for the specific purpose of profiting from its effect, thereby rendering it understandable as a type of market manipulation. Again, then, the role of motive is key.

Investment Advisers and Broker-Dealers. The Supreme Court first considered the legality of scalping in *SEC v. Capital Gains Research Bureau, Inc.*, 375 U.S. 180 (1963), a case which involved recommendations issued by registered investment advisers who published a monthly investment report. The SEC argued, and the Court agreed, that the advisers had committed acts which "operat[ed] as a fraud or deceit" in violation of § 206 of the Investment Advisers Act of 1940. 375 U.S. at 181. The Court focused specifically on the advisers' failure to disclose to their clients their "practice of purchasing shares of a security for [their] own account shortly before recommending that security for long-term investment and then immediately selling the shares at a profit upon the rise in the market price following the recommendation." *Id.* In the Court's view, it did not matter whether the advisers' "advice was 'honest' in the sense that they believed it was sound and did not offer it for the purpose of furthering personal pecuniary objectives." *Id.* at 200. Rather, the Court found in the legislative history an intent "to eliminate, *or at least to expose*, all conflicts of interest which might incline an investment adviser—consciously or unconsciously—to render advice which was not disinterested." *Id.* at 191–192 (emphasis added).

Journalists and Others. An inquiry into the unlawfulness of scalping is more complex outside the context of recommendations by investment advisers or broker-dealers who clearly owe fiduciary duties of disclosure to their clients. Yet in *Zweig v. Hearst Corp.,* 594 F.2d 1261 (9th Cir.1979), the court had little trouble concluding that a newspaper columnist had violated Rule 10b-5 when he touted a stock in his column without disclosing that he had recently purchased 5,000 shares of that stock from the issuer at a discounted price and intended to sell the stock after the column's publication. In finding an omission of a material fact in violation of Rule 10b-5, the court concluded that "[c]olumnists * * * ordinarily have no duty to disclose facts about their personal financial affairs" but that here "the defendant assumed those duties when, with knowledge of the stock's market and an intent to gain personally, he encouraged purchases of the securities in the market." 594 F.2d at 1268.

The *Zweig* court concluded that the failure to disclose an intention to scalp violates Rule 10b-5 prior to the Supreme Court's decision in *Chiarella* holding that "one who fails to disclose material information prior to the consummation of a transaction commits fraud only when he is under a duty to do so." *Chiarella v. United States*, 445 U.S. 226, 228 (1980). *See also Basic Inc. v. Levinson*, 485 U.S. 224, 239 n.17 (1988) (stating that "[s]ilence, absent a duty to disclose, is not actionable as fraud under Rule 10b-5").

Notably, after *Chiarella*, at least one court has affirmed the *Zweig* decision, although in connection with a defendant who was found to have a relationship of trust and confidence with the recipients of his stock recommendations. *See SEC v. Park (a.k.a. "Tokyo Joe")*, 99 F.Supp. 2d 889 (N.D. Ill. 2000) (refusing to dismiss Rule 10b-5 scalping allegations against defendant, a former burrito vendor and present-day "internet guru," who operated a stock-pick and investment advice website for fee-paying subscribers). *See also SEC v. Yun Soo Oh Park and Tokyo Joe's Societe Anonyme*, SEC Litigation Release No. 16925 (Mar. 8, 2001) (announcing settling defendant's agreement that he and his company would disgorge the $324,934 in profits they made (together with prejudgment interest) from 13 instances of scalping).

The SEC may well have faced a higher hurdle in a subsequent enforcement action brought against several Georgetown law students. *See SEC v. Colt*, Litigation Release No. 16461, 71 SEC Docket 2387

(D.D.C. Mar. 2, 2000); *Kenneth Terrell et al.*, Exchange Act Release No. 34-42483, 71 S.E.C. Docket 1863 (Mar. 2, 2000). The SEC's enforcement action against the students likewise involved allegations of scalping, but the recipients of the law student's stock recommendations did not pay a fee to subscribe to the stock selection website in question. The SEC, however, once again did not have the opportunity to test its legal theories in court because the students opted to settle. Notably, the Commission waived the payment of disgorgement and prejudgment interest based on the students' "demonstrated financial inability to pay."

§ 8.5.2   PUMP AND DUMPS (OR DISTORT AND SHORT) SCHEMES

A "pump and dump" scheme undertakes to inflate the market price of a stock through the wide dissemination of false positive information. Then, once the stock price has risen to the desired level, the perpetrator sells off that stock, leaving unsuspecting investors with huge losses once the scheme unravels. "Distort and short" schemes produce the same result, but instead of purchasing stock and disseminating false positive information to drive up its trading price, the perpetrator shorts the stock and then spreads negative rumors about the company or its officials in an attempt to drive down the stock price.

At age fifteen, the New Jersey high school student Jonathon Lebed became the youngest person ever charged with market manipulation by the SEC. *See In re Jonathan Lebed*, Securities Act Release No.

7891, 73 S.E.C. Docket 741 (Sept. 20, 2000); *see also* Michael Lewis, *Jonathan Lebed's Extracurricular Activities*, N.Y. Times Magazine, Feb. 25, 2001, at 26. The SEC's complaint alleged that Lebed had violated § 10(b) and Rule 10b-5 by anonymously posting hundreds of false and misleading messages on investment chat room sites shortly after purchasing large blocks of thinly-traded microcap stocks. It further alleged that "Lebed then sold all of these shares, usually within 24 hours, profiting from the increased price his messages had caused." *In re Jonathan Lebed*, Securities Act Release No. 7891, 73 S.E.C. Docket 741 (Sept. 20, 2000) Although press reports estimated that Lebed's trading profits exceeded $800,000 from this pattern of activity in the stock of dozens of companies over a six-month period, the SEC's complaint narrowed the focus to eleven specific instances between August 1999 and February 2000. Lebed ultimately settled with the SEC, agreeing to pay $272,826 in disgorgement and $12,174 in prejudgment interest, for a total amount of $285,000. Securities law scholars have since questioned whether many of Lebed's alleged material misstatements (*e.g.*, "the next stock to gain 1000%," or "the most undervalued stock in history") may be better described as "puffery" that a court would have found to be immaterial as a matter of law. *See, e.g.*, Donald C. Langevoort, Taming the Animal Spirits of the Stock Markets: A Behavioral Approach to Securities Regulation, 97 Nw. U. L. Rev. 135, 157 (2002) (observing that "[t]he fact that a pseudonymous person on a website says, even repeatedly, that he thinks that a stock is poised to gain an immense amount does not by itself convey any seemingly reliable information").

More recently, the SEC and the DOJ have prosecuted a variation of "pump and dumps" involving phony fax scams and phony voice message scams. In the prototypical case, the defendant purposely dials purported "wrong" numbers, providing recipients of the fax or the answering machine message with a phony stock tip designed to drive up the price of the touted security. Automated calling technology allows for thousands of such "wrong number" calls to be placed in a very short period of time. In one instance, three defendants allegedly conspired to leave messages on thousands of answering machines. *See SEC v. Boling*, SEC Litigation Release No. 20192 (July 11, 2007) (announcing guilty pleas in related criminal securities fraud case and hyperlinking transcript of answering machine message).

§ 8.5.3 CONFLICTS OF INTEREST
ON WALL STREET

Do securities analysts engage in fraud or market manipulation when they publish "buy" recommendations in research reports to brokerage firm customers while actually believing that the recommended stocks are unequivocal losers? What if it could be shown that these analysts intentionally misled investors about the quality of the stocks in order to win lucrative investment banking business for their firms?

These questions and many related ones were at one time at the top of the enforcement agendas for the SEC, the DOJ, the State Attorneys General, and the NYSE and NASD. Indeed, throughout the 2002–03 time period, newspapers were filled with weekly, and often daily, accounts of the various investigations into securities analysts' conflicts of interest, culminating in a historic "global settlement" that required the nation's twelve largest investments banks to pay a combined total of more than $1.4 billion in fines, disgorgement, and funding for independent research and investor education. *See* Federal Court Approves Global Research Analyst Settlement, SEC Litigation Release No. 18438 (Oct. 31, 2003). Two individual analysts were identified and included in the settlement: Jack Grubman, once an analyst at Salomon Smith Barney, who agreed to a lifetime bar from the securities industry and the payment of $15 million in fines, and Henry Blodget, once an analyst at Merrill Lynch, who agreed to a lifetime bar from the securities industry and the payment of $4 million in fines. The global settlement further required the firms to adopt substantial structural changes to ensure that analysts' stock recommendations would not be tainted by efforts to secure investment banking-related bonuses.

The topic of conflicts of interest on Wall Street also received much attention from Congress in the months preceding the Sarbanes-Oxley Act of 2002. Congress ultimately added a new § 15D to the Exchange Act, which required the SEC (or an SRO under the direction of the SEC) to adopt a host of new rules to address the conflict of interest problems that had been brought to light. Reflecting this mandate, FINRA has in place a series of rules designed to prevent member firms and their associated persons from seeking to influence the content of research reports or recommendations for the purpose of gaining or retaining investment banking business. Moreover, FINRA rules now require firms to disclose in research reports if the analyst (or her family member) has a financial interest in the securities of a recommended company.

CHAPTER 9

SEC ENFORCEMENT OF THE FEDERAL SECURITIES LAWS

§ 9.1 INTRODUCTION

Congress has given the Securities and Exchange Commission (the SEC or the Commission) broad powers to investigate whether the federal securities laws have been, are being, or are likely to be violated. Congress has also authorized a wide array of SEC enforcement remedies, most of which are not available in private litigation. In addition to initiating civil enforcement actions either in federal judicial or administrative proceedings, officials in the SEC's Division of Enforcement can refer securities law violations to the Department of Justice (the DOJ) for criminal prosecution.

This Chapter is divided into twelve sections: the SEC's Division of Enforcement (§ 9.2 *infra*); the investigatory process (§ 9.3 *infra*); settlements and consent decrees (§ 9.4 *infra*); available remedies (§§ 9.5–9.9 *infra*); litigating with the SEC (§ 9.10 *infra*); securities industry self-regulatory organizations (SROs) (§ 9.11 *infra*); and parallel proceedings (§ 9.12 *infra*). Later chapters discuss enforcement issues pertaining to actions against attorneys and accountants (Chapter 10 *infra*); criminal prosecutions (Chapter 11 *infra*); and international securities fraud (Chapter 12 *infra*).

§ 9.2 THE DIVISION OF ENFORCEMENT

First organized in 1972 as a separate division of the SEC, the Division of Enforcement investigates possible violations of the federal securities laws, recommends action to the Commission when appropriate, negotiates settlements on behalf of the Commission, and litigates civil enforcement actions in federal court (where the subject is termed the "defendant") or in administrative proceedings (where the subject is termed the "respondent"). An administrative proceeding that requires evidentiary findings is heard initially by an administrative law judge (an ALJ), subject to review by the five-member Commission. The Division also refers cases to the DOJ and to the various U.S. Attorney's offices throughout the country.

§ 9.2.1 ORGANIZATIONAL STRUCTURE

The Division is composed of approximately 1,300 attorneys, accountants, and other professionals (the "staff"). Although most of this staff is based at the SEC's headquarters in Washington, D.C., staff in the SEC's 11 regional offices also pursue enforcement matters within their respective jurisdictions. The Division is headed by a Director who is assisted by a Deputy Director and several Associate Directors. The Division also has its own Chief Counsel and Chief Accountant as well as specialized units in high-priority enforcement areas including: Asset Management (hedge funds and investment advisers); Market Abuse (high-volume and computer-driven trading strategies, large-scale insider trading, and market manipulation schemes); Complex Financial Instruments Unit (particularly derivative products); Foreign Corrupt Practices; and Municipal Securities and Public Pensions.

§ 9.2.2   MARKET INTELLIGENCE AND WHISTLEBLOWING

Also included within the Division of Enforcement is the Office of Market Intelligence, which is charged with collecting, analyzing, referring, and monitoring the more than 15,000 tips, complaints, and referrals received by the Division each year. Market Intelligence also includes the Office of the Whistleblower, which administers the whistleblower program mandated by the Dodd-Frank Act of 2010 (the Dodd-Frank Act). The Dodd-Frank Act added to the Exchange Act a new § 21F, which provides that the SEC shall award a payment when "original information" conveyed by a "whistleblower" leads to a judicial or administrative SEC enforcement action, or related action, that results in "monetary sanctions" exceeding $1 million. Section 21F further specifies that such payments shall be not less than 10 percent and no more than 30 percent of the monetary sanctions collected, with "monetary sanctions" defined to include "any monies" resulting from an SEC judicial or administrative action, or related action, including "penalties, disgorgement, restitution, and interest ordered to be paid."

§ 9.2.3   KEY PRIORITIES

The Enforcement Division's key priorities have stayed consistent in the years following the financial crisis and its aftermath. Financial reporting, accounting, and disclosure violations constitute a continuous focus, as are investment advisers and the funds they manage, municipal securities and public pensions, market abuses (such as insider trading and manipulation), and the Foreign Corrupt Practices Act. In 2015, the Division announced that it was placing a renewed emphasis on securities industry "gatekeepers," including broker-dealers, accountants, investment bankers, and attorneys, because they are uniquely positioned to detect and avert the compliance breakdowns and illegal schemes that cause investor harm.

§ 9.2.4   SEC ENFORCEMENT MANUAL

In response to a Senate Report recommending that the SEC standardize its investigative procedures, the SEC in 2008 made its Enforcement Manual available on its website. http://www.sec.gov/divisions/enforce/enforcementmanual.pdf [hereinafter SEC Enforcement Manual]. Although the Manual states that it is intended to provide guidance only to the staff of the Enforcement Division and "does not, and may not be relied upon to create any rights, substantive or procedural, enforceable at law by any party in any matter civil or criminal," it has nonetheless become an essential guide for securities law practitioners as well as for anyone with a matter involving the Division of Enforcement.

§ 9.3   SEC INVESTIGATIONS

The enormous sweep of the SEC's investigatory powers stems from § 20(a) of the Securities Act, §§ 21(a)(1) and (2) of the Exchange Act, § 209(a) of the Investment Advisers Act, and § 42(a) of the Investment Company Act. These provisions authorize the SEC to investigate past, ongoing, or prospective violations of the federal securities laws, the SEC rules or regulations promulgated thereunder, and the rules and regulations of the various SROs.

The SEC rules governing investigations are set out in the Rules of Informal and Other Procedures, 17 C.F.R. §§ 202.1 et seq. (particularly § 202.5(a)–(f), pertaining to enforcement activities) and the Rules Relating to Investigations, 17 C.F.R. §§ 203.1–203.8. The SEC's Rules of Practice, 17 C.F.R. § 201.100 et seq., also have some relevance in the investigatory phase of an enforcement matter.

Courts have routinely emphasized Congress's intent to grant federal agencies broad discretion in the conduct of their investigations and have generally refused to interfere in judgments by SEC officials that investigations are warranted. *See United States v. Morton Salt Co.*, 338 U.S. 632, 652 (1950) (emphasizing that "law-enforcing agencies have a legitimate right to satisfy themselves that corporate behavior is consistent with the law and the public interest"); *SEC v. Brigadoon Scotch Distrib. Co.*, 480 F.2d 1047, 1052–1053 (2d Cir. 1973); *Treats Int'l Enters., Inc. v. SEC*, 828 F. Supp. 16, 19 (S.D.N.Y. 1993). For a rare determination to thwart such investigatory efforts, *see SEC v. Wheeling-Pittsburgh Steel Corp.*, 648 F. 2d 118 (3d Cir. 1981) (criticizing SEC officials for succumbing to an influential Senator's pressure to investigate a constituent's competitor).

§ 9.3.1 WHAT PROMPTS AN INVESTIGATION?

Complaints received from members of the public, communications from federal or state agencies, and examinations of filings made with the SEC routinely trigger investigation by Enforcement staff. 17 C.F.R § 202.5(a). Other typical sources of SEC investigations include: market surveillance and internet surveillance units in the Enforcement Division; referrals from other divisions and offices within the SEC (such as Corporation Finance and Market Regulation); periodic inspections of broker-dealers, investment advisers, and investment companies by the SEC or SROs; news stories and press accounts of troubled companies; and informants (including those seeking bounties pursuant to the SEC's whistleblower program, discussed at § 9.2.2 *supra*).

§ 9.3.2 AN OVERVIEW OF THE PROCESS

SEC investigations most often begin with a preliminary inquiry, which may be conducted by the staff without the need to obtain formal approval from the Commission or a senior enforcement division official. Thereafter, or as an alternative, the staff may launch an investigation with a "formal order of investigation" that carries with it the authority to subpoena documents and testimony. Both types of investigations are nonpublic, except in the very rare instances when the Commission specifies otherwise. And whether formal or informal, an SEC investigation serves only to find facts. It is thus "an administrative investigation [that] adjudicates no legal rights." *SEC v. Jerry T. O'Brien, Inc.*, 467 U.S 735, 742 (1984).

The time the staff takes to complete its investigation varies greatly with the facts, but may take upwards of two years. If the staff concludes an investigation with the view that enforcement action is warranted, it must prepare a recommendation for the Commission. Whether initiated in federal district court or as an administrative proceeding, an SEC enforcement action cannot be authorized in the absence of an affirmative vote of a majority of the Commissioners.

§ 9.3.3   INFORMAL INVESTIGATIONS/ MATTERS UNDER INQUIRY

If the SEC staff suspects possible violations of the federal securities laws, it generally conducts an informal investigation, sometimes referred to as a Matter Under Inquiry (MUI). Because "no process is issued or testimony compelled," 17 C.F.R. § 202.5(a), the staff is largely dependent on voluntary cooperation. Corporate personnel or other persons deemed to have relevant information may be contacted by the SEC directly or through their counsel when the fact of their representation is known.

The staff typically conducts a thorough investigation before reaching a determination as to whether enforcement action is warranted. Investigations, even informal ones, typically involve the production of documents as well as meetings with the staff, sometimes conducted as interviews in-person or on the telephone and other times involving on-the-record testimony that is transcribed by a reporter. A refusal to provide the information requested by the staff, or an extended delay in doing so, will almost surely result in the staff's seeking a formal order of investigation, pursuant to the process described in the subsection that follows.

At the outset of an informal interview or testimony, the subject is generally told (1) that participation is voluntary; (2) that he or she has the right to have counsel present; (3) that the staff's notes and/or transcript may be shared with other government agencies or regulatory entities; and (4) that the person should understand that knowingly and willfully providing false information to a federal official in connection with a government inquiry constitutes a federal crime under 18 U.S.C. § 1001. *See United States v. Stewart*, 433 F.3d 273 (2d Cir. 2006) (affirming conviction of home designer/ entrepreneur Martha Stewart and her stockbroker, Peter Bacanovic, for making false statements to SEC and DOJ officials in the course of an investigation for insider trading).

§ 9.3.4 FORMAL ORDERS OF INVESTIGATION

If the Enforcement staff's concerns are not resolved in the course of an informal inquiry, pursuant to authority delegated by the Commission, the investigating officials may request a senior officer of the Division (*i.e.*, the Director, Deputy Director, Chief Counsel, Chief Litigation Counsel, Associate Directors, and Regional or Associate Regional Directors) to issue an "Order Directing Private Investigation and Designating Officers to Take Testimony," generally referred to as a "formal order." On other occasions, an immediate request for a formal order may be warranted. For example, if the staff makes an early determination that a subpoena will be necessary to obtain sought-after documents (such as customer records from a telephone company), the investigatory process may begin with the issuance of a formal order.

The formal order generally describes the nature of the investigation that has been authorized and designates specific staff members to act as officers of the SEC for the purpose of issuing subpoenas that require the production of documents or testimony.

SEC Subpoenas. The SEC's authority to issue subpoenas is set out in Securities Act § 19(c), Exchange Act § 21(b), Investment Advisers Act § 209(b), and Investment Company Act § 42(b). Although the reach of an SEC subpoena is nationwide, the staff is free to, and often does, negotiate the location of witness testimony before and after the issuance of a subpoena based on the circumstances of the particular witness or matter.

Persons or companies under investigation by the SEC will sometimes object to the subpoena on grounds of privilege (raising claims of attorney-client, attorney work-product, or Fifth Amendment/self-incrimination privilege, among others). The SEC will often work out these objections with counsel representing the subpoena recipient. The SEC, however, is not required to notify the "target" of a nonpublic investigation, even if that investigation involves subpoenas to third parties that implicate the target's interests. *SEC v. Jerry T. O'Brien, Inc.*, 467 U.S. 735 (1984).

SEC subpoenas are not self-enforcing. This means that if a subpoena recipient fails to produce documents or fails to attend scheduled testimony absent a valid privilege (or when the claim of privilege is in dispute), the SEC must take the subsequent step of applying for a judicial order to enforce the subpoena. The SEC may bring this action by filing a motion and an "order to show cause" in the federal district court where the investigation is being conducted or in any jurisdiction where the subpoenaed party resides. *See, e.g.*, Exchange Act § 21(c). Such actions are conducted as "summary proceedings" under Rule 81(a)(3) of the Federal Rules of Civil Procedure (*i.e.*, there is no complaint and no discovery), and the burden of proof is on the opposing party to demonstrate why the judge should not enforce the SEC subpoena. The failure to obey a court order compelling compliance with a subpoena may prompt the SEC to initiate charges against the recipient for contempt of court.

§ 9.3.5   ADDITIONAL CONCERNS

Securities lawyers and parties under investigation or subject to an SEC subpoena should bear in mind these additional and important concerns:

Obstruction of Justice. "Obstruction of justice" is a broad phrase that may extend to "any attempt to impede the due administration of justice." *United States v. Cihak*, 137 F.3d 252, 262 (5th Cir. 1998). As such, it encompasses conduct involving document destruction as well as witness or evidence tampering. The crime of obstruction of justice may be prosecuted under an array of federal statutes, including 18 U.S.C. § 1519, entitled "Destruction, Alteration, or Falsification of Records in Federal Investigations and Bankruptcy." Pursuant to this statute, a person who knowingly alters or destroys any record, document, or tangible object "with the intent to impede, obstruct, or influence" the investigation of any matter within the jurisdiction of any U.S. department or agency may be subject to a fine and/or imprisonment for up to 20 years.

One example of the enormous liability risk for obstructing justice is the verdict issued against the now defunct accounting firm of Arthur Andersen, LLP, for alleged document destruction and other actions taken in connection with the SEC's investigation into the collapse of Enron, a long-time audit client of the firm. Although that conviction was later reversed by a unanimous Supreme Court, *see*

Arthur Andersen LLP v. United States, 544 U.S. 696 (2005) (holding that the jury was improperly instructed), the case continues to serve as an important reminder of the ancillary issues that may develop in the course of government investigations for possible violations of the federal securities laws.

Whistleblowing and Protections Against Retaliation. In the wake of the scandals at Enron and WorldCom, Congress created a new crime for "Retaliating Against A Witness, Victim, or An Informant," 18 U.S.C. § 1513(e) (providing for up to 10 years of imprisonment for knowingly interfering with the lawful employment of any person who provided truthful information to a law enforcement officer concerning the possible commission of any federal offense, with the intent to retaliate). The Sarbanes-Oxley Act of 2002 (the SOX) also created a private civil action for employees of publicly traded companies who believe that they have suffered retaliation for providing information to any federal agency or Congress about suspected fraud. *See* 18 U.S.C. § 1514A. The Dodd-Frank Act added a special provision to protect "whistleblowers" who report potential violations of the securities laws to the SEC. In addition, the Dodd-Frank Act amended the provision to prohibit the enforcement of pre-dispute arbitration clauses or pre-dispute waivers of retaliation rights and remedies, and to clarify that § 1514A applies to employees of subsidiaries of publicly traded companies "whose financial information is included in the consolidated financial statements of [a publicly traded] company." The Dodd Frank Act also created a new private right of action for employees in the financial services industry who suffer retaliation for disclosing suspected misconduct relating to the offering or provision of a consumer financial product or service.

Multiple Representations. The investigatory stage is also a time when issues may arise concerning multiple representation—*e.g.*, whether a single law firm can represent both a corporation and its individual officers, directors, or employees. Often, to avoid the possibility that a conflict of interest will develop down the road, firms and individuals will retain separate counsel at an early stage of an SEC investigation. State professional responsibility rules, often drawn from the ABA's Model Rules of Professional Conduct, will play a key role in the analysis. Particularly important here is ABA Model Rule 1.13, captioned the "Organization as Client" and ABA Model Rule 1.7, which concerns conflicts of interest involving current clients. For a decision concluding that a single law firm could continue its simultaneous representation of a brokerage firm and 47 registered representatives under investigation by the SEC for securities fraud, *see In the Matter of Merrill Lynch, Pierce, Fenner & Smith, Inc.*, [1973–74 Transfer Binder] Fed. Sec. L. Rep. ¶ 79,608, at 83,630, 83,633 (Ullman, ALJ) (Dec. 6, 1973) (maintaining that "where it is not clear that a conflict of interest will occur between two or more clients of an attorney, the informed consent of the client or clients whose interests more likely would suffer in the event a conflict should develop can provide justification for the continuation of multiple representations").

§ 9.3.6 STAFF RECOMMENDATIONS TO THE COMMISSION

At the conclusion of an investigation, the staff may determine to take no action or to recommend that the Commission bring enforcement proceedings. If the staff has determined not to recommend action against an individual or entity, the SEC staff must notify that person if it is anyone who: is identified in the caption of a formal order; submitted or was solicited to submit a Wells Submission (discussed below); or asks for such a notice. The notification takes the form of a "termination letter." *See* SEC Enforcement Manual, § 2.6.2.

The staff of the Enforcement Division cannot by itself initiate enforcement actions against persons or companies who may have violated the federal securities laws. Rather, if the staff believes that enforcement action is warranted, then a recommendation to that effect must be made to the Commission. This recommendation typically includes the staff's analysis of the facts and the law, and their views with respect to appropriate sanctions. In instances where a person or company is willing to settle and consent to a sanction that is also acceptable to the SEC staff, such a settlement can be accepted only by the Commission.

Wells Notices and Submissions. When the staff has made a preliminary determination to recommend an enforcement action against an entity or individual, it typically provides a "Wells Notice" to the attorney representing the party. This notice identifies the securities law violations that the staff has preliminarily determined to include in the enforcement recommendation and sets forth the party's deadline for submitting a response statement (known as a "Wells Submission") that the staff will forward to the Commission along with its recommendation.

The decision by a prospective defendant or respondent as to whether to make a Wells Submission requires careful contemplation. As the SEC explained nearly 45 years ago, at the time it is asked to consider the staff's enforcement recommendation, "[t]he Commission desires not only to be informed of the findings made by its staff but also, where practicable and appropriate, to have before it the position of persons under investigation." *See* Securities Act Release No. 5310 (Sept. 27, 1972), https://www.sec.gov/divisions/enforce/wells-release. pdf. On the other hand, a Wells Submission that memorializes facts and legal theories while defense strategies are still being formed may create problems for the client down the road. For example, a Wells Submission could reveal facts of which the investigating staff was unaware or it might foreclose alternative lines of argument.

In addition to giving prospective defendants or respondents the opportunity to persuade the Commission that enforcement action is not warranted, the Wells Notice carries with it a second important consequence: § 4E(a) of the Dodd-Frank Act specifies that, not later than 180 days after providing a written Wells notification to any person, the SEC staff must either file an action against that person or provide notice to the Director of Enforcement of its intent not to file an action. A 180-day extension from a senior SEC official is possible for a matter that qualifies as "complex" (with notice to the SEC Chairman), but even for complex maters, an extension beyond the second 180-day period requires approval by the Commission. However, the SEC's failure to abide by these statutory deadlines will not necessarily bar the SEC from instituting an enforcement action. *See Montford & Co. v. SEC*, 793 F.3d 76, 82 (D.C. Cir. 2015) (deferring to the SEC's "reasonable" interpretation that § 4E does not impose a jurisdictional bar).

For years, there was a decided lack of consensus among securities law practitioners as to whether Wells Submissions were an effective vehicle for persuading the Commission to reject an enforcement recommendation that was made by its staff. But a recent study published in the Wall Street Journal confirmed that the Commission does in fact close a significant number of investigations without taking enforcement action. Specifically, of the 797 Wells Notices issued to individuals in the two-year period from September 2010 to 2012, no action was taken in 159 instances—about 20 percent. *See* Jean

Eaglesham, *SEC Drops 20% of Probes After 'Wells Notice,'* WALL ST. J. (Oct. 9, 2013 8:02 PM), http://www.wsj.com/articles/SB100014240527023045004045791256333137423664.

Crediting Cooperation. The SEC frequently credits entities as well as individuals for the cooperation they extend in the course of SEC investigations. As the Commission explained in what has become known as the "Seaboard Report," when companies detect and self-report illegal conduct, and then voluntarily adopt measures to prevent further violations, "large expenditures of government and shareholder resources can be avoided and investors can benefit more promptly." Report of Investigation Pursuant to Section 21(a) of the Securities Exchange Act of 1934 and Commission Statement in the Relationship of Cooperation to Agency Enforcement Decisions, Exchange Act Release No. 44969 (Oct. 23, 2001) (enumerating 13 factors used by the SEC in determining whether, and how much, to credit a company's cooperation). A subsequent release discusses cooperation by individuals. *See* Policy Statement Commission Concerning Cooperation by Individuals in its Investigations and Related Enforcement Actions, Exchange Act Release No. 61340 (Jan. 13, 2010). From time to time, the SEC also enters into Deferred (or Non-prosecution) Agreements, which are formal written agreements in which the SEC agrees to forego an enforcement action if the individual or company agrees to cooperate fully and truthfully and comply with express undertakings. *See* SEC Press Release 2010–6, SEC Announces Initiative to Encourage

Individuals and Companies to Cooperate and Assist
in Investigations (Jan. 13, 2010). *See also* SEC Press
Release 2010–252, SEC Charges Fromer Carter's
Executive With Fraud and Insider Trading (Dec. 20,
2010) (announcing a non-prosecution agreement
entered into with Carter's Inc. in connection with the
company's prompt and complete self-reporting of
financial fraud and insider trading by a former
executive vice president).

<u>Waiver of Privileges</u>. Although the SEC typically
does not condition cooperation credit on privilege
waivers, substantial benefits may nonetheless be
gained from sharing attorney-client or work-product
privileged documents with enforcement officials.
There are, however, significant drawbacks because
most federal circuit courts have refused to allow a
prospective defendant in a government investigation
to selectively waive the privilege and then reassert it
in litigation initiated by third parties. *See, e.g., In re
Pac. Pictures,* 679 F.3d 1121 (9th Cir. 2012); *In re
Qwest Commc'ns Int'l, Inc.,* 450 F.3d 1179 (10th Cir.
2006); *Westinghouse Elec. Corp. v. Republic of the
Phil.,* 951 F.2d 1414 (3d Cir. 1991); *In re Subpoena
Duces Tecum,* 738 F.2d 1367 (D.C. Cir. 1984). Only
the Eighth Circuit has expressly permitted selective
waiver. *See Diversified Indus., Inc. v. Meredith,* 572
F.2d 596, 611 (8th Cir. 1978) (holding that a
corporation participating in the SEC's voluntary
disclosure program retains a privilege as to all third-
party litigants, and noting that "[t]o hold otherwise
may have the effect of thwarting the developing
procedure of corporations to employ independent
outside counsel to investigate and advise them in

order to protect stockholders, potential stockholders and customers"). The Second Circuit at one time indicated that limited waiver may be appropriate where the government has explicitly agreed with the disclosing party to maintain the confidentiality of the disclosed materials. *See In re Steinhardt Partners, L.P.*, 9 F.3d 230, 236 (2d Cir. 1993) (holding that the voluntary disclosure of work product to the SEC waived the privilege for all parties, but leaving open the possibility of limited waiver). But a recent district court decision refused to recognize a limited waiver despite the existence of a confidentiality agreement because the agreement left the SEC with "unfettered discretion" to disclose the protected materials, thereby creating an "illusory" commitment to maintain their confidentiality. *See Gruss v. Zwirn*, 2013 WL 3481350, at *3–5 (S.D.N.Y. July 10, 2013).

Section 21(a) Reports. Section 21(a) of the Exchange Act authorizes the SEC "to publish information" concerning its investigations of possible violations of the federal securities laws. The Commission tends to use this authority to articulate novel legal theories or standards of conduct. By including its views in a report, rather than in an SEC order resolving an enforcement action, the Commission is able to attract public attention without placing the agency in the uncomfortable position of applying its views retroactively to justify the imposition of a sanction. The vehicle of a Section 21(a) report also eliminates the need to hold a hearing to establish the violation and forecloses any judicial review of the theories and standards articulated in the report. The subjects of Section

21(a) reports will often admit to the factual recitations, and agree to specified undertakings, as a means of bringing the investigation to a close.

§ 9.4 SEC SETTLEMENTS AND CONSENT DECREES

The vast majority of SEC enforcement actions (approximately 90 percent) are resolved through a consensual settlement. The SEC regards settlements favorably because they eliminate litigation risk, conserve time and expense, return money to victims more quickly, and allow staff to redeploy resources toward new investigations. Settlements likewise allow the party charged with securities law violations to avoid the expense and uncertainty of a trial. In addition, parties favor settlements because litigating with the SEC and losing may collaterally estop the party from re-litigating facts and issues in related actions filed by private plaintiffs. *See* § 9.10.6 *infra.*

In many instances, even before the Commission has authorized enforcement action, the staff of the Enforcement Division will have had settlement discussions with the prospective defendant's counsel and will have reached a tentative agreement as to the specific charges to be brought, the forum for the relief to be imposed (administrative or judicial), and the sanctions that will be ordered. A party's settlement with the SEC may also include one or more "undertakings," which are prospective actions that are not explicitly contemplated as a statutory remedy. For example, a broker-dealer that consents to a censure and a monetary penalty for improper record-keeping might also undertake to retain a special consultant approved by the SEC staff and to implement any new procedures recommended by that consultant.

§ 9.4.1   THE GENERAL PROCESS

Whether or not the Commission has previously authorized enforcement action, any settlement to which the staff and the party agree in principle must be presented to the Commission for its approval. If the Commission has not previously authorized the filing of a complaint in federal court or an order instituting an administrative proceeding, the staff's recommendation for enforcement action and the proposed settlement are submitted to the Commission simultaneously. If the Commission votes to accept a settlement of an administrative proceeding, then the matter is brought to a close with the entry of a Final Order. Civil enforcement actions filed in federal district court, however, require an additional step. If the Commission votes to accept a settlement of the charges set out in a civil complaint, then the complaint must be filed in federal district court and the consent decree must be approved by the presiding judge. Although the vast majority of proposed settlements are approved without fanfare, federal district court judges have, on occasion, withheld approval, effectively forcing the SEC and the defendant back to the negotiation table. *See, e.g., SEC v. Bank of Am. Corp.*, 2010 WL 624581 (S.D.N.Y. Feb, 22, 2010) (ultimately approving a second proposed settlement which included, among other things, an injunction and a $150 million civil penalty (up from the less "meaningful" figure of $33 million under the terms of the first proposed settlement)). A district court, however, may not reject a settlement simply because it disagrees with the SEC's decisions on discretionary matters of policy. Instead, the appropriate standard is whether the consent decree is "fair and reasonable, with the additional requirement that the 'public interest would not be disserved.'" *SEC v. Citigroup Global Mkts. Inc.*, 752 F.3d 285, 294 (2d Cir. 2014).

§ 9.4.2   NEITHER ADMITS NOR DENIES

Traditionally and still typically, SEC settlements include a provision that the settling party "neither admits nor denies" the allegations in the SEC's complaint or administrative order. A person who subsequently denies the allegations will have breached the terms of that agreement and thereby risks an SEC action seeking to vacate the settled proceeding. The SEC's willingness to allow parties to resolve an enforcement action in that way clearly promotes settlements.

Recently, however, the SEC has been requiring admissions from certain settling defendants or respondents. In 2012, the SEC initially announced that it would eliminate the "'neither admit nor deny'" language from settlements when the party had admitted guilt in a parallel criminal action. *See* Robert Khuzami, Public Statement by SEC Staff: Recent Policy Change (Jan. 7, 2012). Less than two years later, the SEC announced another change whereby it would be seeking admissions in "certain other cases . . . where there is a special need for public accountability and acceptance of responsibility." *See* Mary Jo White, Chair, SEC, Deploying the Full Enforcement Arsenal (Sept. 26, 2013) (noting that admissions may be required in cases where (1) a significant number of investors were harmed or the conduct was otherwise "egregious;" (2) the conduct posed a substantial risk to investors or the market; (3) admissions would help future investors to decide whether to deal with the setting party; or (4) "reciting unambiguous facts would send an important message to the market about a particular case"). However, as the Second Circuit has emphasized, "[t]he decision to require an admission of liability before entering into a consent decree rests squarely with the SEC." *SEC v. Citigroup Global Mkts. Inc.*, 752 F.3d 285, 293 (2d Cir. 2014).

§ 9.5 CIVIL REMEDIES FOR VIOLATIONS OF THE SECURITIES LAWS

"What can the SEC do to me?" "How much money will I have to pay?" "Will an action be filed in federal court?" "Can my case be resolved administratively?" "What collateral consequences result from a finding that I violated the securities laws?"

Ever since the SEC's creation in 1934, concerned clients have posed the above questions, and ones like them, to their lawyers. Yet, while the questions may not have changed, their answers certainly have, as Congress has repeatedly augmented the SEC's arsenal of enforcement remedies.

§ 9.5.1   THE ORIGINAL STRUCTURE

As originally contemplated, violations of the federal securities laws were to be remedied principally through the filing of civil injunctive actions in federal district court. To this end, each of the four principal federal securities acts authorized the SEC to seek injunctive relief. Any additional relief sought in court by the SEC came not from provisions in the federal securities laws but from the exercise of the considerable equitable powers possessed by federal district judges. Congress had also authorized the SEC to pursue relief administratively, but only against specific categories of regulated persons, such as broker-dealers, investment advisers, and reporting companies. Regulated persons could be subject to an array of sanctions ranging from censure, to temporary suspensions, to permanent bars from the industry (in the case of securities professionals), and orders to comply (in the case of publicly traded companies).

§ 9.5.2   AN OVERVIEW OF THE MODERN LANDSCAPE

Today's modern landscape for civil enforcement remedies differs quite dramatically from the schema established by Congress in 1934.

The Insider Trading Sanctions Act of 1984. The expansion of the remedies available began in 1984 when Congress enacted the Insider Trading Sanctions Act, which for the first time authorized the SEC to seek civil monetary penalties in insider trading cases. *See* § 7.6.1 *supra* (discussing Exchange

Act § 21A(a)), under which the SEC may seek a court-ordered penalty of up to three times the profit gained or loss avoided by any person who has engaged in illegal tipping or trading).

The Remedies Act of 1990. The "Securities Enforcement Remedies and Penny Stock Reform Act of 1990" (the Remedies Act and the Reform Act, respectively) authorized the SEC to seek civil monetary penalties in federal district courts for virtually *any* violation of the federal securities laws and, in cases involving securities fraud, judicial orders barring individuals from service as corporate officers and directors upon a showing of "substantial unfitness" to serve. The Remedies Act also broadened considerably the SEC's administrative remedies, providing for the imposition of cease-and-desist orders against anyone found to have violated—or to have caused someone else to violate—the federal securities laws. It also allowed the SEC to impose civil monetary penalties in administrative proceedings brought against certain securities professionals, including broker-dealers, investment advisers, and their associated personnel.

The Sarbanes-Oxley Act of 2002. Congress further expanded the SEC's enforcement arsenal though several provisions in the SOX. First, the Act facilitated the SEC's ability to obtain officer and director bar orders in federal court by changing the former "substantial unfitness" standard to one of mere "unfitness." Congress also acceded to the SEC's request for new authority to impose such bar orders in administrative proceedings without any judicial involvement. Second, in an effort to provide an even more solid foundation for remedies that had been traditionally viewed as part of a federal court's equitable authority, the Act authorized the SEC to seek and federal courts to impose "any equitable relief that may be appropriate or necessary for the benefit of investors." Third, the Act authorized court-ordered temporary asset freezes to prevent publicly traded companies under investigation by the SEC from making "extraordinary payments" to any of its directors, officers, agents, or employees. The Act also authorized courts, in an SEC injunctive action, to bar persons from participating in penny stock offerings if their alleged misconduct related to an offering of penny stock.

The Dodd-Frank Act of 2010. In the wake of the financial crisis of 2008, Congress once again expanded the enforcement remedies available to the SEC. Most notably, the Dodd-Frank Act authorized the SEC to impose civil monetary penalties in cease-and-desist proceedings brought against *any* person or entity. The Act also authorized the SEC to impose so-called collateral bar orders preventing securities law violators from associating with any regulated entity (*e.g.*, in a broker-dealer disciplinary action, the respondent's sanction can now prohibit future association with investment advisers and municipal securities dealers, in addition to broker-dealers). In addition, the Act clarifies that the SEC may bring enforcement actions against and seek applicable remedies in cases in which persons served in a regulated capacity at the time of the alleged violations (*e.g.*, former broker-dealers, investment advisers, officer and directors of SROs).

§ 9.6 JUDICIAL REMEDIES

When the SEC opts to pursue enforcement action against a defendant in federal district court, the following remedies are among the ones that a court may impose:

§ 9.6.1 INJUNCTIONS

Securities Act § 20(a), Exchange Act § 21(d)(1), Investment Advisers Act § 209(d), and Investment Company Act § 42(d) each contain provisions authorizing the SEC to seek an injunction against any person who "is engaged or is about to engage" in a violation of the law. In so doing, the SEC does not have to satisfy the traditional test for equitable relief, which generally requires the plaintiff to plead and prove irreparable injury and inadequacy of remedies at law. Instead, a federal district court may grant "permanent or temporary injunction[s] or restraining order[s]" upon "a proper showing." *Id.*

When seeking a permanent injunction, the SEC must establish a securities law violation as well as demonstrate "some likelihood of a future violation." *Aaron v. SEC*, 446 U.S. 680, 703 (1980). In making that determination, courts consider a host of factors, including the egregiousness of the violation, whether the violation was isolated or part of a pattern, whether the violation was flagrant and deliberate, and whether the defendant's business will present opportunities to violate the law in the future. *See*

SEC v. First City Fin. Corp, 890 F. 2d 1215, 1228 (D.C. Cir. 1989). A court may grant an SEC request for a preliminary injunction or a temporary restraining order (TRO), if the SEC demonstrates a substantial likelihood of success on the merits of the case.

Unless specifically limited in duration, court-ordered injunctions against future violations of the federal securities laws are permanent. However, even permanent injunctions may later be modified or dissolved by a court on a defendant's petition, though the granting of such relief is a rare occurrence. *See United States v. Swift & Co.*, 286 U.S. 106, 119 (1932) (holding that the appropriate standard for vacating an injunction is "[n]othing less than a clear showing of grievous wrong evoked by new and unforeseen conditions"); *SEC v. Blinder, Robinson & Co.*, 855 F.2d 677, 680 (10th Cir. 1988) (confirming that *Swift* articulates the applicable standard and emphasizing the necessity of clear proof of "*unforeseen* conditions" flowing from the injunction).

Because an injunction compels the person subject to it to obey the law, the consequences of violating an injunction are severe. If such a person is found in contempt of the court issuing the injunction, the court can impose a fine, imprisonment, or other civil and criminal penalties.

§ 9.6.2   TEMPORARY ASSET FREEZES

Exchange Act § 21C(c)(3)(A)(i), added by the SOX, empowers the SEC to seek temporary asset freezes. The remedy is available when it appears that an issuer subject to an SEC investigation will make "extraordinary payments" to any of its directors, officers, partners, controlling persons, agents, or employees. In such an instance, the SEC may petition a federal district court for a temporary order requiring the issuer to escrow, subject to court supervision, those payments in an interest-bearing account for 45 days. Without the SEC's initiation of an enforcement proceeding charging a violation of the federal securities laws, the order may be extended only up to an additional 45 days, provided the SEC establishes "good cause." The order, however, may continue subject to court approval if a violation of the federal securities laws is charged, though an issuer or other affected person has the right to petition the court for review.

§ 9.6.3   OFFICER AND DIRECTOR BARS

Section 20(e) of the Securities Act and § 21(d)(2) of the Exchange Act authorize the SEC to seek a judicial order permanently or temporarily barring an individual from future service as an officer or director of a publicly traded company. A federal district court may grant such an order if the SEC establishes a violation of the anti-fraud provisions of the securities laws and demonstrates the defendant's "unfitness to serve." In *SEC v. Patel,* 61 F.3d 137, 141 (2d Cir. 1995) (emphasis added), the Second Circuit identified six non-exclusive factors that were "useful in making the unfitness assessment:" "(1) the 'egregiousness' of the underlying securities law violation; (2) the defendant's 'repeat offender' status; (3) the defendant's 'role' or position when he engaged in the fraud; (4) the defendant's degree of *scienter*; (5) the defendant's economic stake in the violation; and (6) the likelihood that misconduct will recur." The Second Circuit recently affirmed the utility of these factors in *SEC v. Bankosky*, 716 F.3d 45, 48 (2d Cir. 2013) (acknowledging that *Patel* was interpreting prior statutory language that required a finding of "substantial" unfitness, but concluding that Congress's decision in the SOX to lower the threshold of misconduct did not undermine the usefulness of the six factors).

The officer and director bar remedy was one of the more controversial aspects of the Remedies Act, in part because it called into question the interplay between the federal securities laws and state corporate law.

§ 9.6.4   DISGORGEMENT AND OTHER EQUITABLE REMEDIES

Disgorgement is an equitable remedy "designed to deprive a wrongdoer of his unjust enrichment and to deter others from violating the securities laws." *SEC v. First City Fin.*, 890 F. 2d 1215, 1230 (D.C. Cir. 1989). For decades, the remedy was deemed "available simply because the relevant provisions of the Securities Exchange Act of 1934, sections 21(d) and (e), 15 U.S.C. §§ 78u(d) and (e), vest jurisdiction in the federal courts." *Id.* However, the SOX eliminated any doubt as to the authority for court-ordered disgorgement: Section 21(d)(5) of the Exchange Act explicitly authorizes the SEC to seek and any federal court to grant "any equitable relief that may be appropriate or necessary for the benefit of investors."

In addition to ordering disgorgement of ill-gotten gains, courts may use their equitable powers to require a defendant to pay "pre-judgment interest" on any amounts ordered to be disgorged. A number of courts have also invoked their equitable authority to approve consent decrees that include undertakings, such as the retention of a consultant to report on compliance and recommend new procedures. *See* § 9.4 *supra*.

§ 9.6.5   CIVIL MONETARY PENALTIES

The SEC's power to seek monetary sanctions for securities law violations was perhaps the most controversial aspect of the Reform Act. The relevant provisions are set out in Exchange Act § 21(d)(3), Securities Act § 20(d), Investment Advisers Act § 209(e), and Investment Company Act § 42(e), which authorize the SEC to seek monetary penalties against "any" person for "any" violation of the securities laws or for the violation of a cease and desist order issued by the SEC. If the SEC makes a "proper showing," the penalty for "each violation" is to be calculated in accordance with a structure that escalates the penalties to a second-tier when the violation involves "fraud, deceit, manipulation, or deliberate or reckless disregard of a regulatory requirement," and to a third tier when the "violation directly or indirectly resulted in substantial losses or created a significant risk of substantial losses to other persons."

When the defendant in an SEC enforcement proceeding is a publicly traded corporation, civil monetary penalties raise the following question: To what extent is it fair and reasonable to impose a penalty against the corporation for securities law violations that were committed by its agents? The question was frequently posed in the wake of the accounting and corporate governance scandals at Enron and WorldCom, when the penalties obtained by the SEC increased substantially, with some corporate penalties exceeding $100 million. Likely prompted by claims that penalties of this magnitude unjustifiably hurt the shareholders who have already been injured by a drop in stock price resulting from the corporation's damaged reputation, the SEC set forth the considerations it will use in determining whether and to what extent it will impose monetary penalties on corporations. *See* Statement of the Securities and Exchange Commission Concerning Financial Penalties, SEC Release No. 2006-4 (January 4, 2006), https://www.sec.gov/news/press/ 2006-4.htm (observing that the imposition of corporate penalties is often necessary for effective deterrence and highlighting factors used to determine the appropriateness of a penalty, including the presence or absence of a direct benefit to the corporation as a result of the violation as well as the degree to which the penalty will recompense or further harm the injured shareholders).

§ 9.6.6   CEO AND CFO BONUS AND TRADING PROFIT CLAWBACKS

If an issuer is required to restate financial statements because of an error due to misconduct, the SEC may seek disgorgement of any bonus or other incentive- or equity-based compensation paid to the CEO or CFO, or any trading profits realized from the sale of the issuer's securities, during the 12-month period after the filing of the misleading document, in accordance with 15 U.S.C. § 7243(a). *See SEC v. Jenkins*, 718 F. Supp. 2d 1070, 1075 (D. Ariz. 2010) (holding that the SEC may proceed with a clawback action against an issuer's CEO, even if he "was unaware of the misconduct leading to misstated financials").

§ 9.7   ADMINISTRATIVE REMEDIES

When the SEC opts to pursue enforcement action through the initiation of an administrative proceeding against a respondent, the following remedies are among those the SEC may impose:

§ 9.7.1   CEASE-AND-DESIST ORDERS

Securities Act § 8A(a), Exchange Act § 21C(a), Investment Advisers Act § 203(k)(1), and Investment Company Act § 9(f)(1) each contains provisions authorizing the SEC, after notice and opportunity for a hearing, to publish findings and issue an order against "any person" found to have violated "any provision" of the federal securities laws or to have caused any such violation. The SEC may also order the respondent to "comply" with the relevant provision and/or to take steps to ensure future compliance.

The SEC considers a host of factors when deciding whether a cease-and-desist order is an appropriate sanction. These factors include the seriousness of the violation, the isolated or recurrent nature of the violation, the respondent's state of mind, the sincerity of assurances against future violations, the respondent's recognition of the wrongful nature of his or her conduct, and the risk of future violations. *See* In the Matter of KPMG Peat Marwick LLP, Exchange Act Release No. 43862 (Jan. 19, 2001) (observing that while there must be "some" risk of future violation, the amount of risk "need not be very great," since "[a]bsent evidence to the contrary, a finding of violation raises a sufficient risk of future violation").

In extraordinary instances, the SEC may issue temporary cease-and-desist orders against certain regulated entities and associated persons, and such orders may be issued *ex parte* if the SEC "determines that notice and hearing prior to entry would be impractical or contrary to the public interest." Exchange Act § 21C(c)(1), Securities Act § 8A(c)(1), Investment Advisers Act § 203(k)(3), and Investment Company Act § 9(f)(3).

Unlike a civil injunction, the violation of a cease-and-desist order does not put the person subject to the order at risk of contempt. However, if a person violates the terms of a cease-and-desist order, the SEC almost certainly will file an action in federal district court for an injunction requiring compliance with the order. Moreover, pursuant to the authority discussed at § 9.6.5 *supra*, the SEC may also seek the imposition of a monetary penalty.

§ 9.7.2   CIVIL MONETARY PENALTIES

Securities Act § 8A(g), Exchange Act § 21B, Investment Advisers Act § 203(i), and Investment Company Act § 9(d) each contains provisions authorizing the SEC, after notice and opportunity for a hearing, to impose monetary penalties for violating, or causing a violation, of the securities laws. Monetary penalties may also be imposed against broker-dealers, investment advisers, and their associated persons for "failure to reasonably supervise" with a view to preventing violations by another person subject to his supervision. The sections set out a three-tier structure for the calculation of the penalty for each violation and provide that any penalties imposed must be "in the public interest." Prior to amendments made by Congress in the Dodd-Frank Act, the SEC's authority to impose civil monetary penalties in administrative proceedings was limited to matters involving regulated entities and their associated persons. This relatively new and far-ranging authority has sparked some concerns as to the adequacy of the checks on the SEC's power to act both as a prosecutor and an adjudicator. *See* § 9.10 *infra*.

§ 9.7.3   ACCOUNTING AND DISGORGEMENT

Where a violation has been shown in any permanent cease-and-desist proceeding, or in any action in which the SEC may impose a monetary penalty, the SEC may order the retention of an accountant to calculate the profit from the unlawful activity, and may also order the payment of that profit. *See* Securities Act § 8A(e), Exchange Act § 21B(e), Investment Advisers Act § 203(k)(5), and Investment Company Act § 9(e). The CEO/CFO bonus clawback provision, set out in 15 U.S.C. § 7243(a), extends as well to orders of disgorgement issued in administrative proceedings. *See, e.g.,* In the Matter of William Slater, CPA and Peter E. Williams, Exchange Act Release No. 74240 (Feb. 10, 2015) (concluding that, despite the absence of any allegation that the former CEO and CFO participated in the misconduct that resulted in Saba Software's misleading financial statements, they are required to reimburse the company for the stock-sale profits and received bonuses during the 12-month periods following the financial results required to be restated).

§ 9.7.4   OFFICER AND DIRECTOR BARS

Section 8A(f) of the Securities Act and § 21C(f) of the Exchange Act authorize the SEC, after notice and a hearing, to bar a respondent from future service as an officer or director of a publicly traded company if the SEC finds a violation of the anti-fraud provisions of the securities laws as well as the respondent's "unfitness to serve."

§ 9.7.5   BROKER-DEALER AND INVESTMENT ADVISER DISCIPLINARY PROCEEDINGS

Broker-dealers and their associated persons are subject to discipline under Exchange Act §§ 15(b)(4) and 15(b)(6). The analogue for investment advisers and their associated persons is set out in Investment Advisers Act §§ 203(e) and 203(f). The SEC may institute proceedings under these provisions for an entity or individual's violations of the securities laws, or a "failure to reasonably supervise" another person who has violated the securities laws. Possible sanctions, after notice and the opportunity for a hearing, include censures, temporary suspensions, or permanent bars (including so-called collateral bars, which apply across different areas of the securities industry). *See Rizek v. SEC*, 215 F.3d 157, 161 (1st Cir. 2000) (upholding SEC order permanently barring broker-dealer from the securities industry and emphasizing that "[c]onsiderable deference should be given the Commission's ultimate judgment about what will best protect the public").

§ 9.8   DISTRIBUTION FUNDS FOR INVESTORS

Congress has authorized the SEC to create "distribution funds" for the victims of securities law violations. Such funds can be created at the direction of the Commission from any amounts disgorged by a defendant or respondent, together with any civil penalties imposed, in any judicial or administrative enforcement action brought by the SEC under the federal securities laws. The SEC also has authority to add to this fund any "gifts, bequests and devises of property, both real and personal." 15 U.S.C. § 7246.

§ 9.9 COLLATERAL CONSEQUENCES

SEC sanctions often carry with them collateral consequences. Injunctions, for example, might subject a broker-dealer or investment adviser to further SEC disciplinary action, including a bar from the securities industry. *See* Exchange Act §§ 15(b)(4)(C) and 15(b)(6)(A); and Investment Advisers Act §§ 203(e) and 203(f). Certain types of injunctions also disqualify a securities issuer from taking advantage of certain exemptions from the securities registration process (such as offerings pursuant to Regulation A). Although the granting of waivers to these (and other) disqualifications has been fairly routine in the past, there recently has been sharp disagreement as to whether waivers are granted in a way that has made statutory disqualification less meaningful. *See*, *e.g.*, Luis A. Aguilar & Kara M. Stein, Comm'rs, Dissenting Statement In the Matter of Oppenheimer & Co., Inc. (Feb. 4, 2015) (contending that the waiver granted by the majority lacks adequate safeguards to ensure that the firm will comply with the law).

§ 9.10 LITIGATING WITH THE SEC

Although the overwhelming majority of enforcement actions initiated by the SEC are settled, an increasing number of them are litigated, either in an administrative proceeding or in federal court.

§ 9.10.1 LITIGATION IN
ADMINISTRATIVE PROCEEDINGS

Administrative proceedings are governed by the SEC's Rules of Practice. *See* 17 C.F.R. § 201.100 et seq. They typically are initiated with the Commission's issuance of an "Order of Proceedings" that specifies the charges against the respondent, *see* § 201.200, and there is typically a 20-day period for the respondent to file an answer. *See* § 201.220(b). Administrative proceedings that require evidentiary hearings are generally conducted by administrative law judges (ALJs), who are employees of the Commission. ALJs address pre-hearing motions, *see* § 201.221(c)(5), supervise the limited process of discovery, *see* § 201.230, evaluate the testimony and cross-examinations of the witnesses presented by the enforcement staff and the respondent, *see* § 201.326, and render a written initial decision, *see* § 201.360, often after the receipt of post-hearing briefs submitted by both the respondent and the staff, *see* § 201.340(c). In an evidentiary hearing conducted by an ALJ, neither the Federal Rules of Civil Procedure nor the Federal Rules of Evidence applies.

Initial ALJ Decision and Commission Review. The initial decision issued by the ALJ generally includes findings of fact and conclusions of law (supported by reasons for those findings and conclusions) and a recommended sanction. It is final unless either party files a petition for review with the Commission within the time limit specified by the ALJ, generally not to exceed 21 days from the date of decision. *See* 17 C.F.R. §§ 201.360(d), 201.410. On review, the

Commission may affirm, reverse, modify, or set aside
the ALJ's initial decision, or may remand the case to
the ALJ for further proceedings, and may make "any
findings or conclusions that in its judgment are
proper and on the basis of the record." § 201.411(a).
In other words, the Commission's authority on review
is *de novo*. If no review is sought, or if the
Commission declines review where it has discretion
to do so, *see* § 201.411(b), the Commission issues a
final order which sets the date on which the sanction
recommended by the ALJ, if any, takes effect. *See*
§ 201.360(d)(2).

Review by a Circuit Court of Appeals. Each of the
principal federal securities acts provides for judicial
review of a final order by the Commission in the U.S.
Court of Appeals for the circuit in which the
respondent resides or has his principal place of
business or in the District of Columbia Circuit. *See,*
e.g., § 25(a)(1) of the Exchange Act. The acts specify
that an appeal must be commenced within sixty days
after the entry of the Commission's final order, *see,*
e.g., id., and that the SEC's factual findings, if
supported by substantial evidence, are conclusive.
See, e.g., § 25(a)(4) of the Exchange Act. A respondent
may seek circuit court review of an administrative
proceeding only if she has already pursued and
exhausted all administrative remedies available.

§ 9.10.2 LITIGATION IN
JUDICIAL PROCEEDINGS

Enforcement actions initiated by the SEC in
federal court are typically filed as injunctive actions

pursuant to the statutory authority provided in each of the principal securities statutes. *See* § 9.6.1, *supra*. The action commences with the filing of the SEC's complaint, which in cases alleging fraud, must meet the particularity requirements of Rule 9(b) of the Federal Rules of Civil Procedure. In most cases, this is hardly a hurdle because the SEC typically files complaints of considerable length and detail, often described by defense counsel as "speaking complaints."

Pre-Trial Motions. As with private litigation in federal court, in litigation initiated by the SEC, the defendant may file any number of pre-trial motions, including motions to dismiss under Fed. R. Civ. P. 12(b)(6) and motions for summary judgment under Fed. R. Civ. P. 56. The SEC also frequently submits motions for summary judgment, or partial summary judgment, in cases where it is the law rather than the facts that is in dispute. Unresolved issues of material fact must proceed to trial.

Right to a Jury Trial When a Monetary Penalty Is Sought. In cases in which the SEC is seeking the imposition of a civil monetary penalty, a defendant may invoke a Seventh Amendment right to a trial by jury. This right applies only to the determination of the defendant's liability; the determination of the amount of the penalty occurs in a subsequent phase conducted by a judge. *Tull v. United States*, 481 U.S. 412 (1987).

§ 9.10.3   THE SEC's CHOICE OF FORUM

The choice of whether to institute an enforcement action as an administrative proceeding or as a judicial action has been one that traditionally has rested entirely with the SEC. And for many years, the SEC's litigation docket was roughly divided evenly between the two fora. However, for several reasons, including because civil monetary penalties can now be imposed in administrative proceedings against nonregulated persons (*see* § 9.7.2 *supra*), the SEC has been shifting that balance toward its administrative tribunal, which provides for a more streamlined process capable of resolving cases in months (as opposed to what is often years in federal district court). This shift has caused some to question whether the SEC has a "home court advantage" that is unfair to the parties that must litigate before an ALJ—and/or whether the limited scope of discovery, the inapplicability of the federal rules of evidence, the absence of a jury, and the method of appointing ALJs raise due process, equal protection, or other constitutional concerns.

Approximately two dozen legal challenges over the SEC's choice of forum have been brought, with a mixed record of success. Compare *Hill v. SEC*, 114 F. Supp. 3d 1297 (N.D. Ga. 2015) (granting motion for a preliminary injunction against the SEC because plaintiff proved substantial likelihood of success on the merits of claim that ALJ was appointed in a manner that contravened the text of the Constitution's Appointments Clause) with *Jarkesy v. SEC*, 803 F.3d 9 (D.C. Cir. 2015) (affirming dismissal of claim that administrative proceeding violated plaintiff's rights to due process and equal protection because subject matter jurisdiction does not exist while the administrative proceeding is pending). *See also Gupta v. SEC*, 796 F.Supp. 2d 503 (S.D.N.Y. 2011) (refusing to grant SEC's motion for dismissal because complaint pled facts sufficient to state a claim that the SEC's decision to treat plaintiff, a respondent in an administrative proceeding, differently from 28 other defendants in related insider trading federal court cases was irrational, arbitrary, and discriminatory).

In response to criticisms about its procedures and possibly to avert future litigation challenges, the SEC recently proposed changes to its Rules of Practice that, among other things, would allow broader discovery rights in administrative proceedings and allow more time to challenge rulings prior to an evidentiary hearing. *See* Amendments to the Commission's Rules of Practice, Exchange Act Release No. 34-75976 (Sept. 24, 2015), https://www. sec.gov/rules/proposed/2015/34-75976.pdf.

§ 9.10.4 THE BURDEN OF PROOF

Although at one time it appeared that a higher standard should govern in at least some actions brought by the agency, today there is little doubt that "preponderance of the evidence" is the standard that the SEC must meet in civil litigation. *Steadman v. SEC*, 450 U.S. 91 (1981).

§ 9.10.5 STATUTES OF LIMITATIONS

With the single exception of the five-year period specified in Exchange Act § 21A(d)(5) for civil monetary penalties in insider trading cases, *see* § 7. 6.1, *supra*, the federal securities laws do not specify any statutes of limitations for enforcement actions brought by the SEC. And the SEC's unequivocal and longstanding position had been that no such statute of limitations should be implied.

The SEC's advocacy against an implied statute of limitations has met with complete success when the issue has been litigated in the context of remedial relief, such as an action for an injunction or an order of disgorgement. *See SEC v. Rind*, 991 F.2d 1486, 1492 (9th Cir. 1993) ("[p]lacing strict time limits on Commission enforcement actions * * * would quite plainly 'frustrate or interfere with the implementation of national policies' ") (quoting *Occidental Life Ins. Co. v. EEOC*, 432 U.S. 355, 367 (1977)).

If, however, an SEC sanction can be categorized as "punitive," the enforcement action is subject to the general five-year statute of limitations in 28 U.S.C. § 2462, which applies to any government "action, suit, or proceeding for the enforcement of any civil fine, penalty, or forfeiture, pecuniary or otherwise." In *Johnson v. SEC*, 87 F.3d 484, 488 (D.C. Cir. 1996), the court held that a " 'penalty,' as the term is used in § 2462, is a form of punishment imposed by the government for unlawful or proscribed conduct, which goes beyond remedying the damage caused to the harmed parties by the defendant's action." It then rejected the SEC's argument that the broker-dealer supervisor's censure and six-month suspension were "remedial in nature," finding instead that the sanctions "clearly resemble punishment in the ordinary sense of the word." *Id.*

Section 2462's five-year statute of limitations begins to run from the date when the underlying violation occurs, and not from the date of the SEC's discovery of that violation. *See Gabelli v. SEC*, 133 S. Ct. 1216, 1223 (2013) (emphasizing the text of the statute and observing that the policies favoring a discovery-based rule in private litigation by injured parties seeking recompense do not extend to government-initiated civil penalty actions, which are "intended to punish, and label defendants wrongdoers").

§ 9.10.6 COLLATERAL ESTOPPEL EFFECTS

As noted previously, the collateral estoppel effects of litigating with the SEC and losing is a principal explanation for the overwhelming number of enforcement actions resolved through consensual settlement. *See* § 9.4 *supra.* In *Parklane Hosiery Co. v. Shore*, 439 U.S. 322 (1979), petitioners had a "full and fair" opportunity in a prior action to defend against the SEC's claim that the company had issued a materially false and misleading proxy statement in connection with a merger. The Court therefore upheld the offensive use of collateral estoppel by class action stockholders to prevent the company from re-litigating factual and legal issues that had been necessarily determined.

The SEC often invokes the doctrine of collateral estoppel to prevent a defendant in a civil case from re-litigating issues that were "fully and fairly" decided in a criminal trial. *See, e.g., SEC v. Grossman*, 887 F.Supp. 649 (S.D.N.Y. 1995), *aff'd sub. nom., SEC v. Estate of Hirshberg*, 101 F.3d 109 (2d Cir. 1996). The SEC has also successfully argued for collateral estoppel in cases in which the defendant has resolved the prior criminal action through a guilty plea. *See SEC v. Palmisano*, 135 F.3d 860 (2d Cir. 1998).

§ 9.11 SELF-REGULATORY ORGANIZATIONS (SROs) AS ENFORCERS OF THE FEDERAL SECURITIES LAWS

Although Congress established the SEC as the principal enforcer of its newly created federal securities laws, even in 1934, Congress clearly envisioned that the stock exchanges—particularly the New York Stock Exchange (NYSE)—would continue to play a major role in regulating the conduct of exchange members and their associated persons. *See* Exchange Act § 6 (authorizing the SEC to register "national securities exchanges"). Four years later, the National Association of Securities Dealers (NASD) was added to this scheme of self-regulation, when Congress enacted the Maloney Act of 1938, which extended self-regulation to the non-exchange, or over-the-counter (OTC), market. *See* Exchange Act § 15A (authorizing the SEC to register "national securities associations"). Throughout the next 70 years, the NASD and the NYSE, together with a host of other national securities exchanges, regulated the securities industry under the oversight of the SEC. Section 19 of the Exchange Act sets out the general scheme for SRO responsibilities and the oversight role of the SEC.

In 2007, this self-regulatory landscape changed dramatically when the SEC formally approved the consolidation of the NASD and the enforcement, member regulatory, and arbitration divisions of the NYSE into a single self-regulatory organization to be known as the Financial Industry Regulatory Authority (FINRA). The consolidation was intended to help streamline the broker-dealer regulatory system, combine technologies, and permit the establishment of a single set of rules governing membership matters.

§ 9.11.1   FINRA's STRUCTURE AND OPERATION

FINRA is a not-for-profit membership corporation that adopts and enforces rules regulating the activities of nearly 4,000 securities firms with approximately 644,000 brokers. FINRA also contracts to perform market regulation and surveillance functions for many of U.S. stock markets, including NASDAQ Stock Market, Inc., and the International Securities Exchange, LLC.

FINRA is governed by a board composed of a majority of independent directors (*i.e.*, persons who have no material business relationships with its broker-dealer members or the securities exchanges which it regulates). *See* FINRA By-Laws, art. IV,

§ 4(a). In 2016, the Board of Governors consists of 13 seats held by Public Governors, 10 seats held by Industry Governors, and one seat held by FINRA's CEO. The presence of a non-industry majority on the Board and key committees of FINRA has prompted some to contend that there is little "self" left in securities industry self-regulation. Others, however, disagree and emphasize that member firms and associated persons are actively engaged in all aspects of FINRA's work.

§ 9.11.2   FINRA's DISCIPLINARY FUNCTION

As a condition of its registration with the SEC as a "national securities association," FINRA's rules must ensure that members and their associated persons are "appropriately disciplined" for violations of any provision of the federal securities laws as well as FINRA's own rules. *See* Exchange Act § 15A(b)(7). When FINRA's Enforcement or Market Regulation Department determines that such a violation has occurred and formal disciplinary action is warranted, the Department files a complaint and a three-person hearing panel is assigned to any case that has not been resolved through a settlement. FINRA's disciplinary sanctions can run the gamut from "expulsion; suspension; limitation of activities, functions and operations; fine; censure; being suspended or barred from being associated with a member or any other fitting sanction," *id.*, and the rules for FINRA's disciplinary proceedings must provide for "a fair procedure." Exchange Act § 15A(b)(8).

Initial disciplinary decisions rendered by FINRA hearing panels are subject to review by FINRA's National Adjudicatory Council (NAC), an appellate body comprised of fourteen representatives from within and outside the securities industry. The NAC may affirm, modify, reverse, increase, or reduce any sanction or impose any other suitable sanction. The NAC's decision represents FINRA's final action, unless FINRA's Board of Governors decides to review the NAC's decision.

A firm or individual can appeal a FINRA disciplinary decision to the SEC, *see* Exchange Act § 19(d), and an SEC order affirming or modifying a FINRA sanction can be appealed to the Court of Appeals for the circuit in which the respondent resides or has his principal place of business or in the District of Columbia Circuit. *See* § 25(a)(1) of the Exchange Act.

§ 9.11.3 THE STATE ACTION DEBATE

Although they operate under the oversight of the SEC and perform a regulatory function, FINRA and other SROs in the securities industry are generally regarded as private entities and not as government actors. Thus, for purposes of constitutional protections such as the Fifth Amendment's privilege against self-incrimination, the SEC and courts have consistently refused to regard SRO action as "state action." *See*, *e.g.*, In the Matter of Michael Nicholas Romano, Exchange Act Release No. 76011 (Sept. 29, 2015) (citing cases and finding that respondent failed to establish the necessary state action that would implicate a Fifth Amendment privilege against self-incrimination); *United States v. Solomon*, 509 F.2d 863 (2d Cir. 1975) (finding no violation of the Fifth Amendment where the government relied on testimony that was compelled in an NYSE investigation). State action is recognized only on those infrequent occasions in which an SRO engages in "joint action" with the SEC or the DOJ, or when an SRO's action can otherwise be "fairly attributed to the government." *D.L. Cromwell Invs., Inc. v. NASD Regulation, Inc.*, 279 F.3d 155, 161–163 (2d Cir. 2002) (observing that SROs are not inherently state actors based on their regulatory function, even if evidence suggests that SEC or DOJ officials cooperated in their investigations). But *see In re Frank Quattrone*, Exchange Act Release No. 53547, 87 S.E.C. Docket 1847, 1851–1852 (Mar. 24, 2006) (holding that respondent "proffered enough evidence concerning the Joint Investigation to earn an evidentiary hearing").

In the context of claims for immunity, however, a number of courts have recognized that SROs perform a quasi-governmental role in enforcing the federal securities laws and have thus held SRO officials—or the SRO itself—subject to absolute immunity for damages in private actions. *See, e.g., D'Alessio v. NYSE,* 258 F.3d 93, 105 (2d Cir. 2001). But *see In re Facebook, Inc. IPO, Sec. & Derivative Litig.*, 2015 WL 7587357, at *3 (S.D.N.Y Nov. 24, 2015) (denying NASDAQ's motion to vacate and reaffirming previous ruling that " '[w]hile the doctrine of SRO immunity must continue to ensure regulatory independence, it cannot be applied to allow blanket protection for exchanges when they fail to exercise due care in their pursuits of profit' ").

§ 9.12　PARALLEL PROCEEDINGS

The phrase "parallel proceedings" is frequently used to describe concurrent or successive civil and criminal investigations or prosecutions by the SEC and the DOJ, though the phrase can take on an even broader construction if state officials or SRO officials become involved. The general rule is that "[i]n the absence of substantial prejudice to the rights of the parties involved, . . . parallel proceedings are unobjectionable." *SEC v. Dresser Indus., Inc, 628 F. 2d 1368, 1374* (en banc). *See also United States v. Kordel*, 397 U.S. 1 (1970) (government officials may conduct parallel proceedings without violating due process as long as they act in good faith).

The *Dresser* case involved what may be termed "horizontal proceedings"—concurrent or successive proceedings initiated by different agencies in the federal government. The phrase "vertical proceedings" can be used to connote multiple layers of investigations/prosecutions by different authorities, such as multiple proceedings brought by the federal government (the SEC and/or the DOJ), state officials (often involving many different states acting under both criminal and civil authority), and SROs (most often FINRA). These, too, are acceptable and commonplace under the general *Dresser* standard.

§ 9.12.1 SHARING EVIDENCE

Section 21(d) of the Exchange Act authorizes the SEC to transmit information concerning its investigations to the DOJ, which may in its discretion "institute the necessary criminal proceedings" under the federal securities laws. The SEC's Enforcement Manual further encourages Enforcement Division staff "to work cooperatively with criminal authorities, to share information, and to coordinate their investigations with parallel criminal investigations when appropriate." *See* SEC Enforcement Manual § 5.2.1 (2013). The use of SEC investigative material and discovery in criminal cases is thus generally permissible unless circumstances show bad faith on the part of the government in bringing parallel proceedings. *United States v. Teyibo*, 877 F. Supp. 846, 855–856 (S.D.N.Y. 1995), *aff'd*, 101 F.3d 681 (2d Cir. 1996). Such bad faith may exist when "(1) the Government pursued a civil action solely to obtain evidence for a criminal prosecution; (2) the Government failed to advise the defendant during the civil proceeding that it is contemplating criminal prosecution; (3) the defendant was without counsel; (4) the defendant reasonably feared prejudice from pre-trial publicity or other unfair injury; or (5) other special circumstances suggest that the criminal prosecution is unconstitutional or improper." *Teyibo*, 877 F. Supp. at 856–857 (finding that the "Government did not violate Teyibo's constitutional rights by simultaneously pursuing civil and criminal actions against him;" nor were his rights violated when he voluntarily provided information to the SEC after having been advised of his right to be represented by counsel).

§ 9.12.2 DOUBLE JEOPARDY PROTECTIONS

The Double Jeopardy Clause of the Fifth Amendment provides that no "person [shall] be subject for the same offence to be twice put in jeopardy of life or limb." However, as the Supreme Court has long recognized, double jeopardy protection does not "prohibit the imposition of all additional sanctions that could 'in common parlance' be described as punishment." *Hudson v. United States*, 522 U.S. 93, 98–99 (1997). Instead, the "Clause protects only against the imposition of multiple *criminal* punishments for the same offense." *Id.* at 99. Congress's determination to classify a sanction as civil is generally controlling unless the actual imposition of that sanction is "so punitive in nature as to transform what was intended as a civil remedy into a criminal penalty." *SEC v. Palmisano*, 135 F. 3d 860, 864 (2d. Cir. 1998) (finding no double jeopardy violation in connection with district court's order requiring defendant to disgorge approximately $9.2 million and to pay a $500,000 civil penalty, notwithstanding parallel criminal sanction resulting in defendant's sentence to 15 years in prison).

CHAPTER 10

ENFORCEMENT ISSUES INVOLVING ATTORNEYS AND ACCOUNTANTS

§ 10.1 INTRODUCTION

This Chapter examines the role of the federal government in regulating attorneys engaged in securities law practice and accountants responsible for the auditing of companies required to file reports with the Securities and Exchange Commission (the SEC or the Commission). It begins with a discussion of the SEC's power to discipline attorneys, accountants, and other professionals who appear or practice before the Commission (§ 10.2 *infra*). It then turns to the topic of professional conduct for securities attorneys, discussing several general rules promulgated by state bar associations for all attorneys (§ 10.3.1 *infra*) as well as a specific SEC rule applicable to attorneys who represent securities issuers (§ 10.3.2 *infra*). The Chapter then explores different types of enforcement actions against attorneys, including disciplinary proceedings for improper professional conduct (§ 10.4.1 *infra*) and actions against attorneys who commit, or cause their clients to commit, violations of the federal securities laws (§§ 10.4.2–10.4.7 *infra*). Thereafter it examines professional standards for accountants (§ 10.5.1 *infra*) as well as enforcement provisions under the federal securities laws (§§ 10.5.2–10.5.3 *infra*). The Chapter concludes with a discussion of the Public Company Accounting Oversight Board (the PCAOB), a nonprofit organization established by Congress to oversee the accounting firms that audit public companies and broker-dealers (§ 10.6 *infra*).

§ 10.2 SEC DISCIPLINE OF PROFESSIONALS UNDER EXCHANGE ACT SECTION 4C AND RULE 102(e)

Section 602 of the Sarbanes-Oxley Act of 2002 (the SOX) added a new § 4C to the Exchange Act to explicitly empower the SEC to discipline professionals who practice or appear before the agency. Although the SEC has possessed that power since the agency's inception, it previously had been reflected only in Rule 102(e), formerly Rule 2(e), of the SEC's Rules of Practice. *See Touche Ross & Co. v. SEC*, 609 F.2d 570, 577 (2d Cir. 1979) (acknowledging that there was no express statutory provision authorizing the SEC to discipline professionals, but upholding Rule 102(e) as a valid exercise of the SEC's general authority under the federal securities laws "to 'make such rules and regulations as may be necessary or appropriate * * * for the execution of [its] functions * * * '") (quoting Exchange Act § 23(a)(1)). *See also Checkosky v. SEC*, 23 F.3d 452, 456 (D.C. Cir. 1994) ("There can be little doubt that the Commission, like any other institution in which lawyers or other professionals participate, has authority to police the behavior of practitioners before it.") (internal quotation marks omitted).

The text of § 4C and Rule 102(e) each provides that:

(a) AUTHORITY TO CENSURE.—The Commission may censure any person, or deny, temporarily or permanently, to any person the privilege of appearing or practicing before the Commission in any way, if that person is found by the Commission, after notice and opportunity for hearing in the matter—

(1)   not to possess the requisite qualifications to represent others;

(2)   to be lacking in character or integrity, or to have engaged in unethical or improper professional conduct; or

(3)   to have willfully violated, or willfully aided and abetted the violation of, any provision of the securities laws or the rules and regulations issued thereunder. * * *

Rule 102(f) broadly defines "practic[ing]" before the SEC to include:

(1) Transacting any business with the Commission; and

(2) The preparation of any statement, opinion or other paper by any attorney, accountant, engineer or other professional or expert, filed with the Commission in any registration statement, notification, application, report or other document with the consent of such attorney, accountant, engineer or other professional or expert.

Section 4C(b) also defines, for the purposes of that section, what the term "improper professional conduct" means with respect to registered public accounting firms and their associated persons:

(1) intentional or knowing conduct, including reckless conduct, that results in a violation of applicable professional standards; or

(2) negligent conduct in the form of—

(A) A single instance of highly unreasonable conduct that results in a violation of applicable professional standards in circumstances in which an accountant knows, or should know, that heightened scrutiny is warranted; or

(B) Repeated instances of unreasonable conduct, each resulting in a violation of applicable professional standards, that indicate a lack of competence to practice before the Commission.

Rule 102(e)(1)(iv) extends that same definition to any person licensed to practice as an accountant. *See* In the Matter of Aesoph, Admin. Proc. No. 3-15168, at 23–24 (June 27, 2014) (observing that "highly unreasonable" conduct is "higher than ordinary negligence but lower than recklessness," and concluding that while two instances of unreasonable conduct may qualify as "repeated," there must be a separate finding that the instances reflect a "lack of competence").

Neither § 4C nor Rule 102(e) supplies a state of mind for attorneys or other non-accountant professionals charged with "improper professional conduct." Thus, whether the same standards or a different and higher standard shall apply is left to adjudication in an SEC enforcement proceeding (*see* § 10.4.1 *infra*) or to future SEC rulemaking.

§ 10.3 PROFESSIONAL CONDUCT FOR SECURITIES ATTORNEYS

Securities attorneys, like all attorneys, are regulated by state bar associations. Securities attorneys who appear and practice before the SEC must also adhere to the standard of professional conduct set out in Part 205 of the SEC's Rules of Practice.

§ 10.3.1 STATE RULES FOR ALL ATTORNEYS

Most state rules governing the professional conduct of attorneys are based on the ABA's Model Rules of Professional Conduct (the ABA Model Rules) (last revised in 2007). However, some states still draw their rules of professional conduct from the ABA's earlier Model Code of Professional Responsibility.

The ABA Model Rules make it clear that a lawyer may not assist a client in committing a securities law violation or counsel the client to commit such a violation and that the lawyer may not affirmatively make misrepresentations to others. In this regard, ABA Model Rule 1.2(d) provides that a lawyer shall not knowingly assist a client in, or counsel a client to engage in, a crime or fraud. ABA Model Rule 4.1 further states that, in the course of representing a

client a lawyer shall not knowingly "make a false
statement of material fact or law to a third person."

In 2003, after years of debate and in the wake of a
widely-held belief that lawyer malfeasance had
played some role in the accounting and corporate
governance scandals at Enron and WorldCom, the
ABA revised its Model Rules to clarify the
professional responsibilities of a lawyer with
knowledge of misrepresentations or other illegal acts
by a client or by an agent of a client, particularly
when the client is a corporation or other organization.

The Organization as a Client. One rule that
underwent revision in 2003 was ABA Model Rule
1.13 (Organization as Client). That rule now
establishes "up-the-ladder" requirements regarding
a lawyer's obligation to report possible unlawful acts
within the organization. In particular, Rule 1.13(b)
provides that:

> Unless the lawyer reasonably believes that it is
> not necessary in the best interest of the
> organization to do so, the lawyer shall refer the
> matter to higher authority in the organization,
> including, if warranted by the circumstances to
> the highest authority that can act on behalf of
> the organization as determined by applicable
> law.

At least where the organization is a public
corporation, the "highest authority that can act"
typically would be the board of directors. ABA Model
Rule 1.13(c) goes on to specify that if the
organization's highest authority refuses to act and

the lawyer believes that a violation of the law is reasonably certain to result in substantial injury to the organization, then the lawyer "may reveal information relating to the representation whether or not Rule 1.6 permits such disclosure, but only if and to the extent the lawyer reasonably believes necessary to prevent substantial injury to the organization."

<u>Confidentiality of Client Information</u>. ABA Model Rule 1.6(b) (Confidentiality of Information) also underwent a substantial revision in 2003. Whereas the prior rule mandated strict confidentiality, with a client-crime exception that had been limited to disclosures necessary to prevent "reasonably certain death or substantial bodily harm," the present rule provides that a lawyer *may* (but is not required to) disclose client confidences to a third party:

> (2) to prevent the client from committing a crime or fraud that is reasonably certain to result in substantial injury to the financial interests or property of another and in furtherance of which the client has used or is using the lawyer's services;

> (3) to prevent, mitigate or rectify substantial injury to the financial interests or property of another that is reasonably certain to result or has resulted from the client's commission of a crime or fraud in furtherance of which the client has used the lawyer's services.

That revision brought the ABA's Model Rule more in line with the prevailing rule in the vast majority of states. Some states, however, (including California and Washington, as well as the District of Columbia) continue to *prohibit* a lawyer from disclosing to sources outside the corporation that a client is about to engage in illegal conduct. And a few states (including New Jersey and Florida) stand at the other end of the spectrum by providing that a lawyer *must* disclose client confidences to prevent criminal acts. For example, New Jersey's Rule of Professional Conduct 1.6(b) specifies that an attorney with confidential information relating to the representation of a client:

> [S]hall reveal such information to the proper authorities, as soon as, and to the extent the lawyer reasonably believes necessary, to prevent the client * * * from committing a criminal, illegal or fraudulent act that the lawyer reasonably believes is likely to result in substantial bodily harm or substantial injury to the financial interest or property of another.

Securities lawyers must therefore ensure that they are familiar with the current rules of professional conduct that govern their admission to the bar in the relevant jurisdiction(s).

Noisy Withdrawals. Even in the minority of jurisdictions that prohibit lawyers from revealing information necessary to prevent a client's securities fraud, securities lawyers may (and often must) withdraw from representation on account of a client's conduct. Moreover, it may be necessary sometimes for a lawyer to alert a third party to the fact of that withdrawal (termed by some a "noisy withdrawal") and to disaffirm a previously prepared document, opinion, or affirmation. *See* ABA Model Rule 4.1(b) (stating that a lawyer shall not "fail to disclose a material fact to a third person when disclosure is necessary to avoid assisting a criminal or fraudulent act by a client, unless disclosure is prohibited by Rule 1.6"); *see also* Cmt. 3 (observing that "[i]n extreme cases, substantive law may require a lawyer to disclose information relating to the representation to avoid being deemed to have assisted the client's crime or fraud").

§ 10.3.2 SEC RULES FOR SECURITIES ATTORNEYS

Section 307 of the SOX authorized the SEC to issue rules setting forth minimum standards of professional conduct for attorneys who appear and practice before the SEC in any way in the representation of a securities issuer. The SOX further required that these rules include provisions requiring such attorneys to report evidence of a material violation of any federal or state law or breach of fiduciary duty by the company or any agent "up-the-ladder" within the issuer.

The SEC carried out this mandate in January 2003, when it adopted Part 205 of 17 CFR. The rules:

- define "[e]vidence of a material violation to means credible evidence, based upon which it would be unreasonable, under the circumstances, for a prudent and competent attorney not to conclude that it is reasonably likely that a material violation has occurred, is ongoing, or is about to occur." § 205.2(e). The double negative emphasizes that lawyers will be subject to discipline under the rules only if their assessment of the facts surrounding an issuer client's conduct was unreasonable.

- define "issuer" to mean an Exchange Act reporting company. § 205.2(h). *See* § 1.3 *supra* (identifying the three types of reporting companies).

- require an attorney to report evidence of a material violation within the issuer to the chief legal counsel or the CEO or the equivalent. *See* § 205.3(b)(1).

- require an attorney, if the chief legal counsel or CEO does not respond appropriately to the evidence, to report the evidence to the audit committee, another committee of independent directors, or the full board of directors. *See* § 205.3(b)(3).

- provide that a "subordinate attorney" who works under the direction or supervision of another attorney can satisfy the requirements under § 205.3(b)(1) and (3) by reporting to his or her supervisor the evidence of the material violation. The "reporting-up" responsibility thereafter falls upon the supervising attorney. *See* § 205.4.

- provide that the requirements in Part 205 do not apply to foreign attorneys who are not admitted in the US and who do not advise clients regarding US law. §§ 205.2(a)(2) and 205.2(j).

- allow an issuer to establish a "qualified legal compliance committee" (QLCC) as an alternative procedure for reporting evidence of a material violation. § 205.2(b)(3). A QLCC must consist of at least one member of the issuer's audit committee, or an equivalent committee of independent directors, and two or more independent board members. § 2.02(k).

- state explicitly that Part 205 does not create a private cause of action and that authority to enforce compliance with the rules is vested exclusively with the SEC. § 205.7.

- allow an attorney, without the issuer's consent, to reveal confidential information related to the representation to the extent the attorney reasonably believes necessary: (1) "[t]o prevent the issuer from committing a material violation that is likely to cause substantial financial injury to the financial interests or property of the issuer or investors;" (2) to prevent the issuer from committing perjury, suborning perjury, or other act that is likely to perpetrate a fraud upon the SEC; or (3) to rectify the consequences of a material violation or illegal act in which the attorney's services have been used. § 205.3(d)(2).

- preempt inconsistent state rules. *See* § 205.6(c) (stating that "[a]n attorney who complies in good faith with the provisions [in Part 205] shall not be subject to discipline or otherwise liable under inconsistent standards imposed by any state").

- provide that an attorney who violates any provision in Part 205 will be subject to civil penalties and other remedies provided for in the federal securities laws as well as SEC disciplinary action, which could result in a censure or being temporarily or permanently denied the privilege of appearing or practicing before the SEC. §§ 205.6(a),(b).

§ 10.4   ENFORCEMENT ACTIONS AGAINST SECURITIES ATTORNEYS

Securities attorneys who engage in unprofessional conduct may be disciplined by the SEC under Rule 102(e). Attorneys may also be subject to enforcement actions that charge the attorney with causing, or aiding and abetting, a securities law violation by the attorney's client.

§ 10.4.1   DISCIPLINARY PROCEEDINGS UNDER RULE 102(e)

The *Carter & Johnson* Proceeding. Although the disciplinary proceeding dates back more than 35 years, In re Carter & Johnson, Exchange Act Release No. 17597, 1981 WL 384414 (Feb. 28, 1981), is still the most widely-known Rule 102(e)/Rule 2(e) action involving attorneys. The case involved two law firm partners at Brown, Wood who, on numerous occasions over several years, had advised the principal officers of their client, National Telephone Company, to disclose to investors and other third parties material facts about the company's weakening financial condition. The officers, however, repeatedly rejected that advice and, with the assistance of their attorneys, filed misleading financial reports with the SEC. After an extensive hearing, an ALJ found that the attorneys had engaged in unethical and improper professional conduct and had aided and abetted the company's reporting violations. But the SEC reversed that decision—and reversed the attorneys' temporary suspension from practicing before the SEC—because it wanted to provide prior notice of standards that previously may have been under-developed. Looking forward, then, the SEC made clear that:

> When a lawyer with significant responsibilities in the effectuation of a company's compliance with the disclosure requirements of the federal securities laws becomes aware that his client is engaged in a substantial and continuing failure to satisfy those disclosure requirements, his continued participation violates professional standards unless he takes prompt steps to end the client's noncompliance.

Id. at *30. The SEC emphasized, however, that the lawyer is in the best position to choose the next step. Sometimes this might include resignation. Yet the SEC expressly disagreed with those who viewed resignation as the only permissible course when a client chooses not to comply with disclosure advice:

Premature resignation serves neither the end of
an effective lawyer-client relationship nor, in
most cases, the effective administration of the
securities laws. The lawyer's continued
interaction with his client will ordinarily hold
the greatest promise of corrective action. So long
as a lawyer is acting in good faith and exerting
reasonable efforts to prevent violations of the
law by his client, his professional obligations
have been met.

Id. at *31 n.77. The SEC suggested several
alternatives for affirmative steps, including a direct
approach to the board of directors or one or more
individual directors or officers, or enlisting the aid of
other members of the firm's management. But the
SEC also acknowledged that in certain rare
instances, the misconduct may be "so extreme or
irretrievable, or the involvement of his client's
management and board of directors in the
misconduct is so thoroughgoing and pervasive that
any action short of resignation would be futile." *Id.* at
*31.

The *Carter & Johnson* opinion also emphasized
that Rule 102(e) should not be used to discipline
lawyers who in good faith provide legal advice that in
hindsight turns out to be wrong. Instead, securities
lawyers should be encouraged "to bring [their] best
independent judgment to bear on a disclosure
problem," and thus they "must have the freedom to
make innocent—or even, in certain cases, careless—
mistakes without fear of legal liability or loss of the
ability to practice before the Commission." *Id.* at *25.

Intentional or reckless misconduct, as opposed to negligent conduct, was therefore established as the appropriate standard for attorney discipline under Rule 102(e).

The Aftermath of *Carter & Johnson*. The SEC's case against Carter and Johnson remains one of the exceedingly rare instances of a "stand-alone" Rule 102(e) action charging an attorney with improper professional conduct. After an outcry from the legal profession, the SEC went so far as to announce that "as a matter of policy" the SEC will "generally refrain [ ] from using its administrative forum to conduct *de novo* determinations of the professional obligation of attorneys." Disciplinary Proceedings Involving Professionals Appearing or Practicing Before the Commission, Exchange Act Release No. 25893, 41 SEC Docket 465 (July 13, 1988).

§ 10.4.2 RULE 102(e) ACTIONS AS "FOLLOW-ON" PROCEEDINGS

Since the SEC's decision in *Carter & Johnson*, almost all Rule 102(e) actions involving attorneys occur as "follow-on" proceedings. That is, Rule 102(e) findings and disciplinary orders almost always occur *after* a violation of the securities law (or other law) has been established in a federal or state court, or *after* a state bar tribunal has ruled on the attorney conduct at issue. *See* Dixie L. Johnson & David D. Whipple, *Zealous Advocacy and Offending the SEC: The SEC's Lawyer Discipline Program*, 26 INSIGHTS 10, at 2 (Oct. 2012) (discussing research revealing that over a 5 ½ year period from 2007–2012, 81 of the

85 Rule 102(e) disciplinary orders against attorneys constituted follow-on proceedings). In two of the four outliers, the SEC imposed sanctions under Rule 102(e) simultaneously with findings in an administrative proceeding that the attorney had himself violated the federal securities laws or had aided and abetted a violation by his client. *See In re Peter Y. Atkinson, Esq.*, Admin. Proc. File No. 3-13645, SEC Release No. 60806 (Oct. 9, 2009) (attorney and former officer of public company settled proceeding alleging a fraudulent scheme that resulted in material misstatements in the company's periodic reports and proxy statements filed with the SEC); *In re American Pegasus LDG, LLC*, Admin. Proc. File No. 3-14169, SEC Release No. 9167 (Dec. 21, 2010) (investment advisory firm, its CEO, and its general counsel settled proceeding alleging the failure to disclose conflicts of interest, the misuse of client assets, and improper self-dealing).

§ 10.4.3   RULE 102(e) ACTIONS INVOLVING *DE NOVO* DETERMINATIONS

There are rare instances, however, when the SEC acts in a *de novo* capacity to discipline an attorney for unprofessional conduct. In the other two outliers in the above-referenced study, the SEC disciplined attorneys based solely on the agency's own determination that the attorneys had engaged in improper professional conduct. *See In re Spencer C. Barasch*, Admin. Proc. File No. 3-14891, SEC Release No. 67060 (May 24, 2012) (former SEC attorney settled Rule 102(e) action alleging that he violated the federal "revolving door" statute when he represented a client after having "personally and substantially" participated in related matters when he was employed at the SEC); *In re Steven Altman, Esq.*, Admin. Proc. File No. 3-12944, SEC Release No. 63306 (Nov. 10, 2010) (imposing permanent suspension after finding that attorney had violated disciplinary rules of the New York State Bar when he informed his client's former employer that his client would agree to thwart a pending SEC investigation involving that employer in return for a more generous severance package) *aff'd, Altman v. SEC*, 666 F.3d 1322, 1328 (D.C. Cir. 2011) (stating that "[w]hatever ambiguity may exist as to lesser mental states that might implicate Rule 102(e), intentional improper conduct in the nature of extreme departures, such as Altman's sanctioned conduct, falls within the rule's ambit") (internal quotation marks omitted).

§ 10.4.4 ENFORCEMENT ACTIONS AGAINST ATTORNEYS WHO COMMIT SECURITIES LAW VIOLATIONS

Attorneys acting as lawyers—but also in their capacity as investors, entrepreneurs, and corporate officers—all too often commit securities law violations. Sometimes, as with insider trading, even highly publicized scandals and long prison sentences do not seem to function as a great deterrent. On other occasions, as with options back-dating, the scandals and sanctions have prompted definitive change.

Insider Trading. The SEC and the Department of Justice (the DOJ) have been zealous in pursuing attorneys who breach fiduciary duties owed to clients when trading securities on the basis of material nonpublic information. The facts of *United States v. O'Hagan*, 521 U.S. 642 (1997), immediately should come to mind. *See* § 7.4 *supra* (discussing the Court's endorsement of the misappropriation theory of insider trading liability in a criminal case against a former law firm partner who traded stock and options based on confidential information pertaining to a planned tender offer by the law firm's client). More recently, several attorneys—including associates at law firms and in-house company lawyers—pled guilty and were sentenced to prison in connection with the insider trading "ring" surrounding billionaire hedge fund trader Raj Rajaratnam and the Galleon Group. It is also noteworthy that the longest prison sentence in the US for the crime of insider trading—twelve years—was imposed on a former law firm associate who pled guilty in connection with a tipping and trading scheme that lasted more than eight years and involved confidential merger and acquisition information misappropriated from clients at several law firms at which he had been employed, including Cravath; Skadden, Arps; Fried Frank; and Wilson Sonsini. *See United States v. Kluger*, 722 F.3d 549, 570–571 (3d Cir. 2013) (holding that 12-year prison sentence was procedurally and substantively reasonable and thus did not constitute an abuse of discretion by the district court).

Backdating Stock Option Grants. In the mid-2000s, more than a hundred publicly traded companies—and dozens of securities lawyers—were embroiled in DOJ or SEC investigations involving the backdating of stock option grants. The backdating schemes were devised to allow corporate officers to realize larger potential gains without the company having to include those gains as compensation on financial statements filed with the SEC. Many attorneys were ultimately found liable for aiding and abetting, or causing, the company's anti-fraud and reporting violations, and many others were held primarily liable for creating the company records that falsely indicated that the stock option grants had occurred on earlier dates when the company's stock price had been at a low. *See, e.g.,* SEC v. Myron F. Olesnyckyj, SEC Litigation Release No. 20056 (Mar. 27, 2007) (announcing Monster Worldwide former general counsel's settlement of SEC charges and related guilty plea); SEC v. Jacob ("Kobi") Alexander, SEC Litigation Release No. 21753 (Nov. 23, 2010) (announcing Comverse Technology former general counsel's settlement of SEC charges and related guilty plea). *See generally* SEC, *Spotlight on Stock Options Backdating, available at* http://www.sec.gov/spotlight/options backdating.htm. The spot-light serves as an important reminder that attorneys perform a critical gatekeeping role and are expected to fulfill their professional responsibilities by insisting that their clients comply with the law.

§ 10.4.5 ENFORCEMENT ACTIONS AGAINST ATTORNEYS AS "AIDERS AND ABETTORS"

An attorney who aids and abets a client's securities law violation can be held secondarily liable in an SEC enforcement action filed in federal district court. *See* § 2.12.1 *supra* (discussing the SEC's general authority to pursue aiders and abettors under § 15(b) of the Securities Act and § 20(e) of the Exchange Act). Parallel authority for the SEC to pursue "aiders and abettors" is set out in § 209(f) of the Investment Advisers Act of 1940 (the Investment Advisers Act) and § 48(b) of the Investment Company Act of 1940 (the Investment Company Act). To establish liability for aiding and abetting, the SEC must show that the attorney "knowingly or recklessly" provided "substantial assistance" to another person that engaged in a primary violation of the federal securities laws. *See, e.g. SEC v. Fehn*, 97 F.3d 1276 (9th Cir. 1996) (enjoining attorney for aiding and abetting violations of Rule 10b-5 and other Exchange Act provisions that were committed by the company that retained him). The decision in *Fehn*, however, interpreted a prior version of Exchange Act § 20(e) which referenced only "knowing" assistance. In the Dodd-Frank Act of 2010, Congress clarified Exchange Act § 20(e), and the parallel provisions in the other Acts, by specifying that aiding and abetting liability encompasses those who "recklessly" provide substantial assistance as well.

Attorneys who aid and abet a client's securities law violation can also be found criminally liable in an action brought by the DOJ under 18 U.S.C. § 2(a). *See* § 11.6 *infra*.

§ 10.4.6   ENFORCEMENT ACTIONS AGAINST ATTORNEYS WHO "CAUSE" VIOLATIONS BY CLIENTS

An attorney whose legal advice "causes" a client's securities law violation can be subject to a cease-and-desist proceeding under § 8A(a) of the Securities Act, § 21C(a) of the Exchange Act, § 203(k)(1) of the Investment Advisers Act, or § 9(f)(1) of the Investment Company Act. *See, e.g., In re Google, Inc. & David C. Drummond*, Securities Act Release No. 8523 (Jan. 13, 2005) (consent order settling charges that company's general counsel failed to inform the company's board that continued issuance of securities to company employees would cause the company to exceed the dollar threshold in the relevant exemption from SEC registration). *See also* § 9.7.1 *supra* (discussing the SEC's general authority to issue cease-and-desist orders in administrative proceedings).

§ 10.4.7   ENFORCEMENT ACTIONS AGAINST ATTORNEYS AS BROKER-DEALER SUPERVISORS

In-house attorneys at brokerage firms—who may often act in the supervisory chain of command—may face potential disciplinary sanctions under Exchange Act § 15(b)(4)(E). *See* In the Matter of John H. Gutfreund, Thomas W. Strauss & John W. Meriwether, Exchange Act Release No. 31554 (Dec. 3, 1992). Although Salomon Brothers' chief legal officer Donald M. Feuerstein repeatedly advised C.E.O. Gutfreund to report unauthorized U.S.

Treasury auction bids by trader Paul Mozer to the Federal Reserve, Gutfreund did not do so. The SEC did not initiate enforcement action against Feuerstein. But in its report on the conduct of other top Salomon officials, the SEC concluded that Feuerstein was Mozer's "supervisor" for purposes of § 15(b)(4)(E) and as such was obligated to take appropriate steps to deal with Mozer's misconduct.

Questions about whether in-house attorneys should be regarded as "supervisors" arose again in In re Urban, Exchange Act Release No. 66259 (Jan. 26, 2012). In *Urban*, an ALJ determined that the general counsel of a broker-dealer was the supervisor of a former broker who had engaged in a market manipulation scheme. But the ALJ ultimately ruled that the general counsel's supervision was not unreasonable and thus should not be sanctioned under § 15(b)(4)(E). On appeal to the SEC, three Commissioners did not participate, and the remaining two could not agree on a disposition. Accordingly, under the SEC's Rules of Practice, that initial decision had "no effect." But the ALJ's decision did nonetheless raise concerns about the standard that would be used to determine whether in-house counsel should be deemed "supervisors." Partially in response, the SEC issued a FAQ emphasizing that for legal and compliance personnel, the determination of supervisory authority "depends on whether, under the facts and circumstances of a particular case, that person has the requisite degree of responsibility, ability or authority to affect the conduct of the employee whose behavior is at issue." *See* SEC, Division of Trading and Markets, *Frequently Asked*

Questions about Liability of Compliance and Legal Personnel at Broker Dealers Under Sections 15(b)(4) and 15(b)(6) of the Exchange Act (Sept. 30, 2013), *available at* http://www.sec.gov/divisions/marketreg/faq-cco-supervision-093013.htm.

§ 10.5   FEDERAL REGULATION OF ACCOUNTANTS

The regulatory scheme for accountants has changed considerably over the last two decades. The federal securities laws authorize the SEC to regulate the accounting methods used in preparing and auditing the financial statements included in SEC reports, but the SEC for many years delegated most of this standard-setting authority to private independent organizations such as the American Institute of Certified Public Accountants (the AICPA) and the Financial Accounting Standards Board (the FASB), which formulates "generally accepted accounting principles" (GAAP). The SEC did, however, take the lead in promulgating rules setting out "independence" requirements for auditors of SEC reporting companies. The SEC also routinely used its authority under Rule 102(e) to pursue actions against accountants—both for violations of the Securities Act and the Exchange Act and the rules thereunder, as well as the standards set by the AICPA and FASB.

In 1994, Congress stepped in to tighten professional standards for accountants with a provision in the Private Securities Litigation Reform Act (the PSLRA), which added a new § 10A to the Exchange Act. Section 10A places an affirmative duty on auditors to report illegal acts first to a client's senior management and then, if the illegal acts are not rectified, directly to the client's board of directors and to the SEC.

With the Sarbanes-Oxley Act in 2002, Congress again intervened, after the malfeasance of auditors was blamed for the collapses of Enron and WorldCom, as well as for the large number of other earnings restatements by large publicly traded companies. The SOX established a new independent board to regulate auditors under the supervision of the SEC—the Public Company Accounting Oversight Board (the PCAOB). *See* § 10.6 *infra*. The SOX also added to § 10A of the Exchange Act a host of new provisions designed to enhance the independence of the accounting firms that audit public companies. These provisions principally focus on the scope of services provided by the accounting firm as well as on the relationship between the accounting firm and its public company clients.

§ 10.5.1 RULE 102(e) PROCEEDINGS AGAINST ACCOUNTANTS

The SEC applies Rule 102(e) to attorneys and accountants in very different ways. Whereas the SEC almost always initiates a Rule 102(e) action against an attorney as a "follow-on" proceeding after a judicial or administrative finding of misconduct (*see* § 10.4.2 *supra*), the SEC uses Rule 102(e) rather routinely to discipline accounting firms and individual accountants for "unethical and improper professional conduct" and to set standards of conduct for the accounting profession. Moreover, unlike attorneys who are typically pursued under Rule 102(e) only for knowing or reckless misconduct, accountants are subject to a definition of "improper professional conduct" that encompasses gross negligence and even "repeated" instances of simple negligence. *See* § 10.2 *supra* (quoting the text of Rule 102(e)(1)(iv)).

§ 10.5.2   PRIMARY LIABILITY FOR MATERIAL MISSTATEMENTS OR OMISSIONS IN FINANCIAL STATEMENTS

Accounting firms and accountants may be charged with securities fraud under Exchange Act § 10(b) and Rule 10b-5 for acting recklessly in certifying the financial statements contained in a Form 10-K or other document filed with the SEC. Even in the wake of the Supreme Court's decision in *Janus Capital Group, Inc. v. First Derivative Traders*, 564 U.S. 135 (2011), discussed in § 2.11.1 *supra*, accountants can still be held primarily liable when the issuer's financial statements contain material misrepresentations or omissions. *See, e.g., Special Situations Fund III QP, L.P. v. Deloitte Touche Tohmatsu CPA, Ltd.*, 33 F. Supp. 3d 401, 428 n.13 (S.D.N.Y. 2014) (finding auditor to have had "ultimate authority" over its certification). Although the SEC predicates most anti-fraud liability claims against accountants on its Exchange § 20(e) "aiding and abetting" authority, or its Exchange Act § 21C(a) cease-and-desist authority for causing another's violation, the SEC can—and does—charge accounting firms as primary violators. *See, e.g.,* SEC

v. Michael J. Moore and Moore & Associates, SEC Litigation Release No. 211891A (Aug. 27, 2009) (consent order settling Rule 10b-5 and other charges against CPA and his firm for issuing and signing audit reports falsely stating that the audits were conducted in accordance with PCAOB standards).

§ 10.5.3 SECONDARY LIABILITY FOR ACCOUNTANTS

Accounting firms and accountants who "knowingly or recklessly" provide "substantial assistance" to another person in violation of the federal securities laws can be held liable in an SEC enforcement action under Exchange Act § 20(e) or a parallel provision set out in § 15(b) of the Securities Act, § 209(f) of the Investment Advisers Act, or § 48(b) of the Investment Company Act. Accountants who aid and abet a client's securities law violation can likewise be liable in a criminal action brought by the DOJ under 18 U.S.C. § 2(a).

An accountant whose advice "causes" a client's securities law violation can be subject to a cease-and-desist proceeding under § 8A(a) of the Securities Act, § 21C(a) of the Exchange Act, § 203(k)(1) of the Investment Advisers Act, and § 9(f)(1) of the Investment Company Act.

Recent enforcement actions against two national accounting firms and their auditing partners underscore the SEC's continued focus on those gatekeepers that ignore red flags and fail to fulfill their auditing and other financial reporting obligations. *See* In the Matter of Grant Thornton,

LLP, Exchange Act Release No. 34-76536 (Dec. 2, 2015) (firm agreed to cease-and-desist from similar violations, disgorge approximately $1.5 million in audit fees and interest, pay a $3 million penalty, and adopt remedial undertakings as a settlement to charges that the firm was a cause of reporting violations by two public companies and engaged in multiple violations of PCAOB standards); In the Matter of BDO USA, LLP, Exchange Act Release No. 34-75862 (Sept. 9, 2015) (firm agreed to cease-and-desist from similar violations, disgorge approximately $612,000 in audit fees and interest, pay a $1.5 million penalty, and adopt remedial undertakings in settlement of charges that the firm was a cause of a public company's reporting violations, engaged in multiple violations of PCAOB standards, and violated the diligence and reporting requirements of Exchange Act § 10A). Both actions are particularly noteworthy because, as a condition of the settlements, the SEC required admissions of wrongdoing by the accounting firms. As we have seen, the overwhelming majority of SEC settlements include a provision that the settling party "neither admits nor denies" the allegations in the SEC's complaint or administrative order. *See* § 9.4.2 *supra.* But these cases reflect a relatively new policy where the SEC requires admissions in certain types of settlements, including those in which the agency believes that the recitation of unambiguous facts would send a necessary and important message to others. *See id.*

§ 10.6 THE PUBLIC COMPANY ACCOUNTING OVERSIGHT BOARD (PCAOB)

§ 10.6.1 THE PCAOB's STRUCTURE AND PRINCIPAL FUNCTIONS

The PCAOB's five members, including a Chairman, are appointed to staggered five-year terms by the SEC, after consultation with the Chairman of the Board of Governors of the Federal Reserve System and the Secretary of the Treasury. Its headquarters are in Washington D.C., and it has regional offices in NY, Atlanta, Charlotte, Chicago, Dallas, Denver, Orange County, and San Francisco. Its 2015 budget was approximately $250.9 million, which was funded primarily by accounting support fees imposed on public companies by the SOX. The PCAOB has a staff of approximately 850 persons.

The PCAOB's congressionally-mandated oversight of the accounting profession is exercised through four basic functions:

- Registration of accounting firms—No accounting firm may prepare, or substantially contribute to, an audit report for a public company that files financial statements with the SEC, or for a broker-dealer, without first registering with the PCAOB. Registered firms must file annual and other reports that provide the PCAOB and the public with updated information about the firm and its audit practice.

- Inspection of firms and their public company audits—The PCAOB conducts inspections of firms' quality controls and reviews aspects of public company audits.

- Investigation and disciplinary proceedings—The PCAOB has broad authority to impose sanctions on registered firms and associated persons that have violated applicable laws and standards. As provided for in the SOX, all PCAOB investigations and all contested proceedings (*i.e.*, cases in which the Board files charges and the respondent elects to litigate, rather than settle) are non-public. The PCAOB closely coordinates its enforcement efforts with the SEC. In certain instances, the PCAOB investigates the auditor's conduct and the SEC focuses its investigation on the public company, its management, and other parties. In other cases, the SEC's Division of Enforcement takes responsibility for an auditor investigation and requests that PCAOB defer to that investigation.

- Establishing auditing, quality control, ethics, independence, and other standards—The PCAOB is responsible for establishing the auditing and related professional practice standards under which public company audits are performed.

The system of SEC oversight for the PCAOB parallels the recordkeeping, rulemaking, and disciplinary review procedures currently in place for

FINRA and other SROs. Thus, the SEC must approve all PCAOB rules and all sanctions imposed by the PCAOB are subject to the SEC's plenary review. The SEC must also approve the PCAOB's annual budget as well as the formula for the "accounting support fee" that Congress authorized the PCAOB to levy on public companies and broker-dealers to fund the PCAOB's budget.

§ 10.6.2   THE PCAOB's PUBLIC/ PRIVATE STATUS

The PCAOB's unique design as a congressionally-created regulator in the private sector spawned constitutional controversy from the start. The SOX provision that established the PCAOB specified that "[t]he Board shall not be an agency or establishment of the United States Government" and that "[n]o member or person employed by, or agent for, the Board shall be deemed to be an officer or employee of or agent for the Federal Government by reason of such service." 15 U.S.C. § 7211(b). But in *Free Enterprise Fund v. Public Co. Accounting Oversight Bd.,* 561 U.S. 477, 485–486 (2010), the Court made clear that these provisions rendered the PCAOB a private-sector entity for statutory purposes only. For constitutional purposes, "the Board is 'part of the Government,'" and "its members are 'Officers of the United States'" who "'exercis[e] significant authority pursuant to the laws of the United States.'" *Id.* at 486 (quoting *Buckley v. Valeo*, 424 U.S. 1, 125–126 (1976)).

Against this backdrop, the *Free Enterprise Fund*
Court ruled that the PCAOB, as originally
constructed in the SOX, violated constitutional
principles of separation of powers. The Court,
however, chose not to impose the broad injunctive
relief requested by the accounting firm and nonprofit
organization that had brought the litigation. Instead,
Chief Justice John Roberts, joined by four other
Justices, opted to sever the SOX provisions that
limited the way in which the SEC could remove
PCAOB members from office. That is, Congress had
specified in the SOX that PCAOB members could be
removed only by the SEC and only for willful or
unjustifiable transgressions. The Court found that
the PCAOB's insulation from SEC control, when
coupled with the SEC's insulation from direct
presidential control, contravened Article II's vesting
of the executive power in the President.

The majority's decision to excise the restrictive
removal provisions from the SOX also made possible
a quick rejection of petitioners' challenge under the
Appointments Clause. With the SEC now able to
remove the five PCAOB members at-will, those
members were, in the Court's view, subordinates of
the SEC's Commissioners. Thus, the Court found
that the PCAOB members were "inferior officers"
who, pursuant to the Constitution, may be appointed
by the Commissioners acting collectively as the
"Head" of the "Department."

CHAPTER 11
CRIMINAL ENFORCEMENT

§ 11.1 INTRODUCTION

Criminal enforcement of the federal securities laws rests exclusively with the Department of Justice (the DOJ), which operates through U.S. Attorney's Offices across the United States. The DOJ often receives referrals of cases from the Securities and Exchange Commission (the SEC) that the latter deems worthy of prosecution. In addition, the DOJ regularly prosecutes securities cases that result from its own investigative efforts.

In its securities prosecutions, the DOJ has a veritable panoply of crimes from which to choose. Some have been on the books for decades, including those created by the Securities Act and the Exchange Act as well as those of a more general nature, especially mail fraud, wire fraud, and crimes established by the Racketeer Influenced and Corrupt Organizations Act (RICO). Others have come into being as part of the Sarbanes-Oxley Act of 2002 (the SOX), which was enacted in response to the scandals at Enron, WorldCom, and other large companies. The SOX has further enhanced the DOJ's options by increasing the penalties for Exchange Act crimes, mail fraud, and wire fraud.

As to all of these crimes, the DOJ has a burden of proof of beyond a reasonable doubt. *See In re Winship*, 397 U.S. 358, 361–362 (1970). *See also Smith v. United States*, 133 S. Ct. 714, 719 (2013).

This Chapter begins with crimes created by the Securities Act and the Exchange Act (§ 11.2 *infra*) and then turns to SOX crimes (§ 11.3 *infra*), mail and wire fraud (§ 11.4 *infra*), and RICO (§ 11.5 *infra*). Thereafter it examines liability for aiding and abetting these crimes (§ 11.6 *infra*), for conspiring to commit them (§ 11.7 *infra*), and for attempting them (§ 11.8 *infra*). It concludes with a discussion of the applicable statutes of limitations (§ 11.9 *infra*).

§ 11.2 SECURITIES ACT AND EXCHANGE ACT CRIMES

The Securities Act and the Exchange Act are hybrid civil/criminal statutes, that is, they criminalize violations that can give rise to civil liability as well. *See* Securities Act § 24; Exchange Act § 32(a). Criminal liability nonetheless has two distinctive features—the requirement that the defendants have acted "willfully," discussed in § 11.2.1 *infra*, and the burden of proof, which, as noted above, requires that guilt be proven beyond a reasonable doubt.

Willfulness aside, the elements of a securities crime nonetheless do not overlap completely with those of its private civil counterpart. Not germane in the criminal context are the standing requirements applicable to private plaintiffs. *See*, *e.g.*, *United States v. O'Hagan*, 521 U.S. 642, 664–665 (1997) (rejecting in the context of a criminal action Rule 10b-5's purchaser-seller requirement). Likewise not germane in the criminal context is the need for "identification of or reliance by a particular victim."

United States v. Haddy, 134 F.3d 542, 551 (3d Cir. 1998).

The Securities Act and the Exchange Act differ significantly on the subject of penalties. As amended by the SOX, the Exchange Act allows a natural person to be fined up to $5 million and/or imprisoned for up to 20 years. The maximum fine for a non-natural person is $25 million. On the other hand, the Securities Act, which the SOX left alone, authorizes a $10,000 maximum fine and/or a 5-year maximum period of imprisonment.

Another penalty-related distinction between the two statutes is that Exchange Act § 32(a) contains a "no knowledge" clause, whereas Securities Act § 24 does not. The "no knowledge" clause is discussed in § 11.2.2 *infra.*

§ 11.2.1 SECURITIES ACT AND EXCHANGE ACT CRIMES: THE WILLFULNESS REQUIREMENT

Conviction under the Securities Act or the Exchange Act requires proof that the defendant acted "willfully." Neither Act defines the term, however. Moreover, although "willfully" appears frequently in federal criminal statutes, there is no generally accepted definition. *Cf. Bryan v. United States,* 524 U.S. 184, 191 (1998) (describing "willfully" as a "word of many meanings") (quoting *Spies v. United States,* 317 U.S. 492, 497 (1943)).

The Supreme Court has yet to address the meaning of "willfully" in the context of a federal securities crime. The lower federal courts agree that a criminal securities defendant can act "willfully" without knowing that he acted illegally. *See, e.g.,* *United States v. Dixon*, 536 F.2d 1388 (2d Cir. 1976). That consensus has been largely driven by Exchange Act § 32(a)'s "no knowledge" clause, discussed in § 11.2.2 *infra,* which shields a defendant from imprisonment—but not from conviction or a fine—for violating a rule or regulation of which he was not aware.

To be sure, the absence of a "no knowledge" clause from Securities Act § 24 would make it theoretically possible to equate "willfully" with knowledge of illegality, at least for purposes of the Securities Act. But courts have not gone down that road. *Cf. United States v. Tarallo*, 380 F.3d 1174, 1188 (9th Cir. 2004) (describing the meaning of "willfully" in the two statutes as "substantively similar").

The irrelevance of knowledge of illegality aside, the lower federal courts have given "willfully" a variety of definitions:

- that the defendant knew that " 'he was doing a wrongful act,' " but not necessarily an illegal one, provided the " 'knowingly wrongful act involved à significant risk of effecting the violation that . . . occurred.' " *United States v. Cassese*, 428 F.3d 92, 109 (2d Cir. 2005) (quoting *United States v. Peltz*, 433 F.2d 48, 55 (2d Cir. 1970)). *See also United States v. Tarallo*, 380 F.3d 1174, 1187 (9th Cir. 2004) (same).

- that the defendant performed the wrongful acts intentionally. *United States v. O'Hagan*, 139 F.3d 641, 647 (8th Cir. 1998).

- that the defendant "intentionally act[ed] with reckless disregard for the truth of material misleading statements." *Tarallo*, 380 F.3d at 1180.

- that the defendant act either with a specific intent to defraud or recklessly. *United States v. DeSantis*, 134 F.3d 760, 764 (6th Cir. 1998).

Choosing the most appropriate definition is complicated by the arguable need to differentiate the term "willfully" from the following:

Scienter. The civil enforcement of several major securities provisions requires proof of scienter. These provisions include § 10(b) and Rule 10b-5 (*see* § 2.5); Securities Act § 17(a)(1) (*see* § 3.6); and Exchange Act § 14(e) (*see* § 5.3.2). The source of the scienter requirement in each instance has been the text of the respective statutory provision. When enforcement is criminal, causing the willfulness requirement to attach, should scienter retain its own independent significance? This question remains unresolved. *Cf. United States v. Chestman*, 903 F.2d 75, 87-88 (2d Cir. 1990) (Carman, J., concurring in part and dissenting in part) (insisting on the need to instruct the jury on both willfulness and scienter in prosecution under § 14(e) and Rule 14e-3, *vacated on other grounds*, 947 F.2d 551 (2d Cir. 1991).

Recklessly. Acting "recklessly" satisfies the scienter requirement in civil actions under Exchange Act § 10(b) and Rule 10b-5, Securities Act § 17(a)(1), and Exchange Act § 14(e). *See* §§ 2.5.2, 3.6, and 5.3.2 *supra*. Does acting recklessly qualify as acting "willfully" for purposes of a criminal action? The circuits are divided. *Compare United States v. O'Hagan*, 139 F.3d 641, 647 (8th Cir. 1998) (finding recklessness to be insufficient) *with United States v. Tarallo*, 380 F.3d 1174, 1189 (9th Cir. 2004) (finding recklessness to be sufficient). *Cf. United States v. Stewart*, 305 F.Supp. 2d 368, 371 (S.D.N.Y. 2004) (deeming it unnecessary to address the government's argument that civil and criminal actions under Rule 10b-5 have identical state-of-mind requirements). There is irony in conflating the state-of-mind requirements of civil and criminal actions, since the willfulness requirement represents the distinguishing feature of criminal liability. *See* §§ 11.2, 11.2.1 *supra*. To be sure, the term "recklessly" could be defined one way in civil actions and another in criminal actions. But multiple definitions of "recklessness" in the securities law context might be a bridge too far.

Knowingly. Some courts steer clear of equating "willfully" with "knowingly" on the ground that if the two terms meant the same thing, § 32(a) would not require both in connection with the discrete crime of making a false statement in a document, report, or application. *See, e.g., United States v. Lake*, 472 F.3d 1247, 1266 (10th Cir. 2007) ("Although it may be unclear what a 'knowing' requirement adds to the willfulness required by § [32(a)] * * * , there is little doubt that Congress has thought it adds something."); *United States v. Dixon*, 536 F.2d 1388, 1396 & n.7 (2d Cir. 1976). On the other hand, the authors of the leading securities law treatise regard "knowingly" as "redundant" of "willfully." 10 Louis Loss, Joel Seligman & Troy Paredes, SECURITIES REGULATION 424 (4th ed. 2013).

What if the defendant maintains that he lacked knowledge of the underlying facts necessary to make his conduct "willful"? Under such circumstances, the government may be entitled to a "conscious avoidance" instruction directed at whether the defendant deliberately "closed his eyes" to the facts put into evidence. *See, e.g., United States v. Goffer*, 721 F.3d 113, 126–127 (2d Cir. 2013).

§ 11.2.2 EXCHANGE ACT CRIMES: THE "NO KNOWLEDGE" CLAUSE

Exchange Act § 32(a) contains the following language, known as the "no knowledge" clause or the "no knowledge" defense: "[N]o person shall be subject to imprisonment under this section for the violation of *any rule or regulation* if he proves that he had no knowledge of such rule of regulation." *Id.* (emphasis added). There is no counterpart in the Securities Act.

Why would Congress have provided a defense to imprisonment for those who violate rules but not statutory provisions? At the time of the Exchange Act's original enactment, rules promulgated by government agencies were, generally speaking, not readily accessible. It thus would have seemed unfair to send a defendant to jail for violating a rule of which he was ignorant. To be sure, this explanation does not account for the absence of a defense to imprisonment for rule violations under the Securities Act.

To be sure, some rules echo a statutory provision, of which a defendant does have notice, raising the question of how to apply the "no knowledge" clause when such is the case. Consider Rule 10b-5, the subject of Chapter 2. Rule 10b-5 is not only quite similar to its parent statute, § 10(b), but is also almost the same as Securities Act § 17(a) (*see* § 3.6). Relying on these parallelisms, courts have not allowed Rule 10b-5 defendants to invoke the no knowledge clause. *See, e.g., United States v. Knueppel*, 293 F. Supp. 2d 199, 202–203 & n.1 (E.D.N.Y. 2003) (focusing on the parallelism between Rule 10b-5 and § 10(b)); *United States v. Lilley,* 291 F. Supp. 989, 992–993 (S.D. Tex. 1968) (focusing on the parallelism between Rule 10b-5 and § 17(a)). *But cf. United States v. Behrens*, 644 F.3d 754, 757 (8th Cir. 2011) (finding the text of the no knowledge clause to be "unambiguous" and remanding the case to allow the Rule 10b-5 defendant to invoke it).

Complicating the situation further is dictum from *United States v. O'Hagan,* 521 U.S. 642 (1997), describing the no knowledge clause as a "sturdy safeguard[ ]" for criminal defendants and observing that "a defendant may not be imprisoned for violating Rule 10b-5 if he proves that he had no knowledge of the Rule." *Id.* at 665–666. This dictum fueled the Eighth Circuit's decision in *Behrens,* above, allowing a Rule 10b-5 defendant to invoke the no knowledge clause. To be sure, the defendant in that case later failed to meet his burden of establishing the defense, since the evidence established his knowledge of the contents of Rule 10b-5. *See United States v. Behrens,* 713 F.3d 926 (8th Cir. 2013).

In determining whether the defendant has knowledge of the rule or regulation at issue, the focus is on her awareness of the rule's substance, not necessarily its precise formulation or its applicability to the circumstances. Thus, a defendant convicted of violating a rule prohibiting falsification of books and records failed to establish the no knowledge defense where evidence existed that she "tried to hide the backdating scheme and was conscious of her wrongdoing." *United States v. Reyes,* 577 F.3d 1069, 1081 (9th Cir. 2009).

§ 11.2.3   SECURITIES ACT AND EXCHANGE ACT CRIMES: THE RULE OF LENITY

Sometimes the substantive provision at issue in a criminal action presents an ambiguity that cannot be resolved by recourse to statutory language or legislative history. Under these circumstances, should the court simply select the interpretation that best furthers the underlying statutory policies (whether that of the Securities Act or the Exchange Act in general or the provision in particular)? Or must it apply the rule of lenity (sometimes referred to as strict construction) to ensure that the defendant had fair warning given that, if convicted, she may face a prison sentence and opprobrium? The Supreme Court has not been altogether consistent in its answer.

In *United States v. Naftalin,* 441 U.S. 768 (1979), the Court seemed to come down on the side of strict construction. At issue in *Naftalin* was whether the prohibition against using "any device, scheme, or artifice to defraud" in Securities Act § 17(a)(1) (discussed in § 3.6 *supra*) encompasses frauds that are perpetrated on brokers as well as on investors. After giving an affirmative answer, the Court announced that it would have applied strict construction had the statutory language been ambiguous. *Id.* at 778–779.

Yet in *United States v. O'Hagan,* 521 U.S. 642 (1997), the Court eschewed strict construction under circumstances in which *Naftalin* arguably would have required it. In *O'Hagan,* discussed in § 7.4 *supra*, the Court upheld a conviction based on the misappropriation theory of insider trading after concluding that § 10(b) and Rule 10b-5 encompass that theory. The Court anchored the theory in the Exchange Act's policies despite statutory language that could be read to require a closer nexus between the deception and a securities transaction. *See id.* at

658–659. Justice Scalia dissented because of the Court's failure to apply the rule of lenity and read the statutory language in the defendant's favor. *See id.* at 679.

To be sure, the Court did not lose sight of the potential for fair warning problems. In its view, those problems are addressed by the government's obligation to prove that the defendant acted "willfully": "[T]he statute's "requirement of the presence of culpable intent as a necessary element of the offense does much to destroy any force in the argument that application of the [statute]" in circumstances such as O'Hagan's is unjust." 521 U.S. at 665–666. *See United States v. Wenger*, 427 F.3d 840, 851–852 (10th Cir. 2005) (relying on the willfulness requirement to provide fair warning to defendant regarding conduct prohibited by Securities Act § 17(b)). The Court did not, however, specify the definition of "willfully" that would be sufficient to cure fair warning problems.

§ 11.3   SOX CRIMES

The SOX created several new crimes, for which the parameters are still quite sparse:

<u>18 U.S.C. § 1348: Fraud Involving Securities of Reporting Companies</u>. This provision, limited to securities issued by reporting companies (*see* § 1.3 *supra*), creates the crime of "knowingly execut[ing], or attempt[ing] to execute, a scheme or artifice (1) to defraud any person in connection with any security or (2) to obtain, by means of false or fraudulent pretenses,

representations or promises, any money or property in connection with the purchase or sale of any security." Penalties include a fine and a prison term not exceeding 25 years, a length of time that exceeds that authorized by any of the other crimes under the SOX, the Securities Act, or the Exchange Act.

Did Congress mean to make it easier to show that the defendant acted "knowingly" instead of "willfully," the state of mind required by Securities Act § 24 and Exchange Act § 32(a) (*see* § 11.2 *supra*)? There is no definitive answer. One arguable basis for inferring an affirmative answer is that 18 U.S.C. § 1350, enacted contemporaneously and discussed below, distinguishes between a violation committed with knowledge and a "willful" violation committed with knowledge, with harsher penalties authorized for the latter.

Notice that § 1348 explicitly criminalizes attempts, unlike Securities Act § 24 or Exchange Act § 32(a). A defendant convicted of attempted securities fraud can receive the same penalty as someone convicted of the substantive crime. 18 U.S.C. § 1349. For further discussion of attempts, *see* § 11.8 *infra*.

Notice also that § 1348(1) prohibits "defraud[ing] any person in connection with any security" rather than defrauding any person in connection with *the purchase or sale of* any security. The omission of the "purchase or sale" phraseology widens the potential scope of the crime.

To ascertain whether "a scheme or artifice to defraud" is present, the Second Circuit has endorsed consulting the case law that has developed under the mail and wire fraud statutes. *See United States v. Mahaffy*, 693 F.3d 113, 127 (2d Cir. 2012). Those statutes are discussed in § 11.4 *infra*.

18 U.S.C. § 1350: False Certification of Reports by CEOs and CFOs. This provision, limited to reporting companies, *see* § 1.3 *supra*, creates two crimes involving the certifications of the 10-K and the 10-Q that must be made by the CEO and the CFO. The lesser crime consists of certifying "knowing" that it does not meet the Exchange Act's periodic disclosure requirements and does not "fairly present[ ] in all material respects the financial condition and results of operations of the issuer." 18 U.S.C. § 1350(c)(1). The greater crime consists of "willfully" certifying while "knowing" of the same defects. 18 U.S.C. § 1350(c)(2). Penalties for the former include a fine of not more than $1,000,000 and a prison term of not more than 10 years, while those for the latter include a fine of not more than $5,000,000 and a prison term of not more than 20 years.

The appearance of "willfully" in § 1350 raises several questions as to which answers have yet to develop. These questions include not only how to define "willfully" and how that definition compares with the one for "knowingly" in § 1348. In addition, there is the question of whether to import the definition of "willfully" used in crimes created by Securities Act § 24 and Exchange Act § 32(a) and discussed in § 11.2.1 *supra*.

Another unknown involves the phrase "financial condition and results of operations." Does the adjective "financial" modify "results of operations" as well as "condition"? If so, these crimes have a considerably broader reach.

<u>Several Crimes Involving Record Tampering</u>. One such crime concerns the alteration or destruction of a record, document or "tangible object" with the intent to affect a federal investigation (enacted as 18 U.S.C. § 1519). *See* § 9.3.5 *infra*. Another concerns the destruction of federal audit records (enacted as 18 U.S.C. § 1520). A third pertains to the destruction, or attempted destruction of a record with the intent to compromise its "use in an official proceeding" (enacted as 18 U.S.C. § 1512(c)).

§ 11.4   MAIL AND WIRE FRAUD

Enacted in 1872 and 1952, respectively, the mail and wire fraud statutes have long supplemented federal securities prosecutions as well as offered an alternative to them. The penalties for violating these statutes include a fine as well and a prison term of up to 20 years, increased from five years by the SOX. 18 U.S.C. §§ 1341, 1343.

As initially enacted, the mail fraud statute reached only those mailings sent through the US Postal Service. In 1994, Congress amended the statute so that it now also includes "private or commercial interstate carriers" such as FedEx and UPS.

The wire fraud statute reaches communications sent by "wire, radio, or television." The "wire" terminology enables the statute to reach email and Internet communications.

The mail and wire fraud statutes are construed with reference to each other. *Pasquantino v. United States*, 544 U.S. 349, 355 n.2 (2005) (using the Latin phrase "*in pari materia*"). Conviction under either requires proof of these three elements, discussed in the sections that follow:

- a scheme to defraud that involves a material misstatement or omission;

- the defendant's participation in the scheme with the intent to defraud; and

- the use of the mails or wires in furtherance of the scheme.

See, e.g., United States v. Sloan, 492 F.3d 884 (7th Cir. 2007); *United States v. Woods,* 335 F.3d 993 (9th Cir. 2003).

§ 11.4.1 MAIL AND WIRE FRAUD: THE SCHEME TO DEFRAUD

The scheme to defraud can subject the victim to any of three types of deprivation—that involving money, property, or the right of honest services.

These types of deprivation emerge from the statutory language as follows:

- The mail and wire fraud statutes prohibit "any scheme or artifice to defraud, or for obtaining money or property by means of false or fraudulent pretenses, representations, or promises." 18 U.S.C. §§ 1341, 1343.

- The scheme or artifice to defraud can take the form of "a scheme or artifice to deprive another of the right of honest services." 18 U.S.C. § 1346.

The Supreme Court addressed the nature of the property of which a victim can be deprived in *Carpenter v. United States*, 484 U.S. 19 (1987). The *Carpenter* Court affirmed the conviction of a Wall Street Journal reporter who passed along the "timing and contents" of upcoming WSJ "Heard on the Street" columns to two brokers (who then traded securities on the basis of the information). In so doing, the Court held, the reporter deprived the WSJ of the exclusive use of its confidential information, since it was the WSJ's "official policy and practice" to treat the contents and timing of the column as confidential before publication and the WSJ "had a right to decide how to use" the information before disclosing it. *Id.* at 23, 26.

The Supreme Court addressed the meaning of "honest services" fraud in *Skilling v. United States*, 561 U.S. 358 (2010). Deferring to the due process concerns undergirding "fair notice," the Court looked to judicial decisions involving "honest services" fraud that had been issued prior to § 1346's enactment. On the basis of those decisions, it construed § 1346 "to proscribe bribes and kickbacks—and nothing more." *Skilling*, 561 U.S. at 410.

§ 11.4.2   MAIL AND WIRE FRAUD: THE MATERIALITY REQUIREMENT

The "scheme to defraud" must involve an omission or misrepresentation that is "material" in nature, despite the lack of a materiality requirement in the statutory text. *Neder v. United States*, 527 U.S. 1 (1999). The reason, the Supreme Court explained, is that the established common law meaning of "defraud" entails a materiality component. The Court acknowledged that the mail and wire fraud statutes do not encompass every common law element, since some, such as justifiable reliance and damages, cannot be made to fit: "By prohibiting the 'scheme to defraud,' rather than the completed fraud, the elements of reliance and damage would clearly be inconsistent with the statutes Congress enacted." *Id.* at 25. On the other hand, a materiality requirement can be read into the statutes without difficulty.

How should materiality be defined for mail and wire fraud purposes? The *Neder* decision was not altogether clear on this point. Lower courts have read that decision to endorse a variety of definitions, including ones from the following sources:

The Restatement of Torts. According to some courts, *Neder* directs us to look at the definition of materiality from the Restatement of Torts. *Cf. Neder*, 527 U.S. at 22 n.5. The Restatement encompasses two alternative approaches, the first objective and the second subjective, to when a fact is material, namely, when:

(a) a reasonable man would attach importance to its existence or nonexistence in determining his choice of action in the transaction in question; or

(b) the maker of the representation knows or has reason to know that its recipient regards or is likely to regard the matter as important in determining his choice of action, although a reasonable man would not so regard it.

For decisions applying the objective definition, *see United States v. Tum*, 707 F.3d 68, 72 (1st Cir. 2013); *United States v. Gillion*, 704 F.3d 284, 296 (4th Cir. 2012). For a decision applying the subjective definition, *see United States v. Svete*, 556 3d 1157, 1164–1166 (11th Cir. 2009) (*en banc*).

United States v. Gaudin. According to other courts, *Neder* adopted the definition provided by *United States v. Gaudin*, 515 U.S. 506, 509 (1995)—having "a natural tendency to influence, or [is] capable of influencing, the decision of the decisionmaking body to which it was addressed." *Cf. Neder*, 527 U.S. at 14. For decisions taking this approach, *see United States v. Appolon*, 715 F.3d 362, 368 (1st Cir. 2013); *United States v. Wright*, 665 F.3d 560, 574 (3rd Cir. 2012).

Basic Inc. v. Levinson. Some courts have imported the approach to materiality utilized in

Rule 10b-5, *see* § 2.3 *supra*, when the defendant faces securities as well as mail or wire fraud charges. *See, e.g., United States v. Ferguson*, 676 F.3d 260, 273 (2d Cir. 2011) (requiring for all charges a " 'substantial likelihood' " that the misrepresentations "would be important to a reasonable investor") (citing *Basic Inc. v. Levinson*, 485 U.S. 224, 231 (1988)). *Cf. United States v. Johnson*, 297 F.3d 845, 866 n.21 (9th Cir. 2002) (declaring that *Neder* authorizes "alternative meanings of materiality").

The relevance of *Basic*'s materiality standard prompts the question whether other aspects of securities law materiality jurisprudence can be imported into the mail and wire fraud context as well. The courts have indicated some receptivity to so doing. *See, e.g., United States v. Rodriguez*, 732 F.3d 1299 (11th Cir. 2013) (drawing on the doctrine of "puffery" in connection with wire fraud). *Cf. United States v. Morris*, 80 F.3d 1151 (7th Cir. 1996) (assuming, without addressing, the relevance of "the bespeaks caution" doctrine to mail and wire fraud charges). For discussions of puffery and bespeaks caution, *see* §§ 2.3.1 and 2.3.7, respectively.

§ 11.4.3 MAIL AND WIRE FRAUD: THE INTENT REQUIREMENT

The intent requirement for mail or wire fraud can be satisfied by proof of recklessness. *See, e.g., United States v. Flood,* 501 F.3d 888, 897–898 (8th Cir. 2007); *United States v. Coyle,* 63 F.3d 1239, 1243 (3d

Cir. 1995). It does not matter whether the defendant herself concocted the scheme to defraud, so long as she intended to participate in it. *See, e.g., United States v. Manion*, 339 F.3d 1153 (9th Cir. 2003). The necessary intent encompasses only the scheme itself and does not extend to the use of the mails or wires. *See United States v. Serang*, 156 F.3d 910 (9th Cir. 1998). The required use of the mails and wires is discussed in § 11.4.4 *infra*.

What if the defendant maintains that she lacked knowledge of the underlying facts necessary to constitute intent? Under such circumstances, the government may be entitled to a "conscious avoidance" instruction directed at whether the defendant deliberately "closed her eyes" to the facts that have been put in evidence. *See, e.g., United States v. Carlo*, 507 F.3d 799, 802–803 (2d Cir. 2007).

§ 11.4.4 MAIL AND WIRE FRAUD: THE USE REQUIREMENT

The Supreme Court has clarified "the use of the mails and wires" requirement as follows:

- The defendant does not herself have to have used the mails or wires so long as she "caused" the mailing or wiring to happen. *Pereira v. United States*, 347 U.S. 1, 8 (1954). "Cause" entails "act[ing] with knowledge that the use of the mails will follow in the ordinary course of business, or where such use can reasonably be foreseen, even though not actually intended." *Id.* at 8–9. *Cf. United States v. Ratcliff-White*, 493 F.3d 812, 818 (7th Cir.

2007) (noting that "our case law does not require that a specific mailing or wire transmission be foreseen," relying on *Pereira*, above).

- The use of the mails or wires does not have to be an "essential element" of the scheme but only "incident to an essential part of" it. *Pereira*, 347 U.S. at 8. Indeed, the mailing or wiring need not itself be fraudulent in order to provide a basis for prosecution. *See Schmuck v. United States*, 489 U.S. 705, 715 (1989).

The mail fraud statute reaches mailings sent through "private or commercial interstate carriers" such as FedEx and UPS as well as those sent through the US Postal Service. *See* § 11.4 *supra*. Moreover, the wire fraud statute reaches email and Internet communications because they are communications sent by "wire." *See* § 11.4 *supra*.

§ 11.5 RICO

In 1970, Congress enacted RICO in order to combat organized crime. *See* 18 U.S.C. §§ 1961–1968. Since criminalizing mere membership in organized crime would violate the First Amendment to the Constitution, Congress created a complex new set of crimes premised on offenses (including mail, wire, and securities fraud) in which it believed that organized crime often engaged. Penalties include imprisonment for up to 20 years (*see* § 1963(a)) as well as the pre-trial freezing of the defendant's assets (*see id.*).

By far the most frequently invoked RICO offense is § 1962(c), which makes it "unlawful for any person employed by or associated with any enterprise engaged in, or the activities which affect, interstate or foreign commerce, to conduct or participate, directly or indirectly, in the conduct of such enterprise's affairs through a pattern of racketeering activity or collection of an unlawful debt." 18 U.S.C. § 1962(c). Its principal constituent elements, discussed in the sections that follow, are these:

- racketeering activity;

- pattern;

- enterprise; and

- "conduct[ing] or participat[ing] . . . in the conduct of" the enterprise.

In addition to criminal RICO actions, the DOJ can bring civil actions under RICO as well. Private parties can also sue under the statute, a subject discussed briefly in § 11.5.7 *infra*.

§ 11.5.1   RICO: THE LIBERAL CONSTRUCTION CLAUSE

A distinctive feature of RICO is its liberal construction clause, which directs that "[t]he provisions of this Title shall be liberally construed to effectuate its remedial purposes." § 904(a) of RICO, 84 Stat. 947. Although this clause did not make its way into the US Code, it remains an integral part of the RICO statute.

The existence of the liberal construction clause gives rise to two questions. One is how to square it with the rule of lenity (or strict construction) that normally applies in the criminal context. *Cf. United States v. Martino*, 681 F.3d 952, 956 n.16 (5th Cir. 1982) (noting question but not resolving it).

The other is whether it infuses all interpretative questions or enters the picture only to resolve an ambiguity. Compare *Boyle v. United States*, 556 U.S. 938 (2009) (invoking the liberal construction clause to justify a broad reading of the term "enterprise") with *Reves v. Ernst & Young*, 507 U.S. 170, 183–184 (1993) (finding the liberal construction clause to be irrelevant to whether to uphold the "operation or management test").

§ 11.5.2 RICO: RACKETEERING ACTIVITY

A critical element of the § 1962(c) offense is that the defendants have engaged in "racketeering activity," defined in § 1961(1). That six-part definition consists of the following:

- "fraud in the sale of securities . . . punishable under any law of the United States," discussed in § 11.5.3 *infra*;

- bankruptcy fraud and drug crimes "punishable under any law of the United States";

- various crimes such as murder and kidnaping "chargeable under state law";

- mail fraud and wire fraud and other crimes "indictable under" Title 18 of the US Code;

- certain crimes "indictable under" Title 29 of the US Code involving labor organizations and union funds;

- crimes "indictable under" the Currency and Foreign Transactions Reporting Act; and

- certain crimes "indictable under" the Immigration and Nationality Act.

18 U.S.C. § 1961(1)(A–F). The defendant need not have been convicted of the racketeering activity, which must only be "chargeable," "indictable," or "punishable" under state or federal law. *Cf. Sedima, SPRL v. Imrex Co.,* 473 U.S. 479, 488 (1988) (noting that the racketeering activity need not have resulted in a conviction).

The requisite state of mind is the one called for by the specific racketeering activity. *See, e.g., United States v. Blinder,* 10 F.3d 1468, 1477 (9th Cir. 1993).

§ 11.5.3 RICO: RACKETEERING ACTIVITY CONSISTING OF "FRAUD IN THE SALE OF SECURITIES"

What constitutes "fraud in the sale of securities . . . punishable under any law of the United States?" Any of the following can serve as the predicate, together with the corresponding requirement of criminal intent:

- § 10(b) of the Exchange Act and Rule 10b-5 (*see* Chapter 2 *supra*);

- § 17(a) of the Securities Act (*see* § 3.6 *supra*);

- § 14(a) of the Exchange Act and Rule 14a-9 (*see* Chapter 4 *supra*), at least where securities are traded simultaneously with the proxy voting;

- § 14(e) of the Exchange Act (*see* Chapter 5 *supra*); and

- 18 U.S.C. § 1348 (*see* § 11.3 *supra*).

As to the first four, the defendant must act "willfully." *See* § 11.2.1 *supra*. As to the last, he must act "knowingly." *See* § 11.3 *supra*.

In contemplating RICO's embrace of these crimes, consider that "fraud in the *sale* of securities" can be read to reach fraud in the *purchase* of securities as well. *See Pandick, Inc. v. Rooney*, 632 F. Supp. 1430, 1434 (N.D. Ill. 1986). The rationale for this view is that every sale involves a purchase, especially when taking into account the liberal construction clause (*see* § 11.5.1 *supra*).

There is also some support for the view that the failure to satisfy a reporting requirement, at least when part of a scheme to defraud, can qualify as "fraud in the sale of securities." *See United States v. Eisenberg*, 773 F. Supp. 662, 725–726 (D.N.J. 1991) (involving the failure to report beneficial ownership in a registration statement). Proceeding on this rationale, the violation of 18 U.S.C. § 1350 could conceivably qualify also. *See* § 11.3 *supra*.

§ 11.5.4 RICO: THE PATTERN OF RACKETEERING ACTIVITY

To amount to the requisite pattern, there must be at least two acts of racketeering activity within a 10 year period. *See* 18 U.S.C. § 1961(5). Adding further gloss, the Supreme Court has held that the two acts must display "continuity" and "relatedness." *H.J. Inc. v. Nw. Bell Tel. Co.*, 492 U.S. 229 (1989).

Acts are "related," the Court suggested, if they " 'have the same or similar purposes, results, participants, victims, or methods of commission, or otherwise are interrelated by distinguishing characteristics and are not isolated events.' " *Id.* at 239. This formulation was drawn from a provision of the Organized Crime Control Act of 1970, of which RICO was a part.

The Court described continuity as "both a closed-and-open-ended concept, referring *either* to a closed period of repeated conduct *or* to past conduct that by its nature projects into the future with a threat of repetition." *Id.* at 241 (emphasis added). Closed period continuity involves "proving a series of related predicates extending over a substantial period of time," with "[p]redicate acts extending over a few weeks or months and threatening no future criminal conduct" being insufficient. *Id.* at 242. At least some courts applying this concept seem to treat one year as a minimum. *See, e.g., United States v. Wilson,* 605 F.3d 985, 1021 (D.C. Cir. 2010) (17 months sufficient); *Wade v. Gaither*, 623 F. Supp. 2d 1277, 1286 (D. Utah 2009) ("nearly twelve full months" sufficient). *But cf. Primary Care Inv'rs, Seven, Inc. v.*

PHP Healthcare Corp., 986 F.2d 1208, 1215–1216 (8th Cir. 1993) (eleven months insufficient) (collecting cases).

But time may not always be the only consideration. Courts looking at other factors typically take into account "the number of victims, the number of racketeering acts, the variety of racketeering acts, whether the injuries caused were distinct, the complexity and size of the scheme, and the nature or character of the enterprise or unlawful activity." *Resolution Tr. Corp. v. Stone,* 998 F.2d 1534, 1543–1544 (10th Cir. 1993) (citations omitted); *see First Capital Asset Mgmt., Inc. v. Satinwood, Inc.,* 385 F.3d 159, 181 (2d Cir. 2004) (same).

What suffices as open-ended continuity turns on the particular facts of the case. *H.J.,* 492 U.S. at 242. Potentially relevant is whether "the predicate acts or offenses are part of an ongoing entity's regular way of doing business." *Id.; cf. Wilson,* 605 F.3d at 1021 (noting the defendant's statement, " 'Nothing will stop this money train!' ").

§ 11.5.5 RICO: THE ENTERPRISE

Under § 1962(c), the "person" who is the defendant must be "employed by or associated with" an "enterprise." An enterprise, in turn, includes "any individual, partnership, corporation, association, or other legal entity, and any union or group of individuals associated in fact although not a legal entity." § 1961(4). The definition embraces criminal enterprises as well as non-criminal ones. *United States v. Turkette,* 452 U.S. 576, 580–581 (1981).

The enterprise must be distinct from the defendant as well as from the pattern of racketeering activity:

Distinguishing the Enterprise from the Defendant. The enterprise and the defendant are sufficiently separate when the enterprise is a corporation with a single shareholder and the shareholder is the defendant: "The corporate owner/employee, a natural person, is distinct from the corporation itself, a legally different entity with different rights and responsibilities due to its different legal status." *Cedric Kushner Promotions, Ltd. v. King,* 533 U.S. 158, 163 (2001).

Can the enterprise be a sole proprietorship and the defendant be the sole proprietor? Prior to *Cedric*, Judge Posner suggested that the answer to this question turns on whether the proprietorship has employees: "A sole proprietorship is a recognized legal entity, and, provided it has any employees, is in any event a 'group of individuals associated in fact.'" *McCullough v. Suter,* 757 F.2d 142, 143–144 (7th Cir. 1985); *see Wade,* 623 F. Supp. 2d at 1287 (noting that the *McCullough* reasoning has been adopted by all federal appeals courts to confront the issue); *cf. Guidry v. Bank of LaPlace,* 954 F.2d 278 (5th Cir. 1992) (finding § 1962(c) inapplicable to a proprietorship with no employees).

Distinguishing the Enterprise from the Pattern of Racketeering Activity. When an enterprise is a corporation or other legal entity, it typically has a structure wholly apart from the pattern of racketeering activity in which it has allegedly engaged. But when the enterprise is an association-in-fact, such a structure is apt to be lacking. The question thus arises as to what must be shown to distinguish the enterprise from the pattern.

Addressing this question in *Boyle v. United States*, 556 U.S. 938 (2009), the Supreme Court suggested that the answer is not much. On the one hand, the Court held, "an association-in-fact enterprise must have at least three structural features: a purpose, relationships among those associated with the enterprise, and longevity sufficient to permit those associates to pursue the enterprise's purpose." *Id.* at 946. On the other hand, the word "structure" need not appear in the jury instructions and "the evidence used to prove the pattern of racketeering activity and the evidence establishing an enterprise 'may in particular cases coalesce.'" *Id.* at 947 (quoting *Turkette*, 452 U.S. 576 at 583).

§ 11.5.6 RICO: THE CONDUCT OF THE ENTERPRISE

Under § 1962(c), the defendant must "conduct or participate, directly or indirectly, in the conduct of" the enterprise. The Supreme Court has read this language to require the defendant to "participate in the operation or management of the enterprise itself." *Reves v. Ernst & Young*, 507 U.S. 170 (1993). The Court identified three categories of defendants that may satisfy the so-called "operation or management" test:

An Outsider of the Enterprise. This was the category at issue in *Reves* itself, in which the defendant was an accounting firm that prepared fraudulent financial statements for a farmers' coop based on information that the coop had supplied. The Court held that the accounting firm did not operate or manage the coop simply by performing its assigned task (however inadequately it may have done so). Put differently, the accounting firm was "outside the chain of command." *United States v. Oreto*, 37 F.3d 739, 750 (1st Cir. 1994).

Upper Management of the Enterprise. This category, the most self-evident of the three, was explicitly recognized by the *Reves* Court. *See Reves*, 507 U.S. at 184.

A Lower-Rung Insider of the Enterprise. The *Reves* Court likewise recognized that "lower rung" employees were also sometimes capable of operating or managing the enterprise. *Id.* But the Court did not indicate whether to do so, such employees "must themselves play some 'direct[ing]' role, or need only be acting under the direction of upper management." *United States v. Allen,* 155 F.3d 35, 42 (2d Cir. 1998) (alteration in original).

The circuits have come to various conclusions. For example, the Second Circuit conditions liability of lower-rung employees on their

" 'exercise [of] broad discretion' in carrying out
the principal's instructions." *United States v.
Burden,* 600 F.3d 204, 219 (2d Cir. 2010)
(quoting *United States v. Diaz*, 176 F.3d 52, 92
(2d Cir. 1999)). But the First Circuit requires
only that lower rung employees "knowingly
implement[ ] decisions" by those in senior
positions. *Oreto,* 37 F.3d at 750.

§ 11.5.7   RICO: PRIVATE SECURITIES ACTIONS

Until 1995, private plaintiffs bringing federal
securities fraud claims would typically add a RICO
allegation to their complaints. In addition to allowing
recovery of treble damages and attorneys' fees and
costs, civil RICO enabled the plaintiffs to circumvent
various federal securities law limitations, such as the
purchaser-seller requirement (*see* § 2.7 *supra*).

That RICO made possible such circumventions
generated dismay, as did the perception that
securities defendants were being coerced into settling
dubious RICO claims so as to avoid being labeled
racketeers.

Congress responded to these concerns when it
enacted the Private Securities Litigation Reform Act
(the PSLRA) in 1995 (*see* § 1.4 *supra*). The PSLRA
amended § 1964(c) of RICO—the provision
authorizing private actions—by stating that in
connection with such actions, an act of racketeering
activity does not encompass "conduct that would
have been actionable as fraud in the purchase or sale
of securities."

Also noteworthy is the accompanying Conference Report, which expressed Congress's desire that plaintiffs be barred from pleading other offenses, such as wire or mail fraud, as acts of racketeering activity if those offenses embrace conduct prohibited by the federal securities laws. *See* H.R. Conf. Rep. No. 104-369 at 47 (1995).

Courts have displayed a willingness to give effect to this statement in the legislative history. *See, e.g., Calderon Serra v. Banco Santander P.R.*, 747 F.3d 1 (1st Cir. 2014); *see also MLSMK, Inv. Co. v. J.P. Morgan Chase & Co.*, 651 F.3d 268, 277 (2d Cir. 2011) (holding that the prohibition against civil RICO claims alleging predicate acts of securities fraud applies "even where a plaintiff cannot itself pursue a securities fraud action against the defendant"). *But cf. Ouwinga v. Benistar Plan Servs., Inc.*, 694 F.3d 783, 790 (6th Cir. 2012) (finding the securities transactions to be "not integral or 'in connection with' the fraudulent scheme as a whole" (citation omitted)).

The PSLRA does, however, permit a plaintiff to assert a civil RICO claim against a defendant who, in connection with the fraud, was previously convicted of a criminal securities law violation. *See* § 1964(c); *see, e.g., Powers v. Wells Fargo Bank, N.A.*, 439 F.3d 1043 (9th Cir. 2006) (vacating dismissal as to one defendant after taking judicial notice of his conviction for federal securities fraud).

§ 11.6   CRIMINAL AIDING AND ABETTING

The DOJ has authority to prosecute the aiding and abetting of securities and related crimes pursuant to 18 U.S.C. § 2(a):

> Whoever commits an offense against the United States or aids, abets, counsels, commands, induces or procures its commission, is punishable as a principal.

18 U.S.C. § 2(a). Conviction under this statute requires proof that someone committed the crime in question coupled with the aider and abettor's "willing and knowing involvement" in that crime. *United States v. Dowlin*, 408 F.3d 647, 659 (10th Cir. 2005) (prosecution for aiding and abetting Securities Act violation).

In addition to enabling prosecutions of aiders and abettors of Securities Act and Exchange Act crimes, 18 U.S.C. § 2(a) does the same for those who aid and abet SOX crimes, *see, e.g., United States v. Yielding*, 657 F.3d 688 (8th Cir. 2011), and mail and wire fraud, *see, e.g., United States v. Beckman*, 787 F.3d 466, 486 (8th Cir. 2015) (wire fraud). Likewise subject to prosecution under this statute are those who aid and abet one (or more) of the acts of racketeering activity described in § 11.5.2 *supra. See, e.g., United States v. Ramirez-Rivera*, 800 F.3d 1, 20 (1st Cir. 2015); *United States v. Pungitore*, 910 F.2d 1084, 1132 n.68 (3d Cir. 1990) (collecting cases).

§ 11.7 CRIMINAL CONSPIRACIES

The DOJ can charge defendants with conspiracy to commit securities and related crimes pursuant to 18 U.S.C. § 371:

> If two or more persons conspire either to commit any offense against the United States, or to defraud the United States, or any agency thereof in any manner for any purpose, and one or more of such persons do any act to effect the object of the conspiracy, each shall be fined under this title or imprisoned not more than five years, or both. * * *

18 U.S.C. § 371; *see, e.g., Yeager v. United States,* 557 U.S. 110 (2009). Conviction under this statute entails proof of "(1) an agreement among two or more persons, the object of which is an offense against the United States; (2) the defendant's knowing and willful joinder in that conspiracy; and (3) commission of an overt act in furtherance of the conspiracy by at least one of the alleged co-conspirators." *United States v. Svoboda,* 347 F.3d 471, 476 (2d Cir. 2003).

The DOJ can prosecute conspiracy to commit a SOX crime or a crime of mail or wire fraud pursuant to 18 U.S.C. § 1349:

> Any person who attempts or conspires to commit any offense under this chapter shall be subject to the same penalties as those prescribed for the offense, the commission of which was the object of the attempt or conspiracy.

Id; see, e.g., United States v. Beacham, 774 F.3d 267 (5th Cir. 2014) (conspiracy to commit wire fraud); *United States v. Jho*, 534 F.3d 398, 401 (5th Cir. 2008) (conspiracy to commit a violation of 18 U.S.C. § 1519).

RICO contains its own conspiracy provision that makes it "unlawful for any person to conspire to violate" § 1962(c), as well as §§ 1962(a) and 1962(b). *See* 18 U.S.C. § 1962(d). The Supreme Court has held that such a conspiracy "may exist even if a conspirator does not agree to commit or facilitate each and every part of the substantive offense." *Salinas v. United States*, 522 U.S. 52, 63 (1997). That is, all that a conspirator must do is to "agree[ ] to advance a RICO undertaking." *United States v. Mouzone*, 687 F.3d 207, 218 (4th Cir. 2012). He need not operate or manage the enterprise. *See id.* (collecting cases).

§ 11.8   CRIMINAL ATTEMPTS

The DOJ can prosecute an attempt to commit either mail or wire fraud or a SOX crime pursuant to 18 U.S.C. 1349, the text of which appears in § 11.7 *supra. See, e.g., United States v. Webb*, 24 F. Supp. 3d 432 (M.D. Pa. 2014) (attempt to commit wire fraud); *United States v. Johnson*, 553 F. Supp. 2d 582 (E.D. Va. 2008) (attempt to violate 18 U.S.C. § 1512(c)).

§ 11.9   STATUTES OF LIMITATIONS

Prior to the Dodd-Frank Act of 2010 (the Dodd-Frank Act), which became effective on July 22, 2010, the limitations period for federal securities crimes was the 5-year period for federal crimes set forth in 18 U.S.C. § 3282. *See, e.g., United States v. Flood*, 635 F.3d 1255, 1258 (10th Cir. 2011). But as part of the Dodd-Frank Act, Congress enacted 18 U.S.C. § 3301, which extended the period to 6 years for crimes prosecuted under Securities Act § 24, Exchange Act § 32(a), and 18 U.S.C. § 1348. Thus, the limitations period continues to be 5 years for crimes prosecuted under 18 U.S.C. §§ 1350, 1512, 1519, and 1520.

There is no limitations period specifically applicable to the federal mail or wire fraud statutes. Therefore, the 5-year period from 18 U.S.C. § 3282 applies. *See, e.g., United States v. Ciavarella*, 716 F.3d 705, 732 n.18 (3d Cir. 2013).

There is likewise no specific limitations period governing RICO crimes. Those crimes are also subject to the 5-year period from 18 U.S.C. § 3282. *See Agency Holding Corp. v. Malley Duff & Assocs., Inc.*, 483 U.S. 143, 155–156 (1987). The period expires when the defendant has not committed at least one predicate act within 5 years of the indictment. *See United States v. Bruno*, 383 F.3d 65, 81 n.10 (2d Cir. 2004).

CHAPTER 12

INTERNATIONAL SECURITIES FRAUD

§ 12.1 INTRODUCTION

As originally enacted, the federal securities laws did not indicate whether the fraud provisions applied to transactions that cross national boundaries. Congress's silence carried no consequences so long as securities markets were essentially domestic. But beginning in the 1960s, the securities markets grew increasingly internationalized, infusing federal securities fraud actions with numerous permutations of foreign elements—foreign plaintiffs and defendants, foreign securities, foreign exchanges, and negotiations and trades that occurred in foreign countries.

The lower courts had to decide which (if any) of these actions they were entitled to hear. They developed a jurisprudence that focused on the substantiality of the domestic effects and the domestic conduct as well as the nationality of the injured investors and the issuer. They applied this jurisprudence in largely the same manner regardless of whether the action was brought by investors, the Securities and Exchange Commission (the SEC or the Commission), or the Department of Justice (the DOJ).

Two major developments in 2010 radically transformed this landscape: the Supreme Court's decision in *Morrison v. National Australia Bank,*

Ltd., 561 U.S. 247 (2010), followed shortly thereafter by the enactment of the Dodd-Frank Act of 2010 (the Dodd-Frank Act), specifically § 929P(b) thereof. The *Morrison* Court rejected the conduct and effects approach and substituted a transactional test in its place. Section 929P(b) is widely, albeit not universally, understood to resuscitate the conduct and effects approach on behalf of the SEC and the DOJ. *See* § 12.3 *infra*. Because Dodd-Frank is not retroactive, courts have applied *Morrison* to SEC and DOJ actions involving conduct occurring prior to its effective date. *See* § 12.3 *infra*.

This Chapter begins with *Morrison* (*see* § 12.2 *infra*) and then turns to the Dodd-Frank Act (*see* § 12.3 *infra*). It concludes with a brief discussion of the *forum non conveniens* doctrine (*see* § 12.4 *infra*).

§ 12.2   *MORRISON v. NATIONAL AUSTRALIA BANK, LTD.*

The Supreme Court issued its first, and thus far only, decision on transnational securities fraud in *Morrison v. National Australia Bank, Ltd.*, 561 U.S. 247 (2010). To understand this decision, the underlying facts are essential.

Filed under § 10(b) and Rule 10b-5, the action was of the "foreign cubed" variety—that is, the plaintiffs were citizens of a foreign country (Canada), the issuer was a foreign company (National Australia Bank or NAB), and the shares were purchased on a foreign stock exchange (that of Australia).

According to the complaint, the fraud was concocted in Florida by NAB's wholly owned, Florida-based subsidiary. The subsidiary sent materially misleading figures to NAB's Australia headquarters, which in turn transmitted the figures without change to the Australian Stock Exchange and the New York Stock Exchange (the NYSE), thereby distorting the market price of the shares.

The trial court dismissed the action for failure to allege a sufficient quantum of domestic conduct or domestic effects. The Second Circuit affirmed. Both courts treated the question of Rule 10b-5's transnational reach as one involving subject matter jurisdiction.

In its decision affirming the courts below, the Supreme Court did three important things. First, it held that the courts below made a "threshold error" in treating the transnational reach question as jurisdictional rather than merits-related. While this holding did not prompt a remand in *Morrison* it is nonetheless significant for the reasons discussed in § 12.2.1 *infra*.

Second, the Court repudiated the conduct and effects approach lock, stock, and barrel after finding it to contain multiple defects, including its lack of a textual (or other) basis in the Exchange Act; its uncertain and unpredictable application, and its clash with the presumption against extraterritoriality. *See Morrison*, 561 U.S. at 255–261.

Third, the Court replaced the conduct and effects approach with a transactional test which, as the Court saw it, deferred to the presumption against extraterritoriality as well as to the prerogatives of other countries to regulate securities transactions within their own borders. The Court extracted the transactional test from § 10(b)'s prohibition on fraud employed "in connection with the purchase or sale of any security registered on a national securities exchange or any security not so registered." *Id.* at 266–267. Observing that "[t]hose purchase-and-sale transactions are the objects of the statute's solicitude," the Court concluded that § 10(b)'s reach extends solely to fraud in connection with:

- transactions in securities listed on domestic exchanges (*see* § 12.2.2 *infra*); and

- domestic transactions in other securities (*see* § 12.2.3 *infra*).

Id. at 267. *See also id.* at 273 (describing the reach as extending to fraud "in connection with the purchase or sale of a security listed on an American stock exchange, and the purchase or sale of any other security in the United States"). Having bought their shares on a foreign exchange, the *Morrison* plaintiffs were unable to satisfy either prong. *See id.*

§ 12.2.1   *MORRISON*: EXTRATERRITORIALITY AS A MERITS QUESTION

In *Morrison v. National Australia Bank, Ltd.*, 561 U.S. 247 (2010), the Supreme Court held that the courts below had made a "threshold error" in treating extraterritoriality as a jurisdictional question rather than as one involving the "merits." *See* 561 U.S. at 253–254. While this holding did not affect the resolution of *Morrison,* it nonetheless carries significance as a general matter.

When extraterritoriality is jurisdictional, the court must address it first, before turning to any other aspect of the case. *Steel Co. v. Citizens for a Better Env't,* 523 U.S. 83 (1998). The court is "not entitled simply to assume jurisdiction and resolve an easy merits issue." *United Phosphorus, Ltd. v. Angus Chem. Co.*, 322 F.3d 942, 957 (7th Cir. 2003) (Wood, J., dissenting). The jurisdictional inquiry can be wide-ranging and frequently encompasses the resolution of factual disputes.

On the other hand, when extraterritoriality is merely one of many merits issues, "there is no reason why the court cannot resolve the most straightforward [merits] issue first." *Id.* Thus, a protracted inquiry into extraterritoriality can be averted if the case is amenable to dismissal for, say, a lack of materiality or the failure to plead scienter with sufficient particularity.

§ 12.2.2 *MORRISON*: PRONG ONE
OF THE TRANSACTIONAL TEST

The first prong of *Morrison*'s transactional test embraces "transactions in securities listed on domestic exchanges." 561 U.S. at 267. *See also* § 12.2.1 *supra.* When viewed in a vacuum, this language might seem to encompass a purchase or sale effectuated on a foreign exchange so long as the security is also listed on a domestic exchange. But such a reading cannot be reconciled with the following aspects of the opinion:

- The Court drew attention to the Exchange Act's statement of purpose, which declared that "transactions in securities as commonly conducted upon securities exchanges and over-the-counter markets are affected with a national public interest." *Id.* at 263. It then observed that "[n]othing suggests that this *national* public interest pertains to transactions conducted upon *foreign* exchanges and markets." *Id.* (emphasis in original).

- The Court stated that "the focus of the Exchange Act is not upon the place where the deception originated, but upon purchases and sales of securities in the United States." *Id.* at 266.

- The Court indicated its desire to create a test that would allow other countries to regulate their own exchanges. This policy goal would be undercut if § 10(b) applied to a transaction made on a foreign exchange on the ground that the security was also listed on a domestic exchange. *Id.* at 269.

- If the mere listing of a security on a domestic exchange sufficed, the outcome of *Morrison* would have been different. Indeed, NAB stock was available on the NYSE in the form of ADRs. *See id.* at 250.

Thus, satisfaction of the first prong turns on whether (i) the plaintiff made her purchase or sale on a domestic exchange and (ii) that purchase or sale occurred "in connection with" the fraud. While courts have had a relatively easy time applying this prong, the following two difficulties have occasionally arisen:

What is a Domestic Exchange? Plaintiffs have sometimes argued that the Over the Counter Bulletin Board or the Pink OTC Markets qualify as an American exchange. The Third Circuit has rejected this argument:

> Given that a "national securities exchange" is explicitly listed in § 10(b)—to the exclusion of the OTC markets—and coupled with the absence of the Pink Sheets and the OTCBB on the list of registered national security exchanges on the SEC Webpage on Exchanges, we are persuaded that those exchanges are not national securities exchanges within the scope of *Morrison*.

United States v. Georgiou, 777 F.3d 125, 135 (3d Cir. 2015). *Cf. Absolute Activist Value Master Fund Ltd. v. Ficeto*, 677 F.3d 60, 66 n.3 (2d Cir. 2012) (taking "no position on this issue"). *But see SEC v. Ficeto*, 839 F.Supp. 2d 1101, 1112 (D. Cal. 2011) (holding that *Morrison* did not distinguish between domestic exchanges and the domestic OTC market).

When is the Fraud "In Connection With" the Transaction? The issue here is whether the "in connection with" requirement, discussed in § 2.4.2 *supra*, should be read narrowly in deference to the presumption against extraterritoriality. *Cf. In re Optimal U.S. Litig.*, 865 F.Supp. 2d 451, 454 (S.D.N.Y. 2012) (endorsing a narrow reading). The *Optimal* court suggested that the decision in *SEC v. Compania Internacional Financiera, S.A.*, 2011 WL 3251813 (S.D.N.Y. 2011) should have adjusted its "in connection with" analysis to take account of the presumption. *See Optimal*, 865 F.Supp.2d at 455.

At issue in *Compania* was a "contract for difference" (CFD), a security giving the purchasers "the future price movement of the underlying company's common stock * * * without taking formal ownership of the underlying shares." *Freudenberg v. E*Trade Fin. Corp.*, 2008 WL 2876373 at *7 (S.D.N.Y. 2008). Before the CFD is priced, "actual matching shares of the underlying common stock are purchased or sold by the broker on the public securities exchange on which the common stock normally trades." *Id.* In *Compania*, the defendant bought a CFD in London for a specific number of shares of a NYSE-traded company, thereby leading his broker to purchase a corresponding number of shares on the NYSE. The defendant allegedly acquired the CFD based on material inside information. The court held that the defendant's fraud occurred "in connection with" his broker's NYSE purchase. *See Compania*, 2011 WL 3251813 at *6–*7.

§ 12.2.3 *MORRISON*: PRONG TWO
OF THE TRANSACTIONAL TEST

In *Morrison*, the Supreme Court held that even if the transaction did not occur on a domestic exchange, Rule 10b-5 can still apply if the transaction otherwise occurred in the United States. *See* § 12.2.1 *supra*. The Court said nothing more about the parameters of the second prong.

The Second Circuit has provided what is currently the prevailing interpretation of the second prong, pursuant to which the plaintiff must show that:

- irrevocable liability was incurred within the United States by the buyer to take and pay for a security, or by the seller to deliver a security; or

- the passage of title occurred within the United States.

Absolute Activist Value Master Fund Ltd. v. Ficeto, 677 F.3d 60, 67 (2d Cir. 2012). Clarifying this holding in a subsequent decision, the Second Circuit observed that the focus should be on "where, physically, the purchaser or seller committed him or herself, not where, as a matter of law, a contract is said to have been executed." *United States v. Vilar*, 729 F.3d 62, 77 n.11 (2d Cir. 2013).

Why look to "irrevocable liability" in the U.S.? The Second Circuit began with the Exchange Act's definitions of "purchase" and "sale" and noted that these definitions include "any contract to buy" or "any contract to sell." *Absolute Activist*, 677 F.3d at 67. As the court saw it, "these definitions suggest that the 'purchase' and 'sale' take place when the parties become bound to effectuate the transaction." *Id.* The *time when* the parties become bound, the court held, "can be used to determine *the locus of* a securities purchase or sale." *Id.* at 68 (emphasis added).

Why look to the passage of title in the U.S.? The Second Circuit started with the definition of "sale" in Black's Law Dictionary—a sale is " '[t]he transfer of property or title for a price.' " *Id.* This definition led the court to conclude that "a sale of securities can be understood to take place at the location in which title is transferred." *Id.* As the court noted, this conclusion already had the support of the Eleventh Circuit in *Quail Cruises Ship Mgmt. Ltd. v. Agencia de Viagens CVC Tur Limitada*, 645 F.3d 1307, 1310–1311 (11th Cir. 2011).

§ 12.2.4 *MORRISON*: SECURITY-BASED SWAPS

In 2000, Congress amended § 10(b) to encompass securities-based swap agreements: contracts in which the parties agree to exchange payments based on the price of a referenced security. Depending on the particular swap agreement, the referenced security might be one that trades on a domestic exchange, a foreign exchange, or on no exchange at all.

The Second Circuit considered the application of Morrison's second prong to security-based swaps in *Parkcentral Global Hub Ltd. v. Porsche Auto. Holdings SE*, 763 F.3d 198 (2d Cir. 2014). Acquired in the United States, the swaps referenced the stock of Volkswagen (VW), a German company traded only on foreign exchanges. The purchasers brought a Rule 10b-5 action against Porsche (another German company) on the theory that it had distorted the price of VW stock by misrepresenting its intentions about seeking control of VW. The court acknowledged that *if* prong two were invariably satisfied when the United States was the locus of the irrevocable commitment, the plaintiffs would have met their burden. 763 F.3d at 214.

But the court declined to adopt such a position, holding instead that a domestic purchase was not an invariably "sufficient" condition, despite being a "necessary" one. *Id.* at 215. The court noted that nothing in *Morrison* was to the contrary. *See id.* In addition, there was the fact that federal adjudication of the "predominantly German" events at issue would contravene *Morrison* by interfering with Germany's regulation of securities transactions taking place within its own borders. *See id.* at 216. *See also* § 12.2.1 *supra* (discussing *Morrison*). The court cautioned, however, that its holding should not be generalized to other securities-based swap agreements involving different underlying facts. *See* 763 F.3d at 217.

§ 12.2.5 *MORRISON*: THE SECURITIES ACT AND THE TRANSACTIONAL TEST

The plaintiffs in *Morrison v. National Australia Bank, Ltd.*, 561 U.S. 247 (2010), made no claims under the Securities Act. But the Supreme Court arguably invited application of the transactional test to those claims by declaring that "[t]he same focus on domestic transactions is evident in the Securities Act of 1933, enacted by the same Congress as the Exchange Act, and forming part of the same comprehensive regulation of securities trading." 561 U.S. at 268.

No doubt at least partly in response to that invitation, lower courts have applied the transactional test to claims under §§ 11 and 12(a)(2) of the Securities Act. *See, e.g., In re Vivendi Universal, S.A., Sec. Litig.*, 842 F.Supp. 2d 522, 529 (S.D.N.Y. 2012). *See also* Chapter 3 *supra* (discussing §§ 11 and 12(a)(2)).

Moreover, lower courts have likewise applied the transactional test to § 17(a) of the Securities Act. *See, e.g., SEC v. Tourre*, 2013 WL 2407172 at *6 (S.D.N.Y. 2013). The transactional test cannot be applied full-tilt to § 17(a), however, since unlike § 11, § 12(a)(2), and Rule 10b-5 itself, § 17(a) encompasses fraudulent offers, regardless of whether they lead to sales. *See* § 3.6 *supra* (discussing § 17(a)). Thus, when applying the transactional test to a § 17(a) claim involving a fraudulent offer, the focus is on whether the United States was the locus of the "offer," in accordance with the Securities Act's definition of that term. *See Tourre*, 2013 WL 2407172 at *9.

§ 12.2.6 *MORRISON*: THE POSSIBLE STATE-LAW ALTERNATIVE

One way for private plaintiffs to sidestep *Morrison* may be to file common law fraud claims, whether in state court or in federal court under diversity jurisdiction. *See, e.g., Terra Secs. Asa Konkursbo v. Citigroup, Inc.*, 740 F.Supp. 2d 441, 447–455 (S.D.N.Y. 2010) (dismissing federal securities fraud claims on account of *Morrison* but refusing to dismiss diversity-based common law fraud claim "arising out of the same allegedly fraudulent conduct"). Plaintiffs bringing common law fraud claims must avoid those of the class action variety that would invite preclusion under the SLUSA, discussed in § 6.6 *supra. Cf. Terra*, 740 F.Supp. 2d at 443 (lawsuit brought by eight plaintiffs).

§ 12.3   THE DODD-FRANK ACT, § 929P(b)

Section 929P(b) of the Dodd-Frank Act amended the jurisdictional provisions of the Securities Act (§ 22) and the Securities Exchange Act (§ 27) by adding the following language:

EXTRATERRITORIAL JURISDICTION—The district courts of the United States and the United States courts of any Territory shall have jurisdiction of an action or proceeding brought or instituted by the Commission or the United States alleging a violation of the antifraud provisions of this title involving—

(1) conduct within the United States that constitutes significant steps in furtherance of the violation, even if the securities transaction occurs outside the United States and involves only foreign investors; or

(2) conduct occurring outside the United States that has a foreseeable substantial effect within the United States.

Dodd-Frank does not apply retroactively, however, with the result that courts have applied *Morrison*'s transactional test to government prosecutions of conduct occurring prior to Dodd-Frank's effective date. *See, e.g., SEC v. Ficeto*, 839 F.Supp. 2d 1101, 1110 n.7 (C.D.Cal. 2011).

There are currently two quite different understandings of § 929P(b). Under the conventional view, the provision was designed to resuscitate the conduct and effects approach for the benefit of the SEC and the DOJ. *See, e.g., In re Optimal U.S. Litig.*, 865 F.Supp. 2d 451, 456 n.28 (S.D.N.Y. 2012). As it stood prior to *Morrison*, this approach involved the following parameters:

The Conduct Test. Under this test, Rule 10b-5 applied where " 'substantial acts in furtherance of the fraud were committed within the United States.' " *SEC v. Berger*, 322 F.3d 187, 193 (2d Cir. 2003) (quoting *Psimenos v. E.F. Hutton & Co., Inc.*, 722 F.2d 1041, 1045 (2d Cir. 1983)). In applying this test, courts distinguished between the "fraudulent acts themselves" and "mere preparatory activities . . . where the bulk of the activity was performed in foreign countries." *IIT v. Vencap, Ltd.*, 519 F.2d 1001, 1018 (2d Cir. 1975). The nationality of the issuer could matter in this regard. Thus, a foreign issuer's U.S. activities that rose only to the "preparatory" level might appear more significant when undertaken by an American issuer. *See IIT v. Cornfeld*, 619 F.2d 909, 920 (2d Cir. 1980). Likewise relevant was the nationality of the injured investors, with a higher quantum of domestic conduct necessary when those injured were foreign. *See Bersch v. Drexel Firestone, Inc.*, 519 F.2d 974, 993 (2d Cir. 1975). The differences among the circuits were relatively marginal. *See, e.g., Kauthar SDN BHD v. Sternberg*, 149 F.3d 659, 665–666 (7th Cir.1998) (comparing the various approaches).

The Effects Test. Under this test, Rule 10b-5 applies where "the wrongful conduct had a substantial effect in the United States or upon United States citizens." *Berger*, 322 F.3d at 193. To qualify, the effects on U.S. investors or markets must emerge immediately and directly from the transaction itself. *Cf. Bersch,* 519 F.2d at 987–989 (holding insufficient for effects purposes a fraudulent offering that undermined investor trust, leading to a decline in the volume of U.S. securities purchased by foreign investors and consequently a downturn in the price of U.S. securities in general).

The Possibility of Combining Conduct and Effects. Prior to *Morrison*, Rule 10b-5 could become applicable on the basis of a combination of conduct and effects. *See, e.g., Itoba Ltd. v. Lep Group PLC*, 54 F.3d 118 (2d Cir. 1995). But observe that under § 929P(b), the conduct and effects jurisdictional bases are connected by an "or." Query whether the "or" phraseology prevents the use of the combination approach.

The alternative view of § 929P(b) holds that the provision merely reclassifies extraterritoriality as a jurisdictional question for actions brought by the SEC or the DOJ. *See, e.g., SEC v. A Chicago Convention Center, LLC*, 961 F.Supp. 2d 905, 916 (N.D. Ill. 2013) (declining to choose between the two views). The alternative view rests on § 929P(b)'s jurisdictional phraseology coupled with its delineation as an amendment to the jurisdictional provisions of the Securities Act and the Exchange Act. *See id.*

In response to this debate, the SEC adopted the following rule in 2014:

§ 250.1   Cross-Border Antifraud Law-Enforcement Authority

(a)   Notwithstanding any other Commission rule or regulation, the antifraud provisions of the securities laws apply to:

(1)   Conduct within the United States that constitutes significant steps in furtherance of the violation; or

(2)   Conduct occurring outside the United States that has a foreseeable substantial effect within the United States.

(b)   The antifraud provisions of the securities laws apply to conduct described in paragraph (a)(1) of this section even if:

(1) The violation relates to a securities transaction or securities transactions occurring outside the United States that involves only foreign investors; or

(2) The violation is committed by a foreign adviser and involves only foreign investors.

(c) Violations of the antifraud provisions of the securities laws described in this section may be pursued in judicial proceedings brought by the Commission or the United States.

See Exchange Act Release No. 34-72472, 2014 WL 3920307 at *148–*149 (Sept. 8, 2014).

§ 12.4 THE FORUM NON CONVENIENS DOCTRINE

The federal common law doctrine of *forum non conveniens* allows a federal district court to "dismiss an action on the ground that a court abroad is the more appropriate and convenient forum for adjudicating the controversy." *Sinochem Int'l Co., Ltd. v. Malaysia Int'l Shipping Corp.*, 549 U.S. 422, 425 (2007). The doctrine has provided the basis for dismissing many federal securities fraud actions. *See, e.g., Alfadda v. Fenn*, 159 F.3d 41 (2d Cir. 1998) (dismissing in favor of France); *In re Citigroup, Inc., Sec. Litig.*, 2014 WL 470894 (S.D.N.Y. 2014) (dismissing in favor of England); *In re Banco Santander Sec.-Optimal Litig.*, 732 F.Supp. 2d 1305 (S.D. Fla. 2010) (dismissing in favor of Ireland).

A defendant who makes a dismissal motion based on *forum non conveniens* must establish three elements—that "(1) an adequate alternative forum is available, (2) the public and private factors [identified below] weigh in favor of dismissal, and (3) the plaintiff can reinstate his suit in the alternative forum without undue inconvenience or prejudice." *Leon v. Millon Air, Inc.*, 251 F.3d 1305, 1311 (11th Cir. 2001).

The alternative forum typically qualifies as adequate so long as the defendant can be served with process and an acceptable remedy is available. *See Piper Aircraft Co. v. Reyno*, 454 U.S. 235, 254 n.22 (1981). To be unacceptable, a remedy must be "no remedy at all." *Id.* at 254. A forum can also be inadequate if it is "characterized by a complete absence of due process." *In re Arbitration Between Monegasque De Reassurances S.A.M. v. Nak Naftogaz of Ukraine*, 311 F.3d 488, 499 (2d Cir. 2002).

One court found the alternative forum inadequate for an action brought mainly by U.S. investors because of the combined absence of a class action mechanism and a fraud-on-the-market claim. *See In re Lernout & Hauspie Sec. Litig.*, 208 F.Supp. 2d 74, 91–92 (D.Mass. 2002). *But cf. Warlop v. Lernout*, 473 F.Supp. 2d 260 (D. Mass. 2007) (finding alternative forum adequate for a related action brought mainly by foreign investors, despite combined absence of same features). That these quite similar cases led to different outcomes illustrates the highly fact-intensive nature of the *forum non conveniens* inquiry.

The public factors to be weighed include "(1) having local disputes settled locally; (2) avoiding problems of applying foreign law; and (3) avoiding burdening jurors with cases that have no impact on their community." *Alfadda*, 159 F.3d at 46 (citing *Piper* and *Gulf Oil Corp. v. Gilbert*, 330 U.S. 501 (1981)).

The relevant private factors to be weighed include "(1) ease of access to evidence; (2) the cost for witnesses to attend trial; (3) the availability of compulsory process; and (4) other factors that might shorten trial or make it less expensive." *Alfadda*, 159 F.3d at 46 (citing *Piper* and *Gilbert*).

In weighing these factors, the plaintiff's choice of forum is entitled to some deference. However, the deference due is greater when a U.S. plaintiff chooses a U.S. forum than when a foreign plaintiff chooses a U.S. forum. *See Piper*, 454 U.S. at 266.

CHAPTER 13
SECURITIES ARBITRATION

§ 13.1 INTRODUCTION

Arbitration is the principal means of resolving disputes between investors and their brokers. The obligation to arbitrate arises from the pre-dispute arbitration agreement (the PDAA), which is included in the contract that an investor signs when she opens an account with a brokerage firm. The PDAA requires her to arbitrate all future disputes with the firm (or its brokers), regardless of whether those disputes involve state law (*e.g.*, breaches of contact or fiduciary duty) or federal securities law.

The forum for arbitrating virtually all such disputes is the Financial Industry Regulatory Authority (FINRA). FINRA is a self-regulatory organization (SRO) established in 2007 as the result of the consolidation of the National Association of Securities Dealers (the NASD) and the member regulatory, enforcement, and arbitration divisions of the New York Stock Exchange (the NYSE).

Mandatory arbitration of investor-broker disputes has sparked considerable controversy. Supporters maintain that arbitration is fair, efficient, and economical. They also note that judges often recommend it as a form of alternative dispute resolution in a wide spectrum of civil cases.

Critics, on the other hand, contend that investors can be protected only by a trial, conducted by a judge, based on the rules of evidence (not required in arbitration), with a right to appeal (sharply limited in arbitration). In addition, they complain that the system has an inherent pro-broker bias, in part because FINRA's membership consists entirely of brokerage firms. Moreover, a different set of critics, mostly on the defense side, believe that certain features of FINRA arbitration (such as the prohibition on motions to dismiss and the loose approach to evidence) facilitate the assertion of weak claims that would not survive in court.

This Chapter begins with the relation between the Federal Arbitration Act of 1925 (the FAA) and the federal securities statutes (§ 13.2 *infra*), followed by a brief look at securities arbitration procedures (§ 13.3 *infra*). Attention then turns to the availability of punitive damages (§ 13.4 *infra*); the allocation of certain questions as between courts and arbitrators (§ 13.5 *infra*); waivers of the agreement to arbitrate (§ 13.6 *infra*); bars on class-wide arbitrations and class actions (§ 13.7 *infra*); and judicial review (§ 13.8 *infra*).

§ 13.2 THE RELATIONSHIP BETWEEN THE FAA AND THE FEDERAL SECURITIES STATUTES

Enacted the decade before the Securities Act and the Securities Exchange Act, the FAA declares arbitration agreements "valid, irrevocable, and enforceable, save upon such grounds as exist at law or in equity for the revocation of any contract." 9 U.S.C. § 2. The FAA was intended to "revers[e] centuries of judicial hostility to arbitration agreements * * *, to allow parties to avoid 'the costliness and delays of litigation,' and to place arbitration agreements 'upon the same footing as other contracts.'" *Scherk v. Alberto-Culver Co.,* 417 U.S. 506, 510–511 (1974) (quoting H.R. Rep. No. 68-96, 2 (1924)).

For many years, courts struggled with whether a PDAA prevents an investor from suing her broker for federal securities violations. The answer has turned on the far from self-evident relationship between the FAA and the federal securities statutes, a relationship that the Supreme Court has viewed differently at different times. Understanding the evolution in the Court's thinking is crucial for purposes of grasping the current state of securities arbitration and the debates that swirl around it.

The *Wilko* Era. The Supreme Court first addressed the interface between the FAA and federal securities law in *Wilko v. Swan,* 346 U.S. 427 (1953). The *Wilko* Court held that a PDAA did not prevent an investor from suing his broker for violating what is now Securities Act § 12(a)(2). To reach that conclusion, the Court relied on Securities Act § 14, which declares "void" "[a]ny condition, stipulation or provision binding any person acquiring any security to waive compliance with any provision" of that Act. Under § 14, the Court asserted, an agreement to arbitrate amounts to an impermissible "stipulation" to waive the right to sue under the Securities Act. *See Wilko,* 346 U.S. at 434–435.

The *Wilko* Court gave two reasons for reading § 14 in this fashion. One was Congress's desire to protect the hapless investor who waives his right to sue while oblivious to the resulting benefits to his opponent. *See id.* at 435. The other was the Court's perception that the Securities Act would be less efficacious in an arbitration forum than in a judicial one given, among other factors, the lack of judicial oversight and the highly limited nature of judicial review. *See id.* at 435–436.

As a formal matter, the *Wilko* decision voided arbitration agreements only as to claims made under the Securities Act. But in the wake of *Wilko*, lower federal courts likewise refused to order arbitration of claims made under the Exchange Act on the theory that Exchange Act § 29(a) and Securities Act § 14 are virtually identical. *See, e.g., Merrill Lynch, Pierce, Fenner & Smith, Inc. v. Moore,* 590 F.2d 823, 827–829 (10th Cir. 1978).

The Demise of *Wilko*—Early Developments. The Supreme Court abandoned *Wilko* in stages. The process began when the Court required the arbitration of a Rule 10b-5 claim on the ground that the contract containing the PDAA was "truly international." Scherk, 417 U.S. at 515. The Court thereafter mandated arbitration of state securities claims even if they were pendent to a Rule 10b-5 claim that would eventually be litigated. *See Dean Witter Reynolds, Inc. v. Byrd,* 470 U.S. 213, 223 (1985).

The Demise of *Wilko-McMahon*. The abandonment of *Wilko* culminated in *Shearson/Am. Express, Inc. v.*

McMahon, 482 U.S. 220 (1987), which held that § 29(a) did not override a PDAA in connection with a claim under § 10(b) of the Exchange Act and Rule 10b-5. *See* 482 U.S. at 238. To reach that result, the Court read § 29(a) as precluding waivers only as to substantive provisions and not as to those conferring rights to sue (as Exchange Act § 27 did for the implied right of action under Rule 10b-5). *See* 482 U.S. at 228. Acknowledging that this reading of § 29(a) contradicted its reading of § 14 in *Wilko,* the Court maintained that the *Wilko* reading had ultimately been driven by a view of arbitration that was no longer valid: "Even if *Wilko*'s assumptions regarding arbitration were valid at the time *Wilko* was decided, they most certainly they do not hold true today for arbitration procedures subject to the SEC's oversight authority." *Id.* at 233.

Since *McMahon* arose under the Exchange Act, it did not, technically speaking, eviscerate *Wilko,* which arose under the Securities Act. Yet *McMahon* clearly signaled that *Wilko*'s demise was inevitable. The official end came two years after *McMahon* in *Rodriguez de Quijas v. Shearson/Am. Express, Inc.,* 490 U.S. 477 (1989), which required investors to arbitrate claims under what is now § 12(a)(2) of the Securities Act.

Overriding Contrary State Laws. Is a state entitled to enact a law that invalidates PDAAs? Three years before *McMahon,* the Supreme Court held that the FAA preempted such a law. *See Southland Corp. v. Keating,* 465 U.S. 1 (1984) (franchise case). The *Keating* decision took on new significance after

McMahon, when various states adopted regulations aimed at insulating investors from *McMahon*'s effects. For example, Massachusetts adopted regulations prohibiting brokerage firms from turning away those who refused a PDAA and requiring the disclosure of the prohibition to all prospective customers. *See Sec. Indus. Ass'n v. Connolly*, 883 F.2d 1114, 1117 (1st Cir. 1989). Constrained by *Keating*, the First Circuit held that the FAA preempted the regulations. *Id.* at 1124.

A closer case arose in California, where the regulations were more burdensome than NASD's rules but yet not in conflict with them, thereby allowing arbitrators to comply with both. *See Credit Suisse First Boston Corp. v. Grunwald*, 400 F.3d 1119, 1134–1135 (9th Cir. 2005). But in the Ninth Circuit's view, the FAA still trumped the regulations on the ground that the latter thwarted "Congress's chosen approach of delegating nationwide, cooperative regulatory authority to the Commission and the [SRO]" and might "undermine the NASD arbitration system's protection of investors." *Id.* at 1135.

Full Circle with Dodd-Frank? The Dodd-Frank Act of 2010 (the Dodd-Frank Act) grants the SEC new authority over PDAAs, allowing the agency to "prohibit, or impose conditions or limitations on the use of" PDAAs in connection with claims based on federal securities law or FINRA rules. *See* the Dodd-Frank Act § 921 (codified at 15 U.S.C. § 78o). Thus far, the SEC has made no use of this authority. Were it to do so, however, brokerage firms could continue to enforce PDAAs in connection with state law claims.

§ 13.3   A BRIEF LOOK AT SECURITIES ARBITRATION PROCEDURES

As was mentioned in § 13.1 *supra*, FINRA serves as the forum for virtually all securities arbitrations. A discussion of the applicable procedures is available at   http://www.finra.org/arbitration-and-mediation/ arbitration-process.

As that discussion makes clear, the arbitration of securities claims is less expensive than litigation as well as faster. Discovery is obtainable, but the rules of evidence do not apply. The decision of the arbitrator(s) is final, with judicial review available only on an extremely limited basis (*see* § 13.8 *infra*).

Two additional matters merit mention: (i) the circumstances under which arbitrators must explain their decisions; and (ii) arbitrator qualifications and training.

<u>When Arbitrators Must Explain Their Decisions</u>. As a general proposition, arbitrators do not have to explain their decisions. *See* FINRA Rule 2268(a)(4). An explanation nonetheless becomes obligatory when the parties jointly make a request "at least 20 days prior to the first scheduled hearing date." *See id.* That explanation, however, need not include legal authorities or calculation of damages. *See* FINRA Rule 12904(g).

<u>Arbitrator Qualifications and Training</u>. A person seeking to become an arbitrator does not need a law

degree or any previous familiarity with the substantive issues likely to be encountered. All that she must have is five years of "paid work experience" and "at least two years of college-level credits," and even these prerequisites can be waived at FINRA's discretion. *See* FINRA, Become An Arbitrator, available at https://www.finra.org/arbitration-and-mediation/become-arbitrator.

Service as an arbitrator requires completion of online training on arbitration procedures, satisfactory performance on two examinations, and attendance at a live video or onsite training session. FINRA, Required Basic Arbitrator Training, available at https://www.finra.org/arbitration-and-mediation/arbitrator-training. The training does not include instruction in substantive securities law. *See id.*

The standards are stiffer for those chairing an arbitration panel. Chairs must have a law degree and bar membership and also have previously served as an arbitrator in proceedings involving a hearing held under an SRO's auspices. In addition, they must complete FINRA's chair training course. *See* FINRA, Arbitrators Frequently Asked Questions, available at https://www.finra.org/arbitration-and-mediation/faq-arbitrators-faq.

§ 13.4 THE AVAILABILITY OF PUNITIVE DAMAGES

Federal securities claims do not give rise to punitive damages (*see* generally Chapters 2–5 *supra*), but such damages are available in connection with certain state law claims. When a claimant prevails on a state claim of this type, he can be awarded punitive damages, even if his PDAA says otherwise. *See* FINRA Rule 2268(d)(4).

Moreover, investors seeking punitive damages under state law benefit from *Mastrobuono v. Shearson Lehman Hutton, Inc.,* 514 U.S. 52 (1995), where the PDAA was signed before the effective date of the above-mentioned rule (and its predecessor). The brokerage firm argued that punitive damages were barred by the PDAA, an argument that the Supreme Court rejected for reasons reaching beyond contract law: " '[D]ue regard must be given to the federal policy favoring arbitration, and ambiguities as to the scope of the arbitration clause itself resolved in favor of arbitration.' " *Id.* at 62 (quoting *Volt Info. Scis., Inc. v. Bd. of Trustees of Leland Stanford Univ.,* 489 U.S. 468, 476 (1989)).

§ 13.5   THE ALLOCATION OF CERTAIN QUESTIONS AS BETWEEN COURTS AND ARBITRATORS

The fact that PDAAs are enforceable does not take courts out of the picture altogether. They may have a role depending on whether the question at issue is classified as:

- an arbitrability question;

- a procedural question; or

- a fraud-in-the-inducement question.

<u>Arbitrability Questions</u>. A question of arbitrability involves whether the parties agreed to arbitrate the particular type of dispute at issue. An equally important but separate question is who decides whether they did so.

The seminal decision on both questions is *First Options of Chi., Inc. v. Kaplan*, 514 U.S. 938 (1995). At issue in *Kaplan* was an arbitration agreement that had been signed by the plaintiff and a corporation but not by the corporation's sole shareholder. When a dispute arose between the plaintiff and the shareholder, the plaintiff sought to compel arbitration. Over the shareholder's objection, the arbitrators decided that they had the right to resolve the dispute and ruled in the plaintiff's favor. Seeking to challenge that ruling, the shareholder filed a judicial action that eventually reached the Supreme Court.

The Supreme Court began its analysis by distinguishing among the following three questions:

(i)   the merits of the dispute;

(ii)   whether the parties agreed to arbitrate that dispute (the "arbitrability" question); and

(iii) who should address the arbitrability question—the court or the arbitrators.

Id. at 942. The Court assigned different presumptions to questions two and three.

Regarding question three, the Court established a presumption in favor of the judiciary and against the arbitrators (rebuttable by clear and unmistakable evidence). *See id.* at 944. The reason, the Court explained, was that such an "arcane" question may never have occurred to the parties. *See id.* at 945.

Regarding question two (concerning arbitrability), however, the Court presumed *in favor of* arbitration in the event of an ambiguity. *See id.* at 944–945. Why did the presumption flip? Since the parties decided to arbitrate a range of issues, the Court observed, it makes sense to infer that they gave at least some consideration to the width of the range. *See id.* at 945. Also, given the federal policy promoting arbitration, a presumption facilitating arbitration seemed called for. *See id.*

Applying these principles to the record before it, the Court concluded that the plaintiff had not overcome the presumption against a decision by the arbitrators on the arbitrability question. *See id.* at 946. The question thus required independent judicial review. *See id.* at 947.

<u>Procedural Questions Distinguished</u>. The Supreme Court drew an important distinction between arbitrability questions and procedural questions in *Howsam v. Dean Witter Reynolds, Inc.*, 537 U.S. 79 (2002). At issue in *Howsam* was who should decide whether FINRA's six-year time limit on eligibility to arbitrate had expired. The Court held that this was not an arbitrability question (which would call for a presumption against a decision by the arbitrators). Rather, the question fell into the category of dispositive procedural matters emerging from the dispute, a category as to which there is a presumption favoring a decision by the arbitrators.

See id. at 85–86. Other matters in this category, the Court noted, include defenses to arbitration (such as waiver and delay) and conditions precedent to arbitration (such as the completion of a grievance procedure, where the contract made that procedure a prerequisite to arbitration). *See id.* at 84–85.

The Court gave two reasons for carving out these procedural matters. First, the parties likely expected that the arbitrators would decide such questions. *See id.* at 85. Second, the arbitrators would be apt to have expertise bearing on such questions. *See id.*

<u>Fraud-in-the-Inducement Questions</u>. Suppose an investor claims that he was fraudulently induced into contracting with his broker. Who decides the claim of fraudulent inducement—the arbitrators or a court?

The seminal opinion is *Prima Paint Corp. v. Flood & Conklin Mfg. Co.*, 388 U.S. 395 (1967). At issue was who should decide a fraud-in-the-inducement claim directed at the contract of which the arbitration agreement was a part. The Court held the question was for the arbitrators to decide (in the absence of evidence of a contrary intent in the contract). *See id.* at 404. The question would be for the court to decide, however, if the fraud-in the-inducement claim had instead been directed at the arbitration agreement specifically. *See id.* at 403–404.

The *Prima Paint* Court gave two reasons for its holding. One was the language of § 4 the FAA, which provides that "[t]he court shall hear the parties, and upon being satisfied that the making of the agreement for arbitration or the failure to comply therewith is not in issue, the court shall make an order directing the parties to proceed to arbitration in accordance with the terms of the agreement." *Id.* at 403–404 & n.11. The other reason was the presumption in favor of arbitration. *Id.* at 404.

The Court reaffirmed *Prima Paint* in *Granite Rock Co. v. Int'l Bhd. of Teamsters*, 561 U.S 287, 301 (2010), but arguably ran afoul of it in *Rent-A-Center, W., Inc. v. Jackson*, 561 U.S. 63 (2010), which arose in the employment context. The employee alleged that his arbitration agreement was unconscionable, prompting the question of who should decide whether that was so. *See id.* at 68. The arbitration agreement contained a provision (the "delegation provision") expressly giving the arbitrators the authority to decide whether the agreement was "void or voidable." *Id.* at 68. Dividing 5–4, the Court held that the unconscionability question was for the arbitrators to decide, notwithstanding the fact that the arbitration agreement represented the totality of the entire contract. *Id.* at 72. As the Court saw it, this fact "ma[de] no difference." *Id. But cf. id.* at 86 (Stevens, J., dissenting) (arguing that the Court violated *Prima Paint* by "declar[ing] that it 'makes no difference' that the underlying subject matter of the agreement is itself an arbitration agreement").

§ 13.6 WAIVERS OF THE AGREEMENT TO ARBITRATE

There are several possible ways to waive the agreement to arbitrate. Consider the following.

Engagement in Litigation. A party can waive its agreement to arbitrate by engaging in litigation. But what form must the engagement take in order to constitute a waiver? The Second Circuit looks to the presence of three factors: (1) the time elapsed from when litigation was commenced until the request for arbitration; (2) the amount of litigation to date, including motion practice and discovery; and (3) proof of prejudice. *La. Stadium & Exposition Dist. v. Merrill Lynch, Pierce, Fenner & Smith, Inc.*, 626 F.3d 156, 159 (2d Cir. 2010) (citation omitted). Eschewing "any rigid formula," the court regards prejudice as central. *See id; see also In re Pharmacy Benefit Managers Antitrust Litig.*, 700 F.3d 109, 117 (3d Cir. 2012) (identifying six factors, with prejudice being central). *But cf. Kahn v. Parsons Glob. Servs., Ltd.*, 521 F.3d 421, 425 (D.C. Cir. 2008) (noting that "[a] finding of prejudice is not necessary in order to conclude that a right to compel arbitration has been waived" but it is a germane consideration that a court may choose to take into account).

Adoption of a Forum Selection Clause. The Second and Ninth Circuits have held that the parties to an arbitration agreement waive that agreement by adopting a broadly-worded forum selection clause that calls for a judicial forum to decide "all actions and proceedings" between them. *See Goldman, Sachs & Co. v. Golden Empire Sch. Fin. Auth.*, 764 F.3d 210 (2d Cir. 2014); *Goldman, Sachs & Co. v. City of Reno*, 747 F.3d 733, 736 (9th Cir. 2014). The Fourth Circuit, however, has held that no waiver arises under these circumstances. *See UBS Fin. Servs., Inc. v. Carilion Clinic*, 706 F.3d 319 (4th Cir. 2013).

§ 13.7 BARS ON CLASS-WIDE ARBITRATION AND CLASS ACTIONS

FINRA has rules prohibiting the following:

- Class-wide arbitration. *See* FINRA Rule 12204(a); and

- Bars on class-action litigation in PDAAs. *See* FINRA Rule 2268(d) (precluding a PDAA from "includ[ing] any condition that * * * (3) limits the ability of a party to file any claim in court permitted to be filed in court under the rules of the forums in which a claim may be filed under the agreement").

The validity of these prohibitions may, or may not, have been called into question by two recent Supreme Court decisions, both of which arose outside the FINRA context.

The first such decision is *AT&T Mobility LLC v. Concepcion*, 563 U.S. 333 (2011). At issue was a cell phone purchase agreement that required arbitration on an individual basis of all disputes between AT & T and the customer. When a state-law dispute arose under such an agreement, the customers (husband and wife) filed a court action, prompting AT & T to move to compel arbitration. The customers responded by invoking a state judicial rule declaring unconscionable any arbitration agreement with a class waiver. In a 5–4 decision siding with AT & T, the Supreme Court held that the FAA preempted the state rule. *See id.* at 352. In the course of so holding, the Court suggested that a PDAA providing for class arbitration would satisfy the FAA. *See id.* at 348.

Shortly thereafter came *Am. Express Co. v. Italian Colors Rest.* 133 S. Ct. 2304 (2013). Like *Concepcion*, the arbitration agreement contained a class waiver, but unlike *Concepcion*, the dispute arose under federal law—specifically, the Sherman Act. Dividing 5–3, with Justice Sotomayor not participating, the Supreme Court held that the class waiver satisfied the FAA, even if each plaintiff stood to recover less than it would need to arbitrate its antitrust claims individually. *See id.* at 2310–2311. In the Court's view, "the fact that it is not worth the expense involved in *proving* a statutory remedy does not constitute the elimination of the *right to pursue* that remedy." *Id.* at 2311. Moreover, the Court added, the decision in *Concepcion* "all but resolves this case." *Id.* at 2312.

The *Concepcion* and *Italian Colors* decisions prompt the following two questions in connection with PDAAs governed by FINRA:

- Suppose the PDAA requires class arbitration. Would that requirement be enforced as written on the theory that the FAA trumps the prohibition on class arbitration in FINRA Rule 12204(a)? Or would the FINRA rule trump, based on FINRA's authority over PDAAs received from the SEC, whose own authority over PDAAs was recently expanded by Dodd-Frank (*see* § 13.2 *supra*)?

- Suppose the PDAA bars class action litigation. Would that bar be enforced as written on the theory that the FAA trumps the prohibition on class action bars in FINRA Rule

2268(d)(3)? Or would the FINRA rule trump,
based on the same rationale as was mentioned
in the immediately preceding paragraph?

For a while, the second question seemed headed for
judicial resolution. After *Concepcion*, Charles
Schwab, the brokerage firm, adopted a PDAA barring
class action litigation, leading FINRA to file a
disciplinary proceeding against Schwab for violating
FINRA Rule 2268(d)(3). FINRA and Schwab
ultimately settled, however, thereby deferring a
judicial decision on the matters presented.

§ 13.8 JUDICIAL REVIEW

The Arbitration Act gives courts authority to
vacate arbitration decisions only in four narrow
situations:

(1) where the award was procured by
corruption, fraud, or undue means;

(2) where there was evident partiality or
corruption in the arbitrators * * * ;

(3) where the arbitrators were guilty of
misconduct * * * or of any other misbehavior by
which the rights of any party have been
prejudiced; or

(4) where the arbitrators exceeded their powers
* * * .

9 U.S.C. § 10(a)(1–4). For some time, most courts
have upheld the existence of an additional (albeit
limited) ground for vacating arbitration decisions—
"manifest disregard of the law." This ground

originated in *Wilko v. Swan,* 346 U.S. 427 (1953), *rev'd on other grounds,* *Rodriquez de Quijas v. Shearson/Am. Express, Inc.,* 490 U.S. 477 (1989), where the Court stated: "[T]he interpretations of the law by the arbitrators in contrast to manifest disregard are not subject, in the federal courts, to judicial review for an error in interpretation." *Id.* at 436–37.

Modification or vacation of a decision based on manifest disregard requires the court to conclude both "that (1) the arbitrators knew of a governing legal principle yet refused to apply it or ignored it altogether and (2) the law ignored by the arbitrators was well defined, explicit, and clearly applicable to the case." *Lessin v. Merrill Lynch, Pierce, Fenner & Smith, Inc.,* 481 F.3d 813, 821 (D.C. Cir. 2007) (quoting *LaPrade v. Kidder, Peabody & Co.,* 246 F.3d 702, 706 (D.C. Cir. 2001)).

The Supreme Court called into question the continued availability of manifest disregard in *Hall St. Assocs., L.L.C. v. Mattel, Inc.,* 552 U.S. 576 (2008), which held that the grounds for judicial review cannot be expanded by contract. Commenting on *Wilko*'s reference to the "manifest disregard" ground, the Court stated: "Maybe the term 'manifest disregard' was meant to name a new ground for review, but maybe it merely referred to the § 10 grounds collectively, rather than adding to them." *Id.* at 585.

The Supreme Court has acknowledged the uncertain status of manifest disregard in the wake of *Hall Street*:

> We do not decide whether 'manifest disregard'
> survives our decision in [*Hall Street*] as an
> independent ground for judicial review or as a
> judicial gloss in the enumerated grounds for
> vacatur set forth at 9 U.S.C. § 10.

Stolt-Nielsen, S.A. v. AnimalFeeds Int'l Corp., 559
U.S. 662, 672 n.3 (2010). Not surprisingly, the circuit
courts are divided regarding the status of manifest
disregard in the wake of *Hall Street*. *See Bangor Gas
Co., LLC v. H.Q. Energy Servs. (U.S.) Inc.*, 695 F.3d
181,187 & n.3 (1st Cir. 2012) (collecting cases).

When should a court vacate an arbitration decision
under FAA § 10(a)(3) (arbitrator misconduct or
"other misbehavior by which the rights of any party
have been prejudiced")? The Second Circuit
addressed this question in *STMicroelectronics, N.V.
v. Credit Suisse Sec. (USA), LLC*, 648 F.3d 68 (2d Cir.
2011), which involved an arbitrator's alleged
incomplete disclosure regarding his service as a
claimants' expert witness, service that purportedly
"colored his outlook in their favor." *Id.* at 74. The
court found this misconduct unsupported by the
evidence, but made the following observation about
predisposition arguments in general: A "judge's lack
of predisposition regarding the relevant legal issues
in a case has never been thought a necessary
component of equal justice" and that "[t]his is all the
more true for arbitrators." *Id.* at 77 (citations
omitted).

INDEX

References are to Pages